The Language and Sexuality Reader

Deborah Cameron and Don Kulick have assembled a dazzling array of the very best work on language and sexuality, including most (if not all) of the classics as well as a number of important new articles. I highly recommend this work to anyone conducting research or teaching in this area!

Gregory Ward, *Northwestern University, USA*

A well-chosen, prudently edited, and cogently articulated compilation. This cohesive (yet highly diverse) package could elevate the topic of language and sexuality to mainstream status in the language and communication sciences. A unique, invaluable resource, and one of the most complete Readers on my shelf.

Howard Giles, *University of California, Santa Barbara, USA*

An astutely selected and edited Reader, with excellent introductions to each subsection. As well as being an invaluable resource for scholars, this book makes a significant contribution to the development of this exciting new field.

Jennifer Coates, *Roehampton University, UK*

The Language and Sexuality Reader is the first of its kind to bring together material from the fields of anthropology, communication studies, linguistics, medicine and psychology in an examination of the role of sexuality in written and spoken language. Organized into thematic sections, the Reader addresses:

- early documentation of vocabulary used by male homosexuals and later work on the existence of a discourse style signifying gay identity;
- the use of language by individuals to present themselves as sexual and gendered subjects;
- the way language reflects, reinforces or challenges cultural norms defining what is 'natural' and desirable in the sphere of sex;
- the verbal communication of sexual desire in different settings, genres and media.

Extracts from: Hideko Abe, Laura M. Ahearn, Rusty Barrett, Deborah Cameron, Kathryn Campbell-Kibler, Donald W. Cory, Justine Coupland, Louie Crew, James Darsey, Penelope Eckert, Susan Ehrlich, Joseph J. Hayes, Scott F. Kiesling, Celia Kitzinger, Don Kulick, William L. Leap, Gershon Legman, Momoko Nakamura, Sally McConnell-Ginet, Julia Penelope Stanley, Robert J. Podesva, June Machover Reinisch, Sarah J. Roberts, Stephanie A. Sanders, David Sonenschein, David Valentine.

Deborah Cameron is a sociolinguist and currently holds the Rupert Murdoch Chair of Language and Communication at Oxford University. Her publications include *Verbal Hygiene* (1995) and *The Feminist Critique of Language* (1998).
Don Kulick is Professor of Anthropology and director of the Center for the Study of Gender and Sexuality at New York University. His books include *Travesti* (1998) and the co-edited *Fat* (2005).

Together, Deborah Cameron and Don Kulick are the authors of *Language and Sexuality* (2003).

The Language and Sexuality Reader

Edited by

Deborah Cameron and Don Kulick

Routledge
Taylor & Francis Group

LONDON AND NEW YORK

First published 2006
by Routledge
2 Park Square, Milton Park, Abingdon, Oxon OX14 4RN

Simultaneously published in the USA and Canada
by Routledge
270 Madison Ave, New York, NY 10016

Routledge is an imprint of the Taylor & Francis Group, an informa business

Typeset in Perpetua and Bell Gothic by
Florence Production Ltd, Stoodleigh, Devon
Printed and bound in Great Britain by
TJ International Ltd, Padstow, Cornwall

British Library Cataloguing in Publication Data
A catalogue record for this book is available from
the British Library

Library of Congress Cataloging in Publication Data
The language and sexuality reader/edited by Deborah Cameron
and Don Kulick.
        p. cm.
    1. Language and sex.   2. Language and languages – Sex
    differences.   3. Gays – Language.   4. Lesbians – Language.
    5. Sociolinguistics.   I. Cameron, Deborah, 1958–
    II. Kulick, Don.
    P120.S48L348 2005
    306.44 – dc22   2005029140

ISBN10: 0–415–36308–X (hbk)
ISBN10: 0–415–36307–1 (pbk)
ISBN10: 0–203–01337–9 (ebk)

ISBN13: 978–0–415–36308–2 (hbk)
ISBN13: 978–0–415–36307–5 (pbk)
ISBN13: 978–0–203–01337–3 (ebk)

Contents

List of tables   viii
Acknowledgements   ix
List of sources   xi

GENERAL INTRODUCTION   1

PART ONE:
Laying the Foundations   13

Anti-languages: homosexual slang and argot   15

1   Gershon Legman   19
    THE LANGUAGE OF HOMOSEXUALITY: AN AMERICAN
    GLOSSARY (1941)

2   Donald W. Cory   33
    TAKE MY WORD FOR IT (1951)

3   David Sonenschein   41
    THE HOMOSEXUAL'S LANGUAGE (1969)

4   Julia Penelope Stanley   49
    WHEN WE SAY 'OUT OF THE CLOSETS!' (1974)

5   Louie Crew   56
    HONEY, LET'S TALK ABOUT THE QUEENS' ENGLISH (1978)

Gayspeak: language, identity and community 63

6 Joseph J. Hayes 68
GAYSPEAK (1981)

7 James Darsey 78
'GAYSPEAK': A RESPONSE (1981)

8 William L. Leap 86
CAN THERE BE GAY DISCOURSE WITHOUT GAY
LANGUAGE? (1999)

PART TWO:
Contemporary Debates 95

Sexual styles and performances 97

9 Justine Coupland 101
DATING ADVERTISEMENTS: DISCOURSES OF THE
COMMODIFIED SELF (1996)

10 Scott F. Kiesling 118
PLAYING THE STRAIGHT MAN: DISPLAYING AND
MAINTAINING MALE HETEROSEXUALITY IN
DISCOURSE (2002)

11 Hideko Abe 132
LESBIAN BAR TALK IN SHINJUKU, TOKYO (2004)

12 Robert J. Podesva, Sarah J. Roberts and
Kathryn Campbell-Kibler 141
SHARING RESOURCES AND INDEXING MEANINGS IN
THE PRODUCTION OF GAY STYLES (2002)

13 Rusty Barrett 151
SUPERMODELS OF THE WORLD, UNITE! POLITICAL
ECONOMY AND THE LANGUAGE OF PERFORMANCE
AMONG AFRICAN AMERICAN DRAG QUEENS (1995)

Heteronorms 165

14 Celia Kitzinger 169
'SPEAKING AS A HETEROSEXUAL': (HOW) DOES SEXUALITY
MATTER FOR TALK-IN-INTERACTION? (2005)

15   Penelope Eckert   189
      VOWELS AND NAIL POLISH: THE EMERGENCE OF
      LINGUISTIC STYLE IN THE PREADOLESCENT
      HETEROSEXUAL MARKETPLACE (1996)

16   Susan Ehrlich   196
      THE DISCURSIVE RECONSTRUCTION OF SEXUAL
      CONSENT (1998)

17   Deborah Cameron   215
      DEGREES OF CONSENT: THE ANTIOCH COLLEGE
      SEXUAL OFFENSE POLICY (1994)

18   Stephanie A. Sanders and June Machover Reinisch   222
      WOULD YOU SAY YOU 'HAD SEX' IF . . .? (1999)

19   Sally McConnell-Ginet   227
      WHY DEFINING IS SELDOM 'JUST SEMANTICS': MARRIAGE
      AND *MARRIAGE* (2006)

The semiotics of sex and the discourse of desire   241

20   David Valentine   245
      'I WENT TO BED WITH MY OWN KIND ONCE': THE ERASURE
      OF DESIRE IN THE NAME OF IDENTITY (2003)

21   Laura M. Ahearn   258
      WRITING DESIRE IN NEPALI LOVE LETTERS (2003)

22   Momoko Nakamura   270
      CREATING INDEXICALITY: SCHOOLGIRL SPEECH IN
      MEIJI JAPAN (2006)

23   Don Kulick   285
      NO (2003)

      Notes   294
      Bibliography   299
      General index   316
      Index of names   321

Tables

3.1   Comparison of general vocabularies with subject community   45
3.2   Relation of homosexual terms to heterosexual usage in
      subject community   45
3.3   Internal shifts of homosexual terms in relation to heterosexual
      usage   45
12.1 Results for the duration variables (in ms)   147
12.2 Speaker A's durations of /eɪ/ (in ms)   148
12.3 Results for fundamental frequency (f0) variables (in Hz)   148
12.4 Percent of released word-final stops   149
18.1 Percentages for participants answering yes to the question
      'Would you say you have "had sex" with someone if the
      most intimate behaviour you engaged in was . . .'   224
22.1 Use of schoolboy features by female students of
      Baika joshi no den [*The Story of Miss Apricot Scent*] (1885)   276
22.2 Use of *teyo, dawa,* and *noyo* by the four female students
      of *Yabu no uguisu* [*Bush Warbler*] (1888)   278

Acknowledgements

A full list of sources in the order they appear in this volume is given on pp. xi–xii. Here the editors and publishers wish to thank the following copyright holders for permission to reprint material:

Hideko Abe, 'Lesbian bar talk in Shinjuku, Tokyo', in *Japanese Language, Gender and Ideology: Cultural Models and Real People*, (eds) Shigeko Okamoto and Janet S. Shibamoto Smith, 2004. © Oxford University Press, Inc. Used by permission of Oxford University Press, Inc.

Laura M. Ahearn, 'Writing desire in Nepali love letters', Don Kulick, 'No' and David Valentine, 'I went to bed with my own kind once', all reprinted from *Language and Communication* 23. © 2003, with permission from Elsevier.

Antioch College Sexual Offense Policy, extracts reproduced by permission of Antioch College.

Rusty Barrett, 'Supermodels of the world, unite!', in *Beyond the Lavender Lexicon*, ed. William Leap, Gordon & Breach 1995. Reproduced by kind permission of William Leap and the publisher.

Deborah Cameron, 'Degrees of consent', from *Trouble & Strife* 28, 1994, appears by permission of the author.

Justine Coupland, 'Dating advertisements', *Discourse & Society* 7.2, 1996 and Susan Ehrlich, 'The discursive reconstruction of sexual consent', *Discourse & Society* 9.2, 1998. Reproduced by permission of the authors and Sage Publications Ltd.

Louis Crew, 'Honey, let's talk about the Queens' English', from *Gai Saber*, Vol. 1, 1978. Reproduced by kind permission of the author.

James Darsey, '"Gayspeak": a response' and Joseph J. Hayes, 'Gayspeak', from *Gayspeak*, ed. James Chesebro, © 1981 The Pilgrim Press. Used by permission.

Penelope Eckert, 'Vowels and nail polish', in *Gender and Belief Systems,* ed. Natasha Warner *et al.*, Berkeley Women and Language Group 1996. Reproduced by kind permission of the author and publisher.

Scott F. Kiesling, 'Playing the straight man' and Robert Podesva *et al.*, 'Sharing resources and indexing meanings', originally appeared in *Language and Sexuality: Contesting Meaning in Theory and Practice*, Kathryn Campbell-Kibler, Robert Podesva, Sarah J. Roberts and Andrew Wong (eds), © 2002 CSLI Publications, and appear here, by permission of CSLI Publications, Stanford University, Stanford, CA 94305–4115, USA.

Celia Kitzinger, 'Speaking as a heterosexual', *ROLSI* 38 (3), 2005. Reproduced by kind permission of the author and Lawrence Erlbaum Associates.

William L. Leap, 'Can there be gay discourse without gay language?', in *Cultural Performances,* (eds) Mary Bucholtz, A.C. Liang, Laurel Sutton and Caitlin Hines, 1999. Reproduced by kind permission of the author.

Sally McConnell-Ginet, 'Why defining is seldom "just semantics"', in *Drawing the Boundaries of Meaning: Neo-Gricean Studies in Pragmatics and Semantics in Honor of Laurence R. Horn*, (eds) Betty Birner and Gregory Ward. Reproduced by permission of John Benjamins.

Stephanie Sanders and June M. Reinisch, 'Would you say you "had sex" if . . .?' *JAMA* 1999. Reproduced by permission of the American Medical Association.

David Sonenschein, 'The homosexual's language', *Journal of Sex Research* 5.4, © 1969 by the Society for the Scientific Study of Sexuality. Republished with permission (via the Copyright Clearance Center, Inc.).

Julia Penelope Stanley, 'When we say "Out of the closets!"', *College English* 6.3, 1974. © 1974 by the National Council of Teachers of English. Reprinted with permission.

Every attempt has been made to obtain permission to reproduce copyright material. If any proper acknowledgement has not been made, we would invite copyright holders to inform us of the oversight.

Sources

Chapter 1, Gershon Legman, 'The language of homosexuality: an American glossary', from *Sex Variants: A Study of Homosexual Patterns, Vol. II,* ed. George W. Henry (New York: Paul B. Hoeber, Inc., 1941), pp. 1155–79.

Chapter 2, Donald W. Cory [Edward Sagarin], 'Take my word for it', from *The Homosexual in America: A Subjective View* (New York: Greenberg, 1951), pp. 103–13.

Chapter 3, David Sonenschein, 'The homosexual's language', from *The Journal of Sex Research* 1969, 5 (4): 281–91.

Chapter 4, Julia Penelope [Stanley], 'When we say "Out of the closets!"', from *College English* 1974, 6 (3): 385–91.

Chapter 5, Louie Crew, 'Honey, let's talk about the Queens' English', from *Gai Saber* 1978, 1 (3): 240–3.

Chapter 6, Joseph J. Hayes, 'Gayspeak', and Chapter 7, James Darsey, '"Gayspeak": a response', from *Gayspeak: Gay Male and Lesbian Communication*, ed. James W. Chesebro (New York: The Pilgrim Press, 1981), pp. 45–67.

Chapter 8, William L. Leap, 'Can there be a gay discourse without gay language?', from *Cultural Performances: Proceedings of the Third Berkeley Women and Language Conference*, eds Mary Bucholtz, A.C. Liang, Laurel Sutton and Caitlin Hines (IGALA/CSLI Publications, 1999), pp. 399–408.

Chapter 9, Justine Coupland, 'Dating advertisements: discourses of the commodified self', from *Discourse & Society* 1996, 7 (2): 187–207.

Chapter 10, Scott F. Kiesling, 'Playing the straight man: displaying and maintaining male heterosexuality in discourse', from *Language and Sexuality: Contesting Meaning in Practice and Theory,* eds Kathryn Campbell-Kibler, Scott Podesva, Sarah J. Roberts and Andrew Wong (Stanford, CA: CSLI, 2002), pp. 249–66.

Chapter 11, Hideko Abe, 'Lesbian bar talk in Shinjuku, Tokyo', from *Japanese Language, Gender and Ideology: Cultural Models and Real People,* eds Shigeko Okamoto and Janet S. Shibamoto Smith (New York: Oxford University Press, 2004), pp. 205–21.

Chapter 12, Robert J. Podesva, Sarah J. Roberts and Kathryn Campbell-Kibler, 2002. 'Sharing resources and indexing meanings in the production of gay styles', from *Language and Sexuality: Contesting Meaning in Practice and Theory,* eds Kathryn Campbell-Kibler, Scott Podesva, Sarah J. Roberts and Andrew Wong (Stanford, CA: CSLI, 2002), pp. 175–90.

Chapter 13, Rusty Barrett, 'Supermodels of the world, unite! Political economy and the language of performance among African American drag queens', from *Beyond the Lavender Lexicon: Authenticity, Imagination and Appropriation in Lesbian and Gay Languages,* ed. William L. Leap (New York: Gordon and Breach, 1995), pp. 207–26.

Chapter 14, Celia Kitzinger, '"Speaking as a heterosexual": (how) does sexuality matter for talk-in-interaction?', *Research on Language and Social Interaction* 2005, 38 (3).

Chapter 15, Penelope Eckert, 'Vowels and nail polish: the emergence of linguistic style in the preadolescent heterosexual marketplace', from *Gender and Belief Systems,* eds Natasha Warner, Jocelyn Ahlers, Leela Bilmes, Monica Oliver, Suzanne Wertheim and Melinda Chen (Berkeley, CA: Berkeley Women and Language Group, 1996), pp. 183–90.

Chapter 16, Susan Ehrlich, 'The discursive reconstruction of sexual consent', from *Discourse & Society* 1998, 9 (2): 149–72.

Chapter 17, Deborah Cameron, 'Degrees of consent', from *Trouble & Strife* 28, Spring 1994, pp. 32–5. (With extracts from Antioch College Sexual Offense Policy, from Antioch College, Yellow Springs, Ohio, USA.)

Chapter 18, Stephanie A. Sanders and June Machover Reinisch, 'Would you say you "had sex" if . . .?', from *JAMA [Journal of the American Medical Association]* 1999, 281 (3): 75–7.

Chapter 19, Sally McConnell-Ginet, 'Why defining is seldom "just semantics": marriage and *marriage*', from *Drawing the Boundaries of Meaning: Neo-Gricean Studies in Pragmatics and Semantics in Honor of Laurence R. Horn,* eds Betty Birner and Gregory Ward (Amsterdam: John Benjamins, 2006).

Chapter 20, David Valentine, '"I went to bed with my own kind once": the erasure of desire in the name of identity', from *Language & Communication* 2003, 23 (3): 123–38.

Chapter 21, Laura M. Ahearn, 'Writing desire in Nepali love letters', from *Language & Communication* 2003, 23 (3): 107–22.

Chapter 22, Momoko Nakamura, 'Creating indexicality: schoolgirl speech in Meiji Japan', © this volume.

Chapter 23, Don Kulick, 'No', from *Language & Communication* 2003, 23 (3): 139–52.

GENERAL INTRODUCTION

IN AN ESSAY CRITICIZING the pervasiveness of talk about sex in the media, the American novelist Jonathan Franzen remarked: 'If a sexual fetish is understood as a displacement of sexual energies, then language, even more than lingerie, is by far the most prevalent paraphilia in the country today' (2002: 274). Franzen's tart comment implies that talking about sex functions as a substitute for sex itself. But the starting point for this collection of work is that 'sex' and 'talk about sex' are linked in more complex ways. Sex, for humans, is not just something we do, but also something we represent and reflect on: language plays a crucial role in shaping human sexuality and in mediating its various expressions. Speaking (or writing) about sex is not so much a 'displacement of sexual energies' as it is a means for giving those energies direction, shape and form.

It is not only novelists who have made observations about the significance of speech and writing in relation to sex: there is a growing interest among researchers, teachers and students in exploring the connections between language and sexuality. More and more courses are being taught that are either devoted to the subject or include a substantial component dealing with it; and since the mid-1990s there has been a steady flow of publications (e.g. Baker 2002; Cameron and Kulick 2003; Campbell-Kibler *et al.* 2002; Harvey and Shalom 1997; Leap 1995, 1996; Leap and Boellstorff 2004; Livia and Hall 1997; McIlvenny 2002). *The Language and Sexuality Reader* is intended as a further contribution to the development of this field. It brings together in one volume a wide range of material dealing with various aspects of language and sexuality.

For the purposes of compiling that material, we have defined the study of language and sexuality as an inquiry into the role played by language in producing and organizing sex as a meaningful domain of human experience. In keeping with that broad definition, the book's 23 chapters are diverse in their origins, their approaches and their subject matter. Historically, they span a period of more than

60 years: the earliest text reprinted here was first published in 1941, the most recent in 2006, and there is something from every decade in between. The academic disciplines whose literatures we have drawn on include anthropology, communication studies, linguistics, medicine, sexology, sociology and psychology. The subjects examined include lesbian bar talk in Japan and fraternity brothers' talk in the US; British personal ads and Nepali love letters; the linguistic performances of 12-year-old girls and those of African-American drag queens; the conventions of sado-masochistic role-play and Japanese schoolgirl fiction; the use of language in a sexual assault hearing; and the meanings of the English words *sex* and *marriage*. Even with this wide range of topics, though, there are numerous others that we have had to leave out due to lack of space. Later we explain how we have organized our material. First, though, we want to look more closely at what is meant or encompassed by the term *sexuality*, and how it can be related to language.

The meanings of *sexuality*

The on-line *Oxford English Dictionary* (*OED*) lists four main senses for *sexuality*, and as of June 2005, one draft addition (the parenthesized dates indicate the earliest attested usage):

> 1. the quality of being sexual or having sex (1800); 2. possession of sexual powers or capability of sexual feelings (1879); 3. recognition of or preoccupation with what is sexual (1899); 4. appearance distinctive of sex; 5. [*draft addition*] a person's sexual identity in relation to the gender to which he or she is typically attracted; the fact of being heterosexual, homosexual or bisexual; sexual orientation (1897).

Sexuality is a nineteenth-century word, and it originated as a technical scientific term. Sense 1 comes from natural history ('the quality of being sexual' is attributed to those animals and plants that reproduce sexually as opposed to those that do not) and senses 2–4 originally belonged to medical discourse (where *sexuality* becomes a quality of persons rather than organisms or organs – the first quotation given for sense 2, for instance, is 'by removing the ovaries you do not necessarily destroy sexuality in a woman'). Today, the use of *sexuality* to mean a general quality or capacity of human beings to behave, feel and think in sexual ways – a sort of amalgam of senses 1–3 – is part of ordinary English usage.

But, as the lexicographers' draft addition suggests, *sexuality* has also taken on a more specific meaning in contemporary usage: 'the fact of being heterosexual, homosexual or bisexual'. This sense, too, originated in nineteenth-century scientific discourse (the first quotation given for it is an 1897 reference to 'inverted sexuality', i.e. homosexuality, by the sexologist Havelock Ellis). But it has recently become common in everyday English, as is illustrated by the most recent (2002) quotation: 'one belief held that you could tell a guy's sexuality from the way he danced'.

This Reader is about the relationship of language to sexuality in both the more general and the more specific senses, but in our own usage we will distinguish them. We will use *sexuality* to refer to any and all human qualities, behaviours, feelings and preoccupations of a sexual nature; and *sexual identity* to refer to that aspect of sexuality – 'orientation' or 'preference' – which is encapsulated in the *OED*'s sense 5.

The term *sexual identity* is meant to capture an important point about the way modern Westerners think about sexuality. 'The fact of being heterosexual, homosexual or bisexual' is understood in contemporary Western societies not simply as an observation about someone's sexual behaviour, but as a characteristic that, like their gender or their ethnicity, enters deeply into their sense of self and affects every aspect of their life. It is also assumed that the aspect of sexuality that matters in this regard is someone's preference for partners of either the same gender or the other gender. (So important is it to categorize people according to this criterion, we have a separate category – 'bisexual' – for those who show no fixed preference.) Other erotic preferences (e.g. for taking a 'dominant' or 'submissive' role, or for engaging in a particular kind of sex) may influence an individual's behaviour just as strongly, but these are considered less fundamental than the 'hetero versus homo' distinction.

This particular way of making sense of sex is clearly highly significant in the modern West. It has also been important in the study of *language* and sexuality, where the question that has been asked most consistently is along the lines of: 'how does the language of homosexuals differ from that of heterosexuals?' This reflects not only the modern Western perception of identity based on same/other gender preference as the most salient dimension of sexuality (and of homosexuality as the 'marked' variant – the one that is felt to need an explanation), but also the sociolinguistic understanding that language-using is an 'act of identity': speakers use the resources of linguistic variation to signal their identification with one social group and their difference from other groups. If the 'hetero versus homo' distinction marks a socially significant difference, it makes sense to look for linguistic correlates of that difference – though as several chapters of this book suggest, that is not to say you will always find them.

But it needs to be borne in mind that while sex itself is universal – it exists in all cultures and at all times – our ways of understanding and organizing it are not universal, they are variable across cultures and through history. It cannot be assumed, therefore, that either the 'hetero/homo' distinction or the kind of identity associated with it in contemporary Western societies will be found, or accorded the same significance, in every society and historical period. These concepts are not simply given by the nature of sex itself, but are cultural constructs that arise in particular times, places and circumstances.

Michel Foucault tells us in his *History of Sexuality* (1981) that the idea of sexuality as identity, and of homosexuals and heterosexuals as 'types', emerged in the West only in the nineteenth century, when the description and regulation of sexual conduct became a secular and scientific enterprise rather than the province of religious and moral authorities. Previously, 'sodomy' was conceptualized (and punished) as a sinful act to which anyone might be tempted, rather than as the proclivity of a particular kind of person, 'the homosexual'. Even since the invention of the category in the nineteenth century, understandings of 'the homosexual' have changed significantly. Contemporary Europeans and North Americans tend to understand homosexuality as an attraction of like to like, with gay men attracted to other gay men and lesbians to other lesbians. But as recently as 50 years ago, homosexuality was more commonly understood as a matter of gender 'inversion': 'homosexuals' were thought (among themselves as well as by 'experts') to be effeminate males and masculinized ('butch') females who were attracted to their 'opposites', i.e. (straight) masculine men and feminine women respectively. Desire, even among homosexuals, was axiomatically heterosexual – for the 'other' rather than the 'same' gender.

In the (numerous) societies where this understanding of homosexuality remains strong, the locally recognized variants of sexual identity and practice may not be directly comparable to those contemporary Europeans and North Americans are familiar with. For instance, traditional local categories such as the *waria* of Indonesia, *kathoey* of Thailand, *'yan daudu* of Nigeria, Brazilian *travesti* and Indian *hijra* are all (biological) males who are sexually attracted to 'masculine' men, and present themselves as 'feminine' in appearance, dress and manner (Boellstorff 2006; Gaudio 1997; Jackson 2004; Kulick 1998; Nanda 1989). Though they generally do not identify as women, in many ways they are more like what Westerners now call 'transgendered' people than they are like Western gay men. An analogous point could be made about the Japanese women who identify as *onabe*, discussed by Hideko Abe in Chapter 11. *Onabe* are masculine women who are attracted to straight women rather than to other *onabe* or to lesbians.

In most cases, these indigenous forms of minority sexual/gender identity now co-exist with more Euro-American forms of gay and/or lesbian identity. In Japan, for instance, the category of 'lesbian' (called *rezubian*, or just *rezu*), exists alongside *onabe*, with *rezu* denoting women who are attracted to non-*onabe* homosexual women. In Brazil, likewise, men who identify as *gay* emphatically differentiate themselves from *travestis*, partly on the grounds that their own erotic desires are for men who are *gay* like themselves, not for men who identify as straight (Kulick 1998; Parker 1999). What examples like these show us is that there are different ways of organizing the articulation of gender and sexual preference to form sexual identity categories (*onabe* and *rezu* are both identity categories, but they are based on different categorizing principles). In some times and places, too, the notion of sexual identity could not be said to exist at all.

Even where this notion is highly salient, it is only one of a number of cross-cutting systems for imposing structure and meaning on sexual experience. For instance, what Foucault says preceded the emergence of sexual identity in the West – a focus on classifying and evaluating different sexual *acts* – remains part of our cultural apparatus for making sense of sex. All cultures distinguish acceptable sexual acts, practices or relationships from those that are inappropriate, distasteful, disgusting, perverted or wicked. While this may be connected to the dimensions of gender and sexual identity – some people might class the same act as 'normal' when performed in a cross-sex context but 'abnormal' or 'perverted' when those involved are of the same sex — it does not necessarily have to be. Many people consider, say, having sex in public as inappropriate, coprophilia as disgusting, and seeking sexual relationships with young children as monstrous, no matter whether these are same-sex or cross-sex acts. Most people today also make a moral distinction between 'consensual' and 'coerced' or 'forced' sex acts, with any kind of sex that both/all parties do not consent to being seen as unacceptable by definition. The cultural meaning of sex, then, is not only about who is doing it with whom, but also about what they are doing and under what conditions.

If sexuality itself is a variable and multidimensional phenomenon, so too is its relationship to language. We have already mentioned one way in which that relationship is often conceptualized: in terms of language-using being an 'act of identity', which can therefore mark sexual identities such as 'gay' as opposed to 'straight', or *onabe* rather than *rezu*. But another important way in which language is connected to sexuality is as a medium of representation. It is in language (or more exactly, discourse) that we organize our understandings of sex and what it means, elaborating and disseminating definitions, distinctions, classifications and value judgements like the ones we have referred to in this discussion. It is also in discourse that we contest those understandings (challenging, for instance, the definition of 'consent' used in rape trials, or seeking to 'reclaim' derogatory labels such as *queer* and *dyke*). Language is thus an important element in political struggles around sexuality.

Language may also play a significant role in constituting certain acts, relationships or situations as 'sexual'. Consider, for instance, the way of interacting that English-speakers call 'flirting', and that can be identified by a combination of linguistic, paralinguistic and non-verbal features (these may include innuendo, 'personal' questions and references, frequent smiling and laughter, speaking softly, holding and periodically breaking eye-contact, etc.). These features function as what Gumperz (1982) calls 'contextualization cues' — devices that subtly indicate what interpretive frame a piece of discourse should be placed in. Wherever one is (it could be at the dentist's) and whatever the ostensible topic of discussion (it could be last year's sales figures), the use of a 'flirtatious' way of speaking frames an interaction as sexual. Of course, what this accomplishes in context will vary: in different situations flirting may be a joke, a prelude to sex, socially inappropriate behaviour or deliberate sexual harassment. But *recognizing* what someone is doing as 'flirting' does not depend only on properties of the external context. It also depends on properties of the language used — which is why people can flirt in, and thereby sexualize, even the most incongruous settings and situations.

A famous case of linguistic and semiotic resources being used incongruously to sexualize a situation is one we have discussed elsewhere (Cameron and Kulick 2003): the 'faked orgasm' scene in the film *When Harry Met Sally*. In order to prove to Harry that a well-faked orgasm is indistinguishable from the 'real thing', Sally simulates having an orgasm while sitting at a table in a busy Manhattan diner. To do this she makes use of certain conventional signifiers: breathiness, moaning and increasing loudness while uttering sounds like 'Oh', the repetition of words such as 'Yes' and short phrases such as 'Oh God', and what could either be a directive or an exclamation (or both): 'Oh yeah, right there'. These details of language, prosody and voice quality make Sally's performance convincing, at least to the other patrons in the diner. For Harry, on the other hand, and for us as viewers, aware that Sally is faking it, the performance is convincing in a different way: it convincingly dramatizes the point Sally set out to make, that there is no necessary correspondence between the bodily (physical and emotional) experience of sex and the communicative acts that conventionally signify sex. They may go together, but they do not have to.

This point about the potential separation between (subjective and private) bodily experiences and their (intersubjective and public) semiotic coding is analytically important; it is also significant because of its real social consequences. For example, it may prompt anxiety about the 'authenticity' of sexual response (especially women's seemingly less visible sexual pleasure). It is also at the heart of many disputes about whether someone consented to sex. Often the issue in such disputes is not whether the person who claims not to have consented 'really wanted it', but whether it was reasonable for the other party to *believe* that s/he did on the basis of what and how s/he communicated. That such a belief was, indeed, reasonable is a favourite defence of men accused of rape (Ehrlich, Chapter 16). It is also a key component of the Homosexual Panic Defense, where defendants maintain that they were justified in attacking or killing a homosexual man because they believed he wanted to have sex with them (Kulick, Chapter 23).

In this discussion we have tried to show what we mean by saying that the relationship of language and sexuality is one of many dimensions, enabling researchers to approach it from a variety of angles and pose a number of different kinds of questions. We have also tried to suggest that investigating those questions may illuminate issues of more general interest to social science and social theory: issues of, for instance, agency, identity, representation, desire and power. Individual chapters of this Reader show concretely how such issues can be illuminated using the tools of linguistic analysis. At this point, then, let us turn to the Reader's contents and how they are organized.

How this book is organized

The organization of the Reader is partly chronological, and partly thematic. There are two main parts: the first part, 'Laying the Foundations', traces the development of ideas about language and sexuality roughly from the 1940s to the 1980s, while the second part, 'Contemporary Debates', concentrates on texts published between the mid-1990s and the present. Since we take it that most users of this book will be particularly interested in recent and current research, the second part is roughly twice as long as the first. Nevertheless, we believe it is important for a collection on this subject to include some 'historical' material. Part One reprints several texts that are rarely read or cited today – and that in many cases would be hard to find in the average academic library – but that in our view are worth revisiting, both for what they tell us about the history of the field of inquiry they belong to, and for the insights they provide into the social and linguistic realities of the past.

Each of the Reader's two parts is subdivided into sections. In Part One the subdivision is historically based. The first section, 'Anti-languages: homosexual slang and argot', presents a current of research that began as early as the 1920s (e.g. Rosanoff 1927) – though our own selection begins rather later, with Gershon Legman's 1941 'The language of homosexuality: an American glossary (Chapter 1). This is the first comprehensive compilation and discussion of in-group slang terms used by male homosexuals in the US, and it was originally published in a two-volume medical treatise on homosexuality – an unremarkable fact, given that homosexuality at this time was considered to be a pathological condition, and as such to belong 'naturally' within the domain of medical science. The other pieces in this section, however, trace the evolution of a more sociological, and increasingly politicized, view of homosexuality and the language associated with it. In the pieces we reproduce from the 1950s and 1960s, homosexuality – which was still defined legally as a criminal offence and medically as a mental disorder – is treated as a social problem, and its language is taken, like the 'argots' and 'anti-languages' of other socially excluded groups, to express the preoccupations and values of a stigmatized subculture.

By the 1970s, however, that subculture, or at least parts of it, had been caught up in a more militant political struggle for sexual (both gay/lesbian and women's) liberation. In the two chapters we reproduce from this period, the focus is still on vocabulary – gay male slang in particular – but the distribution and significance of this terminology (whether, for instance, it is misogynistic and/or 'self-hating') has become a subject of critical debate within the emerging 'gay community'. By 1981, where our second section, 'Gayspeak: language, identity and community' begins, the focus has shifted from documenting in-group vocabulary to debating the existence and character of what Joseph J. Hayes (Chapter 6) dubbed 'Gayspeak', a discourse style or perhaps even a language in its own right, signifying gay identity in somewhat the same way that features of accent and dialect might signify a speaker's regional, social class or ethnic identity.

The last piece in the 'Gayspeak' section, William L. Leap's 'Can there be gay discourse without gay language?' (Chapter 8), was first published as recently as 1999, and might therefore seem to belong in Part Two, 'Contemporary Debates'. But theoretically and politically, Leap's essay belongs to the 'Gayspeak' tradition, which was inaugurated in the 1970s. As it shows, that tradition has continued rather than disappearing. In our three sections dealing with 'Contemporary Debates', however, we focus on currents of theory and research that have emerged since the beginning of the 1990s.

We can begin our discussion of contemporary debates by noting an obvious difference between Parts One and Two. All the chapters in Part One deal specifically with language and *homo*sexuality: the question they address (though not all contributors give the same answers to it) is essentially what differentiates the language of homosexuals from the usage of the heterosexual mainstream. As we noted earlier, this question, and the associated focus on sexual minority groups (most notably gay men), has historically dominated the field: even now, it is probably what most people think of as the 'core' of language and sexuality research. But during the approximately ten-year period of research activity represented in Part Two, the focus of many investigations has become simultaneously broader (in that groups other than gay men – including straight people – have come under scrutiny) and more specific (in that neither gay/lesbian nor straight language-users are treated as undifferentiated categories). Whereas in Part One many writers discuss '*the* homosexual' and '*the* language of homosexuality', in Part Two we see more emphasis on particularizing the groups a researcher is writing about. These chapters are not about generic 'homosexuals' and 'heterosexuals', but about specific 'communities of practice' (Eckert and McConnell-Ginet 1992) – African-American drag queens, lesbians who frequent bars in Tokyo, a group of sixth-grade 'home girls' or members of a particular college fraternity. Some chapters even examine the behaviour of a single speaker. The aim is no longer to generalize about the linguistic correlates of large-scale demographic categories; rather what is emphasized is the local diversity and complexity of linguistic practice.

This shift reflects wider theoretical and political developments whose effects began to be felt at the end of the 1980s. One development was a certain particularization, and indeed fragmentation, of the groups that had come to be understood as important social and political constituencies in the 1970s and 1980s (e.g. people of colour, women, gay men and lesbians, etc.) Differences and divisions within these groups began to become more salient in political debate; new self-defined constituencies (for instance, transgendered people) began to emerge and to protest against their marginalized status within the established order. The internal diversity of entities such as 'the gay community' (or as many people now say, the 'LGBT – lesbian, gay, bisexual and transgendered – community', a relabelling that illustrates the process we are discussing) became a political issue in its own right, and this was reflected in scholarship dealing with minority communities.

Another significant development was the emergence in the early 1990s of an intellectual current known as 'queer theory'. Though few linguistic researchers have embraced queer theory as a total approach (for a range of views on its usefulness in linguistic scholarship, see Campbell-Kibler *et al.* 2002, chapters 2–6), there are certain key concepts drawn from the work of queer theorists that have been influential in recent research on language, gender and/or sexuality.

One of these concepts, *performativity*, was first elaborated by the philosopher of language J.L. Austin (1962). Austin noted that certain utterances, which he labelled 'performative', did not *describe* pre-existing states of affairs, but rather brought those states into existence (e.g. to say 'I apologize' or 'I promise to do X' is actually to make the apology or the promise). Building on Austin's understanding of language, the philosopher and pioneering queer theorist Judith Butler argued in her book *Gender Trouble* (1990) that identities like 'man', 'woman', 'gay' or 'lesbian' are not just pre-existing attributes of individuals that their behaviour 'expresses', but are actually brought into being, and then sustained, through the repeated actions an individual performs. The social identity 'woman', for example, is constituted by repeatedly acting in ways that are culturally coded as typical of women (and, conversely, untypical of men). These repetitive acts do not depend on, or flow 'naturally' from, the kind of sexed body a person has: they are acquired, like language, as we become acculturated. Because gender is 'performative', it is possible for someone who is not female to 'pass' as a woman, as some drag queens and many MTF (male to female) transsexuals do; conversely, women who *are* female are not exempt from the obligation to perform femininity. In this paradigm, we all perform identity – we all have to work at 'passing' as women or men. As many scholars have pointed out since the early 1990s, language-using is part of gender performativity. Our gender (and also our sexuality) emerges not only through how we move and dress, but also in our speech habits and our linguistic choices.

The first section of Part Two, 'Sexual styles and performances', analyses interactions or texts in which people use language to present themselves as sexual and gendered subjects. The pieces in this section illustrate that there is no single way of performing either heterosexual or homosexual identity, and thus no simple opposition between the two. Both gay/lesbian and heterosexual language-users give a variety of differing performances, which are influenced by the demands and constraints of particular contexts. For instance, heterosexuality will be performed differently by a man designing a personal ad to appeal to a prospective partner (Coupland, Chapter 9) and by one who is hoping to gain status among his friends by boasting about his ability to attract women (Kiesling, Chapter 10). A performance of homosexuality may involve gender 'crossing', as it does for the drag queens discussed by Rusty Barrett (Chapter 13). But for the gay lawyer whose broadcast performance is analysed by Robert J. Podesva *et al.* (Chapter 12), this version of gay identity is contextually inappropriate – the lawyer is a professional expert taking part in a serious debate – and his style, while identifiably 'gay', does not include linguistic features that are stereotyped as 'flamboyant'. Hideko Abe's discussion (Chapter 11) of the lesbians she observed in Tokyo bars makes clear that their performances vary. Gender crossing (for instance, using personal pronouns that are conventionally associated with male speakers) does feature in the speech of these women. But no one does it in every situation; and different forms tend to be chosen by *rezu* and *onabe*.

The other key concept developed in queer theory that is significant for the purposes of this discussion is *heteronormativity*. This term names an overarching system for organizing and regulating sexuality, whereby certain ways of acting, thinking and feeling about sex are privileged over others – they are defined legally, medically, economically and culturally as normal, natural, healthy and desirable. As the 'hetero-' part of the word suggests, one principle of heteronormative social organization is that heterosexuality is privileged over the alternatives: sexual relations between men and women are promoted as normal and desirable, while homosexuality is stigmatized (or indeed, criminalized) as abnormal and undesirable. However, there is more to heteronormativity than the simple elevation of other-sex over same-sex preference. Not all expressions of heterosexuality are equal: the 'ideal' heteronormative sexuality is the kind stereotypically associated with the middle-class nuclear family, involving a stable, monogamous (preferably marital) and reproductive (within 'sensible' limits) sexual relationship between two adults (not too young or too old) whose social and sexual roles are differentiated along conventional gender lines.

Queer theory is an inquiry into the nature and workings of heteronormativity, along with the 'queer' sexualities that heteronormativity produces by stigmatizing, silencing and/or proscribing them. 'Queer' here does not mean 'homosexual', but rather 'non- or anti-heteronormative': straight people and heterosexual practices can also be 'queer' if they deviate from the heteronormative ideal. The 'queer' category would thus include, as well as LGBT people, straight women who initiate sex, older or more powerful women in relationships with younger or less powerful men, single mothers (or fathers) who want to stay single, and anyone who has casual sex with multiple partners or engages in 'perverse' sexual acts (anal sex, sadomasochism, fetishism . . . the list goes on and on). In contemporary Western societies, where sexuality of the 'right' kind is constantly represented as natural and healthy, it is arguably 'queer' to be voluntarily celibate.

The 'Heteronorms' section of this Reader explores how everyday language-use reflects and reproduces heteronormative understandings of sexuality. It begins with two chapters examining the way speakers in their verbal interactions construct themselves as heterosexual – but there is a difference between these pieces and the chapters in the previous section dealing with heterosexual performances. The displays of heterosexuality discussed in this section are not explicitly sexual, but part of what Celia Kitzinger (Chapter 14), using the terminology of Conversation Analysis, calls 'doing being ordinary'. In a heteronormative society, casually displaying heterosexuality is a way of displaying normality, maturity and social appropriateness, whereas analogous displays by non-heterosexuals will often be taken as 'flaunting' sexuality. The other pieces in this section examine the way heteronormativity shapes the definition and interpretation of important concepts and terms in the domain of sexuality: *consent*, *(have) sex*, and *marriage*.

The last section of Part Two, 'The semiotics of sex and the discourse of desire', focuses on language as a medium in which erotic desires are represented and made intelligible. Sexual desire is conventionally thought of as a private, subjective experience, 'too deep', as a romantic novelist might put it, 'to be expressed in words'. But of course, if it is to be communicated, desire often does have to be put into words; and there are clearly codes and conventions – the 'too deep for words' cliché is one example – which both enable and constrain that process. The chapters in this section look at the conventionalized expression of sexual desire (and its inverse, disgust, or fear and loathing) in a variety of (sub)cultures and settings (including New York City, Nepal and Meiji-era Japan), in both face-to-face interaction (Valentine, Chapter 20; Kulick, Chapter 23) and written genres like personal love letters (Ahearn, Chapter 21) and narrative fiction (Nakamura, Chapter 22).

A note on selection and editing

It is not possible in a single collection to provide comprehensive coverage of a field as diverse as this one. We have had to make choices, and inevitably some readers will be disappointed by our failure to include certain pieces or certain topics. Notable omissions include camp (e.g. Harvey 2000), sexual humour, and the construction of sexual experience and/or identity in narrative genres such as pornography and coming-out stories (see e.g. Bolton 1995; Heywood 1997; Liang 1997). In general, we have included very little on narrative, fictional and literary language (but see e.g. Livia 1995; Queen 1997; Talbot 1998). Also absent are a number of media-related topics, such as the portrayal of sexual minorities in news and popular entertainment, the creation and regulation of sexual meanings in commercial advertising (Cameron 2006) and the representation of sexuality in political, educational and public health campaigns dealing with issues like HIV/AIDS and other sexually transmitted diseases, fertility and reproduction, or parenthood and family life (Lazar 1999). Another area of research that is represented only incidentally in this volume examines the relationship of language to sexual identity across cultures. We have not focused on this because up-to-date information is readily available elsewhere (see especially Leap and Boellstorff 2004; also Livia and Hall 1997).

This is one example of a more general principle we have used in making choices. Our aim is to complement rather than duplicate existing resources, so we have chosen where possible to reprint work that would otherwise be relatively difficult to access. Many of our selections come from publications that the passing of time has made obscure or hard to find, from books and periodicals published by small presses when queer scholarship was still a marginal enterprise, from medical or other scientific sources that most linguists would not routinely look at, and from journals or volumes of conference proceedings that are not readily available to students. Conversely, we have avoided reprinting material from the most accessible and widely used recent collections (e.g. Harvey and Shalom 1997; Leap and Boellstorff 2004; Livia and Hall 1997).

In some areas our selection has been constrained by gaps and biases in the literature itself, with perhaps the most striking case being the under-representation of lesbians relative to gay men. Lesbians hardly featured in the early traditions of research and writing that are represented in Part One, and they have remained a fairly marginal presence in more recent collections of work in English dealing with language and homosexuality (though see Moonwomon-Baird 1997; Morgan and Wood 1995; Painter 1981; Queen 1997; Wood 1997). Where lesbians have been studied, researchers have not, on the whole, made claims about their language-use analogous to those that have been made about gay men's. We have discussed some possible explanations for this elsewhere (Cameron and Kulick 2003: 95–7), but in any case, the relative marginality of lesbians in the language and sexuality literature is echoed in our own selection from it.

Another group about which this book says little is transgendered people. Though 'transgendered' as an identity is now commonly placed within the broader 'LGBT' category, which suggests it is conceptualized as a form of sexual identity along with 'lesbian', 'gay' and 'bisexual', our own view is that the study of transgender and language has so far had more to say about the linguistic construction of gender identity than sexual identity or sexuality (cf. Kulick 1999). David Valentine's article (Chapter 20) discusses the links and tensions between these two areas, and shows how a focus on desire in language can highlight theoretical, political and personal difficulties that arise through the separation of gender and sexuality.

Some readers may feel that this collection, while under-representing certain sexual minority groups, contains entirely too much about heterosexuals. We are sympathetic to the kind of 'visibility politics' that wants to focus on subordinated groups in order to disprove negative stereotypes and celebrate their distinctive forms of self-expression, but we also feel it is crucial to study dominant/majority groups. If our political goal is to challenge their power and privilege, we must uncover their sources and critically analyse their workings.

None of the following chapters appears here in its full original form. All have been shortened – some, with their authors' agreement, radically – to fit the requirements of this collection (to enhance readability, we have not marked our edits in the text). The value of a Reader is that it brings together many different contributions, thus providing an introduction to the field as a whole, but readers who are intrigued or inspired by any individual chapter will undoubtedly find it worthwhile to consult the original version (the list of sources on pp. xi–xii indicates, for each chapter, where to find it). We hope users of this Reader will indeed be intrigued and inspired – to think, to argue and ultimately perhaps to do their own research, about the complex, multidimensional relationship of language and sexuality.

Finally, we would like to record our gratitude to those who have helped us in the preparation of this book. We are indebted to all the authors who have allowed us to include their work, but particular thanks are due to James Darsey, Celia Kitzinger, Sally McConnell-Ginet, Momoko Nakamura and David Valentine, who went out of their way to be helpful. We also thank Julene Knox for her extensive assistance with permissions clearance, and Elizabeth Johnston at Routledge.

PART ONE

Laying the Foundations

Anti-languages: homosexual slang and argot

THE FIVE PIECES IN THIS SECTION, all from the US, span a period from the early 1940s to the late 1970s, and can be subdivided into two groups. The first three, by Gershon Legman, Donald W. Cory and David Sonenschein, were produced before the advent of gay liberation, by people who were either outsiders to the community under discussion or else were (understandably) unwilling to identify themselves as insiders, in a context and for an audience that viewed homosexuality as a social problem – while the law, of course, still defined it as a crime. Their treatment of language reflects that historical context. The argot of homosexuals is seen as what Halliday (1976) would term an 'anti-language': a coded way of using otherwise familiar words, which is designed to exclude outsiders (rhyming slang and pig-latin are familiar examples). Anti-languages are generally found among stigmatized subgroups who have reason to be secretive and/or who seek to construct a subterranean social world in defiance of mainstream norms. Homosexuals in the pre-liberation era were a group of precisely this kind.

Julia Penelope Stanley and Louie Crew, by contrast, wrote as members of the politically conscious gay and lesbian community that had begun to emerge at the end of the 1960s. These writers make clear that they are not outsiders pronouncing on a social problem, but insiders contributing to the development of a social movement – one whose goal was, precisely, to challenge the definition of homosexuals as 'deviants' who axiomatically pose a problem for society. Both, however, continue the 'anti-language' tradition by focusing on the already-familiar elements of homosexual argot: in-group vocabulary and the practice of gender inversion (i.e. the use of feminine gender-marking by some gay men).

In this group of contributors only one, Julia Penelope Stanley, is a linguist. Gershon Legman was a folklorist with a particular interest in erotica, and his 'The language of homosexuality: an American glossary' (Chapter 1) appeared in a two-volume survey entitled *Sex Variants: A Study of Homosexual Patterns*, intended for an audience of scientific and medical experts. In this monumental survey of 'the homosexual' as a clinical 'type', which included everything from x-ray photographs of lesbians' pelvises to measurements of male homosexuals' sphincter-tightness, Legman's contribution supplied the linguistic piece of the puzzle. As we have observed elsewhere (Cameron and Kulick 2003: 78–81), glossaries such as Legman's are interesting for what they suggest about the culture of the time and place in which they were compiled (readers today may also find it interesting to count how many of the words Legman categorized as specific to homosexuals are now part of mainstream sexual slang, their 'queer' origins forgotten). Linguistic or cultural historians must treat this evidence with caution, however: mere lists of words tell you nothing about who used them, for what purposes, and in what kinds of contexts. Those questions are given more attention in the two pieces that follow Legman's here, written by Donald W. Cory and David Sonenschein.

'Donald W. Cory' was the pseudonym of the sociologist Edward Sagarin, whose choice of pen-name plays on *Corydon*, the title of a defence of homosexuality – more exactly, of pederasty (i.e. the ancient Greek model of sexual love between an older and a much younger man) – by the French author André Gide. Sagarin did not write under a pseudonym simply because of the subject matter – approached in a certain way, homosexuality was not a taboo subject for 'respectable' social science in the 1950s – but rather because his book *The Homosexual in America* presented what its subtitle explicitly called 'a subjective view'. Though Cory adopts the voice of a sympathetic observer of the homosexual subculture, Sagarin in fact had rather more personal involvement with gay life than his alter ego's self-presentation implies. Though he was married and not, as we would now say, 'out' about his other sexual activities, he was an active member of the Mattachine Society, one of the 'homophile' political organizations that existed before gay liberation, and which argued that in a more tolerant society, homosexuals could be normal and well-adjusted human beings. Later, Sagarin would change his mind on this point and quarrel seriously with his fellow homophiles, but *The Homosexual in America* was an influential statement of the liberal position.

The chapter we reprint, 'Take my word for it' (Chapter 2), is among other things an early meditation on the need for positive terminology. Cory emphasizes the virtues of the in-group term *gay* by contrast with either clinical terms such as *homosexual* or derogatory terms such as *fag*. Some readers may be surprised that *gay* was already being advocated to mainstream English-speakers in 1951; they may also be surprised by some of Cory's other observations about social category labels. Cory takes it for granted that his readership will find *Negro* unobjectionable, *queer* offensive and *straight*, as a term for heterosexuals, completely unfamiliar. Today, of course, it is *Negro* that is avoided, whereas millions are neither offended nor mystified by a mainstream television show called *Queer Eye for the Straight Guy*.

Both the sociologist Sagarin and the anthropologist David Sonenschein are at some pains to counter the perception of what Sonenschein (Chapter 3) calls 'the homosexual's language' as fundamentally an expression of individual sexual deviance or pathology. Instead they stress that its most important function is creating social cohesion within a particular community. Cory makes analogies with 'the argot that is characteristic of any trade or profession', and also with the 'special words' used by and about 'the racial, religious and national minorities of the United States'. He is saying that homosexuals do not stand out from other minority groups – including groups not generally considered 'deviant', such as national and professional ones – in the use they make of language as a symbol of community membership. Sonenschein, couching his argument in the more technical register of 1960s social science, points out that most of the in-group terms his research identified are what he calls 'role terms' rather than 'sex terms' – not references to deviant sexual practices, but terms for describing and evaluating the social roles the community makes available to its members.

Sonenschein also implicitly problematizes his own label 'the homosexual's language' by pointing out that 'homosexuals' do not comprise a homogeneous community from a social or linguistic point of view. He found significantly less use of in-group slang among female, upper-class and 'marginal' homosexuals. From a modern sociolinguistic perspective, this is readily understandable as an observation about the effects of social networks on language-use: speakers who are peripheral to a community's core social networks can be expected to be less advanced in their use of the relevant linguistic variables. Whether, how and to what extent a given homosexual uses 'the homosexual's language' is, then, a question about social relationships rather than sexual proclivities. In the attention he gives to this point, Sonenschein anticipates later discussions more explicitly informed by insights from sociolinguistics. He and Cory are rarely cited in the more recent literature on gay and lesbian language-use, but their work shows that a number of important arguments on the subject go back further than is often supposed.

Though the three authors discussed so far all speak generically of 'homosexuals' and 'homosexuality', they are in fact concerned with the in-group terminology used by homosexual men, and not, or only very glancingly, with that used by lesbians. Legman, in his rather odd remarks on this subject – he goes so far as to propose that lesbian language does not exist because lesbianism itself is 'in a large measure factitious', i.e. most women who claim to be lesbians are only pretending – mentions women's prisons as one location where a more elaborated lesbian argot might hypothetically be found. There is some evidence supporting that suggestion in a classic study of a women's prison published 25 years later, *Society of Women* by Rose Giallombardo (1966). Though language is not a main focus of Giallombardo's work and we have therefore not included it in this volume, it is certainly of interest to students of language, gender and sexuality in the pre-feminist/gay liberation era. The linguistic position of lesbians once that era had dawned, however, is among the issues addressed explicitly by Julia Penelope Stanley, a lesbian feminist linguist who made important contributions to the literature on both gender and sexuality during the 1970s and 1980s (e.g. Penelope [Stanley] 1970; 1977; Penelope [Stanley] and Wolfe 1979; Penelope 1990). 'When we say "Out of the closets!"' (Chapter 4) argues not only that gay men and lesbians have little in common linguistically, but also that the kind of gay male slang discussed by Legman, Cory and Sonenschein is pervaded by sexist, racist and classist values antithetical to feminist (or any other radical) politics.

Although Louie Crew takes issue with Julia Penelope Stanley on whether gay men's use of feminine gender-marking is sexist, his article 'Honey, let's talk about the Queens' English' (Chapter 5), echoes Stanley, and indeed Sonenschein, in questioning the notion that the entire homosexual population has a single way of using language. Not only the differences between lesbians and gay men, but also differences among gay men themselves, come under scrutiny in these pieces. Stanley asserts that there are differences in usage between the politicized, 'out' gay man and the apolitical, 'closeted' homosexual. Crew draws a distinction between some gay men's 'intensification of the masculine' and others' 'identification with females', and suggests that 'nongays routinely ignore the existence of the gay-as-intensified-male, perhaps because the gay-as-effeminate stereotype is less threatening'. He also suggests that a politically radical strategy might involve juxtaposing these 'masculine' and 'feminine' elements so that each undercuts the potentially reactionary meaning of the other. It is interesting to encounter this argument in a piece written in the late 1970s, since a not dissimilar suggestion about the subversive effect of unusual linguistic juxtapositions – including the co-occurrence of markedly 'masculine' with ultra-'feminine' features – has been made much more recently by scholars who see this kind of style or register mixing as an expression of a post-1990s 'queer' sensibility (see e.g. Barrett's discussion of African-American drag queens, Chapter 13; also Queen 1997 on the lesbian comic book character Hothead Paisan).

For Louie Crew, the notion of a 'sexual register of English unique to gays' is a myth subscribed to by prejudiced outsiders for whom the entire culture of male homosexuality is reducible to one thing: effeminacy. Cory had also set out to counter the myth of uniqueness, noting the overlap between homosexual, criminal and theatrical argots. A little later in the history of research on gay and lesbian language, however, the notion of a register or style of speaking 'unique to gays' would become attractive to a number of insider-researchers, prompting a new wave of debates about the existence and distinctive features of 'Gayspeak'.

Chapter 1

Gershon Legman

1941

THE LANGUAGE OF HOMOSEXUALITY

An American glossary

Editors' note: The following extract from the glossary contains only those entries that Legman considered to be 'used exclusively by homosexuals' (139 of the 329 terms). The original glossary also contains a lengthy introduction in which Legman, from a desire, he writes, 'to bring some provisional order out of chaos', coins and defines terms like *penilinctus* and *irrumational*. We have not included this discussion here, but several of these words – most of which did not pass into more general usage – appear in Legman's explanations of the glossary terms. They are:

frictation   Friction of the penis against the abdomen, or between the buttocks and thighs of another person.

irrumation   The introduction of one's penis into the mouth of another.

pedication   Anal coitus, with the active party being the pedicator, and the passive participant the pedicant.

tribady   Confrictation [rubbing together – eds] of vulvae.

———

THE FOLLOWING SLANG GLOSSARY includes only words and phrases current in American slang, argot, and colloquial speech since the First World War, and particularly during the period between 1930 and 1940. The entire sexual vocabulary of the homosexual is not recorded in this glossary, except in the sphere of sexual practice, where every effort has been made to supply a complete and exhaustive record.

A very common usage in the speech of male homosexuals, that should be noted in connection with this glossary, is the substitution of feminine pronouns and titles for properly masculine ones. Male homosexuals use the terms *she*, *her*, *hers*, *Miss*, *Mother*, and *girl* (almost never 'woman') in referring to themselves and each other, where one might expect 'he,' 'him,' 'his,' 'Mr.,' 'Father,' and 'man' (or 'boy'). This usage is sometimes rather confusingly carried over to references to heterosexuals, though an overtone, in such cases, of jocularity or mild contempt usually serves to mark the heterosexuality of the person referred to. These usages are not confined to the very effeminate homosexuals who adopt feminine names, but are current among almost all types. It is worthy of note, too, that Lesbians do not seem usually to refer to each ether by masculine pronouns and titles, even though very many of them adopt masculine or semi-masculine names (such as Toni, Billie, Jackie, Jerry, etc.). However, note the entries *papa* and *daddy* in the glossary.

Very noticeable too is the seeming absence of almost any but 'outsiders'' slang in relation to female homosexuality. It is difficult to assign a reason to this absence, but, if there really is such an absence, and a concealed argot does not exist, two interrelated factors stand out particularly: The tradition of gentlemanly restraint among Lesbians stifles the flamboyance and conversational cynicism in sexual matters that slang coinage requires; and what little direct mention of sexual practice there is among female homosexuals is usually either gruffly brusque and vague, or else romantically euphemistic. This is largely due to the fact that Lesbian attachments are sufficiently feminine to be more often emotional than simply sexual, to which fact the practical non-existence of commercial Lesbianism is also largely due. There is certainly no Lesbian prostitution to compare with the prostitution existing for and among homosexual males. Concomitantly, Lesbianism in America – and perhaps elsewhere – seems in a large measure factitious; a faddish vice among the intelligentsia, a good avenue of entry in the theatre, and, most of all, a safe resource for timid women and *demi-vierges*, an erotic outlet for the psychosexually traumatized daughters of tyrannous fathers, and a despairing retreat for the wives and ex-wives of clumsy, brutal, or ineffectual lovers. All these factors, combined with the greater tolerance in America toward Lesbians than toward homosexual men – due, possibly, to their being less numerous, or, at least, less noticeable – make unlikely any feeling of criminality, let alone criminal community, among Lesbians; two attitudes of mind which seem particularly conducive to the manufacture of slang. I have been assured, however, that the situation is quite different in prisons, and that a fairly extensive Lesbian argot is likely to be found there. I have not had the opportunity to find out.

Finally I wish to point out that the immense territorial extent of the United States, and the flexible and inventive vitality of its spoken language make it impossible to compile a really complete glossary of any current argot, or to define any term positively and forever.

Slang vocabulary

abdicated　Ordered by the attendant to leave a public toilet; said of male homosexuals ('queens' therefore 'abdicated') who frequent park, subway, theatre, barroom, and other toilets. Compare *dethroned*, and see *tea-room queen* and *privy queen*.

angel with a dirty face　A male homosexual who wishes to indulge in homosexual practices, but who is hesitant or inhibited. (In use since the motion-picture, 'Angels with Dirty Faces,' in the mid-1930s.)

auntie   A derogatory term for a middle-aged or elderly homosexual. Also: **aunty**.

badge, To wear one's   To wear a red necktie; in some localities considered the insignia of homosexuality. Obsolescent.

basket   The scrotum, or, rather, the size of the testicles and scrotum as seen or felt through the trousers. (With this term is connected the term *meat* for the penis.) Also, broadly and somewhat incorrectly, the penis and testicles together, or their size. Compare *basketful of meat*, *eggs in the basket*, and *take the meat out of the basket*.

basketeer   To go about the streets – usually in a city or town with which one is unfamiliar – on foot or in an automobile, looking over the genitals of the men as they show through their trousers. Some homosexuals derive complete erotic satisfaction from this; others are simply *cruising*, q.v. Male prostitutes and plain-clothes police officers have been known to stuff their trousers with handkerchiefs, or to wear large dildoes (artificial penises, usually of rubber) or even bananas in their trousers to attract the homosexuals; the prostitutes in order to practice their trade, and the police officers in order to arrest the homosexuals, although provocation to commit a misdemeanor or a felony is specifically prohibited by the laws of most states.

basketful of meat   A large penis. (*-ful* becomes *full* in certain contexts, as: 'What a grand basketful of meat he's got!' but 'His basket is certainly full of meat.') Compare *gobs of meat*, s.v. *meat*.

basket picnic   A *basketeering* expedition.

belle   A male homosexual, particularly if young.

bitch   1. A derogatory term used by one homosexual of another, implying conceit or haughtiness, or general personal unpleasantness. Adjective: **bitchy**. 2. A young pedicant. (Hobo slang)

bleeding dirt   Professional criminals or underworld characters who try to provoke homosexuals to some overt homosexual act, and then extort money from them. This petty racket is known in underworld argot as *the mouse*, but this term does not seem to be known or used by homosexuals. Compare *dirt*.

blind   ADJECTIVE: Uncircumcised; said of the penis. 'Completely blind' refers to a penis of which the prepuce is so long that the glans penis cannot be seen. NOUN: An uncircumcised penis. Also: **blind meat** and **blind piece**. Compare *make the blind to see*.

blind piece, to ride a   To fellate an uncircumcised man, the reference being to the penis, and not to the man. Compare *blind*.

body lover   A homosexual fricator.

brilliant   NOUN & ADJECTIVE: Congenitally homosexual male.

broad   A homosexual prostitute who, himself homosexual, accosts men in the street for sexual purposes. From the common slang term for a female prostitute or a loose woman.

bronco   A boy new to homosexual practices, who is normal, rough, and at times intractable to the wishes of the homosexual. From the cowboy term for an unbroken horse.

brought out, To be   To be initiated into the practice of homosexuality. The active form of the phrase: *to bring (one) out* is rarely used, and in general this locution is losing its original connotation of initiation by another person, and circumstances or fate are coming to be considered the initiatory agents, the phrase therefore coming to be almost the equivalent of *come out*, q.v.

bucket   The anus. Compare *can*.

bugger   A pedicator. The word is used in its actual meaning only by educated homosexuals and others such as seamen and persons of British birth or background. It is used in America usually without realization of, or reference to its true meaning, even by children, as a term of opprobrium; originally a British usage. In rural America *bugger* is used as a term of endearment applied especially to children, and often corrupted to *beggar*, as is done, for purposes of euphemism, in Britain. Compare *bug* and *burglar*.

bull-dike   A homosexual woman, particularly one who wears mannish clothes and is in other ways aggressively masculine. Also: **bull-dyke**, **bull-diker**, and **bull-dyker**. A common corruption is **bull-dagger**. VERBAL ADJECTIVE: **bull-diking** (also spelled: **bull-dycking**). Compare *dike*.

call house   A homosexual brothel which will telephone or send for specific boys called for by homosexuals or pedicators. Compare *show house* and *peg house*. The term exists also in non-homosexual argot, referring to a similar brothel with women prostitutes and male clients.

camp   To speak, act, or in any way attract or attempt to attract attention, especially if noisily, flamboyantly, bizarrely, or in any other way calculated to announce, express, or burlesque one's own homosexuality or that of any other person. As a NOUN, *camp* refers to such flamboyance or bizarrerie of speech or action, or to a person displaying it. The VERBAL NOUN, **camping**, is very common; it should be noticed that camping is largely a practice of male homosexuals, and is not very common among Lesbians. ADJECTIVE: **campy**.

checkers, playing   Moving from seat to seat in a motion-picture theatre to find a willing youth. The homosexual sits down next to a likely subject, and makes either a verbal or an elaborately accidental physical overture or 'pass,' and if rebuffed, gets up and moves to another seat in another row, preferably not too close to the previous location, to try again with someone else.

chicken   A young boy of about fifteen to twenty years, especially one with little homosexual experience; also a generic term for boys of this age and sort, fancied by many homosexuals, both pedicators and fellators, termed **chicken fanciers**.

church-mouse   A homosexual who frequents churches and cathedrals in order to *grope* and *cruise* the young men there. Churches are chosen for this purpose not from any irreverence or cynicism, but rather because crowds of standing and preoccupied people, as in cathedrals, subways, elevators and theatres, are ideal for the homosexual's purpose.

cognoscenti   (Mispronounced in a variety of ways.) Collectively, all persons in the fraternity of homosexuality, including homosexuals, their prostitutes and friends (see *jam*), and others who understand the argot, are acquainted with the current popular meeting places, and share the homosexuals' fear and detestation of the police.

come out   To become progressively more and more exclusively homosexual with experience. This meaning is currently being given also to *brought out*, q.v., which originally had a distinctly different shade of meaning.

cousin   The homosexual lover of another invert.

cruise   To walk or drive in an automobile through the streets, aimlessly but in certain specific and likely areas, looking (if a *hustler*) for a customer, or (if a homosexual – *pay-off* or otherwise) for a companion for homosexual intercourse, whether for money or *pour le sport*. The verbal noun, **cruising**, is very common as a term for this type of street-walking and accosting, and a homosexual or hustler who practices it is termed a **cruiser**. The verb is often used transitively, usually taking the neuter pronoun rather than the masculine, whether the person referred to is homosexual or not, e.g. 'That blond sailor looks good; I think I'll cruise it.' To avoid confusion it should be remembered that the homosexual prostitute may be heterosexual (in which case his prostitution usually consists of allowing homosexuals to fellate him, or allowing pedicators – who may be heterosexual – to pedicate him) or homosexual (in which case his prostitution usually consists of submitting to passive pedication by possibly heterosexual pedicators, or performing fellation upon entirely heterosexual persons). Furthermore, the client may be a homosexual, or a possibly heterosexual pedicator, or a complete heterosexual (who may wish to be fellated because of a superstitious belief that he may be cured of acne in that way, or because women are not available or too costly). This is quite complex, and the above perfunctory elucidation is not entirely satisfactory; but in most cases the technical distinction between client and prostitute – often the distinction *is* merely technical – can usually be made by terming as the client the participant who is more anxious and aggressive, and who pays.

cunt   Actually the external and internal female genitals, considered separately as vulva and vagina, or as a single entity. Transferentially used by pederasts and homosexuals of a boy's mouth or rectum, or of a boy considered merely as a sexual outlet. The slang terms *pussy* and *twat* are also used, in this way, but such usages are rather rare, since, what with the very common use of feminine names, pronouns, and appellations among male homosexuals in referring to themselves and to other men, the female genital and its names are usually reserved to be the one unmistakable mark of reference to an actual woman.

daddy   A Lesbian of the masculine type, especially one who lives or consorts with a Lesbian of the feminine type, a *mama*, q.v. Compare *papa*.

dethroned   Ordered by the attendant to leave a public toilet; said of male homosexuals ('queens' therefore 'dethroned') who frequent the toilet rooms of parks, subways, barrooms, theatres, and other public buildings. Compare *enthroned* and *abdicated*, and see *tea-room queen* and *privy queen*.

dish the dirt   To gossip about the sexual nature, adventures, and misadventures of another homosexual. Also, to criticize anyone who has 'done dirt' to one of the homosexual fraternity; or to criticize anyone generally. Often contracted to dish. See *dirt*.

do   To seduce or enjoy homosexually. Compare *trade, To do for*.

dog's dinner   A term of extreme derogation used among homosexuals, possibly with some reference to fellation and the derogatory term *bitch*.

double-life man   An actively bisexual man, who can, and does, have pleasurable sexual relations with both sexes.

dowager   An elegant elderly homosexual. A **dirty dowager** is one not quite so elegant.

drag   Elaborate feminine clothing, used for transvestist dressing by male homosexuals. Also a party, dance, or costume ball where homosexual men go dressed as women, and, to a lesser extent, homosexual women dressed as men. **In drag** means dressed in the clothing of the opposite sex, that is, the outer clothing; many male homosexuals wear feminine lingerie, but that is not considered *drag*.

drag-queen   A professional female impersonator; the term being transferentially used of a male homosexual who frequently or almost invariably wears women's clothing, often for purposes of homosexual contact, posing as a female prostitute or as a loose girl and fellating men picked up under this disguise, with the excuse that coitus is not practicable because of menstruation. *Drag-queens* are even said to strap their penises up on their abdomens and to submit – without undressing – to pedication in the face-to-face posture, the client thinking that he is having coitus with a woman! Or the penis and testicles, it is said, can be hidden under a menstrual pad, and pedication openly suggested as a substitute for the desired coitus. While many effeminate male homosexuals wear women's underwear – chemises or even panties and brassière – they are not for that reason called *drag-queens*.

duck   To allow pedication. Used for assonance in the phrase: *To fuck, suck, and duck*; and has little or no existence elsewhere.

eggs in the basket   The testicles. See *basket*.

enthroned   In a public toilet; said of homosexuals who frequent toilet rooms looking for *trade*. Compare *dethroned*, and see *tea-room queen* and *privy queen*.

fag   A male homosexual; a derogatory term never used by homosexuals themselves, who use *faggot*, q.v. *Fag* is also used as an adjective, although not so often as *faggot*, of which it is a contraction.

faggot   A male homosexual; a derogatory term, especially when used by homosexuals of each other. Compare *fag*. Also **fagot** and **faggart**, this latter being a Negro corruption, or perhaps it is the original term while the other forms are corruptions. *Faggot* is also used as an adjective (e.g. 'a faggot walk'), another adjective form being **faggoty**, which is mainly used by Negroes (e.g. 'a faggoty man').

fence, To be on the   To forsake homosexual practices for heterosexuality (or vice versa?). Compare *gender, To lose one's*.

fifty-fifty   An adjective phrase referring to alternating fellation or pedication. It is a relatively new coinage and seems to have been invented to differentiate (as for instance in toilet-wall epigraphs and invitations) between simultaneous oragenitalism: 69, and alternating oragenitalism, etc.: 50–50 (or 50/50, the term usually being given in a numerical form). The term, in ordinary slang, refers to even division of matter or labor or to any alternating and turnabout relationship. It may be used as an ordinary adjective (e.g. 'a *50–50 party*'), or as a predicate adjective (e.g. 'I want it to be fifty-fifty'), or it may stand cryptically alone and unmodifying in an epigraph, like *69* scrawled on the door of a Parisian brothel.

fish   Originally a generic term for women or for the vulva; the reference being to the somewhat piscine odor of the female genitalia. The word is used among male homosexuals as a predicate nominative to refer to male homosexuality, especially of the effeminate type, as *to be fish* or *to go fish* (e.g. 'When he touched me I just went *fish*, all over.') Employed as a verb, usually intransitive, meaning to perform cunnilinctus. Other verb forms are: **eat fish** and **chew the fish**. (A popular American song of the late 1930s, 'Seafood Mama,' with the chorus-line: 'I get my favorite dish – fish!' was finally banned from the radio after being innocently allowed for several months.)

fish-queen   A man who enjoys cunnilinctus, or a homosexual (or heterosexual) male who practices it for pay. The term is quite derogatory, and, in the case of a homosexual male, is sometimes contracted to *fish*, q.v. I do not wholly understand the organization of this type of prostitution to women, although it has been reliably reported in New York, Los Angeles, and New Orleans, and probably exists in metropolitan and resort cities (Chicago, San Francisco, Reno, Atlantic City, Miami, etc.); nor do I understand whether the women involved are Lesbian or vicious or what, nor why it is necessary for them to pay for their sexual pleasure. The 'queen' in *fish-queen* does suggest, however, that the term (and possibly the commercial practice) was originally current only among, and in reference to homosexuals, and that it was later transferentially applied to a heterosexual cunnilinctor, whether amateur or professional. What confuses the matter even more is the common and vociferous distaste among homosexual men for women and for their vulvar odor, which makes it hard to understand how homosexuals could become professional cunnilinctors.

flaming   VERBAL ADJECTIVE: Obviously homosexual; using cosmetics, wearing flamboyant clothes and suede or high-heeled shoes, and generally affecting exaggeratedly feminine mannerisms in order to announce, and attract attention to one's homosexuality. Most used in the term **flaming queen**, a homosexual who attempts thus to attract attention and drum up trade. Both parts of this term may be modified, as, e.g. 'a very flaming young queen.' Compare *queen*.

floater   A boy or man not a resident of the town or city where he prostitutes himself to homosexuals, certain of whom will consort only with this type of trade in order to reduce the danger of gossip or exposure in the locality where they live.

fuck   To pedicate, or, less commonly, to irrumate. Compare the two following entries.

fuck in (or **up**) **the ass**   To pedicate. Compare *ass-fuck*.

fuck in the mouth (or **face**)   To irrumate.

ga-ga   **1.** The first of 'seven recognized stages of homosexuality, from *ga-ga* to the "deeper tones" of lavender.' (There do not seem to be terms for each stage, and it is possible that seven distinct stages are not actually thought to exist, the phrase being merely a way of indicating the progressive nature of homosexuality.) **2.** An immature or inexperienced homosexual. **3.** The preliminaries of arousal between two homosexuals who enjoy sexual intimacy with each other and are therefore looked down upon by many experienced homosexuals (compare *ki-ki*).

gang-fuck   An instance of pedication or irrumation of a single boy or homosexual by two or more men (usually more) consecutively, and with or without his consent. Also used as a verb; and, in both senses, heterosexually, of the consecutive copulation of two or more men with a single willing or unwilling woman, in which case it is also called *gang-shagging*. Compare *line up*.

gay   An adjective used almost exclusively by homosexuals to denote homosexuality, sexual attractiveness, promiscuity ('camped' as *promiscruity*, on *screw*, meaning to copulate), or lack of restraint, in a person, place, or party. Often given the French spelling, *gai* or *gaie* by (or in burlesque of) cultured homosexuals of both sexes.

gender, To discover one's   To *come out*; to become progressively more homosexual with experience. 'One who "hasn't discovered his (her?) gender" hasn't achieved the "deeper tones" of lavender.'

gender, To lose one's   To leave homosexual practices and become heterosexual. Compare: *fence, to be on the*.

glut   A homosexual, particularly a fellator, with an insatiable sexual appetite. Contraction of *glutton*.

glutton for punishment   A fellator who has already experienced his indirect orgasm, but who continues fellation out of sheer lubricity. No connection with *punishment*, q.v.

go all over town (with)   To administer a t*ongue-bath* to another person; to lick a person all over the body, usually ending with fellation (or cunnilinctus). See *trip around the world*.

goofer   A male prostitute to homosexuals, who prostitutes only his penis (that is, to fellators, to mutual masturbators, or to passive pedicants), and not his anus, as do *punks*, q.v., nor his mouth, as do those prostitutes who are willing to take on a *french job* (i.e. a job of *frenching*, q.v.). Compare *prick-peddler*.

grand bag   A large scrotum, which is very pleasing to fellators. 'Grand' and 'gorgeous' are very common adjectives of approbation among homosexual males. Compare *basket*.

grope   To feel and handle another person's genitals, thighs, or buttocks, especially when he is clothed. Used as a noun in the verb phrase, **get a grope**, but not so much as is *feel*, q.v., although *grope* is by far the more common term in all contexts in the speech of homosexuals.

hair, To let down one's   To drop all restraint in displaying one's homosexuality, or to admit to being homosexual. The use of this phrase in common American slang, as meaning to drop all pretense or finally to tell the truth, seems to stem from the homosexual meaning.

have   To have sexual relations with; more usually meaning to pedicate than to fellate. Heterosexually, the word is used only of a man who copulates with a woman, and not vice versa.

head   A generic noun or predicate nominative referring to a fellator, as, e.g. 'looking for head.' Term reported from Montreal in 1940. Compare *head-worker*.

hidden queen   A male homosexual who conceals, or tries to conceal the fact of his homosexuality. Compare *veil*.

hose   To pedicate. The verbal noun, **hosing**, usually refers to a specific act of pedication, rather than to pedication generically. These terms are also used heterosexually of the copulation of a man with a woman, e.g. *to give her a* (*good*) *hosing*.

husband   The normal or else more aggressive member of a homosexual liaison, male or female; a favorite lover who sees the homosexual regularly. Compare *wife*.

hustler   A male prostitute to homosexuals, especially so called if he is himself heterosexual. A common slang term for an accosting female prostitute.

incest   A sexual liaison between two homosexuals, such an association being held in comparative contempt by most homosexuals. Compare *ki-ki*.

it   The usual pronoun of reference used by homosexuals, instead of 'he' or 'him' in speaking of heterosexual men accosted or *picked up*. See the quotation s.v. *cruise*. Another such substitution is the use of 'something' for 'someone.' *It* is also used as a noun or pronoun in referring to a homosexual of either sex, especially a male homosexual, this usage being derogatory and confined to 'outsiders.'

jam   **1.** A non-homosexual male (the term is said to be an abbreviation of just a man, but this derivation may be merely a *camp*), especially if he is acquainted with another person's homosexuality but does not divulge it. The term is usually employed as a predicate nominative, and has no connection with *eat jam*, q.v. **2.** Preliminaries of homosexual eroticism between a homo- and a heterosexual.

jam fag   A congenitally and completely homosexual male.

jam pot   The anus. See *eat jam*, referring to anilinctus.

jockey   A Lesbian, particularly one of the masculine type, who takes or is imagined to take the superior position in tribady. Compare *top-sergeant*.

John   The regular lover – paid or paying – of a homosexual male prostitute.

keister   The anus or buttocks. Also: **kiester**, both being pronounced *kee-*.

kidney trouble, To have   To frequent toilet rooms for homosexual purposes; from the diuresis commonly accompanying kidney ailments.

ki-ki   (Pronounced with both 'i's' long, as in ice, and with both syllables stressed equally, or with only a slightly greater accent on the first syllable.) A homosexual male who is sexually attracted only to other homosexuals, or who engages in an affair with another homosexual for want of the money or personal attractiveness necessary for contact with heterosexuals. Such homosexuals are commonly considered to indulge in mutual fellation, simultaneous or turnabout, or, less commonly, in mutual pedication. Variant: **kiki**. As an adjective in **ki-ki queen**; and as a predicate adjective as, for instance, in *to go ki-ki. Ki-ki queens* are held in mild contempt by *pay-off queens* (q.v.), and vice versa.

knights, To be one of the   To have syphilis.

lace curtain   A long foreskin.

live one   A male prostitute's homosexual client who is generous with money and valuable gifts. 'Live' is an adjective; the 'i' being long as in *ice*.

long-winded   Not likely to ejaculate quickly in being fellated, a quality much sought after and appreciated by many fellators.

lover   A non-homosexual man who is sustaining, or has sustained sexual relations
or a liaison with a homosexual or with several homosexuals. Many such men
are bisexual rather than heterosexual, although the precise distinction between
these two psychosexual states seems to be a matter of some question.

low neck and short sleeves   A circumcised penis. A related term, similarly
drawn from the feminine pursuits of decoration and dress, is *lace curtain*, q.v.

madam(e)   The proprietor, usually homosexual, of a *peg house* or *show house*.
From the slang appellation for the proprietress of an ordinary heterosexual
brothel, with women inmates.

mama   A Lesbian of the feminine type, especially one living or consorting with
a *papa* or *daddy*.

man   When pronounced emphatically by a homosexual, this term refers to a man
who is definitely not homosexual. Also: **he-man** and **real man**.

meat   The penis. Also: **the meat** and **piece of meat**. Compare fish, for homosexual men; **meat** being used generically to refer to heterosexual men. See
also *basket* and *take the meat out of the basket*. To have **gobs of meat** is to have
a large penis: compare *basketful of meat*. I am informed that it is considered
humorous to refer to a very large penis as 'phenomenal.'

Miss   A title imputing homosexuality to the man whose name follows. Compare
Ma and *Mother*; and note the remarks preceding this glossary concerning
feminine titles and pronouns as used among homosexuals. Note also that
male homosexuals will call most anyone Bessie or Mary, e.g. 'Oh, Bessie,
you're a camp!' Furthermore, the more effeminate male homosexuals –
particularly those given to feminine mannerisms and pursuits (such as needle-
work) and those who dress in women's clothes whenever possible – often
assume feminine names such as 'Mae West,' 'Spanish Annie,' 'The Duchess,'
and other similar appellations.

mother-love   **1.** Copulation or oragenitalism between a homosexual male and
a woman. **2.** Sexual intimacy between two homosexuals; derogatory.
Compare *ki-ki*. The term does not refer to love given by a mother, but rather
to incestuous love directed toward a mother, one of the most powerful
taboos of our civilization, with which is connected the superlatively derogatory colloquial epithet, *mother-fucker*, with its burlesque synonym, *granny-
jazzer*; note the assonance in both. Compare *sister-act* and *incest*.

mug   A derogatory term used by male prostitutes to denote a homosexual client.

muscle in   To attempt to divert the affections of a male prostitute's homosexual
client to oneself. The term is borrowed from criminal slang.

muzzler   A homosexual, a derogatory term used by male prostitutes, and usually
denoting a fellator. The term is also used in ordinary slang with, aside from
its derogatory force, some reference to handling a girl's breasts or, possibly,
to kissing.

near-sighted   Uncircumcised, but with the tip of the glans penis showing under
the foreskin; the term is used of the penis itself, and not of its owner. Compare
blind.

oncer   A homosexual who will have only one sexual experience with any single
person. VERBAL NOUN: **oncing**, the practice of refusing to have, more than
a single sexual experience with any particular person. The terms are not very
common, but the practice is.

one-way man   A male prostitute who, if himself heterosexual, will allow himself to be fellated but not pedicated; or, if himself homosexual, will allow himself to be pedicated but will not perform fellation. This is not a very stringent definition, and there are many exceptions, but in general it is correct. Compare *two-way man*.

papa   A Lesbian of the masculine type, especially so called if living or consorting with a *mama*, q.v. Also *daddy*.

pay-off queen   A homosexual who pays for the privilege of practicing his particular type of eroticism upon another man. This type of homosexual is held in great contempt by homosexuals who do not pay the other participant, who is cooperating simply for pleasure, and by homosexuals who are prostitutes and receive money for homosexual practice.

pee-pee lover   A homosexual, particularly a fellator, who fancies very young boys.

pee-pee meat   A small penis; *small meat*. From the nursery term, *pee-pee*, meaning the penis considered as a urinary organ (*pee* is a euphemistic contraction of *piss*; but compare the French *pipi*).

peg-house   A house, or, more often, an apartment, given over to male homosexual assignation and prostitution. (The name is from the East Indian homosexual brothels, where young boys are said to be kept sitting on a pegged bench to keep their anuses distended until they are required for pedication. This does not exist in America (where homosexuals are usually fellators and pedicants rather than pedicators), and is quite probably only apocryphal elsewhere). Compare *show house* and *call house*.

pervert   A colloquialism very current in America for a homosexual or for any other sex deviator: rapist, sadist, pederast, coprophile, etc. Compare *degenerate*.

phoney   A homosexual whom a male prostitute suspects or knows to be stingy, and likely to cheat or bilk him.

pimp   A person who procures male prostitutes for homosexuals. There does not seem to be any appreciable actual pimping in male prostitution, since most of the boys and men so employed are heterosexual, and have male 'lovers' only for pay, and do not require a pimp, as do female prostitutes, as a business manager and lover. Male prostitutes who are themselves homosexual often live with heterosexual male prostitutes who may pimp for the homosexual consort. Also: **p.i.** (pronounced as the letters)

privy-queen   A homosexual who frequents toilet rooms, looking for trade. Compare *tea-room queen*.

prospect   A man or boy who might be willing to fall in with a homosexual's erotic or erotico-financial purposes; potential *trade*.

proud   Having deserted homosexual company, and having discontinued homosexual practices. Compare *gender, to lose one's*.

punishment   Accepting orally or anally a penis which is uncomfortably large. No connection with *glutton for punishment*.

queer bird   A female homosexual.

railroad queen   A homosexual who *cruises* the 'jungles' where tramps live and congregate.

R.F.D. queen   A homosexual who lives in the country or in a small town, and who has homosexual impulses and desires, but who does not understand the argot and ways, or know the habits and places of congregation of the homosexual fraternity in cities and metropolitan centers. From *Rural Free Delivery*, a term which immediately suggests the rustic scene to the urban mind.

rough trade   An uncultured, roughly-dressed and -spoken man 'picked up' by a homosexual, or such men generically. See *trade*.

say a mouthful   To reprove or reprimand another homosexual verbally, incisively, and at great length. This idiom has a slightly different meaning in popular slang, to which I have been informed that it was brought over from homosexual argot. Also: **To lay (one) for filth**.

sea-food   Generic for sailors; a term used by male homosexuals, especially fellators (but note the implication of cunnilinctus in the song 'Seafood Mama' mentioned s.v. *fish*).

sell   To sell a boy is to procure him for a homosexual for a set price. Compare *pimp*.

show-house   A brothel for male homosexual clients unlike a heterosexual brothel in that it is used more as a place of assignation than as a place of prostitution, the sexual contact often – though not invariably – taking place elsewhere. See *peg-house* and *call-house*.

sil   A Lesbian who is currently in love with another woman. A contraction of *silly*, meaning infatuated (usually in combination as *silly* about). Also: **sill**.

sister-act   **1.** Copulation or oragenitalism between a homosexual male and a woman. **2.** Sexual intimacy between two homosexuals; compare *ki-ki*. Derogatory in both senses; compare *mother-love*.

slay   To injure a homosexual by dishing the dirt about him or informing on him.

small meat   A small penis; compare *meat*. It should be remembered that fellators and pedicants are usually fond of large penises, and they might term *small meat* a six- or seven-inch penis, which an ordinary heterosexual man would consider eminently satisfactory.

straight   Not a *clip-artist* or a *phoney*, q.v. Also employed as meaning not homosexual. **To go straight** is to cease homosexual practices and to indulge – usually to re-indulge – in heterosexuality.

swing   To fellate. The object is the penis, not the person; e.g. 'to swing a *blind*.' Also: **swing on**, the object here being either the person or the organ; in the latter case the phrase is usually **swing on it**.

swish   ADJECTIVE: Have male homosexual characteristics. Even inanimate objects may, be referred to, e.g. 'But dearie, isn't that tie too swish?' Also: **swishy**. The reference is to the peculiarly effeminate walk of many male homosexuals, suggesting the imaginary rustle of skirts; and *swish* is also used verbally to refer to this gait, the verbal noun being **swishing**.

tail   Generic for boys considered as the object of pedication; a boy so considered, or his pedication, being a **piece of tail**. The term is also used heterosexually in all senses in reference to copulation with women. Compare *ass* and *cunt*.

take the meat out of the basket   To undo the clothing and expose the penis of another person or of oneself. See *meat* and *basket*.

tea-room queen   A homosexual who frequents toilet rooms to find persons amenable to his erotic or erotico-financial plans, or to scrawl homosexual dithyrambs or invitations on the walls. The ironic 'tea-room' for toilet does not seem to occur in any other connection.

temperamental   Homosexual. Usually an adjective; as a noun the term is obsolescent.

top-sergeant   A Lesbian of the masculine type, who takes, or is imagined to take the superior position in tribady. Compare *jockey*.

trade   Generic for male prostitutes to homosexuals, or for heterosexuals to whom homosexuals prostitute themselves; the existence or direction of any exchange of money being irrelevant. **Do for trade** to have homosexual relations with a heterosexual male (prostitute or otherwise), usually referring to fellating him, the object usually being interpolated into the idiom, as, e.g. 'to do him for trade.' *Trade* may be used as a predicate nominative in referring to a single person generically, e.g. 'He is trade,' such a person also being called a **piece of trade**. Compare *rough-trade* and *uniform*.

triangle   The situation in which a man and a Lesbian are both in love with the same woman; or in which both have sexual relations with her without any jealousy. Probably also applied to similar situations involving a male homosexual, a woman, and a more or less normal man; but I have never personally heard the term so used. This usage of *triangle* derives directly from the colloquial usage of the term to refer to the rivalry of two men over a woman married to one of them, or of two women over a man married to one of them.

tricks, To do   To be willing to fellate or to submit to pedication; said of a male prostitute of any type and sexuality.

turn over   To allow oneself to be pedicated. Also: **turn one's back**.

turn the tables   To blackmail a heterosexual client, said of homosexuals; the term implies, and correctly, that it is more often the homosexual who is blackmailed. The tables may also be turned on a homosexual client, a homosexual who would blackmail another being considered the lowest kind of *dirt* by the fraternity.

two-way man   A male prostitute who, if heterosexual, will not only allow himself to be fellated, but will *turn over* too, that is, will also allow himself to be pedicated; or who, if himself homosexual, will not only allow himself to be pedicated, but will perform fellation also. See *one-way man* and *take it any way*.

uniform, a   A soldier, sailor, or marine (only very seldom, if ever, used to apply to a fireman, policeman, postman, or messenger boy); as opposed to civilians or to *rough trade*, q.v., who are roughly dressed.

veil, To wear a mourning   To attempt to conceal the fact of one's homosexuality. An obvious homosexual who tries ineffectually to conceal his state is said to **wear a cut-glass veil**, that is, his concealment is perfectly useless and transparent.

vibrations, To pick up the   To watch others indulge in homosexual practice, some homosexuals paying for the privilege of this voyeurism, and achieving automatic orgasm during its course.

virgin   A man who has never been pedicated. Compare *cherry*.

white-liver   A male or female homosexual who is completely indifferent to the
opposite sex.

wife   The less aggressive member of a homosexual alliance, male or female. See
husband.

wise   Acquainted with the fact, the practices, and the locales of homosexuality;
said of boys and young men by homosexuals.

words and music, To know the   To use or recognize typically homosexual
locutions (such as *gay* and *camp*), suggesting that one is homosexual or under-
stands the other person to be so.

Chapter 2

Donald W. Cory

1951

TAKE MY WORD FOR IT

THE SPECIAL LANGUAGE CREATED by a minority group may have several purposes. It can be aimed at making unintelligible to others that which is perfectly understandable to a few; it may have a more or less euphemistic aim, softening the blows carried by certain words, although expressing their meanings; and it may seek to be descriptive in a colorful manner.

The language of homosexual life has in it an element of cant – the keeping in secrecy from the out-group that which is clear to the in-group; it has the argot that is characteristic of any trade or profession; the slang that is on the fringe of our language just as the homosexuals are on the fringe of society; the euphemisms and their counterpart from which they grew, the hostile words and expressions. It is a language similar in some respects to that of the underworld; in others, to that of the theater; and finally, it is suggestive of the language of a professional minority, such as the physicians. Actually the two phases of the special language of homosexuality – the words and phrases used by the world at large, and those employed by the inner circle – are almost unrelated to each other.

There are two broad characteristics of what I should like to call the homosexual 'cantargot': first, that it has failed to develop in the natural way because of the conspiracy of silence in which the subject is enshrouded; secondly, that in the connotations, pro and con, that are implied by special words, the cantargot is remarkably suggestive of that of the racial, religious, and national minorities of the United States.

How widespread is the silence and how far-reaching its effects are indicated by the fact that even the scientific terminology is frequently absent from otherwise complete and authoritative dictionaries; and that even the authorities cannot agree on the meanings that should be assigned to such words as *homosexual*, *invert*, *pederast*, and *sodomist*.

As for the connotations of special words, the homosexual is sensitively aware of the stigma attached not only to his practices and desires, but to terms associated therewith, and he seeks to create or to utilize synonyms with a more agreeable connotation. Sometimes the outside world is hardly cognizant of the origin of a term it is employing, nor of the aura of ill-feeling that it will engender. The majority will use words like *wop*, *chink*, or *boogie* with no conscious malice, believing them to be nothing but descriptive, and ignorant of their deep and hurtful meanings. Even more subtle are the reasons that certain terms become unacceptable. For example, *Negress* and *Jewess* are no longer respectable words, although no one would object to the terms *Negro* or *Jew*.

The homosexual in America has been described by people in society at large by various words and phrases, each of which usually carried a sneering connotation. Best known among these words are *fairy*, *pansy*, *nancy* or *nance*, *Mary*, *sissy* or *sis* (sometimes *sister*), *fag* or *faggot*, *queen* (an important variation being *fish-queen*), *queer*, *homo*, *c——r* [probably 'cocksucker' – eds], *freak*, *fruit* (he is *a fruit* or he *is fruity*), *man-lover* or *boy-lover*, and on occasion a *Wildeman*. In England, and in legal and some other circles in the United States, *bugger* has been in frequent usage, and the practice called *buggery*. My English friends tell me that in England the word *bugger* has an extremely hostile connotation, comparable to the worst terms used in the United States.

The female homosexual has been called, almost universally and with considerable acceptance, a *Lesbian*, sometimes (although rarely) a *Sapphist*. Sometimes *lady-lover* or *woman-lover* is heard. In the inner circles, the cantargot includes such terms for the Lesbian as *dike* (or *dyke*), *stud*, and *bull* (more frequently *bull-dagger*).

The homosexual feels that the many terms used for male inverts are all inadequate. First, they describe a stereotype, the effeminate male: *fairy*, *queen*, *sister*, *nance*. Secondly, those that did not originate as description of an effeminate person became that through the evolution of language and through association; an example is *pansy*. *Queer* is obviously unsuited, because of its typing of an individual's personality. Many homosexuals are, in the totality of their lives, not queer people at all, and many heterosexuals are extremely queer. The word *queer*, in every other sense, leaving aside its colloquialism, has a tainted characterization about it that is unattractive, and therefore is to be shunned. The word *fag* is particularly humiliating. The evil that it carries can only be compared, as I see it, to some of the worst terms that America's dominant culture has used to humiliate and suppress racial groups. And, finally, the making of a slang synonym for almost anything or anyone nefarious, with no regard to his sexual inclination, of the term *c——r*, is comparable only to the hatred expressed by our society against out-of-wedlock children, who in addition to being characterized as illegitimate, are called *bastards*. Like *c——r*, the word *bastard* is used to describe anyone on whom contempt is heaped. In this way, an insulting connotation is implied in a word which, in its literal meaning, should merely describe the status or activity of a person.

It is a curiosity worth noting that in many lands the description of homosexuality has been associated with things foreign. The English word in common favor, *buggery*, is derived from *bougre*, which means *Bulgar*. A French book of the nineteenth century, whose title may perhaps have been inspired by the traditional Franco-German rivalries, was called, *Homosexualité, l'amour allemand*. Homosexuality, the German love! Indeed, at a time when France was becoming increasingly aware of the widespread nature of sexual inversion within her own confines. Certain of the forms of homosexual practices, and for that matter of heterosexual indulgences, namely fellatio and cunnilingus, are called in America *French love*, with the verb to *French* frequently used. *He Frenches* or *she likes to French* will be said, and almost any adult knows the meaning of these expressions. A homosexual is sometimes called a *Greek*, or more often a *Greek lover*, and homosexual friendship called *Greek love*. One of the many underworld synonyms for an active pederast is *turk*.

In conjuring up the Bulgar, the Frenchman, the German, the Greek, or the Turk (and, no doubt, there are other examples), the dominant heterosexual society has often sought to characterize homosexuality as foreign; seeks to associate it with immigrants and sometimes with enemies; and would therefore give the impression that it is not indigenous but rather un-American. It is ironical, but understandable, that the name of one nation that has been a traditional friend should have been employed; and of another whose civilization people are taught to admire and to emulate!

A minority group frequently reacts to the name-calling by similar activity against the majority. The homosexual, in inner-group language, is likely to call a heterosexual girl a *fish*, and a man who is attracted only to women is *butch*, but neither of these words is considered derogatory by those who use them.

For many years, homosexuals found a burning need for a language that would not have unpleasant connotations. The words must be free of the stereotype concepts, free likewise of hostility, and less cumbersome and heavy than such a word as *homosexual* itself. The language must be utilizable to describe all those sexually directed in their passions toward their own sex, regardless of virility, or lack of it, regardless of the type or age of the person coveted, or of the character of the physical relationship entered into. It was in this spirit that Ulrichs, a German writer and civil servant, proposed that homosexuality be called *Uranism*, and the individual a *Uranian* or *urning*. Ulrichs found inspiration for his etymology in the planet Uranus, which, of all the planets visible to the naked eye, is furthest from the sun and therefore nearest to heaven; love for one's own sex was likewise the most heavenly of physical passions, he contended. The derivation, with its glorification, might have been overlooked, but the word had a particularly foreign flavor and never seems to have become popular in our tongue, despite rather widespread employment by Edward Carpenter and other glorifiers of homosexuality around the turn of the century.

Carpenter himself used other euphemisms. He liked to call homosexuals *the third sex* or *the intermediate sex*, but in these words, heavy and long, were scientific connotations unacceptable to the Freudians. Another writer, André Tellier, called his subjects *twilight men*, whereas Radclyffe Hall referred to inversion as the *no-man's land of sex*.

In the meantime the scientific terminology was rather obscure. Somehow the word *invert*, although quite acceptable, never became widely used within the group. Suffice it to say that its meaning is known, but it is seldom heard in conversation. Entirely unacceptable, on the other hand, is *pervert*, which brings forth the ugly picture of an elderly man accosting a child (the latter may be male or female, but the criminal inclination of the older man is described as a perversion). I have opened library books in which the homosexual is referred to as *pervert*, and in the margins are vehement notations: *No, invert — not pervert!* Many of my friends have expressed similar distaste for the word *deviate*, for they resent the repulsive grouping of homo-sexuals with all sexual nonconformists: the sadist, the child-molester, and others.

In most of the English-language literature, *invert* is used interchangeably with *homosexual*. It is Gide's contention – and his opinion is shared by many – that *an invert* is an effeminate homosexual; he is the woman of the love-match seeking a man; his personality and sexuality, and some of his characteristics, are inverted, so to speak. The *pederast*, Gide maintains, is the lover of youth, the older man of the Greek man-boy relationship. The *sodomist* (or shall we say *sodomite?*) is the lover of the older man, the boy seeking maturity. Such lines of demarcation and absolute classifications are difficult to make and the arbitrary definitions are disputed both in the scientific and in the legal literature. In such writings, sodomy is usually not confined to homosexuality, and pederasty only to a certain type of physical relation-ship, which is usually of a homosexual character. At any rate scientific and popular, not to mention legal, confusions, and the removal of these words from the everyday language, combine to exclude them from serious consideration.

Needed for years was an ordinary, everyday, matter-of-fact word, that could express the concept of homosexuality without glorification or condemnation. It must have no odium of the effeminate stereotype about it. Such a word has long been in existence, and in recent years has grown in popularity. The word is *gay*.

How, when, and where this word originated, I am unable to say. I have been told by experts that it came from the French, and that in France as early as the sixteenth century the homosexual was called *gaie*; significantly enough, the femi-nine form was used to describe the male. The word made its way to England and America, and was used in print in some of the more pornographic literature soon after the First World War. Psychoanalysts have informed me that their homosexual patients were calling themselves *gay* in the nineteen-twenties, and certainly by the nineteen-thirties it was the most common word in use among homosexuals them-selves. It was not until after Pearl Harbor that it became a magic by-word in practically every corner of the United States where homosexuals might gather, and in the decade following America's entry into the Second World War I find that it was used with increasing frequency not only by novelists, magazine writers, and gossip columnists, but even by radio announcers. And yet, even to this day, despite its decades (if not centuries) of use, it is practically unknown outside of homo-sexual circles, except for police officers, theatrical groups, and a few others. Mencken, in his studies of the American language, shows no indication of famil-iarity with the word, despite his going to some pains to mention several synonyms of secondary importance.

Gay . . . gay . . . gay! Life is gay, the party is gay, the bar is gay, the book is gay, the young man is gay – very gay – or, alas! he is not gay! 'Look up my friend – he's gay' . . . 'youth, gay and witty, seeks correspondent' . . . 'did we have a gay weekend!'

Gay! The word serves many purposes. It is like the Z. of Tchaikowsky's diaries and letters, a secret code that will always be understood by some, never by others. 'There was much Z.,' Tchaikowsky wrote in his diary about a party he attended on April 23, 1884, and the diarist of today would express it in almost the same words: 'The party was so very gay!' Not only is correspondence quite safe from being understood in the event of interception, but even conversation can be held in which the homosexuals in a room use a language which they alone understand, but, unlike the situation prevailing were a foreign tongue being spoken, the others present are unaware of their ignorance.

Gay is simple and easy to say and free from the usual stigmas. Its usage has thus grown with great rapidity. A few homosexuals object to it, but, for lack of a better term they, too, employ it. One of the most desirable purposes it serves is that it facilitates discarding the mask by offering a language free of odium. Thus, among homosexuals, the euphemism brings franker and fuller discussion. One seldom would hear it said: 'At the age of thirteen, I realized that I was a *fairy*,' nor would this be said substituting the word *queer*. One version might be: '. . . that I was a homosexual,' but most frequently the word *gay* would be used.

The word serves as a signal, a sign of recognition. In a conversation there is an exploration, a search to know whether the other is likewise hiding behind a mask. And then one person uses the word and awaits a response. The cue cannot be misunderstood.

The secretive and fraternity-like language has its dangers. The homosexual world is not completely isolated. The man who is planning to lure the homosexual in order to victimize him, to assault and to rob him, or to set a trap for blackmail, frequently employs the language of the group in order to allay fears. And the probation officer or detective, interrogating a suspect, uses the inner-group language likewise to trap:

'This man who you were out with tonight – you know he's gay?'

A denial brings a torrent of new questions: what do you understand by the question? – did you understand it to refer to his being queer? – how do you know that's what the word means?

Within homosexual circles, the use of the word is almost universal, but its acceptance is often with reluctance. Some object to its ambiguous meaning, which is precisely what the group has found most advantageous about it. An advertisement for a roommate can actually ask for a gay youth, but could not possibly call for a homosexual. Even *Lesbian* would be an impossible word to use in this connection, and hence the female inverts are beginning to use the word *gay*, although less frequently than the males. Those who contend that it is a distortion of the language, because many homosexuals are not gay in the traditional meaning of the word, whereas many heterosexuals certainly may be, are actually consistent, for they protested with equal indignation against the appellation *queer*. But a word like *gay* is manifold in its uses and is not so easily discarded.

Some of the usefulness of *gay* diminishes as its meaning becomes more widely understood. New and wider circles are constantly becoming familiar with the word, although the public at large, except for theatrical and artistic people, literary groups, bohemians, underworld characters, and police officers, are unaware of its slang meaning. However, as it becomes better known, its secret character, and the advantages derived therefrom, are to a certain extent vitiated.

Gay requires an antonym, and the antonym is *straight*. This, too, is widely known and used among homosexuals, and has thus become a magic password. The conversation at the bar between two strangers:

'I've been in this town for a week, and it's dull as hell.'
'What's the matter – everybody you meet straight?'

The word in one sense is even more valuable than *gay*, in that its confinement to homosexuals has been so carefully guarded. There is hardly a homosexual in certain parts of the United States who does not know and use it, just as he knows and uses *gay*, but it is extremely rare to find it known among those people whom it is meant to describe.

But, in another sense, it has always been considered an unfortunate word, because it characterizes the heterosexual and, therefore, by implication, the homosexual. The former is straight; therefore the latter is not straight, he is crooked. *Straight* is the slang word for legal and moral correctness: *to go straight*. Hence the homosexual is not straight, does not go straight. This is euphemism in reverse. Instead of finding a mild and delicate word for something disagreeable, the homosexuals have found a manner of expression which, by implication, is harsh and indelicate for something which, to them, is quite agreeable.

Although *gay* is used throughout the United States and Canada, *straight* is hardly known on the West coast, except among those who have migrated from the East. In San Francisco, for example, the gay circles refer to other people as *jam*: 'She's gay, but her husband's jam,' a person will say. *Jam* is used in the East, but would hardly be considered an everyday word.

In fact, the geographical variations in the homosexual language are probably more severe than are to be found in most of the analogous slang, because of the lack of any volume of printed literature. The words cannot be used on the radio, and are seldom found in print. Visitors traveling from one part of the country to another find it impossible to introduce the slang of their native region, and soon begin to use the terms that are understood in their new surroundings.

It is characteristic of the special nature of the semantics of gay life that the peculiar usage of words in a given context is readily understandable even to those who have never before encountered them. A well-known novelist to whom I was introduced was exchanging questions and answers with me about my experiences. After I told him that I was married, he asked, 'Does your wife know the facts of life?' I had never heard this cliché used in this particular connotation, but sensed immediately that *to know the facts of life* meant, for him, and for many others, as I was to discover, *to be aware of the homosexual stream of life*. A few weeks later I posed the same question to a friend who had asked me to look up a companion of his on my vacation. 'Does he know the facts of life?' I queried, and he immediately replied as if my expression were an everyday one to him, although he later confessed that he had never before heard the words used in that particular sense. In similar manner, many other expressions might be cited which would be incomprehensible to the straight person, but immediately understood, on first usage, by the gay world.

Because there is no organized society of gay life, no recognized source of authority, no book of rules, no lexicons and lawmakers, no public press that gives permanent form to the language, there is considerable fluidity in the use of special expressions. Even spellings can differ. More than once I have received correspondence concerning *gae life*, although this struck me as an affectation until I realized that it was close to the French, *gaie*. But the expression *in the life* is used to mean, on the one hand, 'being gay,' or on the other, 'living a gay life.' If employed in the first sense, it would include the suppressed married person, but in its second sense only those who, in one form or another, give expression to their homosexuality. An everyday word in the gay life is *trade*; it is common for a person to refer to another as *trade*. 'Out looking for trade tonight?' someone will jokingly ask; or, 'There goes the best trade in town.' To me, the word originally meant a young person who accepted money in return for sex. My friends are quite vehement in insisting, however, that *trade* is the person indulging only in certain types of physical homosexual relations – the meaning which seems to be prevalent at this time in the larger cities of the United States. And on inquiry I found one person who rejected both of these definitions. 'If you and I should shack up for a one-night stand,' he said, 'then I would just be trade for you, and you would be trade for me.'

One should not overlook the many expressions of a regional or national character, in addition to the sharp geographical differences on which I have already commented; and also the words used by hoboes, underworld men, and police, all of whom have special terms for homosexuals. Their expressions are seldom known and never used by the gay world itself. I learned from a book, for instance, that the British hoboes call the homosexual a *pouf*, but I have never heard this word in America. *The Dictionary of Underworld Lingo* makes a strong distinction between the active and passive pederast; for the former, such words as *daddy*, *joker*, and *wolf* are used, among others. The passive is defined by no less than sixty-eight different words or phrases, from *apple pie* to *works*. Most of these are unknown in homosexual circles (unless they may be known to homosexual criminals, a matter on which I am not competent to offer comment). Some of the words are most colorful: the passive pederast, caught in the act, has his *jeans* at *half mast*. In *The American Dictionary of Slang* I counted 174 synonyms for *homosexual*. Among these were some repetitions and some variations that consisted of slight changes in spelling. Most of the words were of infrequent usage: *agfay*, *lavender boy*, *mason*, *nola*, *queervert*. Although this book contains a supplement dated 1947, and although the underworld lingo book cited earlier was published in 1950, neither of them mentions the word *gay*, which for years has been the most common synonym for *homosexual* used by the homosexual.

Other words are of passing fancy, taking themselves from a song hit, a movie, or perhaps even a book of popular interest, or from the humorous allusions to sex that gay and straight people encounter in life. One evening I was invited to a gay bar that had been nicknamed *the snake pit*; while there, a companion to whom I was talking excused himself, saying that he had to go to *the advertising club*.

'In our particular theater of war,' a veteran related to me, when we were discussing the terms used by and for gay people, 'they were called *night-fighters*. It all started by their being called *night-cruisers*, but this became a little too obvious, and so it was changed to *night-prowlers*, and finally to *night-fighters*.' Most veterans insist that they did not encounter this word in the service.

All in all, the homosexual groups do not create an entire and self-sufficient argot of their own, in the manner of the underworld, the jazz followers, and others. Their terms are few in number and are mainly confined to descriptions of their own activities. The bisexual companion is *ambisextrous*, the gay group is *the circle*, the masquerade ball is *a drag*, the transvestist is *dressed in drag*, to behave effeminately is *to camp*, the person who is effeminate is called *a camp*, his opposite number is *rough trade*, the obvious crotch is *the basket*, or sometimes *the canasta*, to look for a temporary love-mate is *to cruise*, and a partner whom one meets and never sees again is *a one-night stand*, while the middle-aged man still seeking a young lover is *an auntie*. A few of these terms, as one can see, are used in a similar sense by heterosexuals: *to cruise* and *a one-night stand*, for example. Some words have synonyms: *a camp* is also *a bitch*; but change the vowel, and one has the antonym, *a butch*.

Much of the resentment against individual words is due to the conditions under which they are spoken. In the mouth of a friend or a sympathizer, or particularly a member of the circle, the words lose much of the hostile tinge given to them by the world at large. 'What is that guy you had lunch with – a queer?' is a question that carries with it all of the semantic implications of a similar sentence in which a racial epithet is used. But the homosexual can use the word *queer*, and many other words, with comfort, because inherently lacking is condemnation. There is no air of superiority, no slur nor sneer. The word is no more than a communication of a thought. 'I want you to meet a friend of mine,' a gay person will say to me. 'He's a grand guy – and as queer as a three-dollar bill.'

The homosexual society requires a word like *gay* so that conversation can be free and unhampered; the fetters of conventional condemnation have not yet relegated this word to the realm of the outlawed nor associated it with a stereotype. The group, and its individual members, can only profit by every device that makes possible the act of unmasking. Any semantic effort that facilitates free conversation is desirable. The secret and code-like character of the *gay* and *the straight*, so reminiscent of words and signs of fraternal orders, will be needed so long as there is a submerged and semi-legal society of homosexuals, and new words to meet new exigencies will have to be found.

In the meanwhile, the world at large, comprising those of all sexual temperaments, lacks an acceptable term that is the male counterpart of *Lesbian*. Like *Lesbian*, such a word might logically come from the great civilization where homosexuality flourished as an accepted part of the mores and where it was an inspiration to philosophy and art – the culture of ancient Greece. A word like *Dorian*, for instance, might be valuable as a part of our language. It would, like *fairy*, be synonymous with the male homosexual, but without the implication of effeminacy and without the hostile sneer associated with *fairy*. Like *Lesbian*, the word *Dorian* could encompass a relationship, a thought, a philosophy, an individual, without regard to the sexual fulfillment of the desire.

Chapter 3

David Sonenschein

1969

THE HOMOSEXUAL'S LANGUAGE

O NE OF THE MAIN INTENTS of the ethnographic approach to the study of groups, whether cliques or cultures, is to see why that group carves up the world as it does and to analyze the mechanisms used to do so. These mechanisms may be psychological and individual, they may be social and particular to a small part of a larger group, or they may be cultural, typical at some level of all (or as far as we can see, most) members of that group.

In this paper, we are interested in the special language or slang of a sexually deviant group and the ways in which it is connected to a homosexual's view of the world and himself and is influential in his relations with his own group. There has been a shift from the many earlier studies of slang which were largely philological in nature to the more recent research which takes slang words and usage to be in various ways indicative of the sociocultural qualities of the group that uses them. We are interested in characterizing language as a message system which is enacted through interpersonal relations; as such, it carries a sociocultural value content which may be analyzed to give indications of 'meaning' in a wider sense than mere definition. The ethnographic approach used here attempts to outline the ways in which a special language provides a cultural base for the definition and evaluation of sociosexual roles and their performance. To this end, this paper presents some data on a specific slang vocabulary and its characteristics of formation and use in a specific social context.

The vocabulary represents the slang of a homosexual community in a city of the Southwestern United States. The subject community was considered by its members to be stratified roughly into two parts on the basis of relative prestige; the lower status group served as the focus unit and displayed more frequent use of the slang. Some of the social characteristics of this group have been reported on previously (Sonenschein 1968). During a one and one-half year period of field work (1961–3), the terms were gathered both by asking informants to define and explain the various words and by observation and recording of their usage and meaning in actual interaction events.

The social context

Continuing to consider slang as a special language, we can say that the homosexual is in a sense 'bilingual' in that he has the choice of using 'Everyday English' or the slang in appropriately defined situations. The definition depends upon whether the individuals concerned are homosexual or not and whether the environment is homosexual or not. The vocabulary presented here was used almost entirely in the context of the homosexual group. As members moved in and out of the subculture, their language changed accordingly; most words were not used 'outside' (especially those in the 'unique' category; see below). The meaning of the 'shared' terms became socially reapplied to carry the heterosexual connotations when homosexuals were in this company.

The special language of the homosexual is the language of his special world: its roles, values, and activities. All of this has been implied in other studies of slang but we shall develop this further here. Contrary to views that see slang as a mechanism of 'secrecy' or mere linguistic 'play' (Jespersen 1946: 137), we see slang as a form of verbal communication and identification between individuals and thus amenable to sociocultural analysis. Therefore, the emphasis to be placed on slang is not that it is indirect and isolative but rather that it is cohesive, consistent, and above all, communicative. It is one of the direct and fundamental mechanisms of special group relations and control.

Processes of verbal distinction

Slang is thus the language of specific social contexts and specific types of interpersonal relationships. It is to be noted that slang is also more of a *spoken* rather than written language and thus has the added dimension of face-to-face verbal interaction which is important to the sociocultural perspective taken here. On this verbal level, we may describe a number of processes that center about the unit of the word itself which help characterize (but not completely define) some of the homosexual's language.

1. Effeminization. Effeminization is often considered to be the outstanding mark of the homosexual; effeminate lisping speech is thought to be naturally expressive of the ultimate nature of homosexuality: women trapped in men's bodies. The verbal effeminizing process may in fact be a consciously learned form of behavior. Aside from the fact that speech patterns of one sex are resistant to transfer to the other because of the force of gender role definitions (Weinreich 1953), effeminate behavior in homosexuals is, generally speaking, sporadic, situational, and satirical rather than the result of a consistently maintained self-concept (Simon and Gagnon 1967; Sonenschein 1968).

When effeminacy is enacted however, the attempt to emulate female speech patterns may involve the following specific areas: (a) In general, there is an attempt to imitate the verbal sound of female conversation; this involves primarily the copying of inflectional and stress patterns and rarely the stereotyped lisp. This sound pattern may then underline the uses of the words. (b) There may be frequent use of what are popularly seen as feminine adjectives. Words like 'darling' and 'lovely' and phrases like 'terribly sweet' are used to describe people and things of interest. (c) The use of feminine familiars such as 'honey' and 'darling' as well as the pronouns 'she' and 'her' are used both as terms of address and reference to males. (d) With considerably less frequency, general nouns and other words are feminized with the result of sounding much like baby-talk. 'Cigarette' becomes 'ciggy-boo' and 'beer' becomes 'beersy.' (e) Related to point (c) above, is the effeminization of masculine names. 'Harry' becomes 'Harriette' and 'David' becomes 'Daisey.' The designation or acquisition of a role may thus become strongly based in verbal behavior and interaction.

· The following processes refer more to the slang words themselves and the way in which they become part of the homosexuals language.

2. Utilization.   In this Category, there is a simple and straightforward borrowing of both form and meaning of slang terms as used in other groups. In the subject community, almost all of these were terms that referred to sexual activity and the few that were related to behavior or roles (e.g., 'queer,' 'fairy?') were rarely used.

3. Redirection.   Here the form remains but the meaning changes from a heterosexual referent to a homosexual one. An example of a redirected role term is 'bitch,' meaning a male homosexual with certain unpopular characteristics and style though not necessarily effeminate.

4. Invention.   Words are taken and given a new and unique meaning, the use of which in a slang sense is not to be found outside the homosexual circle. These are the most salient words of a slang vocabulary because of their esoteric nature. In the subject community, most were role terms, an example being the word 'nelly' to mean effeminate.

The vocabulary

The language of homosexuality is basically the language of social and sexual relationships rather than of the sexual act itself. The deviancy of homosexual sexual orientation has been so salient in the past that previous research has ignored two main and very real factors of homosexual life: (1) its social complexity and (2) its relatively unexotic (even unerotic) nature as a *total* life-style (Simon and Gagnon 1967). The homosexual's social relationships and their mechanisms have particularly suffered from this neglect (Sonenschein 1966, 1968; Simon and Gagnon 1967). To illustrate this: when, in the subject group, homosexuals talked about sex it was for the most part in the context of *who* had sex with *whom* and *why* that particular relationship might or might not have taken place; it was in other words, talk about sexual *partners* rather than sexual outlets.

Clearly then, we must take a broader view of sexual behavior. We shall want to look at sex as being more than a mere coupling and friction of genitals and orifices; it is in many important ways what William Simon and John Gagnon call 'socially scripted behavior' (Gagnon and Simon 1967). Sex is in fact, a specific form of inter-personal interaction, the meaning of which is defined by the culture or values of particular groups as well as the personal histories and experiences of their members. The eroticism of sex, including homosexual sex, derives in large measure from, the definitional and conceptual components of the subcultural values of such things as attractiveness, availability, and the definition of what constitutes, adequate and exciting sociosexual behavior. Obviously, many of these definitions are carried through the use of language.

Such conceptions were behind the gathering of the vocabulary. By making a gross distinction between terms that reflected a purely sexual versus behavioral interest, it was felt that quantitative support would be given to the qualitative analysis outlined above. The criteria for dividing the descriptive corpus were simple: 'sex terms' were those that referred to a purely sexual activity, sex organs, and so on (e.g., 'cock' or 'brown' [anal intercourse]). 'Role terms' were those that referred to aspects, forms, and patterns of behavior and orientations (e.g., 'nelly' or 'queen'). As seen in column two of Table 3.1, what were designated as 'role terms' emerged much more predominantly in the subject community than those purely sexual items.

An examination of the literature, both popular and professional, revealed a number of other glossaries of homosexual slang. Some were subjected to the analysis used above and are offered for comparison in Table 3.1, but only in a very rough and approximate way for several reasons. Firstly, those who present such glossaries may attempt to cover all homosexual slang; they make no claims to draw from a specific socially defined group of homosexuals. Secondly, they rarely allow for or indicate variance in meaning and definition, socially or geographically. Thirdly, some items may be omitted, especially those words that may have overlapping usage with heterosexuals. Obviously, there is a need for more exactly defined comparative research to provide similar vocabularies. Even so, in our analysis here, the disjunction between role and sex terms was upheld in a relatively even way as seen in Table 3.1.

For further analysis, overall comparison was sought with the heterosexual mean-ings of the shared terms in the same city. One-half of the total homosexual vocabulary was shared either wholly ('same usage;' e.g., 'dike' for lesbian) or in part ('redirected usage;' e.g., 'wife' for a partner in an affair). As can be seen in Table 3.2, both of these kinds of words were predominantly sexual in reference; sex terms amounted to 31% while role terms comprised 19% of the total corpus.

This separation is supported by observational and other ethnographic data from the subject group on two main points. Firstly, the predominant sharing of sexual terms is supported by the homosexual philosophy of 'sex is sex' no matter with whom. There is, in other words, from the homosexual's view, a common bond of sexuality plus the supposed 'latency' in 'everybody' that binds all men together, and the homosexual points out that his orientation is but one of several possible. Secondly however, the minority of the shared role terms reflected the behavioral and value distance (deviance) that did in fact separate the group from the hetero-sexual society. It is of note that of those terms holding the exact same meaning for heterosexuals in the role category, all in the subject group were derogatory and of relatively infrequent usage; words such as 'queer' and 'fairy' were used with no small amount of hostility in situations of conflict. By the use of role terms in certain

Table 3.1   Comparison of general vocabularies with subject community

Content	Legman (1941)	Subject community	Cory (1963)	Strait (1964)	Guild (1965)
Sex terms	39%	36%	40%	23%	35%
Role terms	61%	64%	60%	77%	65%
(N=)	(316)	(74)	(89)	(127)	(467)

Table 3.2   Relation of homosexual terms to heterosexual usage in subject community

Content	Same	Redirected	Unique
Sex terms	23%	8%	5%
Role terms	7%	12%	45%

Table 3.3   Internal shifts of homosexual terms in relation to heterosexual usage

Content	Same	Redirected	Unique
Sex terms	71%	43%	11%
Role terms	29%	37%	89%

situations, the boundaries of behavior as based on subcultural values and meanings were clearly and quickly outlined for those in the interaction situations.

Table 3.2 also indicates the distribution of the 'unique' terms in the subject group. These were words that were used only in the context of the homosexual group and ones whose meanings were not known outside. Most important to note is the fact that they were *all* role terms. Many consisted of the various words for 'queens.' In this case a 'queen' was only superficially meant as a term for an effeminate homosexual. Being a 'queen' or a certain kind of 'queen' (e.g. 'drag queen' as one who frequently wears women's clothing) is, as one informant put it, 'being queer for something.' Certain tastes, orientations, and values within the subculture are thus highlighted by the word and evaluated by the intonation and context of usage.

To further highlight the trends that reflect group influence, on words, the terms in each column of Table 3.2 were percentaged. The results recorded in Table 3.3 show that while the terms shared completely with heterosexuals were sexual in nature, the 'unique' language of homosexuality was a language of roles and relationships. The homosexual roles and orientations were unique and terms were needed to conceptualize them. The language of homosexuality then contains the vocabulary of its interests and behaviors. The less sharing of roles and concepts with the heterosexual community may be closely related to the smaller number of shared terms. In a more general way, it can be suggested that the more behaviorally isolated a homosexual group is from the hetemosexual population, the higher will be the incidence of uniquely devised role terms.

It can be expected that in larger cities that have more differentiated homosexual subsocieties, the total area vocabulary will be correspondingly larger to cover the wider range of roles and activities. Members of each homosexual subtype will cluster together and have a slang vocabulary specialized in terms relating to the interests of that particular group. In addition, any one individual may have various degrees of knowledge of the terms and usages of groups other than his own.

Speech of groups within the subject community

In addition to the data drawn from the lower status group of the subject community, some data were gathered by interview and observation from the other divisions of the homosexual population in the city. These may be summarized here as follows.

Upper status homosexuals.   This group of males comprised the other half of the subject community but they were very isolative and discrete, hence assemblages were carefully arranged to include only a well-defined membership (usually on the basis of sexual participation). Most members were in the higher socioeconomic levels of the city and were more integrated with the heterosexual world.

The use of slang was limited in both quantity and quality. Slang was regarded as rather unsophisticated in the first place but when it was used, it was employed only in exclusively homosexual settings. The active vocabulary was smaller than that of the lower status group although all terms seemed to be known. On the other hand, the higher usage of slang in the lower status group was accompanied by several contrasting characteristics including an openness of homosexuality and more effeminacy, younger members, and a general recency of having entered the homosexual subcultural life.

Marginal homosexuals.   Male homosexuals who had little or no group contact or identification, including male prostitutes (Reiss 1961), were referred to as 'marginal.' These people seemed to know most of the vocabulary but active usage was rare and minimal and only in instances of group participation.

Female homosexuals.   Lesbians shared only infrequently in male group activities; the homosexual subculture is in fact a male subculture. The females seemed to have little group structure beyond small cliques of their own; there were no lesbian bars in the city. They shared a number of the more common terms (such as 'gay' and 'butch' [masculine]) but the word 'fluff' (a very feminine lesbian) was their only unique term found in use. It was also used by the males.

Discussion

The use of slang to sensitize one to social structures and cultures is not entirely new. Goffman (1959) uses slang words to name types of roles in interaction situations where they may help summarize for the participants the qualities of those roles. Orrin Klapp (1962) takes slang terms for personality types and surveys the extent of their commonly recognized characteristics. In much the same way, in the subject homosexual group, role terms became summaries of constellations of sociosexual, behavioral, and attitudinal characteristics, the evaluation of which was a function of the various subgroups (e.g., cliques) and situations (e.g., private versus public behaviors). The flux or turnover of members in the subject community was fairly rapid and adequate guides underlined by some relatively consistent value system were, therefore, needed to quickly characterize the people one met. Most of the terms used were terms not of address but of reference.

On the other hand, while one may talk about others, he may also talk about himself. It becomes evident that this kind of discourse of roles is also just as important antly a placement of the self in the immediate interaction as well as in the larger social and value systems. The use of role terms allows the allocation of behaviors along the more salient dimensions of interests, such as focal points of sexual likes and dislikes and continua of masculinity and femininity. These categories indicate not only the parameters of social interaction but also social and self-evaluation where individuals may evaluate the bounds of propriety in behaviors through a contrast with their own personal style.

Because the homosexual, like anyone else, must operate within a framework of interpersonal relations to attain some measure of physical and emotional satisfaction, the language he uses reflects a codification of status-role expectations. Enculturation into a community entails the learning of the language and the normative behavior at the same time; one is embodied in the other. The new member is thus shown his behavioral alternatives, or the place in which his present activities put him, and learns to attach to these activities the relative prestige values that come with the terms or phrases. It seems that the degree of universality of homosexual behaviors in the United States can be connected to a basic universality of language meaning and communication (cf. Hertzler's process of 'social uniformation' 1966). Through this linguistic identification, the slang terms do in a very real and important sense reinforce group cohesiveness and reflect the common interests, problems, and needs of the population. When homosexuals travel to a new city, the recognition of the language is usually one of the first modes of social and sexual access — not to mention the personal comfort felt in finding others much like oneself.

Many homosexuals spend some amount of time in a highly yet implicitly structured and codified subculture and thus a minimum level of adherence to common behavioral patterns is expected of all who function within the group. The quest for sex and love is an important concern of the homosexual and certainly one of the bases of the structure of the group. Other factors, however, are also important in the maintenance of the homosexual group and the homosexual's life in and out of the subculture. The heart of the cultural system is the value system. Just as 'social judgments . . . reach us in the form of words' (Bram 1955), homosexual slang role terms evaluate as well as designate behaviors. Social judgments then refer not only to the rightness or wrongness of certain acts but to whole patterns of behaviors. Schwartz and Merten (1967) use the phrase 'status terminology' to point up the fact that the prestige value of these patterns is sharply noted in the language of the group. The placement of the self discussed above then becomes a working-out of a self-concept based on the evaluation of immediate events and situations – evaluations made both by individuals and groups which are communicated through the language. The mediation of values between the slang terms and the application of them by and to individuals in a given social system is a direct reflection of the kind and extent of social support a group gives to the behavior of its members. The congruency of the communication net and the 'community of discourse,' one which reflects common experiences, allows a homosexual individual to move through his worlds with as little psychological and social friction as possible. Thus the language of a special nature is one of the primary ways in which a group can help pattern and give meaning to the experiences of its members.

Chapter 4

Julia Penelope Stanley

(1974)

WHEN WE SAY 'OUT OF THE CLOSETS!'

I N SPITE OF OCCASIONAL ARTICLES in newspapers and journals dealing with the phenomenon of camp (e.g., Sontag 1964; Brien 1967) there have been no systematic or scholarly investigations of the language of the gay community in America. There is only one dictionary devoted exclusively to gay terminology, *The Queens' Vernacular: A Gay Lexicon* by Bruce Rodgers, which boasts over 12,000 entries. As the title specifies, the language documented in the lexicon belongs to gay men, or 'queens,' as some call themselves. Rodgers' extensive lexicon provides quantitative insight into a vital interest of gay men, sexuality; and individual terms reveal the extent of the bitterness that gay men feel toward the larger society. As Rodgers himself points out in his introduction, many gay militants regard gay slang as 'another link in the chain which holds the homosexual enslaved.' Gays in the liberation movement have come to see the most prevalent uses of gay slang as forms of self-oppression, in particular those terms that perpetuate the trivialization and degradation of gay people.

Too much of the lexicon of gay slang is given over to a preoccupation with sexual objectification and social stratification, both economic and racial, characteristics typical of relationships in the larger, heterosexual society. Insofar as gay slang reflects and encourages the value system of a racist, patriarchal culture, those gays who use it are engaging in self-oppression. But gay slang, like the slangs and argots of other subcultures, has also functioned as a bond among gays, signaling one's identification as a member of the gay community. But one must speak of a 'gay community' with caution, since only the most fragile bonds link the lives of lesbians with those of gay men. Gay slang belongs primarily to the men, and the extensive lexicon reflects more accurately their lives and their interests. Lesbians are familiar only with a few terms from the gay vocabulary, among them *bull dyke, dyke, butch, camp, closet queen, drag, drag queen, femme, gay, one-night stand, queen, straight,* and *trick*. If there is such a thing as gay slang held in common by lesbians and gay men, it consists of the few terms I've listed here, and these terms are the ones that have come to have political meaning among gay activists.

In order to understand the growth taking place in the gay community, it is necessary to understand first where we were when gay liberation became a political movement. Gay people have always existed at the periphery of the larger society as outcasts yet, by remaining covert about their identity, they have also been able to maintain themselves within heterosexual society. Gay slang reflects this dichotomy in the lives of gay people, on the one hand pointing to the transient nature of gay relationships and our rebellion against the kinds of lives that our society would have us adopt; on the other hand embodying certain of the values of heterosexuals, indicating a desire to blend into the larger culture. Although gay slang is primarily a male terminology, oriented toward male sexual interests, the vocabulary demonstrates the degree to which lesbians and gay men have fallen back on the models provided by straight society. Thus, although gay slang is the vocabulary of people who are themselves outcasts from the straight culture, it is also sexist, classist, and racist, and the existence of terms that reflect such attitudes binds us to the same value system that makes us outcasts. Such a conflict within the gay subculture will not be resolved easily, and there are two possible solutions that gay militants have chosen as strategies for eradicating such values from the liberation movement. The first solution is the more radical and difficult: one simply stops using gay slang altogether, but whether or not this really indicates a change of attitudes within the individual is something we can only ascertain through behavior. The second solution has been somewhat easier on an individual level, although it introduces new conflicts when there is misinterpretation, and it follows the precedent set by the black liberation movement. Certain terms, those shared by lesbians and gay men, have ceased to be used with sexual meanings and have, instead, taken on new, political meanings as the movement has expanded and become more vocal. Also, within the gay political context, there are efforts to take terms that were formerly pejorative and make them into positive vocabulary items. Again, such efforts introduce conflicts among gays, and I will describe some of these terminological problems at the end of this article.

Outside the movement, however, gay slang is still being used as it has always been used by those gay people who wish to live anonymously. These gays, in trying to define themselves and their relationships with other gay people, have relied heavily on the sex-role stereotyping so commonly used in straight relationships. In addition, terms exist within the gay vocabulary for classifying other gays according to their social and economic status. Racism in the gay vocabulary is more difficult to describe, since it is directly related to the sexual preferences of gay men. Nevertheless, the terms for describing racial preference are common, and although I will not hazard an explanation for their necessity, I will discuss them briefly.

Sexism, as I've already mentioned, turns up in the terms that denote relationships among gay people. The two terms that draw most directly on straight definitions of the roles appropriate to women and men (respectively) are *femme* and *butch*. The butch in a gay relationship, regardless of its duration, is the person who exhibits those positive personality traits associated with males: aggressiveness, self-confidence, self-assertiveness, independence, strength, and activity. People who regard themselves as butch usually wear the clothing appropriate to the role: pants, boots, T-shirts, severely tailored shirts, etc. Some gays also go out of their way to display or act out some of the negative characteristics associated with the male role, such as physical violence, hostility, promiscuity, and claiming a powerful sex-drive. These persons are dominant in their relationships, they're 'on top' in the sex act, and they make the initial overtures in the bars.

The femmes, on the other hand, imitate the patterns of behavior reserved for women in our society. They become passive, dependent, weak, emotional, and they tend to acquire the negative characteristics associated with dependent persons. They become manipulative, petty, whining, and nagging. Please note that I'm not saying that these traits are inherent in either the person or the role. I am saying that persons who cast themselves in the role assigned to women assume some of these behaviors. The femmes sometimes dress in accordance with the code established by straight society for the dependent person: dresses, lace underclothing, long hair, makeup, long nails, skirts, heels, etc. They are passive in their relationships and they rarely make the initial overtures.

The lines are not always as clearly drawn as I've made them appear, however, and one finds variations in every relationship, just as in straight relationships. But the basic ingredients of sex-role stereotyping are obvious; gays have accepted the dual premises that there is behavior appropriate to 'masculine' people, and there is behavior appropriate to 'feminine' people. Once a person discovers that she's attracted to persons of the same sex, she tends to acquire the behavior assigned to the sex empowered to love her sex. Because our society rewards the behavior assigned to the male sex, gays also place a high value on 'masculine' behavior. To be a butch is always somehow 'better' than being a femme, insofar as more privileges inhere in the role itself. It is the butch who can behave promiscuously, and it is the butch who can come home and prop her feet up while the femme cooks dinner. Among such gays, masculinity is as highly prized as it is among heterosexuals, and some gay men refuse to associate with other gay men who display any of the characteristics linked to the female role. In fact, there is a subset of terms within the gay vocabulary reserved for describing a man's effeminacy. Most of the terms for men who are not 'masculine' enough incorporate the word *queen*, a general term for a homosexual male who acts in ways defined as female. It is the queen who affects so-called 'female' behavior, and generally only queens are said to like queens by those who consider themselves above such things. Homosexuals (and I use the word advisedly) who affect 'masculine' behavior usually put it this way: 'If I wanted a woman, I'd go find a real one; who wants a man who thinks he's a woman?' As a consequence of this sexist attitude, we find the word queen in combination with other words that make specific the degree to which a male affects 'feminine' behavior, e.g., *nellie queen, swishy queen, flaming queen* (or *flaming faggot*), or *nell, swish*, or *limp-wrist*. It's the queen who is said to 'drop hairpins' (let someone know he's gay by dropping hints), or 'drop beads' (let someone know he's gay accidentally). Extending the comparison of themselves to women, many of the queens refer to themselves as 'dizzy bitches,' 'vicious cunts,' 'the girls,' or as 'pieces of ass,' thus incorporating many of the destructive definitions of women favored by our society into their own self-images. Extreme identification with the roles of women is manifested by the wearing of women's clothing, which is called *drag*. To *go in drag* is to wear clothing designed for women. A *drag queen* is a man who wears women's clothing, often performing in bars.

A lesbian can also wear drag; that is, she can dress in clothing designed for men, but current fashions make drag for a woman less distinctive. Formerly, it was the 'butch' who went in drag, wearing pants, shirts, men's shoes, and jackets. But with the breakdown of the role structure in lesbian relationships, such a distinction is harder to justify. Now perhaps the only way for a lesbian to be in 'drag' would be to wear a tuxedo. *Drag butches* have also been reported to wear jockey shorts and tape their breasts down in much the same way that drag queens tape up their genitals.

Classism among gay men draws upon stereotypes of social/economic classes among men, especially elevating certain conceptions about the masculinity of men engaged in the kinds of labor which require physical strength, occupations like truck driving, factory work, construction, farming, etc. Among the gay men who emphasize characteristics like calloused hands, toughness, crudity, roughness, the possession of such features by another man is a prerequisite to desire. In fact, the men who are called *trade*, the men who make a living catering to a sexuality dependent upon the male stereotype, cultivate those characteristics associated with extreme masculinity. Apparently gay men have two conflicting perceptions of these hustlers, on the one hand assuming them to be straight, wanting to think of them as straight, on the other regarding them as 'closet cases' who are using hustling as a rationalization for their own homosexuality, pretending to themselves that they're only 'doing it for money.' One expression used by some gay men captures both perceptions: 'Today's trade is tomorrow's competition.' *Rough trade*, as distinguished from *trade*, refers to straight men who occasionally relate sexually to men, but such men are especially feared by most gay men because these are the men who frequently beat up gay men, using their sexuality as an·excuse for extreme violence and, sometimes, murder. One other term that reflects the existence of classism among gay men is *piss-elegant*, a pejorative term used to characterize gay men who aspire to 'the finer things in life,' and who often adopt certain affectations of dress and speech in order to impress others with their affluence (real or imaginary). These are the men who try to 'pass for straight,' and who won't be seen with the more 'obvious faggots,' since it might endanger their own precarious existence. As a result of these classist attitudes, the men who are ostracized by other men refer to them as 'piss-elegant,' and there is a great deal of resentment between the two extremes in the gay male culture.

With the word *trade*, we've entered that area of gay slang borrowed entirely from the slang of prostitutes, which includes *trick*, *number*, *John*, *cruise*, *seafood*, and *one-night stand*. The men who sell themselves to other men are called *meat*, and the places where they make themselves available are called *meat racks* or *meat markets*. By using terms borrowed from prostitutes to refer to their sexual activities, gay men transfer the social attitudes toward prostitutes to themselves and their behavior, switching their sexual objectification from women to men, but maintaining the destructive attitudes inherent in such objectification.

The relationships among women may not be as clearly defined in terms of sex roles, and the women have terms for women who are comfortable in either role, *ki-ki* and *bluff*. *Bluff* is a blend, and combines the terms *butch* and *fluff*. *Fluff* is another term for the passive partner in the relationship. Some women know the terms *one-night stand* and *trick*, although most of the relationships between two women last longer than one night. Few women actually 'trick.' One might guess that this behavior is due more to the heavy conditioning toward monogamy that women go through than to anything inherent in the nature of women, regardless of what we're taught. But it's among the women that we often find the strongest orientation toward monogamy, held up to us by our society as the most positive relationship between two people. It's the men who are called *street fairies*, *tea room queens* (men who frequent toilets for sexual purposes; the toilet is a *tea room*), and only the men have terms for sex in which more than two people are involved, *team creams*, *group gropes*, and *circle jerks*.

In spite of the difference between gay men's and women's attitudes, monogamy nevertheless is valued among gays, or has been. The ideal relationship of this kind supposedly is one in which the 'wife' stays at home and does the cooking and cleans the house. In addition, gays have worked out a kinship terminology which closely parallels that of straight society. A *father* is a woman who brings out another woman, and a *mother* is a man who brings out another man. Butch lesbians may call themselves as *sisters*. An *auntie* is an older male homosexual.

The terms for lesbians also reflect some of the ambiguity inherent in sex-role stereotyping. I'm assuming that gay men coined these terms, since very few lesbians used them until recently. Gay men assert that these terms are used positively or neutrally, while gay women have found them offensive in the past. Among gay men the term *dyke* is synonymous with *lesbian*. It refers to any gay woman. It can, however, be used with reference to a woman who is 'mannish' in her appearance. The rest of the terms are used as the 'masculinity' of the woman increases. Thus, one may be a *bull dyke*, a *diesel dyke* or a *truckdriver*, a *stompin' diesel dyke*, or a *rompin' stompin' diesel dyke*. Among conservative gays, there is disdain for the man who takes on the characteristics of social inferiors or women, and resentment toward the woman who aspires to membership in the ruling class, men. For a woman, it's all right to be a *tomboy* up to about the age of 14; a man cannot be a sissy at any age, because of the negative attitudes toward the female role as our society defines it.

At present, most of the terms that comprise gay slang refer to the activities of gay men. The sexual activities themselves are reflected in terms such as *brown*, *butt fuck*, *fist fuck*, *suck*, *eat*, *do*, *rim*, *go down on*, *give head to*, *grope*, and *blow job*. To go out and look for sex is to *cruise*, a toilet is a *tea room*, and a gay man who cruises toilets is a *tea room queen*. The male genitals may be called *crown jewels*, and if they're uncircumcised they may be called *lace curtains* or a *roll-away set*. If the genitals are unusually large, they're called *miracle meat*. A gay man who seeks other men with large genitals is a *size queen*. A man interested only in men with well-developed bodies is a *body queen*, and an older man who prefers boys or young men is a *chicken queen*. In fact, that portion of the gay lexicon which deals with sexual preferences, sexual activities, and physical attributes is by far the most extensive and detailed, and the terms listed here are only meant to be indicative of its range. A more extensive analysis of all the words and phrases dealing with gay male sexuality would provide a more accurate picture of the system of self-classification that gay men have developed for seeing themselves and other men as sex objects. Apparently they have adopted the view that people can be most safely treated as sex objects, and they have incorporated this approach to relationships as an inherent part of their social structure.

Just as gay men have developed terms for classifying themselves and other men according to their social status and sexual preferences, they have also made up words and phrases which categorize gay men with respect to their racial preferences. White males who seek out black men (*dinge*) are *dinge queens*, while black men who prefer white men are *social climbers* or *oreos*, and they have *white fever*. Spanish men are called *Taco queens*, *chiquita banana*, or *south of the border*. In a similar fashion, Chinese males have been characterized as *tiny meat*, *chinese food*, or just *yellow boys*. Such terms are usually used by the men who disapprove of the preferences of other gay men, and they represent the same bigotry found in the larger society.

Although the preceding discussion has been necessarily brief, one can see in the terms and their meanings the prejudices and categorizations of other human beings typical of the straight culture. But there are signs, as gays become increasingly aware of who they are, that there are efforts to do away with the attitudes that such terms represent. We have begun to understand that much of gay slang is self-destructive and demeaning, especially when it is directed at another gay person. Many of the gay activists are now concentrating on creating new, more positive references for some of the most common terms in the gay lexicon, such as *closet*, *drag*, *dyke*, *faggot*, *flame*, *come out*, and *cocksucker*. The underlying assumption of these efforts is that as gays come to associate such previously negative terms with their own political awareness, they will develop a positive image of themselves and, out of this, gay pride.

In 1969, gays began marching, chanting 'Out of the closets, into the streets,' 'Ho-ho-homosexual, sodomy laws are ineffectual,' 'Two–four–six–eight, gay is twice as good as straight,' and 'Better blatant than latent.' Words that had formerly referred only to one's sexual identification, like *gay* and *straight*, or that had been pejoratives, like *dyke*, *faggot*, and *cocksucker*, had become instead politically charged terms that affirmed the new identity of gays. *To come out of the closet* now has a political meaning; the phrase refers to the assumption of one's identity as a positive thing, something to be yelled in the streets, rather than hidden and whispered about behind closed doors. And once you are out of your closet, you no longer cringe when someone calls you a *dyke* or a *faggot*. To be a dyke or a faggot refers to one's political identity as a gay activist. Being *gay* no longer simply refers to loving one's own sex, but has come to designate a state of political awareness in which one no longer needs the narrowly defined sex-role stereotypes as bases for identity.

But redefining old terms that have been pejoratives for so long is not an easy process, nor is it something that takes place overnight. Among the women, new distinctions are being made among the usages of the old terms. As we redefine the old pejorative labels, making them our own, what we choose to call ourselves also takes on political meaning, defining one's political position. A *dyke* is a woman committed to revolution, the most radical position. A lesbian is committed to a more liberal position, and she is more willing to compromise and work within the system. A *gay woman* affirms her commitment to a 'gay community,' and sees nothing wrong with working with men. Whether or not she calls herself a *dyke*, a *lesbian*, or a *gay woman* is directly related to the extent of the influence of feminism on her political views. The influence of feminism within the lesbian community can be seen most clearly in the politics of *dyke separatism* and *lesbian separatism*. Both positions assert that women have to develop their own consciousness of themselves as women separate from men and their politics and movements. The difference in application of the two phrases is apparently related to the degree of one's radicalism, and the extent of the compromises with men that one is willing to make.

Among the men the same process of redefinition is going on, but the political ramifications are not as clear to this writer. For example, most of the men within the movement refer to themselves as *faggots* or *gay men*, and they reject such terms as *queen* and *swish* as derogatory. The apolitical men, those not involved with gay liberation, refuse to call themselves gay because they feel that it connotes a false happiness about their lives. In fact, they see the term *gay* as trivializing and inane, and prefer to be called homosexuals, which they say is more honest and neutral. Male gay activists sometimes refer to themselves as homosexuals, although they tend to see the term as clinical and associate it with the psychological profession. For them, to call oneself a homosexual signifies that one is still in the closet politically. For the men, then, what one calls oneself is related to the extent of one's involvement in the gay liberation movement, but the political implications are not as clear as those of the women's terminology.

As I've indicated throughout this article, many changes are currently going on in gay slang as a result of the gay liberation movement. The terms that reflect sexism, classism, and racism are not used among gay activists, and their continued usage with the gay subculture is condemned. Other terms, regarded as somehow 'salvageable' or useful to the movement, have been retained, but with radically different usages and meanings, including connotations. Because of the conflicts that arise when connotative values are not understood or explained, I have been primarily concerned with describing the process of redefinition of terms as it is taking place, a difficult and dangerous task because of the further misunderstandings such a discussion could create. What does emerge quite clearly from such an examination, however, is the enormity of the task that lesbians and gay men have undertaken as we move toward constructing positive self-images of ourselves and move away from the destructive definitions that straight society would have us accept.

Chapter 5

"The Language and Sexuality Reader,"
Honey, Let's Talk about the Queens'
English Edited by Deborah Cameron and
Don Kulick. London: Routledge, 2006.
336 pp. ISBN: 0415363071. Pages 56-

Louie Crew

1978

HONEY, LET'S TALK ABOUT
THE QUEENS' ENGLISH

SPECIALIZED GAY USE OF ENGLISH is a very explosive and unpopular subject, rarely treated at all by linguists and only begrudgingly mentioned or demonstrated in most of the gay press. When linguists do discuss it, they usually note only its slang, often lighting on items for their colorfulness and rarity rather than for their pervasiveness in the speech of gays who actually make specialized use of English. Yet conflict over gay specialized language takes much energy in gay experience, both from the users and the avoiders. I dare here to ignite only a few of the gay male parameters of the subject.

All gay male usage bespeaks a criminal underground, whether the use is the cleverly concealed homosexual allusions that have periodically occurred in centuries of English literature or the cant of the streets. As recently as 1857 gay males were put to death in Great Britain, and homosexual acts are still [in 1978] felonies in thirty-three of the United States.

The incentive to use language uniquely comes from the natural desire to communicate, to be known as we are and to be understood by others, particularly by others similarly stigmatized and sharing our language. Shared specialized language bonds people, and for gays it can be a way of self-affirmation, a way of rejecting the taboo. Specialized language *builds* as well as *responds* to community.

Yet the ubiquitous threat of disclosure as a criminal is the major deterrent to widespread specialized use of language by gays. Of course, people are never jailed for the way they talk, nor can gay language legally mark its users as persons who perform homosexual acts. The penalties for using language in specialized gay ways are more subtle, typically in the social and economic ostracization that can result. Given such penalties, it is not surprising that most gay males do not speak a special language, or at least try to control very carefully the contexts in which they do so.

Survival and anonymity are not the only reasons many gay males avoid or minimize specialized gay uses of language. Some want to escape identification with various gay ghettos where such language is more common fare. Others relish their male privilege and power. Some are fighting accepting the facts of their own predominantly homosexual orientation and view any compromise of nongay language standards as tantamount to becoming that much more what they fear they are.

Distinctive gay male uses of language?

There is no sexual register of the English language unique to gays. The language has sexual references only in feminine, masculine, and neuter; and sex minus or neuter is equally available to all females and males without regard to sexual orientation.

When gay males use English differently from other males, their differences can take only three directions with regard to sexual registers of English:

A.   A greater than average density of items from the male registers of English.
B.   A greater than average density of items from the female registers of English.
C.   Distinctive blends of items from both registers.

The linguistic difference common to all three of these directions is a heightened experience of the choice as choice. For most heterosexual males, male language is perceived by definition as simply the way any one of them speaks, allowing for a range (if narrow) of difference so long as other signals reveal that the genital plumbing is hetero. Most gay males are not allowed the luxury of easy self-acceptance, but face a culture which denies at every level the reality they are facing with the involuntary arousal of their genitals. Long before most gays knowingly meet any other gays we are questioning all aspects of behavior, particularly our linguistic behaviors, to discover any other ways we might be different. That very introspection often leads to much greater experimentation with different alternatives from the available sexual registers, and often leads to much greater precision with any register we adopt. Furthermore, our hetero teachers tell us most readily that gay males are *supposed to be* effeminate; and thus many gay males either adopt that stereotype or react to it in the extreme by intensifying their male registers of English.

Too often heterosexual outsiders view any gay decision on these matters as mere role-playing; yet for the choosers the alternatives are potentially just as much ways of being as is the hetero practice of matching biological and linguistic gender rather less self-consciously.

The difference between nongay and gay roles is not a difference of authenticity, but a difference in the great degree of stress placed on gay people merely for being, particularly for affirming who we are, by whatever choice.

Gay male intensification of the masculine

Intensified same-gender linguistic choice is at once the most common choice of gay males who decide to speak differently from other males and at the same time the gay male use least noticed by the public, often even by the scholars ostensibly concerned with gay male language. Its utility as vehicle for communication exclusively with the desired audience, especially when nongays are present but unaware, is a major appeal to its users. More essentially, for many gay males the *homo-* or sameness of sexual attraction is precisely the attraction to and amplification of the gender one is. Nongays routinely ignore the existence of the gay-as-intensified male, perhaps because the gay-as-effeminate stereotype is less threatening except when heteros want to talk about 'saving our children.' Most hetero males seem never even to hear the exaggeration and the difference, as can be readily demonstrated by taking them to a non-dancing leather bar, one scene where one variety male-intensified language is routine. To the heterosexual unaware of where he is, the scene is just another all-male setting, unless he happens to notice the hungry eyes.

Male-intensified language is the language of body builders, the football team, and some other male congregations. It represents a glorification of masculinity and power almost in the same self-conscious way that parody can. A fairly unequivocal literary source for such use is gay male pornography, whether the brute vignettes on men's rooms walls or the cheap novels which eschew any delicacy whatsoever. Yet it is no accident that *Out*, a short-lived NYC gay publication, featured Norman Mailer in drag on the cover of its first issue, or that Hemingway-ese to some ears often doth protest its toughness too much. Much macho culture is a gay male camouflage or celebration. Writers such as John Rechy, James Baldwin, and Jean Genet have always recognized these charades, as did Proust with his Albert and Albertine.

Gay male identification with females

Cross-gender identification may be very slight (and for the closeted, unintentional), as for the gay male whose only departure from the general male standard is a predilection for *so* as an intensive; or the identification may be fully comprehensive, as for gay males who are female impersonators. Obviously, not even heterosexual males completely avoid at all times any use of language more readily associated with women. Some heterosexual men are female impersonators and others are transvestites, particularly in the privacy of their home. Sociologists tell us that only about four percent of the gay male population can be consistently identified as such by clear cross-gender reference. Furthermore, since cross-gender identification is more highly stereotyped as gay, even those gays who are included thus to identify themselves are greatly pressured not to do so or to restrict the places where they would do so.

The origin of the inclination of some gay males to identify themselves with women is unclear, particularly in terms of whether the inclination is self-willed or involuntarily imposed. Early art and literature demonstrate cross-gender identification to have been around a long time. Greek pottery sometimes depicted older men with exaggerated gestures of delicacy being derided by handsome younger men. Some of the American Indian tribes recognized female-identified men as different and responded by giving them specialized training to be holy men. Some have argued that the celibacy of the Roman priesthood, while not designed to do so, had the valuable effect of giving meaningful development to the talents of persons who might otherwise have been anathema. The official church position was much more hostile, particularly with regard to homosexual practice, and the Levitical text specifically stressed the cross-gender behavior of those men who lie with themselves 'as with a woman.'

Some whole cultures, such as most of the Arab world, parts of the Orient, and some of the American proletarian culture, as well as same-sex institutions in schools, the military and prisons, have much weaker taboos against concealed homosexual practice, and are particularly lighter in their stigmas for the penetrator as compared with the penetrated. In such settings the penetrator is always male-identified and considered to be still heterosexual, while the penetrated is female-identified and considered to be homosexual. Significantly it is the experience of being penetrated which such a view says *makes* one a homosexual. In such settings a young male who acknowledges deep involuntary arousal by same-sex stimuli can often resolve much of his ambivalence by adopting the feminine mannerisms culturally prescribed for such persons, such as cross-gender language. In Austin, Texas, for example, where blacks are only about 15 percent of the population, black males represent about 50 percent of the female impersonators in the gay bars. Similar figures are available for other cities. Many see this higher incidence of one form of cross-gender identification as an index of the greater tolerance the black culture affords gay males who will meet heterosexual expectations. The black penetrators are similarly rewarded by not being pressured to define themselves as gay at all.

Others have seen cross-gender identification as more intrinsic, less a matter of choice. A recurrent theory about homosexuals, ascribed to in the 19th century and popularized by English gay liberationist Edward Carpenter, has been that 'the gay male is a woman in a male body,' and that 'a lesbian is a man in a woman's body.' Most such theories are now usually limited to describing a new breed, the transsexual, who is so thoroughly identified with the opposite sex as to feel best served by a sex-change physical operation. Most *homo*sexuals appear to be just that, persons attracted to what they perceive as their own sex rather than to what they perceive as their opposite sex. Even those who initially attract men by their cross-gender references report a high incidence of 'flip-flop,' or as one queen describes it. 'There are more and more of those men who do me and lo and behold turn over and expect me to do them.' By the same token, many queens are insisting that they do not have to give up *any* of their male privileges merely because they are queens.

Some of the uses of cross-gender identification have very clear results for gay males who use them. They can minimize a self-defined heterosexual's fear of being sexually involved on a part-time basis. They can also establish casual, nonsexual registers for gays to relate to each other. Almost never does one hear two lovers using cross-gender references with each other, certainly not in prelude to sexual behavior. Using cross-gender language in response to another's use of it can fairly well guarantee an understanding of no genital expectations unless the language shifts into another register for at least one of the two.

Cross-gender references function effectively as rejections to sexual overtures not welcomed, as in 'Sorry, I don't go to bed with a sister' (this from a female-identified gay male) or 'I don't like nellie people' (from a masculine-identified gay male to a female-identified gay male).

A more positive and very recurrent use of cross-gender reference is the establishing of supportive bonds of nongenital friendship, as in the telephone opening from one gay male to another: 'Hey, girl, give me some dirt!'

The better-known uses of cross-gender references are the more dramatic, vicious ones. Lesbian linguist Julia [Penelope] Stanley has noted the sexism involved in the fact that when such gay males want to hurt one another, they do so by applying all of the verbal opprobrium men have used on women. It is often alleged that there is no 'bitch fight' comparable to a gay-male bitch fight.

Sometimes a group of gay males talking as women will refer to a male of unidentified sexual orientation as 'she' in his presence, in ways that are very indefinite in reference. The use here is to discover whether the person is closeted and gay (often revealed by his protesting too much that he isn't, in response to the game) or that he is a heterosexual outsider. (Heterosexuals rarely even notice what is happening, and if they do, they are typically not threatened, even if scornful.)

Cross-gender references by gay males very often offend women, particularly if they do not know the source of such references in response to the shared heterosexual male oppressor. Feminists resent in such males what they view as the very trivialization of self which they are trying to avoid. Women who are not feminists are likely to consider such males as silly and obnoxious, or in some cases as unfair sexual competition. Many women view the cross-gender language as an insensitive or cruel parody of their own lot in life, particularly since such males can drop the language at any point and walk right back into positions of male privilege and domination.

When heterosexual males detect or think they detect a gay male by crossgender reference, they see the variation from the language of male peers as a surrender of that male privilege and domination.

From one gay male perspective, cross-gender identification is a gesture of defiance of the hetero culture which defines all males as feminine who do not want sexual intercourse with women. 'I'm a queen and proud, honey!' is a verbal thrust towards personal freedom, even if not always efficacious. For an isolated gay male audience the statement may have no direct bearing on women. The rub is that women perceive the statement as derogatory. What is bonding and self-assertive in a gay male context is a painful put-down when transported. The choice of whether to use such cross-gender references is a conflict for gay males who want to increase bonds with other gay males already using the cross-gender standard and who also want to increase bonds with lesbians and other women who suffer oppression from the same hetero males. One can hardly resolve the difficulty by speaking one language with one group and another language with the other, particularly when a goal is to bring the two groups closer together. Lesbians report similar conflicts over whether to refuse cooperation with the users and remain ardent separatists or silently to endure continued humiliation.

These conflicts are rich with irony. For example, there is often more serious sexism in the behavior of gay males who eschew cross-gender language than in the behavior of the gay males who use it. Strict avoidance of cross-gender references often correlates with a clear resentment the non-user has of women, whom he likely sees as a symbol of his only measure of weakness in the masculine culture which he prizes – namely, he has not subdued a woman and begotten a family.

By contrast, many of the users of cross-gender language identify themselves as allies of women and are often supportive of measures to end sexism in our society. Privately they often give much reverence to female figures of strong will, such as Judy Garland, Bette Davis, Joan Crawford, Shirley McLaine, *et al.*

Distinctive blends of items from both registers

Julia [Penelope] Stanley has frequently observed that gays now are working to forge new gay standard [see, e.g., Chapter 4, this volume]. These efforts yield what I have identified as the third specialized direction for gay usage to take, viz., distinctive blends from both male and female registers. Already such blends are appearing unawares in the public media, as in much that is called the *New Yorker* style and in much that informs the chatter style of talk shows. Hopefully these blends will minimize sexism with all of the attendant abuses and maximize individual freedom in shared community. Hopefully too it will be less and less a code language sneaking through because not easily codified and dismissible, and more and more a language of directness and gentle candor.

I personally am particularly concerned that such blends not cancel altogether the cross-gender registers of gay males, as there is increasing pressure from feminists and many gay males to require. Witness the plea of Richard Wood (1977: 131), a Dominican Priest at Loyola, from whom one would perhaps not expect a feminist analysis:

> A final talk-trap associated with camp is the use (mainly if not exclusively by males) of cross-gender reference. While it may be superficially just 'campy' to refer, for instance, to a man as 'she,' such inversions are indicative of deeper attitudes, specifically a sexist bias. For feminine pronouns and nicknames are used basically as camp – for comic effect, mild irony and sometimes vicious verbal abuse. But never in anything but a condescending manner. Authentic liberation in the gay world demands the eradication of such degrading patronization of both women and men.

Fr. Wood's analysis is simply inaccurate and incomplete. From my own files I can find hundreds of letters from all over the English-speaking world employing cross-gender, references without condescension, comic effect, mild irony, or verbal abuse.

The most poignant of many cases that counter Fr. Wood's claims occurred last Thanksgiving at the National Council of Teachers of English when I was the guest of a gay Episcopal priest in Chicago. My host took me when he was summoned to a rescue mission to counsel a very depressed gay wino who was threatening suicide. He had twice before been hauled out of the Chicago river in below freezing weather. On this occasion he was in grief over the recent death of his lover of ten years, another wino who was a gay American Indian. The two of us arrived dressed in stark contrast to this needy man. There was a long pause on his part and ours, a clear question whether there could be any communication across the obvious boundaries. Then he blinked his eyes at us in Scarlet O'Hara fashion, though from a toothless face, and said coquettishly and tentatively: 'It's a tough world for a girl these days.' Without hesitation and with full certainty whereof he spoke, my priest friend replied, 'We're two girls here who know you're telling the truth!'

Much need of cross-gender identified gay persons will simply not be met if gay people are intimidated out of using a language, however stigmatized, that has a long history of support. No thoughtful feminist would suggest that this needy person was really attacking females and needed to be told first to watch his language.

Much too much prescription about language occurs at too remote a distance from the persons who use language. The *OED* is filled with reports of words that in origin are opprobrious, but have undergone amelioration. An important fact about human life is that symbols belong to people, not people to symbols; hence our symbols don't remain fixed, and our language changes. Analysis would be much easier for linguists if cross-gender usage were less complex, but complexity is less fearful than linguistically blind moral purges. For my part, I would rather weigh each use of language on its own merit for real sexism rather than try to purify my mind by cutting out my tongue. For a certainty the minority of gays who use cross-gender references are not going to quit doing so under any kind of prescriptive linguistic force from outside their felt needs, and they are right to suspect the motives of the majority of the more 'respectability conscious' gay males who would like to minimize identification with them.

There is a clear danger in merely celebrating ourselves in the roles of our oppression rather than tackling the harder task of creating new ways of being. There is a parallel danger in giving up our present way of being completely before we have self-defined alternatives free from the imposition of aliens. Right now it seems that only women and gays are concerned to effect change of any kind. I suspect that until the powerful heteromales enter the dialogue, we will remain voices of the powerless in our several ghettos.

Gayspeak:
language, identity
and community

IN *EPISTEMOLOGY OF THE CLOSET* — one of the books that defined queer theory in the early 1990s — the literary scholar Eve Kosofsky Sedgwick (1990) introduced a distinction between what she called 'universalizing' and 'minoritizing' discourses on homosexuality. Universalizing discourses portray homosexuality as a potential of all humans (as in the Freudian view that infantile sexuality is 'polymorphously perverse', capable of developing through subsequent experience in either a hetero- or a homosexual way). Minoritizing discourses, on the other hand, promote the view that homosexuals are particular kinds of people, very different from non-homosexuals (as in the hypothesis that there is a 'gay gene' or a 'gay brain').

Sedgwick's distinction is helpful for thinking about the discussions of gay language that appear in this section. In the three articles we reproduce here, already-existing tensions about the precise relationship between language and sexuality come to a head. Early work such as Legman's (Chapter 1) assumed that 'the language of homosexuality' is part of a package deal: if you are homosexual, you have a particular kind of body — recall that Legman's study was originally published in a medical volume that measured pelvises and pubic hair growth in homosexuals — and you speak a particular kind of language. In Sedgwick's terms, this is a minoritizing view. It is at least implicitly rejected, however, in the pieces by Sonenschein, Penelope Stanley and Crew (Chapters 3–5), who all argue that gay slang follows the same principles and serves the same kinds of purposes as the slang of other subcultural groups (a universalizing view). In addition, these scholars point out that knowledge and use of gay slang co-varies with sociological factors such as sex, geographical region, social class and level of political awareness. This kind of variation makes it difficult or impossible to speak of a single 'gay community' with a single and distinctive 'gay language'.

Understandings of language, however, never arise in a social vacuum. In the years following the Stonewall rebellion of 1969, there was an unprecedented emergence of homosexuals into public life. This period, the early years of the gay liberation movement, was a universalizing moment – a time when lesbians claimed that all women were potentially lesbian, and gay men declared themselves to be in the vanguard of a sexual revolution that would liberate everybody's sexuality. The moment passed quickly, however, and the late 1970s and 1980s saw the ascendance of a new minoritizing view of homosexuality. As more and more women and men came out as homosexual, as distinctively homosexual neighbourhoods and businesses began to grow in places such as San Francisco and New York, and as homosexual activists increasingly demanded that homosexuality be regarded not as a harmful perversion or personal defect, but as a legitimate sexual orientation that should be protected against harassment and discrimination, the idea of 'the gay community' (note the definite article) became a culturally salient and politically important one. It was at this time – when gay rights movements were presenting homosexuals as a minority group that, like other minority groups, could claim legal protection and civil rights – that the idea of 'Gayspeak' emerged.

'Gayspeak' is a word coined by Joseph J. Hayes in the paper we reprint here (Chapter 6), first published in 1976, and reprinted in a 1981 anthology of the same name. Hayes argues that homosexuals are 'America's largest subculture' and that they (the men at least) have their own language. He discusses three settings in which he says Gayspeak is used. These are the secret setting, where gays are circumspect about expressing their homosexuality; the social setting, in which gays speak to other people they know to be gay; and the radical-activist setting, in which gays monitor their language in what we today would call 'PC' ways. Hayes identifies a number of linguistic features that correspond to these settings, for example, euphemism and innuendo in the secret setting, in-group slang in the social setting, and conscious avoidance or resignification of particular terms in the radical-activist setting.

But to what extent is any of this 'gay'? This is the question asked by James Darsey in his response to Hayes's paper (Chapter 7). Darsey criticizes Hayes for making claims that Hayes's own data do not support. His major criticism is that none of the uses of language discussed by Hayes as being characteristic of Gayspeak are in fact unique to gay men. For example, it isn't just gay men who use innuendo or evasion when they don't want their sexuality to be known: 'a college student with a roommate of the opposite sex, unbeknown to his or her parents, might employ the same tactics Hayes claims to be peculiar characteristics of Gayspeak'. It isn't only gay men who have in-group slang or engage in camp talk. And it isn't only gay radical-activists who avoid certain terms and consciously try to resignify others.

Darsey wants to maintain a clear distinction between what he calls 'generic' and 'idiographic' phenomena, meaning that we need to separate general features of language-use (such as the use of innuendo, or in-group terms), from the specific way in which particular groups of people may actually use language in situated interactions. Phrased in Sedgwick's terms, we might say that Darsey wants to distinguish between the universalizing and the minoritizing dimensions of language used by homosexuals. What Hayes's observations about secrecy, in-group sociality and radical activism tell us, he says, is how people in general (i.e. anyone) may use language in certain kinds of situations. They don't tell us much about any specific-ally gay way of using language. This is the meaning of Darsey's point that 'a study that uses gays as a source of data does not necessarily say much about gays' (for a similar kind of criticism, see also Podesva *et al.*, Chapter 12).

Darsey does not deny that some gay men may use language in specific ways. He even suggests specific dimensions of language-use among gay men that deserve more attention, such the co-occurrence of particular verbal and non-verbal signals. But he urges caution: rather than look at how gay men talk and claim that those ways of talking are gay, he suggests doing ethnographic work to determine the precise ways that general features of language-use are deployed in particular contexts by specific kinds of homosexual speakers. In addition, he reminds us that there is not just one gay culture:

> Blacks can be gay; Chicanos can be gay; Native Americans can be gay; women can be gay ... Persons interested in gay studies need to ... be aware of the interactions among subsections of a culture. What unites them? How do traditional divisions on one level and common oppres-sion on another affect interaction?

Even though the *Gayspeak* anthology in which Hayes's and Darsey's articles appeared was the first scholarly volume to address the issue of gay language and gay representation, it was not widely cited in subsequent work. Why is not entirely clear, but it may be because the majority of authors were scholars working in speech communication, a discipline whose literature is not widely read by linguists, sociologists or anthropologists. Perhaps for this reason, the same arguments that structured Hayes's article and Darsey's criticism of it reappeared in later work, for example in the third article in this section (Chapter 8), the linguistic anthropolo-gist William L. Leap's paper entitled 'Can there be gay discourse without gay language?'.

Leap's article is a concise summary of an argument he develops in his mono-graph *Word's Out: Gay Men's English* (Leap 1996). The appearance of *Word's Out* was an important moment for the field of language and sexuality. Though work on language and homosexuality had been appearing since the 1930s, it often appeared in obscure and difficult-to-obtain publications, was not widely known, and made little impact on discussions within linguistics or sociolinguistics. Leap's monograph changed this. The book was published by a respected university press, and it was widely publicized and read. In 1993, Leap had also founded an annual conference, 'Lavender Languages', devoted to research on language and homosexuality. The con-ference is still hosted by Leap every year, attracting a wide range of scholars who are working with or interested in the topic. Both Leap's book and his conference were decisive for establishing language and sexuality as an area of scholarly study.

Leap does not refer to Hayes's work, but the similarities between his approach to what he calls Gay English, and Hayes's approach to Gayspeak, will be appar-ent. Like Hayes, Leap asserts that Gay English fulfils two main functions: one secretive, the other social (he does not address Hayes's third category, gay activist rhetoric). Leap labels the secretive function 'language of risk'. This language consists of euphemism, code words and innuendos that both signal a man's own gay sexuality and ascertain the sexuality of other men in settings in which a question such as 'Are you gay?' would be inappropriate or even dangerous. The social function of Gay English is termed 'co-operative discourse' in Leap's framework, and is characterized more fully in *Word's Out* as 'carefully negotiated styles of turn taking, the use of descriptive imagery and metaphor, inference strategies, and a range of additional techniques ensuring listener – as well as speaker – involvement in each exchange' (Leap 1996: 16). Leap's article can usefully be evaluated by asking the same questions of it that Darsey asked of Hayes's paper: is he describing language specific to gay men, or is he describing general features of interaction that are being used by gay men? What makes Gay English gay?

In fact, Leap goes a step further than Hayes in arguing for the existence of a specifically gay language. Whereas Hayes sees Gayspeak as a discourse style that gay men use in different contexts to signal their homosexuality, Leap wonders whether gay men's use of language might not be an expression of a specifically gay ontology. The question posed in Leap's title, 'Can there be a gay discourse without a gay language?' means 'Can gay men use language in particular ways if they don't have a gay-specific form of linguistic competence that differs from heterosexuals?'. This is a robustly minoritizing question; it asks not only whether gay men use language in specific ways, but also whether they may actually acquire and process language in gay-specific ways. Without actually mentioning it, the question raises the possibility of a 'gay brain' – a topic that is regularly ventilated in public discussions about homosexuality. But it also relates to debates that had been occurring among language and gender scholars in the wake of Deborah Tannen's bestselling 1990 book *You Just Don't Understand*.

Tannen had popularized the idea that men and women have fundamentally different communicative styles, acquired, she claimed, because the peer groups in which girls and boys learn to communicate are largely segregated throughout childhood. The different communicative styles that develop in these different peer groups (boys emphasizing competition and girls emphasizing cooperation) are unconscious and unrecognized, and are the root of miscommunication between women and men (Tannen's arguments are discussed in more detail by Ehrlich, Chapter 16). In asserting that there is a specifically gay form of English that differs from heterosexual English, Leap appears to have been influenced by this approach. Tannen's claim that men and women, in effect, speak different languages, is reformulated by Leap as a claim that gays and straights may speak different languages. Of course the parallel falters as soon as we consider that homosexuals do not grow up in peer groups segregated from heterosexuals. Because Leap does not propose a social mechanism or process through which a specifically gay grammatical competence might be acquired, it is difficult not to conclude that the 'gay language' he discusses must arise from some innate characteristic.

A further distinction that Leap discusses in his article is between 'authentic' and 'inauthentic' uses of Gay English. Leap argues that this distinction is politically important because it allows him to foreground what he calls the 'optimal, valuable and life-cherishing' dimensions of gay experience. One may sympathize with that as a political goal, but there are also some political problems with it – who defines what is or is not 'authentic', and how are the 'inauthentic' cases to be treated?

Leap's analytic moves – first, claiming a Gay English distinct from other forms of English, and second, defining some forms of that Gay English as more 'authentic' than others – can be seen as reflecting the workings of identity politics. As homosexuals became 'gay', and as 'gay' was increasingly understood as an identity category whose members could claim rights and protections on the basis that they belonged to it, it became more important to establish both the existence of a coherent community and criteria for legitimate membership. An 'imagined community' of homosexuals emerged, defined by their politics, their identity and their language.

Both Leap's and Hayes's articles are examples of language being used to make arguments, not about sexuality, but about sexual *identity*. This concern to delineate a linguistic correlate of gay male sexual identity in the form of Gayspeak/Gay English was always subject to challenge (as Darsey's response to Hayes demonstrates), but it would soon encounter a new and powerful wave of criticism, as queer theory, with its critique of identity politics, emerged in the 1990s. Leap's article, first published in this form in 1999, illustrates that the Gayspeak approach has not disappeared, but as Part Two of this Reader will show, it is no longer such a dominant current in the study of language and sexuality.

Chapter 6

Joseph J. Hayes

1981

GAYSPEAK

IN THIS ESSAY I EXAMINE some aspects of language use in America's largest subculture, homosexuals. It is not my purpose to offer a descriptive analysis of syntax, morphology, or phonology, but to analyze the social functions of language in this particular group. I wish to see the ways in which the language used by gay men reflects and affects the relationships between dominant culture and subculture, and, in turn, to evaluate the relationships between normative and special dialects in the way they influence the self-image of their speakers.[1] To facilitate a discussion which must include lexicon, usage, imagery, and rhetoric, I call the language of this community Gayspeak.[2]

Since any special language must be evaluated within a contextual framework, I have divided the body of my essay into three sections in order to account for some specific behavior patterns in the subculture, which are directly reflected in language use: the secret, the social, and the radical-activist settings.[3] At the conclusion of this analysis of social context I offer some hypotheses on the effects which the normative and special dialects have on each other and their users, and some comments on the unique functions of language in gay culture.

In this analysis I have drawn primarily on observations of my own language and that of other gay people. I have listened over a long period of time to a wide range of people talking in bars, clubs, meetings, and social gatherings, and to the voices of novelists and periodical writers. These people are my informants; their linguistic behavior forms my 'data'. My analysis explores the linguistic behavior of the gay community within the three settings listed above. The criteria for such an analysis come from the behavior of each speaker toward other gays and toward the dominant culture, as well as from language differences. It is important to understand, however, that any member of the gay community may function in any one or all three of these settings. They are not exclusive to any individual or subgroup.

In the *secret* setting, gays are covert in expressing their gay identity, separatist (from the straight world especially, but often from the gay community as well), apolitical, and conservative. They are often painfully self-conscious about the stigma imposed on them by the straight world and take great pains to avoid any mannerisms or language which would stereotype them. The *social* gay setting is the most traditional one. It is best known to the dominant culture, since its linguistic behavior is often the butt of comments and jokes. The central meeting place for social language is the gay bar or club, and as the name suggests, gays in this setting frequently engage in social activity with other gays, either privately or in gay meeting places. Gays who frequent the social scene, however, may be open about their subcultural identity with friends or fellow workers in the straight world. Gays in the third setting, the *radical-activists*, are currently the most visible in their behavior. Although they may not have formal ties with the gay liberation movement, they are usually highly political and freely expressive about their identity. Because of their association with the counterculture they are sometimes alienated from people who move only in the secret and social settings, although radical gays may themselves move in the secret or social setting at various times.[4]

The secret setting

The gay who is in a covert setting may be distinguished from one in a social or activist setting by his refusal to use any Gayspeak or only as much as is necessary for making social contacts. Even in a gay social group or alone with a friend the secret gay may refuse to refer to his subculture life in any but the mildest euphemisms. This typical exchange of two men at a straight social gathering might serve as an example:

> Mr. X: You certainly have on a colorful tie!
> Mr. Y: Yes, I really like gay apparel.

The information, 'I am gay and I believe you are, too', has been transmitted in what amounts to code language. In this setting, guarded use of Gayspeak allows people to hint at their sexual orientation, but never in a way which jeopardizes their ability to pass. Even among friends the secret gay may eschew gay terminology, preferring to call his lover of many years his *friend*, his circle of gay acquaintances the *kids*, and all gays *members of our book club* or *people of our faith*. The simple question, 'Is he?' in many contexts asks any or all of the following questions: 'Is he gay?', 'May I use Gayspeak in his presence?', 'Do you want him to know that you (or both of us) are gay?', 'Is he straight but hip to the scene?', 'Would he be available as a potential sex partner?'.

Another prominent feature of secret Gayspeak is the tendency to avoid specific gender reference. In describing a weekend trip, a gay person might begin: 'I went to the mountains with this person I know and they enjoyed the view from the summit.' Gays may also become adept at switching gender reference when there is a perceived threat. Chatting on the telephone in a public office, the covert man or woman may refer to Elliott as Ella or to Jill as Joe in order not to arouse suspicion.

In questions which anticipate a specific gender response, this person may respond vaguely as follows:

X: Who'd you go to the movies with last night?
Y: Oh, this friend of mine.

Secret gays may also use innuendo in referring to other gays, calling them *artistic*, *liberal-minded*, *understanding*, or *sensitive*. People with *tendencies* – *artistic tendencies*, *unusual tendencies* – are hinted to be gay. This usage may have developed from a standard locution on employment or security-clearance forms: 'Have you ever had homosexual feelings or tendencies?'

For gays in a secret setting, the development and maintenance of a code language form a protection against exposure. As certain words or phrases pass into general usage or become generally familiar, some gays must develop new phrases or employ more arcane synonyms, in order to maintain secrecy. They are always on stage and usually on guard. However, it must be remembered that the language habits in the secret setting are used by most gays whenever they perceive a threatening situation.

The social setting

Unlike the covert gay, for whom Gayspeak helps to maintain a rigid separation between minority status and mainstream acceptance, the gay who is in a social setting uses language to express a broad range of roles both within and outside the subculture. Social Gayspeak emphasizes the importance of acting in language behavior. If I were to summarize the social setting simplistically, I would say that it employs a vast metaphor of theater, which includes role stereotypes, clear notions of approved sexual behavior, and the rewards and punishments that are assigned according to one's ability or failure to use the symbols assigned by sex role. 'Scanning the possibilities' – being always on the alert for contexts in which various modes of expression are either allowed or appropriate – requires one to perceive the total spectrum of distinctions between what people say and what they do.[5] Thus, the humor in Gayspeak, especially camp, is often cynical because it is based on a serious relation to the world. In the social setting, Gayspeak suggests that there is always a vast gulf between what people pretend to be and what they are.

Closely related to the acting behavior is the habit of categorization. Although all speakers make categorical distinctions, gays do so along specific parameters: 'The important point is that everyone (and every kind of sexuality) be accounted for by some linguistic category of the gay world. Words, then, function to separate outsiders from insiders, to account for ambiguous persons within sociable or sexual interaction, and to describe the primary, close, and unique relationships of insiders with one another' (Warren 1974: 114). In the social setting people are not only typed by the usual distinctions (height, weight, race), but by sexual preference (*bottom boy*: anal receptor, *suck queen*: fellator), intimacy of relationship (*auntie*, *sister*, *husband*), rank within the subculture (*queen bee*: social arbiter, *nelly number*: effeminate and insignificant), and eccentricities within the norms of the subculture (*leather*: motorcycle crowd, *drag*: transvestites, *S/M*: sadomasochists). In general, a person's occupation, status within the dominant culture, or family are not described in Gayspeak except as they have some bearing on events in the subculture.

As we would expect from the process of categorization, the richest features of social Gayspeak are found in the lexicon, particularly in compound constructions. Perhaps the most widely employed stem word for building compounds is *queen*. The more traditional meaning of the term implies effeminate behavior in a man. In its wider context, however, it may be used to build a limitless series of images: to describe sexual preferences – *dinge queen* (one who prefers blacks), *size queen* (one who likes men with large penises); to describe a subculture type – *queen mother* (older man who serves as counselor or social arbiter), *queen of tarts* (a pimp for hustlers); to make fun of a man's hobbies or interests – *Chippendale queen* (likes antiques), *poker queen* (likes to play cards); or as an all-purpose term of derogation – *Queen Mary* (large or fat), *Queen of Spades* (black with high status).[6] There is no limit except each speaker's imagination, and neologisms are constantly being coined. In all the forms I have cited, *queen* refers simply to gay man. In certain instances where the speaker refuses to consider any event or person outside the terms of Gayspeak, *queen* may simply refer to all men in general. Thus, a gay man noticing the impeccable clothes of a public official might observe, 'Oh, she's such a neat queen!' (one obsessed with cleanliness and order). He does not mean that the mayor is gay; rather that the speaker is gay and that he recognizes in the mayor a stereo-typed trait of the gay community, that all gay men are fastidious housekeepers or dressers.

As is true of American slang in general, social Gayspeak has an especially large number of synonyms for sexual organs and sexual acts. To the extent that the dominant culture defines gays largely in terms of specific sexual practices and the imagined role and behavior changes that these acts must bring about, the sub-culture reflects this labeling in the richness of its vocabulary for proscribed sexual acts. It is outside my scope here to resolve the chicken/egg question of whether the sexual vocabulary developed in response to outlaw status or whether it merely generated itself.

However, as an adjunct to the acting skills of 'scanning the possibilities', social Gayspeak has developed an important cluster of images from stage and film. Famous Hollywood stars of the thirties and forties figure importantly, especially if the roles they play are campy or treat of tragic love. A melodramatic loser, for instance, is a *Stella Dallas*. A man who is suspected of actually enjoying his constant misfortune becomes a *Camille* or a *Sarah Bernhardt* (sometimes *Sarah Heartburn*). Stars such as Mae West, Bette Davis, and Carmen Miranda are mimed along with some of their famous scenes or routines probably because they exaggerate the various stereotyped roles that women play in general society. Gayspeak has, thus, an idea of acting within acting. Mimicking the tone, diction, rhetoric, and speech mannerisms of these camp heroines would seem to show the subculture's perception of how seriously the dominant culture takes the language by which it maintains rigid images of sex stereotyping. At its very core, camp is the art of the put-down, especially of one's self and culture. Behind the irony of camp, however, is the awareness of the roles played outside the culture as well. By pretending to be a vamp or a sexpot, gay men manifest an implied awareness that language may be used as a means to reshape attitudes toward social roles. Through camp, stereotyped behavior is revealed as nothing more than another form of playacting.[7]

Some articles have offered evidence to show the extent to which women's language makes use of the expressive as opposed to the instrumental mode. This is certainly true of gay men's language to some extent. There is a difference, however. The metaphor of acting in Gayspeak implies that the process of trivialization, when put on or off at will, is a form of mockery, perhaps a flaunting of 'abnormality'. What would appear to be a trivialization of the world, because social Gayspeak is often frivolous, comic, precious, or fleeting, amounts to a trivialization through parody of the dominant culture.

The radical-activist setting

The rhetoric of gay liberation is often indistinguishable from the rhetoric of the general counterculture. It is distinguished from the rest of the gay community, however, by its deliberate reevaluation of Gayspeak. As is true of the counterculture at large, the gay activist believes that a change in the way people use language can bring about a change in society's structures and values. If language can create attitudes and modes of behavior in a subculture, they argue, then a change in Gayspeak can bring about changes in the dominant culture. Julia [Penelope] Stanley [Chapter 4, this volume, p. 50] summarizes the relationship clearly:

> Thus, although gay slang is the vocabulary of people who are themselves outcasts from the straight culture, it is also sexist, classist, and racist, and the existence of terms that reflect such attitudes binds us to the same value system that makes us outcasts. Such a conflict within the gay subculture will not be resolved easily . . .

The first strategy is to avoid any special jargon at all. This attitude links the radical group with the secret group. While the more conservative secret group wishes to distinguish itself from the gay subculture, the activists, who also wish to distinguish themselves from gays in a social setting, avoid Gayspeak not to hide their gay identity but rather to stop both the process of alienation and ghettoization and to reject the value system which Gayspeak has incorporated from the mainstream culture.

As the feminist and black movements have worked out a new set of values for the terms woman and black, the task of value redefinition occupies a central position in gay liberation theory. In an article on the general subject of his personal identity, Allen Young (1974: 31) describes the process of redefinition in its largest context:

> Saying 'I am gay' has the important element of *self-definition* to it. It is not the negative definition of others (homo, lezzie, queer, pansy, fruit) but a positive term we can call our own. (Even if the term is not an ideal one – there have been objections to the trivializing aspects of the word 'gay' from within our community – still it is the one most generally favored by gay people.) . . . The term homosexual does not comply

with the need of self-definition, because the term was given to us by doctors and other 'scientists' who have not generally been our friends. 'Faggot' and 'dyke' are used in a special way, turning terms of put-down into proud affirmation . . . The affirmation of gay identity allows us to get together and achieve unity with others of like identity. This has obvious advantages for our sexual and social needs, but it also means we can share life experiences which cannot be shared with people who are not gay . . . This leads quite naturally to the discovery of gay media, international communications and understanding among gay people, and perhaps most important, action against our oppressors. The price of suppressing one's gay identity, the price of closetry, is a very high one to pay.

A similar attempt at definition is found in D. Cartier's 'A Dyke's Manifesto'. In asking the question, 'where does the woman from a dyke-masculine background fit into the women's liberation movement?', the author describes her response to the position of the lesbian in the general feminist movement (Cartier 1973: 19):

Crap on society, I say, when I walk into a bar and see the rigid faces of women who have forgotten or who never learned how beautiful it is to be loved as a woman by a woman. Anger and rage when I look over the years at the unreality of being ostracized from straights and men because I am a woman, and alienated from other women, and my very identity, because I played to win on a losing side.

These are my sisters who like myself are just beginning to recognize that their real strength and beauty lie in being their own self-denied women. These are my sisters who have come to realize that that little gun is a crippler and the very chain that separates us from an honest love for other women like ourselves.

It's a strange sort of sisterhood because we have enemies on all sides and inside. Our enemies are society and its sex-roled oppression that has alienated us from half of ourselves and the women we purport to 'love.' Our enemies . . . are ourselves and internalized illusion that what this society says is 'strong and right' is really crap – and was never us to begin with.

Like the style of the social setting, gay radical rhetoric often has a 'spoken' quality to it, although this tone resembles the rhetoric of political conflict (the 'speech') more than 'gossip'. The language attempts to dramatize and intensify rather than trivialize. Terms of *anger* and *rage* – the *crippler gun*, the *chain*, *enemies* – and the images of deceit, alienation, sell-out, delusion, and ostracization give Cartier's passage a vivid and aggressive tone. The situation discussed is termed significant and dramatic. In this sense, radical Gayspeak, like its other versions, is also a form of acting. Since Cartier's piece is meant to be taken seriously, it adheres to a 'masculine' tone, that is, it does not qualify the action, dwell on decorative elements, or use ironic parody. This tone is employed by both men and women.

The writer creates a persona who is neither arch nor coy. She wishes to convey strength and determination. Like other radical activist writers she has learned from the subculture to use 'male' language to make 'power' statements.

However, the frequently expressed belief that the dangers of *posing* are as inimical as those of *passing* makes many activists distrustful of all language. For them words are very important; but the use of language as a tool for changing behavior is occasionally met with suspicion. In a humorous column on radical rhetoric, Rita Goldberger reflects the gay world's heightened awareness of euphemism and cant:

> *Movement* people do not 'gossip.' They 'discuss intra-*Movement* personal dynamics.' They do not 'cruise' because cruising is sexist. And *Movement* women do not 'trick,' they have 'short term,' but 'meaningful' relation-ships . . . One last word that is necessary of a *Movement* person's vocabulary is 'high.' One meaning of 'high' is 'stoned.' . . . *All Movement* people get 'high' because getting 'high' is illegal and therefore very radical . . .
>
> However, when used with the word 'consciousness,' 'high' takes on a new connotation. Someone with a 'high consciousness' is someone who is politically aware and understands her oppression. One can tell how 'high' a person's consciousness is by how many meetings she goes to and how often she uses the words in this article. Thus, to demon-strate a 'high' consciousness, *one does not really have to change one's ideas, but merely one's vocabulary*.
>
> (Goldberger 1973: 7, emphasis added)

Thus, radical gays are committed to the notion that 'language uses us as much as we use language'. Many radical gays feel that Gayspeak holds them to the ghetto, either because gays subsume in their dialect the contempt manifested by the straight world or because it reflects the oppressive values of that world. By making over pejorative terms (*faggot*, *dyke*) radical gays are attempting to turn back these terms into symbols of defiance of the dominant culture. From other stigmatized groups, radical gays have learned to put their special dialect to use as a focus of pride and identification. Radicalesbian provocateurs label themselves The Dyke Patrol. A group of Berkeley gays picketed a San Francisco gay bar called The Stud to urge a name change to The Fairy (from straight machismo to gay affirmation). A Boston quarterly calls itself the *Fag Rag*. Just as Black is Beautiful, Gay is Good.[8]

Indeed, one important way to distinguish radical from social Gayspeak is by the differences in understanding of contextual meaning. Kinship and rank terminology may serve as a representative example. The circumstantial nature of relationships in a stigmatized community seems to act as an impetus to the creation of alternative structures modeled on the dominant community. Since the acting nature of social Gayspeak emphasizes caricature and exaggeration, these kinship terms are intended to be parodic. A gay man might refer to his *sisters*, who are his close friends with whom he enjoys the confidentiality and close ties that the siblings of the idealized family enjoy. His *mother* is the person who first introduced him to gay society (a *father* for gay women). An *auntie* affords him the indulgences, kindness, and general entertainment that a visiting relative might provide for her adored nephews. A gay *son* or *daughter* may have been housed or educated by an older member of the community. In many larger cities, elaborate costume balls are held to elect an *emperor*, *empress*, *princesses*, and a *royal court*. In the spirit of Mardi Gras and King Momus, the strictest etiquette is observed, but in a spirit of merrymaking.

Except in the egalitarian sentiment of *sisterhood* and *brotherhood* radical gays abjure the use of these kinship terms as 'elitist' and 'sexist', as well as a waste of time better spent on social work or political activity. They perceive the use of social Gayspeak as inimical and serious, a manifestation of ghetto sycophancy. In their concern for the values implied in social Gayspeak, radical gays seem to have a more restrictive understanding of contextual meaning than gays in the social setting. The lexicon of social Gayspeak may be 'elitist' or 'sexist' only if the social context is taken seriously. If, as I suggested, the acting metaphor of social Gayspeak presents language as potentially comic or parodic whenever it deals with sex roles or stereotypes, then gays in the radical setting can properly be accused of a failure to understand social Gayspeak.

An overall perspective

Gayspeak has some unique aspects which make it especially interesting to the study of language behavior. It is always acquired as a second dialect or register, yet its features are not generally known to the mainstream community. Unlike black English or Chicano Spanish, which are the normative dialects in their own communities, Gayspeak is not ever used by many gays, although they are normally exposed to it in late adolescent or early adult life. While most bidialectals learn the dominant culture's language at least by their early school years, gays learn to acquire the special dialect well after learning the normative one, usually at the time of entry into the gay community. Within that community, moreover, there is much debate about the value of Gayspeak. For some it is a source of pride and self-affirmation; for others it is an embarrassment or a threat.

Gays who remain only in the secret setting face problems in understanding and using social Gayspeak. Since the development of some Gayspeak was brought about by the need to remain covert, the secrecy of the language makes it difficult to acquire for people who wish to come into contact with the gay subculture. The process of coming out is both aided and inhibited by the existence of Gayspeak. Since there has been a manifest conspiracy of silence in all media when dealing with the subject of homosexuality, except in a degrading or lurid fashion, the language used to describe the gay world relies almost solely on stereotypes. For even the most secretive gay person, it is almost impossible not to become familiar with some Gayspeak. Yet it is the knowledge of Gayspeak which may potentially expose the covert gay to the straight world and is treated by many gays as a mark of the ghetto mentality. Certainly, this is a situation of 'damned if you do, damned if you don't'. In the short run, a knowledge of Gayspeak may ease the transition into the gay world during the coming-out process. In the long run, however, Gayspeak has a potential for harm.

As the radicals point out, much of gay lexicon is sex-linked. The association of women with passivity and men with aggression finds exaggerated expression in the subculture. No one has ever satisfactorily determined to what extent language influences our behavior. But there is a danger that Gayspeak may develop in men the *belief* that they are sexually abnormal, weak, silly, passive, and unstable creatures. To the extent that the speaker is aware that these poses are ironic, it can be a healthy antidote to repression. To the extent that linguistic behavior determines psychological behavior, it can be dangerous.

Inevitably, the gay who moves in more than one setting must evaluate how his use of language will affect intra-group prestige and standing. The queen, whose social status is low because of his 'feminine' traits is often marked by his witty chatter. The 'strong silent type', however, is much sought after because his apparent verbal inabilities are taken to be a sign of masculinity. In our society, silence is frequently associated with power. Women are often denigrated for 'chattering', or in the male view, trivializing the world by talking about it too much. However, outside the sexual marketplace, linguistic 'cleverness' may be a valuable skill, especially if one is good at the brand of repartee called dishing.

The final problem for the secret gay is the passing of Gayspeak into the main-stream language. When code language appears in normative language it threatens those who seek protection behind it, because once-secret signals are now open to public scrutiny. Lakoff suggests that gays always use the dominant culture's language, whereas the dominant culture abjures minority language (Lakoff 1975). I do not think this is true for gays in the radical setting or to the extent that the language of gay activists has been absorbed into everyday speech. As the taboo against talking openly about sex has abated somewhat recently, many terms from Gayspeak have entered the language, just as terms from black English relating to drug usage have done. Films such as *The Boys in the Band* have made Gayspeak words like *auntie*, *butch*, *cruise*, *drag*, *queen*, and *gay* more familiar to the general public. There has also been a cross-fertilization in the political realm as well. The process of coming out or the trap of being in the closet, for instance, are discussed widely in weekly newsmagazines and film reviews. One may come out to the women's movement or be a closet radical. One might also come out as a member of a party to which one does not nominally belong. A film motif might be described as closet Gothic. The controversial Madalyn Murray O'Hair appealed to American 'closet atheists' to 'come out of the closet' (Dart 1975).

In the course of this essay I have suggested that the straight world's narrow focus on abnormality and sexual 'deviance' is incorporated to some extent in Gayspeak. To put the case somewhat simply, I feel that Gayspeak reflects this pejoration in two ways: extreme euphemism, even to the extent of denying Gayspeak altogether, and extreme dysphemism, a mark of the parodic nature of Gayspeak. In Gayspeak this is the difference between *dropping your hairpins*, giving subtle hints about your sexual orientation, and *throwing your beads* (or *pearls*), being dramatically open about your gayness. An alternative response in the gay community comes from the radical group, which attempts to reverse the pejoration by redefining certain terms to give them positive values. Perhaps ironically, the proudest affirmation of one's personal identity and the most paranoid repression of it in the gay community are achieved principally through the existence of Gayspeak.

Final observations

A proper conclusion must certainly include a perspective on problems in current and future research. Until recently, research on the gay community has followed principally one interest: the investigation of the etiology of 'abnormality'. As a result, we have little phenomenological or ethnographic information about gay life. We do not know, for instance, much about the ways that gay people in various contexts and settings view each other. Nor are there data for distinguishing between male and female language in the gay community. Are the differences related to class, sex, adaptation, or position in the dominant culture? Why is male Gayspeak so full of pejorative terms for women while the reverse is not true?

When linguists write about black English, Chicano Spanish, or women's language, some assume that all speakers come from the same class. Is the bond of a subculture stronger than the class structures developed by the main culture? This question is important in discussing Gayspeak since there is such a strong stigma attached to being gay. We also need to study the use of nonverbal language in the gay community and its relationship to the spoken dialect.

We can only guess how widely Gayspeak is used. Who employs it? Can we discern patterns in those people who will not use it other than to serve their desire to remain covert, appear more masculine or feminine, or to avoid the oppression of a ghetto mentality?

Finally, we need to examine Gayspeak in greater detail precisely because its speakers come from all races, classes, and occupations, and because it exists in many languages. In pursuing the answers to some of the questions I have raised, researchers will bring us closer to a complex and sophisticated model for understanding the reciprocally affecting influence of language and behavior.

Chapter 7

James Darsey

1981

'GAYSPEAK'

A response

[*Editors' note:* Quotations from and page references to Joseph Hayes's article correspond to the page numbering in Chapter 6, this volume.]

> *Of course the first thing to do was to make a grand survey of the country she was going to travel through. 'It's something very like learning geography,' thought Alice as she stood on tiptoe in hopes of being able to see a little further.*
> (Lewis Carroll, *Through the Looking Glass*)

T HIS ESSAY ATTEMPTS TO PROVIDE some preliminary views on what areas are the legitimate province of a legitimate gay studies, especially gay language and communication studies. No one would like to play chess from the perspective of one of the pieces, yet gays risk the consequences of just that unless they make some attempt to reflect on their claim to academic uniqueness. They, like Alice, must occasionally stand on tiptoe to get the lay of the land if they are to be effective.

The claim I pursue here is that it is profitable for those involved in shaping gay studies to think of scholarly endeavors as either generic – those that are concerned with broad, generalizable classes of phenomena – or idiographic – those that are devoted to establishing and understanding the unique characteristics of an event, person, or group. For example, a study that demonstrates the unique effects being black has on behavior is idiographic. In contrast, a study that uses a black ghetto population as an example of the effects of lower socioeconomic status on behavior is generic. Similarly, a study that uses gays as a source of data does not necessarily say much about gays. For instance, a study of the rhetoric of Mattachine Midwest that I prepared several years ago says something about agitative rhetoric but little about gays; it was properly included in an extant tradition of scholarship that has such questions as its concern; it was a generic study.

It seems apparent to me that gay studies, if there is to be such a thing, must concentrate on the idiographic, that is, precisely what no one else is going to study. The traits that are unique to gay men and lesbians must be isolated, and their impact on various phenomena, such as language usage, must be studied. Unfortunately, at the present time, we often lack the basic knowledge to make that distinction – the distinction between the generic and the idiographic. If we fail to make and use this distinction, we run the risk of failing our essential function in gay studies. If we confuse this distinction, we run the risk of creating outright falsehood.

A close examination of 'Gayspeak' by Joseph Hayes clarifies the nature of the idiographic/generic distinction and its importance, and suggests some possible directions for future research.

Joseph Hayes and the nature of Gayspeak: a view from across the hall

Joseph Hayes deals with the 'social functions of language' in the gay subculture. Within his scope he includes 'lexicon, usage, imagery, and rhetoric,' all under the rubric of Gayspeak. To facilitate analysis Hayes divides Gayspeak into three social contexts: the secret, the social, and the radical-activist settings. In the secret setting Gayspeak is apparently a restricted language code used to identify other gay people without jeopardizing one's own identity. The other function attributed to secret Gayspeak is evading the inquiries of others concerning one's identity and the nature of specific relationships.

From Hayes' description the latter function is simply filled by lying about the nature of these relationships, activities, and attachments. There does not appear to be any peculiar linguistic usage. For example, a college student with a roommate of the opposite sex, unbeknown to his or her parents, might employ the same tactics Hayes claims to be peculiar characteristics of Gayspeak. One wonders if this example provides any insight into the social functions of language in the gay subculture.

The former function – identification – is more interesting. Hayes maintains that 'for gays in a secret setting, the development and maintenance of a code language form a protection against exposure' [p. 70]. In other words, Hayes sees this activity as analogous to the highly popularized citizens' band codes – a code specifically created to facilitate communication within an in-group while excluding members of an out-group. In making this assumption, Hayes ignores the full implications of the term he uses to describe the gay community: subculture.

Cultures and subcultures have histories. Some histories may be more highly developed and explicated than others, some long and some short, but all cultures and subcultures have continuity in time. To have a history means that the events that constitute this history are defined in terms of people, places, things, and times. Often these events have significance to the culture of which they are part but not to other cultures. More to the point, an event that is significant to a particular subculture may go largely unnoticed by the larger, surrounding culture. In other words, *cultures and subcultures have a host of events – including people, places, things, and times – that largely attain significance only within that culture or subculture.* These events, people, places, things, and times have symbolic referents (names) quite aside from any nonexternally grounded attempt to create a 'secret code.' For example, several years ago there existed in Atlanta a gay bar known as Bayou Landing. The surrounding straight culture was largely unaware of the bar, but it was known by virtually every active gay male in the Southeast. Thus, using Hayes' scenario, two strange men at a straight social gathering, after the preliminary nonverbals, might engage in some conversation. The discussion would be directed to Atlanta (considered a gay city), further to places to go there ('Oh, really? Where do you go when you're there?'), and finally, someone would drop the name Bayou Landing. Appropriate recognition of the name serves to fill all the functions Hayes describes.

The same kind of interaction could take place with events (the Stonewall rebellion), people (a local gay person, or a literary figure like Christopher Isherwood), literary works (*Teleny*, *City of Night*), gay publications (*The Advocate*, *Christopher Street*), or places (San Francisco, Polk Street, The Gold Coast). Hayes' citation of certain cult heroes and heroines is a further example of this [p. 71]. Mae West may be part of the subculture because she wrote plays with lesbian themes as much as for any exaggeration of 'the various stereotyped roles that women play in general society' [p. 71]. Bette Midler started her career in the gay baths of New York and became a gay idol. Montgomery Clift owes much of his gay following to gay identification with his own homosexual torment, and Tennessee Williams' plays have a loyal gay audience, partially because of Williams' own homosexuality and his use of homosexual themes (Silverstein 1972). Sometimes heroes and heroines are part of the gay subculture because of a real or believed participation in this subculture's history.

This cultural view of Gayspeak grants it new dimensions for which Hayes cannot account. The difference in origin between what Hayes presents as a code expressly created for limited communication, and what I have presented as a code growing out of a history with significance limited only to an in-group might be expected to create differences in function as well.

In the secret setting, for example, Hayes sees Gayspeak limited almost in contradiction to his definition and certainly more limited than the historical/cultural view would dictate. The question Hayes presents – 'May I use Gayspeak in his presence?' – is never really raised. If, by its nature, Gayspeak 'allows people to hint at their sexual orientation, but never in a way which jeopardizes their ability to pass,' the question Hayes presents is not really important [p. 69]. A better way to conceptualize it is the question 'Would it be profitable (friendship, sexual encounter, etc.) for me to use Gayspeak in his presence?'

In the social setting none of the questions Hayes presents in the secret setting are relevant. All these questions are tacitly answered by participation in the group. The situation is no longer one of being identified, resolving doubts, and making contact. Social-setting Gayspeak, then, serves a distinctly different function than does secret-setting Gayspeak.

Small-group theorists give insight into the function of social-setting Gayspeak in talking about the social rewards of groups (e.g. Bormann 1969: 149–50). Extending this notion of rewards, one can begin to understand why a heavily stigmatized group would create social climates that build a defense against the attacks of a larger, surrounding culture. In keeping with current sociological thought on the topic, *stigmatized groups socialize in an effort to create an alternative social reality to the one held by the oppressing society of which they are a part* (Berger and Luckman 1967).

This effort manifests itself in social-setting Gayspeak through the use of camp. Hayes talks of camp in general terms. Vito Russo (1976: 17) describes it particularly as it relates to and reflects the gay subculture:

> Since camp flourishes in urban cliques and is something of a secret code, it has become one of the mainstays of an almost ethnic humor which has been formed for defense purposes over the years. Because camp seeks to comfort and is largely a generous rather than a selfish feeling, it has also operated in a human sense, aiding people in forming images with which they feel comfortable in a hostile culture.

Except for the appearance of certain words believed to be peculiar to the gay subculture (apparently because they describe acts or relationships largely restricted to that group), most of the characteristics Hayes ascribes to the social setting are more properly characteristic of camp. The sexism (use of *queen* and *she*), the exaggeration, the trivialization, and the self-deprecation are all qualities of camp (Russo 1976: 17–18). This distinction is important, because camp is neither exclusive to the gay subculture (Sontag 1964) nor universal within that subculture. Gayspeak in the social setting, then, may not be Gayspeak at all, but camp.

If the predominance of camp in the social setting grants insights into the function of social-setting Gayspeak, then the marked absence of camp in the radical-activist setting may indicate something about a difference in function. Russo (1976: 18) says: 'Camp, because it deals only frivolously with the roles we've been assigned and entails no criticism of them, is totally apolitical.' The exclusion of, even contempt of, camp in the radical-activist setting rests on this apolitical nature that is dysfunctional to the distinctly political function of the radical-activist.

> We perceive our oppression as a class struggle and our oppressor as white, middle-class, male-dominated, heterosexual society, which has relentlessly persecuted and murdered homosexuals and lesbians since the oppressor has had power.
>
> (Jay 1972: 1)

This excerpt from the introduction to 'a collection of the experiences and philosophies of *radical* lesbians and homosexuals' (Jay 1972: 1) illustrates the radical-activist stance, which is anything but a frivolous treatment of the gay person's status in America. In fact, implicit in the radical-activist stance is a rejection of such an orientation, often accompanied by scorn for those who participate in the social setting (see e.g. Wittman 1972).

In a like manner the secret homosexual is the philosophic antithesis to the radical-activist. The idealized version of the radical-activist never worries about his ability to 'pass.' This type of behavior is injurious to one's goals. With this orientation, use of a restricted language code – as Gayspeak is defined in both the secret and social settings – is philosophically repugnant and counterproductive.

Wide-scale change in the sociopolitical sphere is not facilitated by communicating with only a few. An elaborate language code is necessary for effective sociopolitical dialectic. Thus, the Gayspeak of the radical-activist is not the Gayspeak of the social or the secret setting.

Perhaps the most important statement made by Hayes about the radical-activist Gayspeak is that, it 'is often indistinguishable from the rhetoric of the general counterculture' [p. 72]. This observation is further supported by a notion of an undifferentiated radical-revolutionary rhetoric developed in an article by James Chesebro, who specifically includes gay liberation in his study as an example of a cultural revolutionary group (Chesebro 1972).

Here Hayes falls prey to the same criticism raised in connection with the social setting. He is exploring a phenomenon that is not exclusively a product of the gay subculture, nor universal within that subculture. Perhaps his insights are more applicable to radical-revolutionary rhetoric than particularly to a type of Gayspeak. This argument gains impetus when one realizes that this mode of Gayspeak is so different from, and even critical of, other modes that it is doubtful they have anything in common, except the fact that all three are used by members of the gay subculture.

Substantively, then, Hayes has made a basic confusion between the generic and the idiographic. In an attempt to tell us something about the unique behaviors of the gay subculture, he has stumbled into larger areas of behavior with no compelling evidence that they are in any way uniquely employed by gay persons. Each of the three settings serves a different, sometimes antithetical function, and even on a lin-guistic level, Hayes fails to provide us with any words or word patterns that have a constant function and usage across settings which might indeed illuminate something uniquely and universally gay. Rather than a singular Gayspeak that appears in three settings, it seems that a more appropriate conception is Gayspeak$_1$, Gayspeak$_2$, and Gayspeak$_3$, the latter two being subsets of generic behaviors (linguistic and otherwise) known as camp and the rhetoric of the radical-revolutionary, respectively. An artifi-cial association of the three results in a confusing picture of linguistic behavior in the gay subculture, with little clear indication of its importance and no clear directive as to where we go from here.

Future directions for Gayspeak

The above analysis is not intended to minimize the contribution of Hayes' work. In fact, it may be seen as a tribute to the breadth of Hayes' work, since it seeks to reduce it to more manageable portions. Very little of the substance of Hayes' essay has been contested; it has only been put into a new framework.

Given this body of data as a starting point, where do we go from here? Those who are interested in using gays as data for more generic concerns might expand the notions of camp and radical-revolutionary rhetoric. Consciousness-raising is still another, quite new setting in which gays participate but which is also charac-teristic of women's and men's liberation (Chesebro *et al.* 1981). Many fields have ignored the gay subculture as a valuable source of data. Those who are interested in pursuing the idiographic approach – creating a distinctive area of gay studies – will indirectly benefit from the encouragement of this generic work.

There are also immediate possibilities for those interested in the idiographic aspects of the gay community. As claimed earlier, this depends on isolating distinctive qualities of the gay subculture and looking for the effects of those qualities on behavior.

Both on the basis of the foregoing analysis and on outside documentation, the secret setting seems to be the area in which gay persons claim their greatest distinctiveness. The issue of identification never materializes for other similarly oppressed groups. Stuart Byron (1972: 58) explicates the view that the 'particular problem of homosexuality itself – the thing about the state of being gay which distinguishes it from other "oppressed" conditions . . . is that one can hide one's minority group status: "staying in the closet" is a phrase that has little application to women or blacks or chicanos.'

For students of language and communicative behavior such isolation suggests questions like the following: How does this ability (for anonymity) affect language use? Does 'identification' create unique patterns of interpersonal satisfaction (of following up a hunch, feeling of mutual membership in a clandestine community, sexual encounter), and if so, are they distinguishable from the interaction patterns?

The issue of concealed identity also raises a host of questions concerning different levels of membership and the effect of varying degrees of involvement with the subculture on interaction patterns. The gay community has a remarkable latitude in the degree to which its members identify themselves as such, ranging from the married businessman who stops off at a local tearoom on the way home from work and hustlers who just 'let the "Johns" do them' to the radical-activists who assert their sexuality as an integral part of themselves that cannot be compromised. Ironically, those who least identify themselves as members of the subculture are those most in need of some unique form of communication. Presenting oneself as gay (or at least as desirous of homosexual contact) is often a necessary prerequisite for identifying others as gay. Only when the conditions of wanting to identify (i.e., be identified) and not wishing to 'jeopardize one's ability to pass' are simultaneously present is there a need for unique modes of interaction. The radical-activist and even many regular participants in the social setting are seldom confronted by both exigencies at once.

One potentially fruitful line of pursuit would be the exploration of how nonverbal modes of communication supplement verbal modes, particularly in secret-setting identification rituals. Hayes [p. 69] represents the process linguistically through the following exchange:

Mr. X: You certainly have on a colorful tie!
Mr. Y: Yes, I really like gay apparel.

The problem with this representation is that it lacks context; Hayes gives no hint that any but linguistic cues have been employed here. Martin Hoffman, however, describes something of the intricate, subtle nonverbal type of behavior that usually predetermines the safety and desirability of any further interaction:

> It is not true that the majority of homosexuals are recognizable on sight by the uninitiated. It is often true, however, that they can recognize each other. This is not because of any distinguishing physical characteristics, but, rather, because when cruising, they engage in behavioral gestures which immediately identify themselves to each other. A large part of cruising is done with the eyes, by means of searching looks of a prolonged nature and through the surveying of the other man's entire body.
>
> (Hoffman 1968: 45; see also Goldhaber 1977)

The importance of the nonverbal is carried even further when one realizes the pervasiveness of object language cues in the gay subculture. Some of the artifact displays are widely known even in the larger heterosexual community; pinky rings, for example, commonly make the wearer suspect. Gay persons have an elaborate set of object language symbols that not only indicate membership in the homosexual community, but also sexual preferences. Wearing an exposed key chain is an old indicator of interest in S & M (sadism and masochism). A cowboy-type handkerchief (bandana) has also been used as an indicator of sexual preference. This is worn in the back pants pocket – one side for 'active' and the other for 'passive' – or around the neck – if one will 'swing both ways.' The color of the kerchief determines the type of sexual activity. What is significant about these object cues in relation to Hayes' essay is that they usually are the basis for and precede any verbal interaction.

Another area in which work obviously needs doing is nonmale, nonwhite gay communication. Homosexuality more thoroughly transcends other minority memberships than does any other identification: blacks can be gay; Chicanos can be gay; Native Americans can be gay; women can be gay. In a sense it can be viewed as an additive process – e.g., a black female homosexual. Most of the work to date deals only with the white, male segment of the subculture. This essay exhibits the same male bias that Hayes notes in his essay. Persons interested in gay studies need to overcome this bias and be aware of the interactions among subsections of a subculture. What unites them? How do traditional divisions on one level and common oppression on another affect interaction?

Related to this problem of minority membership is the lack of role models in the gay community. Unlike blacks, Chicanos, Native Americans, or women who have someone with whom they share their identity and oppression, gay persons generally do not have gay parents. In fact, they usually have no role models at all until they have managed to find their own way into the gay community. How does this affect language use and interaction patterns? In fact, how do people learn Gayspeak at all? With no role models until they have already penetrated the gay community to some extent, the process of acquisition is itself problematic. These are the kinds of questions and problems to which persons interested in promoting gay studies as an idiographic area of study must devote their attention.

Excitement, shortsightedness, and a trip down the rabbit hole

In the above comments I have intended to suggest that gay studies must develop a clear understanding of its unique purpose – to inform us of gay persons *qua* gay persons. Every eleventh-grade poetry class studies Walt Whitman as a poet. But gay studies has the responsibility of studying Sappho, Whitman, Dickinson, Ginsberg, Auden, and so on as *gay* poets and the responsibility of establishing that there is validity in doing so, or there is no reason to use gayness as a division of study. The issue is, of course, larger than poetry.

The gay subculture provides an excellent example for the necessity of giving such an overview and outlining the research possibilities. With most communicative bodies, including that of the black rights and the women's liberation movements, the activity is aboveboard; it is there to be observed by anyone who cares to look. Not so with the gay subculture. Much of the significance of Hayes' remarks lies in the fact that the uninitiated may be involved in a gay exchange and never know it. This has a tremendous significance for future research unless we are to leave it all to those who already possess a familiarity with the cues and symbols, and hope that they also possess the training and methods.

Essentially, the problem I have raised here is one of definition. Especially for a young and burgeoning area, it is important for those developing the area to be somewhat introspective; to actively consider the area's purpose, substance, and province; to define. Earlier I said that my criticisms of Hayes' article would reflect most obviously the infant state of gay studies. I hope that it is now apparent why. Ethnic and minority studies are a relatively new idea. Psychologists hypothesize that such studies are a result of a newfound determination for gays to be themselves that they achieved through countless repetitions of 'the gestalt prayer' as they negotiated the 60s. Now that gays have decided to be themselves and to be proud of who they are, they are desperately searching to find out who they are and what it is they are proud of. In the 80s they are all looking for their roots.

Gay studies is the newest of the new. As an inaugural venture, Joseph Hayes has provided a great service by supplying future scholars with a wealth of data that requires further exploration and, more than that, by providing a backdrop against which gay studies can begin to find itself. He has given gay persons that grand survey of country they must travel through which Alice sought by standing on her tiptoes. But just as Alice's broad survey failed to provide an understanding of the forest, where even names were lost, or of the shop, which eventually faded into a rowboat, a closer examination of Hayes' broad view reveals that things are not always what they seem at first glance. Although it is vitally important to keep gay studies grounded in phenomena, it is also important in gay studies to be reflective. Without such an examination gay men and lesbians may find themselves calling hills valleys and doing all the running they can do just to stay in the same place.

Chapter 8

William L. Leap

1999

CAN THERE BE GAY DISCOURSE WITHOUT GAY LANGUAGE?

Introduction

FOR A VARIETY OF REASONS, discourse has become one of the key concepts in gender research and in other studies of popular culture. Different authors associate rather different meanings with this term; still, analysis of discourse (more properly, discourses) consistently centers around relations of power that are produced through the interactions of social institutions and practices and that contribute heavily to the reproduction of those institutions and practices over time.

As an ethnographer, I am interested in how these forms of discourse play out in particular social and historical settings. And as a linguist, I am interested in identifying and describing representations of that discourse as they unfold in the language of site-specific text-making.

My research to date has centered around the English of some gay men in the United States – primarily urban white gay men from academic or professional backgrounds and male college students with similar home/family profiles. My data-gathering for this project takes place in explicitly gay-identified, gay-defined spaces (e.g., in bars, restaurants, and bookstores; at meetings of gay support groups; during at-home dinner parties; in outdoor cruising areas) as well as in more neutral places shared by gay men and persons of other genders (e.g., in department-store sales areas, in coach-class cabins during airplane flights, and in work-out areas, locker rooms, and saunas at health clubs).

Through observations of gay men's use of language in different social settings, discussions of gay language themes during one-on-one interviews and focus-group sessions, and comparison of findings with comments about gay language and communication in the literature, I have been able to develop some general claims about gay men's text-making skills.

I have found evidence that gay men follow any number of linguistic strategies to ensure that conversations with other gay men are cooperative, not exclusionary or antagonistic. In settings where common gender interests may be suspected but cannot immediately be confirmed, gay men use additional strategies to ensure that conversations become carefully controlled opportunities for risk-taking.

Unclear in my work to date is whether cooperative discourse and language of risk are in fact linguistic properties or properties that are expressed in linguistic terms but are derived entirely from elements of social discourse external to that linguistic system. Under the first alternative, cooperative discourse and language of risk are in fact linguistic properties – that is, part of a speaker's grammar (his knowledge of language) or part of the rules of text-making that enable a speaker to make use of grammatical knowledge in situated social exchange. If this is the case, the presence of such features in gay men's text-making suggests that gay men's knowledge of English is substantially different from the knowledge of English maintained by heterosexual persons. This difference in turn argues in favor of the uniqueness of Gay English and raises a series of additional claims about gay men's socialization and identity construction.

At the same time, it is possible that cooperative discourse and language of risk are not implicit in gay men's knowledge of language at all but are refictions in linguistic terms, of the more general interplay of power and social process that informs gay discourse at all sites, in the sense just explained. Gay English, under this alternative, is still a viable component of gay culture, but the contributions of Gay English to the integrity and authority of gay culture are now somewhat scaled down. The uniqueness of Gay English (if in fact this is a unique variety of English at all) now derives from sources external to linguistic knowledge – speaker identity, speech context, content or topic of discussion. Under this formulation gay language becomes a specialized vocabulary (or, at best, an inventory of idiom and metaphor), so that researchers now have no reason to take the details of linguistic form into account when exploring gay culture or communication. Finally, the absence of a uniquely gay Gay English suggests that gay resistance to heterosexual oppression is also not linguistically dependent; hence any variety of English can be a suitable format for such resistance, and any speaker of any variety of English can participate knowledgeably and with authority in its construction.

Discussions of the 'place' of language 'at the site' of social experience, and discussions of the connections between language and social discourse, are in no sense restricted to studies of lesbian and gay experience. Still, they raise what I believe are important questions about the nature of Gay English grammar and text-making, such as: What does a text need to contain in order to be considered a 'gay' text by speakers, by listeners, or by researchers? What does a person need to know in order to be considered a 'fluent' speaker (writer, signer, artist, craftsperson) of this variety? The goals we set for description and theory-building in the newly emerging field of 'queer linguistics' depend quite closely on the answers we give to these questions.

On authenticity in lesbian and gay cultures

One way to explore these questions is to focus attention on the uniqueness of Gay English – that is, to find and inventory features of grammar and text-making that are characteristic of Gay English grammar and text but not of other English codes. A second approach – and the one I am going to follow here – shifts the focus of the analysis from uniqueness to authenticity in language. Gilbert Herdt and Andy Boxer (building on ideas developed by Edward Sapir ([1924] 1949: 314–16]) explain the meaning of authenticity in the following terms:

> Authenticity as a criterion of gay culture is meant to indicate here what is genuine as opposed to spurious in gay men's world views and relationships . . . To ask, What is authentic in gay men's lives? is to [ask] what is optimal, valuable, and life-cherishing? Ultimately, gay culture is a perspective on human nature and the world, not just on sexuality and consumerism. The search for authenticity thus leads to an understanding of meaning and purpose in adult lives today and to a consideration of the institutions and opportunities for socialization that will be available to the gay youths of tomorrow.
>
> (1992: 3–4)

Sapir himself, when exploring similar issues some seventy years ago, noted that 'the whole terrain through which we are now struggling is a hotbed of subjectivism' ([1924] 1949: 312). Subjective this may be, but it is necessary if we are ever to understand what is (in Herdt and Boxer's words) 'optimal, valuable, and life-cherishing' in gay male experience. If nothing else, studying authenticity in gay cultures provides information that will better enable gay men and their allies to subvert misconceptions about gay men's experience that have become fully entrenched in the heterosexual mainstream and that provide ammunition and incentive for homophobic discourse.

Any consideration of authenticity in culture depends on finding evidence for authenticity. Again following Sapir's argument quite closely, Herdt and Boxer address this task by establishing criteria for authenticity, then evaluating the content of particular events and activities within a culture (and ultimately the configuration of the culture as a whole) in the light of those criteria.[1]

On authenticity in gay men's English

My interest in authenticity is text-centered, and I focus my analysis around the processes contributing to text-making as well as the consequences enabled through text constructions. I want to present an analysis of two texts (see examples (1) and (2) below) to suggest what an analysis of gay men's English in these terms might entail.

I have chosen these texts because they suggest the contrasts in text form and content that recur throughout my Gay English data base, and because they demonstrate other problems associated with the interpretation of Gay English authenticity. Example (1) comes from Steve Murray's (1979) article 'The Art of Gay Insulting'; example (2) is one of many texts that I have collected and analyzed during my studies of Gay English discourse in recent years.

Both of these texts emerged in the context of all-gay dinner parties, that is, dinner parties in gay men's homes where all of the invited guests were gay. In both cases, all participants in the text-making – actors and audience – already knew each other prior to the beginning of the exchange.

(1) 'Gay Insulting' at the Dinner Table (source: Murray 1979: 216–17)

Scene: During an after-dinner dinner-table conversation. A and B are 'recognized masters at producing exotic insults in quick repartee' (Murray 1979: 216), and have been invited this evening in hopes that they will demonstrate their talents. As this passage opens, the anticipated exchange has already begun.

1 A: We can't afford to lose another sofa, Chapped Cheeks.
2 B: Your ass is so stretched you should put in a drawstring.
3 A: Word is you've had your dirt chute mack-tacked.
4 B: And you've wall-papered your womb.
5 A: Where do you find tricks who'll rim your colostomy?
6 B: You douche with Janitor in a Drum.
7 A: Slam your clam.
8 B: Slam it, cram it, ram it, oooo but don't jam it [demonstrating].
9 A: Cross your legs, you're showing your hemorrhoids.
10 B: You need to strap yours forward so you'll have a basket.
11 A: Better than back-combing my pubies, like you do.
12 *Preparation H* is a great lubricant.
13 B: This girl's hung like an animal – a tsetse fly.
14 A: Four bulldogs couldn't chew off this monster.
15 B: I don't think even a bulldog would want that in his mouth.
16 Besides, I've seen chubbier tits.
17 A: Peeking under the door in the washroom again? [and the exchange continues]

(2) What Color Is the Water Pitcher? (source: WLL fieldnotes)

Setting: An at-home dinner party, two hosts and six guests. Dinner has ended. One host (A) is washing dishes in the kitchen while other guests continue to chat in the dining room. A guest (B) moves into the kitchen to get some water.

1 B: Can I get a glass of water? [moves toward sink where A 2 is washing dishes]
3 A: There is ice water in the fridge.
4 B: OK. Thanks. [opens refrigerator door, looks inside]
5 A: [notices pause in action] In the brown pitcher.
6 B: [continues to look; raises head toward A].
7 I don't see a brown pitcher in here.
8 A: Sure. It's brown, and round, and on the top shelf.
9 B: [looks inside again] Nope.
10 A: [stops washing dishes, dries hands, moves to fridge,

11   removes pitcher, pours water]
12 B: That pitcher is not brown, it is tan. [pause. A remains silent.]
13   It is light tan.
14 A: It is brown to me.
15 B: No, you said brown; so I looked for something dark
16   chocolate.

Example (1), as Murray presents it, is part of a ritualized drama ('gay insulting') that Murray likens to instances of 'playin' the dozens' in urban African American discourse. Both of the speakers in this example are experts at 'insulting' and were invited to this party in hopes that they would engage in such an exchange for the entertainment of the other guests. As one can tell from a review of this dialogue the guests were certainly not to be disappointed in this regard.

Also apparent is the persistent use of sexual and erotic reference, comments that confirm (on first reading at least) arguments from Frank Browning (1993), Richard Mohr (1992), and others that the common theme in all gay experience is a shared 'culture of desire.' Another characteristic is the persistence of women-related imagery and metaphor, so much so that (as I first read it) the progress of the entertainment depends directly on a participant's willingness to create gay-centered text references at women's expense.

Example (2), on the other hand, contains no evidence of misogynist ritual. Rather, this was a spontaneous conversation between two friends, a guest at a sit-down dinner for eight and one of the hosts. The conversation took place after the meal had ended, while the host was washing dishes and the co-host and guests were in the living room enjoying spirited chitchat. The exchange began with a familiar guest-to-host request (for a glass of water), shifted in a miscued discussion about the location of the water pitcher in the refrigerator, and ended with a debate over the correct way to identify the color of the water pitcher. As in example (1), strains of conflict contribute to text-making here; deliberately crafted insults were not exchanged directly at any point in this exchange.

It seemed tempting, when I began the analysis of these texts, to summarize these contrasts by arguing that example (1) (given its misogynist tone) is much less 'optimal, valuable, and life-cherishing' than is example (2) and hence that example (2) is a more 'authentic' text. A more detailed review of this material, combined with discussions of its significance with other gay men, swiftly provided different ways to interpret the data.

For example, example (1) does have a certain statistical authenticity, given that speakers A and B may be familiar characters for some readers of this essay (the phrase *a bunch of bitchy queens* may already have come to mind, although that also associates negative value to women's behavior). The style of conversation may also be familiar to some readers – even though they recognize that they cannot construct texts in similar terms themselves.

And it is possible that the women-centered imagery in the text may not be an attack on women, or action at women's expense, so much as an attempt to depict the uniqueness of gay men's gender identity by reworking female imagery rather than recasting images associated with heterosexual males. Viewing such usage as a form of resistance does not excuse the misogyny, but it does help me account for it somewhat more easily.

Example (2) raised somewhat different problems in interpretation. Unlike (1), with its familiar gay-associated 'bitchy' style, example (2) does not appear to be 'gay' (in any essentialized sense) at all. My partner reminds me, for example, that this is a conversation that his parents could have standing in their kitchen in Puerto Rico. And the novelist Nora Ephron (1983: 20–1) provides interestingly similar dialogue (in this case, the exchange centers around the question *Where's the butter?*) to explain why 'Jewish princes are made, not born' (1983: 20). Hence, example (2) may be authentic in some evaluative sense, but the distinctiveness of the text detail and the close connections to gay experience are initially anything but self-evident.

To move beyond these contrasts and conflicting interpretations, I decided to orient my analysis around a situated, actor-centered analysis of text construction. Here are some of the things that I learned from that analysis. To begin with, think of both of these texts as instances of cooperative discourse, in which primary emphasis on mutually negotiated maintenance of text prompts speakers to curtail their use of divisive, disruptive, or agonistic commentary. Hence, while example (1) is competitive, there is no evidence of speaker intent to subjugate the opponent or vanquish him from the text-making scene. Instead, speakers appear to me to be working creatively and cooperatively to prolong the exchange and see how many different references each speaker can, supply before the exchange, by mutual consent, comes to an end.

Example (2) shows similar concerns with cooperation and mutuality. There is also evidence of friction in this exchange, which becomes more evident as the conversation progresses. Still, neither party allows disagreement to disrupt their communication. Hence, for example, speaker A introduces silence and nonverbal action at a strategic point in the conversation (lines 10–11) – a time when prolonging the 'yes-it-is/no-it-isn't' debate would have erupted into more serious consequences.

Speaker B shows similar concerns with text maintenance in his response to this action. By shifting discussion from 'the pitcher's location' to 'the pitcher's color,' speaker B focuses the final segment of the conversation (lines 12–13) around a comical parody of the initial dispute, and ultimately (lines 15–16), he introduces an exaggerated parody of the parody. Speaker A supports speaker B in the resulting minstrelsy. In fact, speaker A ends up playing the 'straight man' opposite speaker B's comic relief, further ensuring that any lingering threat of disruption is dispelled.

Example (1) also contains ample instances of parody, minstrelsy, and exaggeration (lines 1, 5, 8, 11–12, and 16–17). Again, it is true that the content of the word play emerges at women's expense, and that alternative frames of reference could have been employed – such as example (2)'s satire of the widely held belief that gay men are instinctively skilled at color recognition and other forms of interior design. Still, it is important not to lose sight of the process of word play evidenced here or the speakers' uses of other components of grammatical skill to transform this occurrence of verbal dueling into something with a special message and appeal to gay men and to ground the location of text-making even more securely within gay experience. The text-making strategies may differ in these examples, but the consequences of text-making – the transformation of place into space – are very much the same.

I want to mention one more area of textual similarity. Not all instances of gay men's use of language will occur in private, protected, and gay-positive domains, or in settings that (while ostensibly gender-neutral) can easily be recast into gay space without serious threat of controversy, through a judicious use of imagery and metaphor. In fact, much of gay discourse – the linguistic and the social kinds – unfolds in public domains, in settings where the interlocutors' sexuality and erotic interests are not necessarily constructed in similar ways and gender itself may become a point of contestation and conflict.

Given such realities, the knowledge of language contained in Gay English grammar has to include language skills that enable maintenance of self and assurances of safety in non-gay as well as gay environments. Fluency in the 'language of the closet' is one viable option under these circumstances; learning how to code gay messages within seemingly 'gender-neutral' references, and how to identify and decipher messages that others have packaged in neutral terms, is another such option. Direct confrontation with oppressive heterosexuality is a third option, one that has increasingly become a popular gay discourse strategy in recent years.

Whatever the gay man's strategy of choice in any setting, all three options require acquisition of specific linguistic skills, and all three require some opportunities for rehearsal. I suggest that both of these activities – learning and rehearsal – are taking place in the speech events displayed in examples (1) and (2). Both of these examples, while socially productive in their specific domain, provide gay men with opportunities for gay-centered language development and safe havens for experimentation with these skills.

At issue here are the types of language skills that all of us, as gay people, may be called upon to employ – or may hope we will be able to employ – when confronted by homophobic or heterosexist discourse in the workplace, in the classroom, on the street corner, while visiting with family and friends back home, or while on vacation. I suggest that the audience fascination (and tolerance) with the give-and-take in example (1) can be explained, at least in part, by recasting this exchange as an instance of gay language socialization.

Conclusion

I began this paper by raising questions about the uniqueness of gay language and moved from those questions into a discussion of authenticity and authentic qualities in gay English text-making. I have suggested that a text-making that enables cooperative discourse between interlocutors, that makes use of imagery and metaphor to transform 'neutral' place into gay space and uses other grammatical strategies to ground text production within gay terrain, and that provides opportunities for rehearsal to ensure that participants will be able to transfer language skills from gay-positive to less-positive speech domains speaks to authenticity in gay experience because it enables the seemingly ordinary, mundane, and offensive in gay life to become 'optimal, valuable, and life-cherishing' to the human spirit.

I realize that this is a somewhat different conclusion about language, gender, and authenticity than that reached by feminist scholars who are probing authenticity in women's voice. For example, Irigaray's discussion of what it means to 'speak as woman' (1985, *passim*) associates *parler femme* with uses of language that occur when 'women (are)-among-themselves,' not when women are in 'dominant language domains.' Indeed, she explains, *parler femme* is appealing to women precisely because it provides an alternative to dominant language discourse and thereby offers women a means of placing themselves at a distance each time they construct discourse within such domains.

Alternative discourse and separatism may provide the cornerstone for authenticity in *parler femme* but gay language, as I have just explained, is ultimately constructed in relation to, not at a distance from, dominant discourse. The fact that gay men are men, and therefore are aligned with dominant language even when we try to sabotage or conceal those alignments, may account for this contrast between gendered codes. But adding *in-relation-to* to the other elements of authenticity discussed in this paper returns the analysis to the issue raised in my title: If an authentic language is a language that conveys or enables qualities of authenticity onto other components of speaker experience, then there surely cannot be authentically gay discourse without gay language.

PART TWO

Contemporary Debates

Sexual styles
and performances

THE ARTICLES IN THIS SECTION illustrate the influence of recent theoretical ideas on language and sexuality research from the mid-1990s onward. The most important of those ideas is that identity is 'performed'. The idea that people perform their identities swept through the humanities and social sciences in the early 1990s with the force of a revolution, but at first glance it may be difficult to see what is revolutionary about it. Everyone knows the Shakespearean truism 'All the world's a stage, and all the men and women merely players'. One of the earliest lessons we learn as children is that we need to behave – that is, perform – differently in different situations, even if we don't want to, so that others won't think us rude or stupid or badly brought up. Sociolinguists, too, have long maintained that speakers engage in 'acts of identity'; that is, they employ linguistic resources such as word choice or intonational patterns to present themselves as particular kinds of people.

So why did the seemingly obvious idea that we perform our identities cause so much excitement? The answer is, because it was reformulated in a way that reversed the taken-for-granted relationship between identity and actions. The commonsense view is that we act a certain way because we are a certain kind of person. A woman, for example, acts like a woman because she 'is' a woman and her actions reflect her identity as a woman. This understanding, however, was turned on its head in the philosopher Judith Butler's 1990 book *Gender Trouble*. Rather than acting in a certain way because you are a certain kind of person, Butler argued that you feel yourself to be a certain kind of person because you act a certain way. Phrased in the kind of philosophical terms Butler uses, this means that ontology (being; our subjective sense of who we are) does not produce practice – on the contrary, practice produces ontology.

This way of understanding the relationship between what a person is and what she or he does was not, in itself, new. Ethnomethodologists and social psychologists

had long argued that identities are collaboratively constructed in situated interactions. French poststructuralists such as Althusser, Bourdieu and Foucault had
made similar points about how practice (that is, habitual actions) instils in us a
sense of who we are. Centuries earlier, the philosopher Blaise Pascal (1623–62)
advised a non-believer: 'Kneel down, move your lips in prayer, and you will believe.'
In other words: perform conventional actions and the feelings and identities associated with those actions will instil themselves.

Judith Butler's contribution was to bring these insights together into an argument that our actions do not just reflect our social positions: they attach us to
those positions. Four important consequences follow. First, identities are made over
time. This means, second, that identities have to be continually re-made in order
to convince. It wouldn't do, for example, for a fraternity brother such as those
described in Scott F. Kiesling's chapter to only ever tell a 'fuck story' once. Once
is never enough: identity is always at risk of failing if the actions that invoke it
are not repeated. That suggests, third, that what produces and sustains identity is
not some mysterious essence 'inside' a person, but rather the system of signification (i.e. language, in the broad sense of all kinds of signifying practices) into
which people are socialized and through which they interact. And fourth, since
signifying is something we do, doing things in novel or unexpected ways can have
consequences for the system in which we live and for the kinds of identities that
are conceivable in that system.

Butler's ideas were formulated as part of a radical sexual politics. In addition
to being feminist, her work is generally regarded as 'queer'. One of the things that
makes it queer is her assertion that particular kinds of gender-performances – the
paradigmatic example in Gender Trouble was drag queens – are not necessarily
reactionary reinforcements of gender inequality, as had often been argued in
previous analyses (cf. the chapters in this Reader by Julia Penelope Stanely and
William L. Leap). Butler argued that because drag queens achieve the effect of
femininity using the same means as women (such as clothing, make-up, movement,
speech styles), they call into question the idea that there is such a thing as a
'natural' femininity that is 'owned' by women. If femininity inheres in the actions
that produce it, then it can logically be produced by anyone who performs the
actions. Furthermore, exaggerated and stylized performances of gender such as
those enacted by drag queens need not simply reproduce misogynist stereotypes
about women. Instead, by drawing explicit attention to the signifying practices that
construct femininity, drag queens mock the idea that particular genders arise 'naturally' from particular kinds of bodies. This mocking, Butler suggested, can be a
destabilizing and subversive act. (The chapters of Part One in which Louie Crew
and Joseph J. Hayes defend gender reversal among homosexuals can be re-read in
the light of Butler's arguments; Hayes's observation (p. 72) that '[w]hat would
appear to be a trivialization of the world, because . . . Gayspeak is often frivolous,
comic, precious, or fleeting, amounts to a trivialization through parody of the
dominant culture', prefigures Butler's analysis.)

Not all the chapters in this section refer to Butler's work, but they share a
concern with the way linguistic resources are used by individual speakers in styling

themselves sexually for particular purposes, occasions and audiences. The first two chapters, by Justine Coupland and Scott F. Kiesling, focus on performances of heterosexuality. Coupland's article (Chapter 9) examines the structure and content of both written and spoken dating advertisements. Dating advertisements are fruitful places to explore the discursive construction of self-identities because, as Coupland notes, their form requires advertisers to be unusually concise in how they label and categorize both themselves and their desired other. The attributes and qualities that advertisers offer and seek provide valuable information about the statuses, appearances, characteristics and roles that are positively valued in different kinds of romantic and sexual relationships.

Coupland is also interested in dating advertisements for what they tell us about the linguistic management of self-promotion and self-display – by comparison with politeness and self-effacement, neglected topics in sociolinguistics. Self-promotion and display are also prime characteristics of the talk analysed in Scott F. Kiesling's 'Playing the straight man' (Chapter 10). Kiesling investigates how young men in a US college fraternity perform heterosexuality through narratives that foreground the speaker's desirability to women and interactions in which brothers vie for dominance through oppositional moves and linguistic gender reversal. It is interesting to note that 'the substitution of feminine pronouns and titles for properly masculine ones', as Gershon Legman called it, is not unique to the speech of homosexual men. Kiesling's fraternity brothers are adept at casting other men as women – by giving them female names, by addressing them with phrases such as 'Honey, I'm home', which calls to mind 1950s television representations of a man greeting his domesticated wife as he returns from a long day at the office, and by calling them 'bitch' or 'bitch boy'. Unlike the practices of gender reversal discussed by Butler, Hayes and Crew, calling a fraternity brother 'Hazel' has little to do with mocking or parodying gender roles: rather, Kiesling analyses such practices as verbal strategies of dominance. His chapter demonstrates that heterosexuality is very much a homosocial affair, enacted verbally not just through the denigration of women and homosexuals, but also through the display of dominance over other men in same-sex groups (see also Cameron 1998).

Hideko Abe's 'Lesbian bar talk in Shinjuku, Tokyo' (Chapter 11) is a further example of how individuals use specific linguistic resources to effect particular sexual styles. Here, however, it is not heterosexuality that is being articulated, but rather culturally specific forms of lesbianism. Abe explains that an important distinction exists in Japan between women who are *onabe* and those who are *rezu* (or *rezubian*). The difference is not unfamiliar to Westerners: *onabe* are similar to butch lesbians who take on masculine roles and want relationships with obviously feminine women, whereas *rezu* do not maintain those kinds of role distinctions. Abe shows how *onabe* and *rezu* identities are performed partly through the first-person pronouns that speakers use. Women who style themselves as *onabe*, for example, make more use of a first-person pronoun (*jibun*) that is associated with and frequently used by men, while female to male transsexuals use a form, *boku*, that is even more strongly marked as male, and *rezu* women use more gender-neutral forms. However, none of this is categorical, and Abe demonstrates that grammatical indexes of gender do not have invariant associations for all speakers (some women, for example, think that forms linguists have identified as gender-neutral are 'too feminine').

Like Abe, the sociolinguists Robert J. Podesva, Sarah J. Roberts and Kathryn Campbell-Kibler (Chapter 12) note that linguistic forms typically serve more than one function or achieve more than one effect. This poses problems for the kind of argument about 'Gayspeak' or 'Gay English' that depends on identifying the use of certain features, such as ambiguity or cooperation, uniquely with the social category 'gay men'. Analysing phonetic features used by a gay lawyer speaking on a radio programme, Podesva *et al.* affirm that there is no necessary or predictable relationship between linguistic forms and social categories. Instead, they argue that it is important to examine the *co-occurrence* of different features in speech, and to understand that the talk people produce in different contexts does many more things than position them in relationship to simple oppositions such as 'gay vs. straight'.

A similar point is made by Rusty Barrett's 'Supermodels of the world, unite!' (Chapter 13), which is about the kinds of drag queens that Judith Butler may have had in mind when she wrote *Gender Trouble*. Barrett draws on Butler's point that oppressed groups may rework the terms of their domination by appropriating and resignifying the language of the dominant culture. He maintains that African-American drag queens' use of what he calls 'white women's speech' (an exaggerated form of what Robin Lakoff (1975) described as 'women's language') is not an indication that the drag queens want to be white. This is an important argument, since it is commonly supposed that speakers who use prestige forms seek to align themselves with the social prestige of the groups who prototypically use those forms. Barrett however suggests that in context, the white woman style mocks the idea that whiteness is superior to blackness. This effect is achieved in part when the drag queens shift between the white woman style and other styles, such as African-American Vernacular English. A valuable part of Barrett's argument is his observation that subversion and queerness are discursive achievements produced not by the use of forms in isolation, but by the co-occurrence of different linguistic features that normally do not appear together (for example, uttering obscene words with hypercorrect pronunciation).

The most significant feature of work on language and sexuality done since the early 1990s, then, is a shift from asking how sexual identity is *reflected* in language to a focus on how different identities are *constructed* through the co-occurrence of linguistic forms in specific contexts and genres. One consequence of this shift was to bring heterosexuality into focus as an object of investigation. Researchers came to see heterosexuality as just as constructed, just as performed, as homosexuality. This has opened up other new avenues for language and sexuality research, which we pursue further in the section that follows this one.

Chapter 9

Justine Coupland

1996

DATING ADVERTISEMENTS

Discourses of the commodified self

Introduction

> Sensual, imaginative brunette, 25, artistic, intelligent, with a sense of
> humour. Enjoys home life, cooking, sports, country life. No ties, own
> home. Seeking a tall, strong, intelligent fun companion with inner depth
> for passionate, loving romance, 25–35. Photo guarantees reply. Must
> feel able to love Ben my dog too. London/anywhere.

DATELINE, A MAGAZINE PUBLISHED by a UK dating agency,
claims this to have been the most successful personal advertisement they have
ever published, having received 241 replies (reported in the *Daily Mirror*; Bowden
1994). Self-advertisement for the purpose of meeting a partner has, since the early
1980s, gained acceptance among a wide set of users and since the early 1990s,
written advertisements such as the one above and, more recently, in television
text pages, have been supplemented by telephone voicelinks, whereby interested
parties can follow up written advertisements by telephoning to listen to advertisers'
pre-recorded messages.

Using a media self-advertisement, an advertiser bypasses what might be
construed as more conventional uncertainty-reducing first stages of relationship
formation by referring to, labelling and generally constructing the self and the
wanted other as products in the dating market-place. This packaging process results
in a text genre closely allied in its formal characteristics to media advertisements
for the selling and buying of houses, cars or second-hand furniture – 'small ads'
which, interestingly enough, are conventionally used for trading in used rather than
new goods. In dating advertisements, the identities of the advertiser and her/his
would-be partner are managed in an initially static way, as brief and categorical
textual representations. Consumers observe these representations and decide
whether to invest time and effort in 'detextualizing' them. Advertisers embark on

the discourse practice of self-advertising equally strategically, producing versions of themselves for selective consumption by recipients.

This paper develops a discourse-analytic approach to dating advertisements, focusing on how individuals construct identities for themselves and others within this constrained and (at least in its written textual aspects) highly formulaic practice. The data comprise written advertisements and, in some cases, their voicelink counterparts from two local newspapers, television text pages and one magazine source. Dating advertisements can be considered a limiting case for the discursive construction of self-identities (Potter and Wetherell 1987; Shotter and Gergen 1989), requiring highly direct self- and other-representation within a sparse textual framework. They are an ideal site in which to observe the constructive function of linguistic labelling and categorization (Kress and Hodge 1979; Lee 1992). Given that in the data clear preferences emerge in the selection of demographic and social categories and then in the traits associated with categories, the advertisements provide insights into advertisers' idealizations of self-identities – for example in terms of physical attributes, age, personalities and interests.

The central theoretical construct which informs this paper is Giddens' notion of the commodification of the self in late modernity and the speculation, therefore, that dating advertisements are an almost prototypically contemporary discourse practice. Giddens (1991) identifies the late modern potential for consumers to buy a lifestyle, by making consumer decisions about how to live, how to behave, what to wear and what to eat. He interprets this as evidence of the interpenetration of commercial practices into the lifeworld and into selfhood (see Habermas 1984). Self-identity, Giddens argues, is constituted less in the roles and structures of the traditional order and more in individual market-place decisions: 'To a greater or lesser degree, the project of the self becomes translated into one of the possession of desired goods and the pursuit of artificially framed styles of life' (Giddens 1991: 196).

Within this general framework, dating advertisements again seem to be a limiting case, this time of the self-commodification process – the textual reduction of selfhood to a small set of somewhat predictable attributes, verbally packaged into a few lines of newspaper print or television text and 'floated' onto the public market-place. However, while the basic reading of dating advertisements as a commodifying discourse practice seems appropriate, the data I examine also raise questions about how we should model commodification and respond to it evaluatively in this context. A closer look at commodification in social theory is merited.

Commodification and self-advertising

Fairclough (1995) gives a useful review of current approaches to commodification in introducing his own perspective on the marketization of public discourse. Briefly, he points to Beck's (1992) theorizing of the risk society, Wernick's (1991) characterization of contemporary culture as being 'promotional' and Featherstone's (1991) observations on contemporary 'consumer culture'. These theoretical approaches point to 'the incorporation of new domains into the commodity market . . . and the reconstruction of social life on a market basis' (Fairclough 1995: 141).

Examples include the 'culture industries' and the commodification of leisure. In each of these domains, discourse is implicated 'as a vehicle for "selling" goods, services, organizations, ideas or people'.

The evaluative loading of the terms commodification, marketization and promotionalization is altogether negative in Fairclough's account. He suggests that one consequence of these processes is 'the subordination of meaning to, and the manipulation of meaning for, instrumental effect'; another consequence is 'synthetic personalization', that is the 'simulation in institutional settings of the person-to-person communication of ordinary conversation' (p. 141). Fairclough goes on to suggest that 'the colonization of discourse by promotion may also have major pathological effects upon subjects, and major ethical implications' (p. 142). These include uncertainty about the distinction between the authentic and the promotional (the problem of trust) and the 'deeper' problem that 'self-promotion is becoming part-and-parcel of self-identity'. His critical perspective on marketization is to expose it, as a step towards resisting it (p. 159). In a similar way, Giddens (1991: 201) problematizes commodified experience, under the rubric 'tribulations of the self'. He writes of the 'narrative of the self' being 'constructed in circumstances in which personal appropriation is influenced by standardised influences on consumption'. Knowing how to act and how to represent the self is seen as a mediated process, under the influence of sources such as images (usually narrativized) in advertising and media entertainment such as soap operas, which act as 'substitutes for real satisfactions unobtainable in normal social conditions' (Giddens 1991: 199).

For the analysis of dating advertisements, commodification theory is appealing in many respects. First, it allows us to locate analyses within a specific cultural context, which is lacking in existing, mainly psychological studies. Dunbar's (1995) review of research on dating advertising locates it within a Darwinian perspective, for example noting that males regularly look for younger females and females for older males. Also:

> Older women (who are less fertile) were less demanding in the traits they asked for in prospective mates than younger women. Similarly, when matched for age, women who considered themselves physically attractive were more demanding than those who made no mention of appearance.
>
> (Dunbar 1995: 29)

This approach in fact decontextualizes dating advertising and fails to consider it as a temporally and socially specific practice. In fact, dating advertisements have been viewed principally as a source of information on relationships generally (Lynn and Bolig 1985). Based on content analyses, research has examined the regularities of personal traits offered and sought and linked these to implicit notions of attraction and role expectations (Davis 1990; Koestner and Wheeler 1988) or it has attempted to correlate aspects of reported physical appearance with rates of response to adverts (Lynn and Shurgot 1984). Bolig et al. (1984) invoke social exchange theory which has traditionally suggested that women were more likely to offer physical attractiveness and seek professional status, while men were more likely to offer professional status and seek attractiveness, consistent with traditional sex-role expectations.

As we shall see, some of these trends are also apparent within the present data. Previous studies maintain strikingly apolitical and non-strategic stances in relation to their data. Dating advertisements have generally been presented as a textual barometer measuring the relational preferences of particular subgroups, without consideration of how advertisers and respondents are engaging with the constraints of their media. That is, studies have tended to leap from textual data to relational configurations, without sensitivity to the discourse practices of mediated dating and its historical and cultural constitution.

However, it is not clear that we should follow Fairclough's unequivocal line on pernicious commodification in this context. As noted earlier, dating advertise-ments do apparently short-circuit 'normal', negotiative relation processes, involving a gradual reduction of uncertainty (Berger and Bradac 1983). In written personal advertisements, most norms relevant to the early stages of face-to-face relation-ships are flouted and impression formation becomes a static process of display and evaluation. Commodification can also be thought of as relationally efficient and a 'natural' response to a particular configuration of societally imposed, modern life circumstances – time-pressured, work-centred, mass mediated. As one of the advertisers in the data under consideration comments in her audio-recorded telephone message:

> um and why I'm advertising 'cos it's not a thing I (laughs slightly) ever thought about doing before is because I do find it difficult to meet the type of person I'm looking for in a in a pub or whatever.
>
> (*Making Friends*, December 1993)

It would be important, then, to avoid over-romanticizing the 'normal', tradi-tional relationship or overstating the depersonalization of commodified self-representations. Similarly, we need to be circumspect about the apparently marked discursive behaviours that commodification brings with it. For example, positive face enhancement, representing the self in a directly positive light (Penman 1990) is held to be, with few contextual exceptions, a relational taboo. The commodi-fication of personal attributes and the selling of one's merits in public arenas might appear to be forcing a relational brashness upon participants. On the other hand, it is interesting that sociolinguistics has developed models of 'polite', self-restraining, other-protecting discourse strategies (Brown and Levinson 1987) without corresponding attention to self-promotional and self-display strategies. Thus there is a risk that sociolinguistics and discourse studies may romanti-cize relationships and we have perhaps disattended to strategies of visual self-commodification in 'normal' relationships and their function as attention-grabbing, self-promotional relationship openers. Dating ads may not be as marked or as 'inhuman' as we might assume.

Finally, it is important not to homogenize the process of commodification in dating advertising. Advertisers display a range of different orientations to the process of self-representation, as the present data show later. And as a discourse practice, such advertising is involved not only with the promoting or 'selling' of selves but with the attracting or 'buying' of others. Advertisers are not simply in the thrall of market forces, occasioned by the mass media institutions. Whether aggressively or under-confidently, they are active players or investors in the personal commodity markets and sustainers of its ideology. They offer commodified versions of their own selves but only as a first move towards a negotiated matching or complementarity of commodified attributes. Many of the advertisements are strongly directive in defining the attributes of their desired matches, they wish to 'buy' under strict conditions of their own establishing. Overall, then, the paper's analyses of dating advertisements allow us to reflect on the process of commodification itself and perhaps to highlight some previously unrecognized definitional and moral complexities.

Sources

Heterosexual dating advertisements from three different sources were collected; two offer a voicelink service. The written texts, 200 in all, were sampled between December 1993 and November 1994:

1. Advertisements from regular sections of two independent local newspapers: *Making Friends* (45 texts) and *Meeting Point* (34 texts).
2. The Independent Television (ITV) Information Service Teletext, *One-2-One National Dating Service* (67 texts) (hereafter Teletext One-2-One).
3. Advertisements from a regular section of *Saga* (a national magazine marketed for the over 50s), *Penfriends and Partnerships* (54 texts).

The spoken texts were the 45 voicelink messages connecting to the texts from *Making Friends* and the 67 messages connecting to the *One-2-One* texts. Voicelink messages were not a facility available to *Saga* readers, for whom the next point of contact would be by mail; one of the two sets of local newspaper voicelinks was considered sufficient. The samples reflect the diverse media contexts where dating advertisements appear. The *Saga* data allow my analyses to connect in some ways with broader research interests in discourse and ageing, as well as emphasizing the broad age-spectrum of dating advertisers. Voicelink messages were audio-recorded and transcribed. As the text and audio materials are in the public domain, they are available for research scrutiny. However, all names, locations and box numbers have been replaced by fictional alternatives in the transcripts.

The generic character of textual dating advertisements

Hodge and Kress suggest that 'the site in which a text occurs typically contains instructions as to how it should be read and what meanings should be found in it' (1988: 68). Such instructions, for both encoding and decoding, are very precise and widely known for 'small ads' and are increasingly well known for dating advertisements. Texts show a high level of generic predictability, with rhetorical structure and ideational field tightly specified. In the printed medium, dating advertisements share features with, and sometimes metaphorically evoke advertisements for selling cars, household equipment, furniture or pedigree animals. Selves are projected as short lists of predominantly positive characteristics, such as *attractive, pretty, friendly, slim, fit, loving, honest*. There is occasional metaphorical reference to the wider genre, for example *vintage model, house-trained, luxury-sized* (of a woman), or *well-built* (of a man). The metaphor is occasionally sustained throughout an advertisement:

> CLASSIC LADY limousine, mint condition, excellent runner for years seeks gentleman enthusiast 45+ for TLC and excursions in the Exeter area BOX 555L.
>
> (*One-2-One*, March 1994)

Layout in newspaper and magazine sources is again evocative of personal commodity sales in the 'small ads'. Abbreviations, such as VGSOH (very good sense of humour), WLTM (would like to meet) and, as above, TLC (tender loving care), reflect the principle of economy (since text lines are paid for) and an acculturated readership, familiar with textual norms. Shared also is a need to communicate positivity but sometimes also to incorporate hedges on positivity, or even negativity: *insolvent, smoker, fat, tall* (if female) *short* (if male) (see Shepperd and Strathman 1989). Selling is a strategic practice and hedged-positive or negative self-ascriptions can boost buyers' confidence in the seller as an 'honest' or possibly a 'modest' or 'realistic' person. They can also be important in achieving an 'appropriate' match and in signalling attributes stereotypically seen as less desirable which can then be set aside as a relationship possibly develops.

The structure of written adverts was investigated in a sub-sample of 100 advertisements, chosen randomly but in equal numbers from the three written sources, as follows:

1. *Meeting Point* (6 October 1994) (34 instances: 17 men, 17 women).
2. *One-2-One* (8 March 1994) (33 instances: 20 men, 13 women).
3. *Penfriends and Partnerships*: (November 1994) (33 instances: 9 men, 24 women).

The highly conventionalized structure provides limited opportunities, in comparison with the spoken genre, for advertisers to be creative. Texts are most frequently organized sequentially as:

1. **ADVERTISER**	2. *seeks*	3. **TARGET**
4. **GOALS**	5. (**COMMENT**)	6. **REFERENCE**

The **ADVERTISER** (1) is represented by a list of attributes from the following sets, presented in frequency order. Percentages of occurrence are followed by raw numbers from the three sources (*Meeting Point*; *One-2-One*; and *Penfriends and Partnerships*, consecutively) and some examples of labels used under each type of self-categorization:

gender: 100% (34; 33; 33) – *female; widow/er; woman; mother; lady; gal; male; gentleman; businessman; Mr Nice Gay; Tarzan; bachelor; guy.*

age: 87% (33; 28; 26) – simple disclosure of chronological age (*23; 36; 43*; etc.) or other age-marking devices, such as *60ish; young 70; active 58; young-at heart 53; 33 going on 13; early 40's.*

location: 73% (14; 33; 26) – *Cumbria; E. Anglia; Nottingham.*

appearance: 60% (24; 22; 14) – *tall; attractive; good-looking; ordinary-looking; brunette; long-haired; with blue eyes; slim; not dark, not handsome: fat; wrinkly.*

personality/behaviour traits: 55% (22; 18; 15) – *friendly; honest; GSOH; genuine; intelligent; loyal; romantic; lively; happy; shy.*

interests: 51 % (18; 9; 24) – *many varied interests; music; cinema; cooking; home-life; wining and dining; walking; travel.*

career/solvency/status: 34% (10; 8; 16) – *company director; professional; home/car owner; insolvent; unemployed.*

generational/marital status: 33% (9; 8; 16) – *single; divorced; single mum; no ties; widow/er; bachelor.*

ethnicity: 7% (0; 6; 1) – *mixed race; white; Asian; Australian.*

In the context of heterosexual self-advertisements, gender data can be thought of as establishing a basic, qualifying criterion. Location addresses a convenience criterion, but the other dimensions can be taken to constitute the conventional repertoire of self-commodifying attributes for self-selling in this medium. Age, appearance and personality are therefore the most heavily promoted 'internal' traits. However, within each dimension of self-categorization, the strategic impact of an item such as *widower*, or of *gentleman* versus *male*, or of *blonde* versus *fair-haired*, of *bubbly* or *vivacious* versus *cheerful*, is masked in the frequency data. Also, as a methodological problem for categorization, labels are not mutually exclusive to categories; widower, for example, informs the readership at least of gender and marital status and is also potentially loaded as a way of doing painful self-disclosure (Coupland *et al.* 1991) and may function as a warning to potential respondents.

Seeks (2) is the most common lexical item in this textual slot, with *WLTM/would like to meet; looking for; is missing* as other possibilities. Only three per cent of instances begin with a question such as *Are you a tall intelligent professional man?* followed by a characterization of the advertiser: I am. . . .

Attributes for **TARGET** (3), show different frequencies of essentially the same set of personal dimensions as for **ADVERTISER**:

gender: 89% (28; 32; 29) – *female; lady; woman; girl; Jane; male; guy; gentleman; gent; widower; Mr. Wonderful.*

age: 54% (19; 24; 11) – *18–27; 27–40; 40's; 31–39; 46–55; under 70; 70–80.*

personality/behaviour traits: 45% (16; 17; 12) – *honest, caring and romantic; sensuous . . . kind, generous; sincere; with sense of humour; trustworthy; gentle.*

appearance: 26% (4; 15; 7) – *feminine; slim; attractive; refined; smart; good-looking; handsome.*

career/solvency/status 9% (2; 3; 4) – *professional*; *educated*.

generational/marital status: 6% (1; 3; 2) – *widower*; *single dads welcome*.

interests: 5% (0; 3; 2) – *similar interests*.

ethnicity: 5% (0; 5; 0) – *white*; *any race, colour*.

location: 1% (0; 0; 1).

Age, appearance and personality are again the highest-ranked personal dimensions (excluding the qualifying gender criterion) but personality overtakes appearance as a frequent dimension for target. Most advertisers clearly have strong preferred models of age-appropriate relationships (see Coupland and Nussbaum 1993). They appear to invest significance in own-appearance as a selling strategy, but claim to prioritize a target's personality traits over her/his appearance in the buying mode. The issue of age merits its own treatment, and is beyond the remit of the current paper.

The **GOALS** (4) slot gives any non-inferable goal/purpose for placing the advert: for friendship, possibly romance; to bring sparkle into life; for fun nights in, no ties relationship; for companionship, visits and holidays. The **GOAL** is sometimes encoded as an attribute of **TARGET** (e.g. future husband).

The **COMMENT** (5) is a fleeting opportunity in the written mode to deconventionalize the advert, only used by two advertisers in the sample:

> *call you might be surprised; let's see how it goes.*

The **REFERENCE** (6) is the means of moving from this initial event into a next event (suggesting that a target write or leave a telephone message in the voicelink box).

The traits commonly chosen to portray individuals positively are grounded in cultural stereotypes about youth, femininity, masculinity, attractiveness, etc. The advertisement text that heads this paper exemplifies this well, with the female advertiser offering traits positively marked for sexuality, personality, solvency and a wide range of interests including domestic activities. However, it is important not to oversimplify the positivity/negativity dimension. Self-categorizations such as *fat*, *smoker* or *insolvent* may function as invitations as well as disinvitations. It is noticeable that the very few negative characteristics that are referenced relate to the appearance and solvency dimensions and not to personality. Although advertisers can refer to themselves as *curvy in all the wrong places*, or *not dark, not handsome*, or *moulting*, there is no reference in the data to 'bad tempered', 'disloyal' or 'fickle'.

Selling and buying through the audiorecord

Voicelink messages are 'spontaneous', relative to their written counterparts, but they are nevertheless likely to be scripted, rehearsed and polished. Companies offering the voicelink facility offer guidance, regulations and (in some cases) model recordings which, in various ways, normalize and constrain spoken performances.

Advertisers are given guidance towards structuring their messages ('a . . . brief description of yourself your likes and dislikes and the partner you are seeking') and a model recording. Similar constraints, as well as some less specific advice, are mentioned in the Teletext instructions (printed on screen):

> Your call will last at least three minutes . . . entertaining ads work best, but all must be decent and legal. Gays must be over 21 and hetero-sexuals over 18. Overtly sexual messages will be refused . . .

The message left for people dialling one voicelink number to listen to a message was as follows (in the transcription, (.) is a short, untimed pause, and numbers in parentheses are timed pauses, so (2.0), for example, is a 2-second pause):

> hello (.) and thank you for calling Making Friends (.) the message you're about to hear has been left by the advertiser in their own voice to give you a better insight as to what they're really like (.) after you have heard their message you will be asked to leave a message for them in their voicebox . . .

The notion that the advertiser's *own voice* will give the listener a *better insight as to what they're really like* invokes the voice evaluation material which becomes available to the consumer on dialling the voicelink number and this must be interpreted as an important feature of the commodity under consideration, in that aspects of voice quality (e.g. breathiness, pitch range, vocal setting, speech-rate and regional/social accent) will predictably be used to make judgements about the speaker (Giles and Powesland 1975; Scherer and Giles 1979).

The discourse structure of spoken self-advertisements certainly suggests conformity, if not to the precise models offered, at least to a general, conventionalized norm. Instances in the data display a generalized sequencing of moves, as follows:

1. Greeting: *hi, hello, hiya.*

2. Self-introduction: *this is Rose; my name is Mike.*

3. Thanking: *thanks for showing an interest in my ad; thanks for ringing.*

4. Metacommentary: *as you already know; what else should I tell you? hope you're not as nervous as me; it's not easy making one of these tapes.*

5. Listing of traits offered: *I'm five foot three bluey-grey eyes and have long natural blonde hair; I'm twenty-nine (3.0) reasonably or quite good looking or so I've been told; I'm friendly and I have a warm personality (.) I also have a good sense of humour.*

6. Listing of interests: *I love going to the films movies theatres concerts things like that; I like playing golf (.) I like driving in the country (.) I like pubs; I enjoy cooking entertaining and cosy nights in with a good bottle of wine.*

7. Personal narrative/account for single status: *I've been on my own for the past year now; I've just moved into the area so I don't know many people yet; I've been a widow for nearly two years.*

8. Listing of traits wanted: *I'm looking for a handsome intelligent white male*; *I am looking for somebody that's (.) easy going or not only that but caring*; *looking for a warm sensitive lady slim attractive*; *I'm looking for a broad-minded lady any size (.) looks are not as important as a friendly nature*.

9. Statement of goals: *I'm looking for a future husband*; *I'm not interested in marriage only friendship*; *I'm looking for a no-ties relationship*; *I'm looking for someone to add sparkle excitement and romance into my life*; *a lady (.) er to share my life with er possibly get married*; *to help me to mend a broken heart*.

10. Challenge: *if you think you can do this*; *if you think this is you*; *if you think you're interested*.

11. Referencing information/exhortative comment on future contact: *leave your number and I'll give you a call*; *I hope to hear from you soon*; *see you soon*.

12. Promises: *I promise to call you back*; *you won't regret it*.

13. Location: *by the way I live in Bristol*.

14. Thanking/farewell/pre-closing: *thanks for calling*; *bye*; *bye for now*; *that's about it*.

Rarely there are also play elements, such as the telling of jokes or setting of riddles. However, most of the 14 individual elements of structure are optional so that the set is never fully realized (in the present data at least). However, the above sequencing reflects the most common ordering of moves.

Commodification, marketization and personalization in the two modes

A straightforward overview, as in the previous section, of the normative structures of written and spoken modes of dating advertisements shows that both are circumscribed and conventional, but that the written advertisements are more rigidly so. I have assumed that formulaicity and rhetorical structure are key aspects of discursive commodification and marketization and there is a clear sense of advertisers in both modes confining their self- and other-characterizations to a fairly predictable set of marketable traits and of designing their texts to conform to marketplace norms, including the discursive norms of marketing genres. If there is a moral case against 'relational trading' through dating advertisements, it is presumably that the practice is de-individuating. The argument might run as follows:

> Generic constraints reduce selves, on either side of the trade, not only to lists of traits but very largely to gross demographic and physical traits. Personal qualities need to be cast as 'personality types', forcing the categories of reductionist social psychology onto individuals' representations of themselves and their prospective partners. The rhetorical format requires brief, serial representations and this in turn works to deny distinctions between listed personal 'attributes': physical attributes seem to be equated with emotional attributes, ephemeral with profound. Dating advertisements presume and expound a

model of relational adequacy or 'compatibility' premised on either the matching of attributes (shared interests or goals) or the complementarity of attributes (males in their fifties with females in their forties, etc.). The practice oozes categoriality, conventionality and social stereotypes, to the detriment of 'the complex individual' and 'the successful unconventional relationship'. Text is allowed to lord it over interaction, which is the 'proper ground' of relational development. Perhaps above all, dating ads require seekers and targets to identify with those and other labels and generally to lexically represent ineffable aspects of selfhood and interpersonal relationships.

I would not want to deny the potential force of this general argument but it certainly over-generalizes. It is informative to look, in fact, at the personalizing potential of dating advertisements, as well as their marketized character: strategies of personalization are quite readily apparent, particularly in the spoken data.

The structural summaries in the previous section show there is potentially very considerable overlap of content and structure in the written and spoken modes. At the same time, different resources are available to users of the two modes. In the spoken texts, the greeting, naming, thanking, metacommentary, challenging and farewell moves are obviously structural elements not shared with the written advertisements and they are embedded in a rather more loosely organized sequence of structural possibilities. Spoken advertisements tend to incorporate sequences and orientations associated with what Malinowski characterized as phatic communion (Coupland *et al.* 1992, 1994; Layer 1975, 1981; Malinowski 1972). We might see this as the re-introduction of personalization, in however limited ways, into commodified discourse.

Even spoken ads which are closely based on their prior, written counterparts show phatic elements:

Text 1

(a) Written

> YORKS LADY 39 DIVORCED VGSOH GOOD LOOKING, LONG
> NATURAL BLONDE HAIR SEEKS FUTURE HUSBAND IN
> CORNWALL 40–50 BOX 212.

(b) Spoken
(sounding calm, in control)

> hello I'm Jenny and I live in Yorkshire (.) thirty-nine and have been
> divorced almost ten years (.) I'm five foot three bluey-grey eyes and
> have long natural blonde hair (.) I'm considered to be very attractive or
> (.) well so people say (laughs) and I have a good sense of humour (.) to
> get to the point I'm looking for a future husband preferably in Cornwall
> (2.0) so leave your number and I'll give you a call (.) thank you.
>
> (Teletext *One-2-One*, March 1994)

The advertiser self-presents consistently with socio-cultural stereotypes of female desirability in appearance. As Giddens notes: 'Self-actualisation is packaged and distributed according to market criteria . . . Commodification promotes *appearance* as the prime arbiter of value and sees self-development above all in terms of display' (1991: 198). However, in the spoken version, as well as adding some commodifying detail to her written physical self-description (height and eye-colour), she hedges the positivity of 'good looking' by repositioning the judgement of her own appearance, locating the judgement in the views of others ('I'm considered to be very attractive'), and then retreating from this claim by acknowledging it to be a claim about others' claims ('or (.) well so people say'). The discourse marker 'well', the hesitation and the laughter around the claimed evidence could all be taken as strategic mitigation of the positive threat to own-face (Brown and Levinson 1987) entailed in self-directed positivity-strategic because it allows attributions of modesty and therefore, presumably, likeability. Similarly, her 'to get to the point' humanizes the text by retrospectively downplaying her assessment of her own attributes in favour of an 'open' statement (in a genre where many are coy) of her goals. In both modes, the very fact that she sets no qualifying standards beyond location as a desired attribute of the other seems to resist the full-blown commodification process. She commodifies herself physically but she does not locate her prospective partner categorially.

Advertiser 2 is again sparing in her specification of commodified attributes.

Text 2

(a) Written

> WELL-BUILT MANCHESTER LADY 32 SEEKS SOMEONE
> SPECIAL, HONEST, CARING AND ROMANTIC, TO PUT
> SPARKLE BACK INTO HER LIFE! SO DO YOU? SNAP! BOX 500.

(b) Spoken
(brightly)

> hi! my name is Jane thanks for ringing (.) hope you're not as nervous
> as me (.) well what should I tell you about myself (.) I'm thirty-two
> (.) and I've done all those easy things to try and resolve my life back
> (.) buying a new house changing my car (.) and now it's time for the
> difficult one (2.0) someone special to make me smile again (.) and
> share some fun (.) happiness and hopefully romance (2.5) please leave
> me a message including your name and phone number or your address
> and I'll contact you as soon as I can (2.0) hope I've not scared you off
> (.) (even more brightly) I'm *quite* nice *really* (.) hope to speak to you
> soon (.) bye!

> (Teletext *One-2-One*, March 1994)

'Well-built' is in fact strangely physicalist in relation to the focus of the remainder of this advertisement, both written and spoken. Although the advertiser anticipates a list of personal attributes in the spoken text ('well what should I tell you about myself'), she selects only her age from the conventional set of demographic, physical, personality and social categories. She locates her spoken ad overtly within the domain of commodification, referring to her desired partner as one of a list of three lifestyle commodities she is in the process of acquiring ('buying a new house changing my car (.) and now it's time for the difficult one'). But her overt references to acquiring a partner and especially as 'the difficult' transaction for her self-project seems to undermine the effect of commodification. Her oblique references to personal crisis ('I've done all those easy things to try and resolve my life back') set a more weighty emotional agenda that breaks out of the marketized genre. She is presumably aware of and in control of this rupture, since she signals that her approach (and perhaps her personal disclosiveness) could be challenging for listeners ('hope I've not scared you off I'm *quite* nice *really*'). These efforts to humanize the marketing procedure through communicating uncertainty and hesitation echo her stance earlier on in the spoken ad: 'hope you're not as nervous as me'.

This mix of conforming to commodification principles and strategic humanizing devices is the norm for spoken advertisements, although in widely different proportions and with very different ultimate effects. Commodification theory in fact accounts for this pattern of inconstancy and resistance. Giddens comments that commodification is not all-triumphant at either an individual or a collective level, with individuals partaking in active discrimination among available material: 'The reflexive project of the self is in some part necessarily a struggle against commodified influences . . . plurality of choice is in some substantial part the very outcome of commodified processes' (1991: 198).

Some texts in the sample quite actively contest the need to present the self as a commodity, at least through discursively resisting stereotyped formulations of female desirability and submissiveness of the type that Text 1 espouses.

Text 3

(a) Written

> FAT SINGLE MOTHER WITH HOUSE FULL OF ANIMALS,
> LANCS, SEEKS SMALLISH MALE WITH GSOH, ANY RACE
> COLOUR BUT NO BALDIES, 27–40ish FOR FUN AND
> FRIENDSHIP BOX 792.

(b) Spoken
(brightly, confidently)

> hello! my name is Sue I am single twenty-seven and have a fifteen
> month old daughter (2.0) I only want to hear from people who have a
> genuine interest in animals and *don't* have a macho attitude (2.0) I am
> not interested in marriage only friendship (.) and would like to meet
> someone who'll share in *my* interests for a change.
>
> (Teletext One-2-One, March 1994)

As in Text 2, the focus is on buying capital rather than selling it. But advertiser 3 flouts the stereotypical 'ideal woman' norms by categorizing herself in the written format as a 'fat single mother'. Her closing words in the spoken advert, 'someone who'll share in *my* interests for a change', invoke and reject the stereotyped dominant male image, incorporating an element of challenge into the advertisement. Although this is still an opening move to a market-place transaction, it is a transaction which rewrites the conventional rules for marketing females. At the same time, advertiser 3 aggressively commodifies her target by listing not only desired but also undesired attributes.

Some advertisers deploy strategies for resisting marketization more thoroughly, in both written and spoken modes.

Text 4

(a) Written

> NOT UNATTRACTIVE MALE, 56, INSOLVENT, INTO THEATRE, WRITING, MUSIC, COOKING, WINING AND DINING SEEKS FEMALE 35–40 FOR FUN AND FRIENDSHIP BOX 111.

(b) Spoken
(very slowly and carefully)

> hi! my name's Tim (2.0) thank you for showing an interest in my ad (3.5) if you'd like to leave your name and number (.) I'll get back to you as soon as possible (2.0) by the way (.) I live in Plymouth.
> (Teletext One-2-One, April 1994)

In the written advert, this advertiser hedges positivity on his appearance (syntactically, through a hedged negative – 'not unattractive') and his financial security ('insolvent') and so subverts two norms of positive self-marketization. This may offer attributions of 'openness', 'a mature ability to self-criticize', 'non-materialism' or even 'a sense of humour'. But the brief spoken advert strikingly suspends all overtly marketizing initiatives (unless the thanking: 'thank you for showing an interest in my ad' is seen as thanking the respondent for showing an interest in the advertiser as a commodity). After the naming, no new information about the advertiser is offered (his place of abode is apparently added as an afterthought) and there is no interpenetration of the written text into the spoken version. The effect is of a minimalist and severely understated self-projection which is likely to appeal to targets only through its *non*-compliance with market norms. There are still marketable qualities to the self-projection, through prosodic and paralinguistic aspects of the performance and the social meanings culturally associated with them. But this is a category of vocal cues available to any audible interactional encounter and what is striking about instances like Text 4 is the advertiser's withholding, in a marketing context, from the conventional marketized formats.

The moral contexts of self-marketization

I embarked on this analysis out of interest in identity-management processes in discourse (Goffman 1959) and the constitution of formulaic communication (Coulmas 1981; Cheepen 1988). Behind the data lie the unresolved moral questions raised in Fairclough's and Giddens's theories of commodification and marketization (discussed earlier). To some extent, by demonstrating how advertisers construct personal ads with differing degrees of conformity to the 'fully marketized' generic ideal and with different amounts and means of personalization, I have already challenged the most negative moral readings of dating ad marketization. I would like to take the debate a step further.

Returning to Fairclough's earlier-quoted concerns (in the specific and wholly different context of British university management), we might extrapolate and argue that dating ads are censurable as another late-modern discursive context in which (to recap) meanings are subordinated to and manipulated for instrumental effect and person-to-person communication is colonized by a discourse of promotion, perhaps with major pathological effects upon subjects; they blur the distinction between the authentic and the promotional and, as Giddens has it, offer no more than substitutes for real satisfactions.

But this stance (which I am of course not attributing to either Fairclough or Giddens in the context of my own data) raises highly problematic questions of how to define and locate non-instrumental, non-promotional, authentic and truly satisfying discourses or relationships. Just as the definitional basis of 'small talk' presumes the (illusory) existence of a normatively 'full', 'serious' or 'committed' mode of discourse (Coupland et al. 1992), we need to recognize the presence of self-promotional elements in all discourses and most certainly in relational encounters. Dating ads are indeed circulated through technologies that are well-adapted for economic market transactions but they do not appear to have duped users into wholly marketized formats for their interpersonal dealings. The data, and especially the audio-recorded self-promotional follow ups to written advertisements, show that advertisers who have initially subjected themselves to the formulaicity of the written mode do also command resources to resist and undermine the process of commodification itself. Some facets of dating advertising, then, actually show people playing creatively with the strictures of the media and reconstituting themselves as 'human', de-commodified beings. To this extent, commodification can sometimes be only a technical constraint on the communicative range of dating advertisements and a stimulus to self-expressive creativity, rather than a persistent threat to late-modern identities.

Finally, a factor which has not emerged clearly enough from the examples I have included so far is the great diversity of footings or stances adopted by different advertisers. Some are fully absorbed into relational commercialism. However, there are instances where the spoken texts move well beyond the trading of attributes into confessional data, appeals and the disclosing of apparently painful personal information (see Coupland et al. 1991).

Text 5

(a) Written

> MUST BE SEEN to be appreciated. Tall slim, widow, 50's looks younger, seeks tall gentleman with an adventurous spirit. Tel: 0011 444 555.

(b) Spoken
(slowly, carefully)

> hello (.) my name is Mary (.) I've been a widow for nearly two years
> (.) and I thought (.) that my memories would sustain me for the rest

of my life (.) but I now realise that I didn't die as well (.) (faster) I want to love again I want to be happy (.) with a kind (slower) gentle man I never thought that I would use this method to find a partner but being on my own I cannot go out and search for mister right (.) so are you this man (breathes) I have *many* pastimes I enjoy walking eating out (.) I like all types of music I'm very very fond of animals I have a dog and a cat (.) I retired (.) er from work when my husband was ill and obviously now have a full day to myself and er (.) I get a bit fed up with my own company so I really am looking for somebody to fill my days as well as my evenings (1.0) I really haven't a *lot* more to say about myself I'm (.) as I said tall and slim um (.) I keep fit go to (.) er leisure centres for (.) er games of badminton or (.) into the jacuzzi and sauna (.) I try to fill my time as much as I can but I must admit I dread the thought of another lonely Christmas (.) so if you are this gentleman and you *are* looking for somebody who's genuine (.) kind and honest *please* get in touch with me.

(Making Friends, December 1993)

The shift from written to spoken medium sees a radical shift of key. The written text, perhaps parodically, aligns the discourse practice with small ads: 'must be seen'. The advertiser emphasizes positive aspects of her appearance and the emotional loading of 'widow' is attenuated - as little more than just another demographic attribute. It is only in the spoken advert that the loneliness and dis-engagement of the advertiser become apparent, both in content and prosodically. She discloses her bereavement and her intense emotional response to it 'I now realise that I didn't die as well' and leaves an impression of vulnerability and lack of purpose or direction: 'I really am looking for somebody to fill my days as well as my evenings'; 'I must admit I dread the thought of another lonely Christmas'. The move that I previously characterized as fulfilling a 'referencing' function is rather an appeal to be rescued from a lonely life: '*please* get in touch with me'.

At another extreme, an advertiser can make blatant, immodest claims and offer a self fully loaded with stereotypically valued market attributes, demanding the equivalent, in very precise terms, in return:

Text 6

(a) Written

> GORGEOUS MIXED RACE FEMALE 22 SINGLE PARENT SW AREA, SEEKS SMART, CLEAN SENSUOUS, RICH, KIND GENEROUS GQ-READING WHITE MALE FOR FUN AND FRIENDSHIP BOX 086.

(b) Spoken
(slowly and confidently)

> hi this is Sarah (.) I'm half-caste (.) twenty-two years old five foot four (.) very slim and *very* attractive (.) my interests include dancing (.) cooking (.) good clothes (.) and looking after my young daughter (2.0)

I'm looking for a handsome (.) intelligent (.) white male (.) in
between twenty-five to thirty-five who is strong yet sensitive to the
needs of a good woman (2.5) I also need someone with a *wicked* sense
of humour (.) an up-to-date wardrobe and a finely-cut physique (.)
you will need to live in or around Bristol (.) so if you fit the bill leave
your name and number and I promise I'll call you back.

(Teletext One-2-One, April 1994)

How might these two last instances be evaluated, relative to the charge of
'pernicious commodification'? While it might be argued that Text 5 exposed a
vulnerable and genuinely needy individual to the rigours of the relational market-
place, the advertiser managed to resist the more obvious marketizing imperatives
of the medium. Her 'human' and troublesome circumstances were self-evident, to
the extent that there was scarcely any plausible confusion in the minds of her target
audience between 'real' and 'fictional' meanings. Commodification signally failed
to override her moving account of painful circumstances.

In the last and very fully marketized instance, the confident hard-sell, with
unmitigated claims about appearance ('gorgeous'; 'very slim and very attractive'),
is fully acculturated to marketized genre and the advertiser, 'Sarah', appears to be
in full control of the practice itself. We might doubt the 'authenticity' of her self-
portrayal and some might be concerned about the 'authenticity' of the relationships
that it may trigger. But Sarah's self-promotion follows an instrumental agenda and
we are not entitled to assume that the instrumental goals of players in this exchange
(Sarah potential respondents) derive from any source other than their own (rather
than 'the media's' or 'the culture's') relational priorities.

It is of course true that the victims of discursive shifts are often ignorant of
the constraints that new discourse formations bring with them and that victimization
can often look like complicity or even control. As Fairclough notes, commodification can produce a bogus intimacy, masquerading as the stuff of 'genuine' intimate
relationships. However, there is also the fact that human relationships can legit-
imately be defined by their own members to be physicalist, materially reciprocal
or ephemeral. Before demonizing marketization in all of its discursive manifestations, we should at least consider the potential of individuals, on the one hand to
challenge and subvert the discourses of the marketplace and, on the other hand to
endorse and use marketized practices where they meet their personal or relational
priorities.

Chapter 10

Scott F. Kiesling

2002

PLAYING THE STRAIGHT MAN

Displaying and maintaining male heterosexuality in discourse

IN THIS CHAPTER I EXPLORE the discourse of heterosexuality: how a group of men define, police, and display heterosexual relationships within their same sex group, and how these practices also help to create and display relationships among the men – relationships of homosocial desire and dominance.

The heterosexual identities I explore are not just displays of difference from women and gay men. They are also, more centrally, displays of power and dominance over women, gay men, and other straight men. A discourse of heterosexuality involves not only difference from women and gay men, but also the dominance of these groups. In fact, we will see that, through the use of address terms, men display same sex dominance by metaphorically referring to other men as 'feminine', thus drawing on the cultural model of the heterosexual couple to index a homosocial inequality.

'Greek' society and compulsory heterosexuality

The men's discursive indexing of their heterosexuality is embedded in a community of practice that is organized around heterosexuality and sexual difference. Thus, not only the practices within speech activities, but also the organization, purposes, and rituals of speech events and activities in this community help to create a heterosexual and homosocial community. This heterosexual organization begins with a separation of genders: The 'greek' letter society system is arranged through an ideology of sexual difference, such that fraternities are all-male, sororities all-female.

The system also polices heterosexuality through its organization and naming of social speech events and activities. The most obvious example of this is a 'mixer' speech event, at which one fraternity and one sorority hold a joint party, and 'mix' with one another. This terminology also reinforces an ideology of difference: Men and women are metaphorically different ingredients that must be mixed.

'Open' parties, while not being so overtly focused on heterosexual desire, nevertheless are similar in their focus on sex and alcohol. This focus is seen most in how the men evaluate parties, as Flyer does in the following excerpt. He is speaking during a meeting held to discuss fraternity problems. In this context, he compares his fraternity's parties to another's:

Excerpt 1

01	Flyer:	I- I- I went-
02		I even went to a party the other night to investigate
03		just to see who was gone
04		not that I really wanted to go there
05		I didn't have a great time
06		I tried to get the fuck outta there but my ride dumped me.
07		I went to- what the fuck-
08		I went to see what happened.
09		it was fuckin packed.
10		it was wall to wall chicks.
11		chicks hookin' up with guys everywhere
12		they're havin such a great time
13		they decided to fuck on the floor or whatever (??)
14	??:	(who?)
15	Flyer:	this was Sig Ep OK.
16		and this- what this-
17		I- I thought *Jesus Christ*.
18		this was our parties.
19		good music,
20		they had a couple of trash cans of beer
21		and a couple bottles of liquor.

In this excerpt, Flyer is in fact implying that Gamma Chi Phi's parties have become too focused on drinking and homosocial activity, by suggesting another fraternity's party was better primarily because *it was wall to wall chicks* (*chicks* is the term the men most often use for women, especially young women to whom they are sexually attracted). Moreover, these women are *hookin' up* with the men, and are having such a great time, claims Flyer, that they *decided to fuck on the floor*. Thus it is because of this heterosexual activity that the party is rated highly – notice that Flyer goes out of his way to suggest that the drinks were not special (line 20: *they had a couple trash cans of beer*). This high evaluation of heterosexual activity creates a social context in which heterosexual sex is glorified as an end in itself, thus creating an ideology of heterosexual desire as an important social goal.

Some heterosexually organized speech activities constitute these larger speech events, and have been named by the men and women. Flyer's phrase 'hook up' is an example. These named sexual speech activities were explained to me by Saul in an interview:

Excerpt 2

01 SK: there's hookin' up, there's scamming,
02   what other words are there like that?
03 Saul: throwin' raps hhhhhhh
04 SK: I never heard that one, what's that?
05 Saul: throwin' a rap is just basically
06   you go up to a girl you think is attractive and uh
07   y'kno:w you try to be as outgoing as you can. normally-
08   the best way
09   that I've found
10   to get a girl
11   to hold a conversation
12   #is to entertain em.#
13   an' basically throwing a rap is entertaining a girl
14   *with* the intent to try to bring her back that night he he he he
15 SK: yeah
16 Saul: or with the intent of eventually setting something up.=
17 SK: =is there any difference,
18   like if you just go an t- an an an
19   and talk to her
20   like is there is there any way that *she* knows that?
21   [in that throwing raps]
22 Saul: [the smart] the smart girls do he he he he he he
23   they they they know that um::
24   but . . . we do our best to say, y'know
25   like, we'll throw in all kinds of disclaimers when we're talkin y'know
26   'y'know hey::'
27   'y'know but we you know what I mean'
28   'y'know what I'm sayin?'
29   that kind of things
30   and you'd even say that to a girl.
31   You'll be talkin'
32   and you'll say somethin' a little promiscuous maybe like
33   'aw you know know what I mean' type of deal so-
34   so yeah
35 SK: OK, so, and hookin' up is- is that different?
36   that's more of a . . . after the fact kind of thing
37 Saul: tha- tha- that's the action, he he he he he
38   that's the action and that's uh . . . uh
39   ah:I mean y'know you find a gir:l,
40   you throw your rap,
41   you hook up,
42   and uh, usually no strings attached.
43   but a lot of times- not a lot of times
44   depending on who the girl is
45   if it happens to be a drunk thing

46   and it's late night
47   and you hook up
48   it's usually something you try to keep as a drunk story.
49   but um, but, I mean, sometimes hookin' up leads to y'know
50   y'know you li- you end up likin' the girl y'know
51   and then you go into your commitment thing.
52 SK: yeah all right now then there's some other ones like scamming.
53   do you guys use that at all?
54 Saul: yeah:: well
55   scamming is interchangeable with throwing a rap.
56 SK: is that uh- . . .
57   in my experience that's more of a female term.
58 Saul: yeah gir- girls- yeah that's the way to look at it
59   if I go to a girl, I'm throwin a rap.
60   but if I'm a girl, getting the rap thrown to me,
61   and I'm catching on to this,
62   this guy's scamming on me.

In this excerpt, Saul explains a constellation of terms describing heterosexual speech activities: *throwin' raps, scamming, hookin' up*. He also names some different kinds of heterosexual relations without describing them in detail: *a drunk thing* and *do your commitment thing*. The latter two illustrate the distinction the men make between short- and long-term relationships respectively, and their importance as immediate goals of the fraternity men. Saul comments that *a drunk thing* is an experience *you might want to keep as a drunk story* (for 'Gavel', as described below). This way of viewing 'one-night stands' suggests that they are as much for the homosocial enjoyment of the fraternity, and a display of sexual prowess, as they are actual sexual attraction (although sexual attraction should be understood socially as well). The *commitment thing*, on the other hand, implies that the man actually likes the woman and enjoys her companionship whether or not sex is involved. In fact, men were often ridiculed by other members for spending too much time with their girlfriends at the expense of the fraternity.

The men thus have a range of named heterosexual speech events, activities, and sexual relationships. Other social displays, such as the display of posters of nude or nearly-nude women in their apartments and dorm rooms, are similarly heterosexually-focused. In sum, the institutions of greek society, the speech events that make up this society, and the speech activities within those events are constructed principally around the display of sexual difference and heterosexual desire. They reflect the cultural models for men and women as different and unequal: men as dominant and hunting for sex, women as submissive and existing as sexual prey for the men.

The heterosexuality of homosociability in the fraternity

Now let us turn to how the men talk in these interactions, and how this talk serves to create and reinforce the heterosexual model. The men use several different strategies to police and construct sexuality. However, most involve the taking or assigning of specific stances either to themselves or to others, including women and subordinated men. Specifically, one revolves around the telling of stories, both performed in meetings and told in more private conversations. Another type is speech in which men take on roles of women and homosexual men – or have these roles forced upon them. A man is 'assigned' the role of a woman or gay man when he is in a subordinate position.

Cultural models of sex in interaction: public valorization of 'man as hunter for sex'

Many of the stories the men tell present women and men in sexual relationships. These stories comprise a recognized, ratified genre in which men display sexual relationships. This 'genrification' of such narratives is an important component for policing/reinforcing hegemonic heterosexuality, because it means that one kind of sexual relationship is valorized in narrative performances.

This genre is a linguistic object, and its importance in the verbal repertoires of the men is a way of valorizing this kind of heterosexuality. There is status (and solidarity) to be gained from telling a story of this sort, or in being a character of one of these stories. In investigating how identities are created and how social values are transmitted, we need to look at the deployment of genres in the community, which includes the content of these genres.

'Fuck stories' in gavel

Gavel is a story round at the end of Sunday meetings in which men often tell of their sexual exploits over the weekend. These are explicitly named by the men as 'fuck stories'. They can be particularly graphic, and portray women as sexual objects for the men, including for men who are voyeurs. The gavel stories were one of the highlights of the week for the men; they were performances for the entertainment of the members, usually told at the expense of the performer or one of the other members. (Fuck stories are not the only kind of narrative; another common type is the 'drunk story', in which one member tells about the usually embarrassing actions of another member while very intoxicated; drunk stories and gavel stories are often the same.)

During most of my research I was not permitted to tape-record gavel. This fact shows how important this story round is for the social cohesion of the group – it is a form of ritual gossip which may never leave the group. The stories are a powerful way of creating a cultural model and placing value on it.

Conversational narrative and alternate sexual identities

While fuck stories are perhaps the most overt and obvious genre in which a certain heterosexual norm is reproduced, the men do not see this as the only kind of relationship with women, although it is the most 'public' representation their relationships with women. Let's have a look at one of the members who displays this public/private dichotomy. First, consider a portion of Hotdog's report to Mack of his trip to Atlanta, in which he creates a stance with respect to women similar to that in gavel stories. This excerpt is from the beginning of the narrative, on the day Hotdog arrived in Atlanta.

Excerpt 3

01	Hotdog:	Then we went to a Ma::ll
02		and just like sat in the food court
03		and just looked at all the *beau*tiful fuckin' hot ass chicks
04	Mack:	(are they) really dude.
05	Hotdog:	Oh my *go:d*
06	Mack:	Where was it?
07	Hotdog:	In Atlanta
08	Mack:	I know but what school?
09	Hotdog:	Ahh Georgia Tech.
10	Mack:	I'm movin' to Atlanta dude
11	Andy:	We're movin' there
12	Hotdog:	We weren't like at the school
13		we were like
14		we were like in like the business district
15	Mack:	Oh
16	Hotdog:	So it was just like all business ladies dressed up
17		and they're like (.) *in*credible.
18		then that night we registered
19		that's that *first* night is when we went to Lulu's,
20	Mack:	Let's move to Atlanta when we graduate [dude.
21	Hotdog:	[I want to.
		I *def*initely want to. Definitely.
22	Andy:	I told you I wanna move down there.
23		I'm movin down there as soon as I graduate.

In this excerpt, Hotdog evaluates a shopping mall in Atlanta by describing the physical appearance of the women he sees there. We can see the impact of this evaluation and the importance of the appearance of women through the reaction of the men: Just this description of the women prompts them to talk about moving there when they graduate. This response constructs Hotdog's evaluation, then, as the highest compliment for the city.

Contrast this positioning with the one Hotdog presents in the interview situation, and with only myself present. The following excerpt begins after I have asked Hotdog about his plans for the future, specifically marriage.

Excerpt 4

01	Hotdog:	I don't ever intend to be close to getting married any time soon.
02	SK:	You think you'll get married eventually?

03 Hotdog: Yeah. (0.8) Probably (1 .0)*lets see today's ninety three*
04   I probably could see myself getting married by like
05   nineteen ninety seven nineteen ninety eight.(1.4)
06   So about (.) four years.
07 SK: Wow. Do you- I mean- do want to or is that just a matter of-
08 Hotdog: No I-
09   it's not that I want to I have I have had a girlfriend sinc:e
10   *I guess we were*
11   I was in high school we've been datin' on and off.
12   Kinda got a little more serious once we went away believe it or not.
13   and uh (.) yknow if things stay the same way with her,
14   I could see us getting married like: ninety seven ninety eight
15   but if: we-
16   if things don't stay the same
17   I can't see u- me gettin' married
18   until after the year two thousand (laughing).
19   [So]
20 SK: [Laugh] (1.7) So you guys are pretty close then.
21 Hotdog: Yeah. We're very close.

Because Hotdog evaluates all the women he sees in the Atlanta mall as sexual objects, we would get an impression that his status on the heterosexual market-place is unattached: for most of the men, the definition of having a 'girlfriend' is monogamy with that person. Thus, if Hotdog publicly shows a face of sexual voracity, it would be logical to think that he does not have a girlfriend. However, he *does* have a girlfriend, one with whom he is 'very close', and one whom he is considering marrying in the near future. So Hotdog represents himself with respect to women and that he represents his sexuality quite differently in two different situations with different audiences and purposes: he performs two different kinds of identity in each of these situations.

In fact, it seems that he is a little unsure of exactly how to perform his iden-tity with me in the interview. My status is not one he is familiar with: I am similar to a member, but not quite a member. At the beginning of this excerpt, Hotdog seems to want to present the same kind of identity as he did in the Atlanta recount. He denies quite strongly an interest in getting married: *I don't ever intend to be close to getting married any time soon.* But after I rephrase the question, he reveals that marriage may only be four years off. It takes several moves on my part before Hotdog tells me about his girlfriend, even though he later says 'we're very close' (line 21).

Hotdog's relationship with me has shifted over these turns, so has his identity. He begins with a stance similar to the one he takes publicly in the fraternity, and eventually admits to having a close, loving relationship with a woman. We thus see how the linguistic construction of sexuality for these men is based not just on the actual relationships they have with women but also on the relationships they are creating with other men. This allows the men to 'have' in fact more than one (hetero)sexual identity.

Metaphorical representations of other members as women

Morford (1987) and Hall and O'Donovan (1996) show that an address term indexes not simply such things as power and solidarity, but specific cultural models which are part of speakers' knowledge, and which interact with context to create local relationships between speakers. To the extent that speakers share these cultural models and scripts, the address terms are interactionally successful. Address terms in the fraternity work in this way as well, on several levels of linguistic and cultural awareness. All of the address terms I consider position a man as subordinate through the use of a female address term.

In the first case, the address term occurs within a culturally recognized phrase, thus indexing a certain heterosexual cultural model. It occurs while the men are playing Monopoly, in which players pass through other players' property and pay rent. I will particularly focus on line 26, but I reproduce here some relevant context as well.

Excerpt 5

```
09 ((Pete rolls, moves))
10 Dave:    Nice, pay me. (2.3)
11 Pete:    I can't. Aren't you in jail or something?
12          Don't I not have to pay you this time?
13              [Free pass]
14 Boss:    You[got a] free pass.
15          He's got one more.
16 Dave:    No that's your last one.
17 Pete:    I have one more.
            I've got one left.
18 Dave:    No that's it
19 Pete:    I have one left. I've only used two.
20 Dave:    That's right. And these over here. OK.
21 Pete:    The deal was for fi:ve.
22 Dave:    God damn I needed that money too you son of a *bitch*.
23 ((Dave rolls))
24          The deal was for TWO.
25 (4.3)
26 Pete:    HI: HI: hi: honey I'm home.
27 Boss:    I'm gonna blow by Dave right here.
28 ((Boss rolls))
```

The phrase 'Hi Hi honey I'm home' in line 26 does a large amount of contextually-dependent identity work for Pete. First, we need to understand the game situation: Pete has landed on a property owned by Dave, which would usually mean that Pete has to pay rent to Dave. However, because of an earlier deal in which Dave gave Pete a number of 'free passes', Pete is allowed to 'stay' at Dave's property without paying rent. Pete draws on this metaphor and extends it. The metaphor taunts Dave and puts him down, in part by metaphorically vandalizing Dave's property, but also through the phrase 'Hi Hi honey I'm home'.

Without the correct background knowledge and cultural ideologies, the remark makes no sense, especially as a taunt. The phrase brings to mind the stereotype of a husband returning from work to a 'housewife' in a stereotypical American nuclear family. So it metaphorically positions Pete not only as one of the family staying for the night, but as 'the man of the house', in a dominant position over his wife. This interpretation was confirmed through an informal poll of the members. Dave is then put in a metaphorically subordinate position as a housewife in a particular stereotype of a family. It thus makes sense as a taunt because Pete is not only staying for free but claiming that Dave is in a servant position to him. Without this background knowledge, the phrase makes little sense. Thus it reinforces an ideology as a woman/wife in that subordinate servant role for the man/husband, even as it is constructing a local dominance relationship between Pete and Dave.

This kind of dominance relationship was even clearer in the naming of one of the pledges. During the pledge period, the members gave all the pledges nicknames which were often insulting or highlighted the subordinate position of the pledge. One pledge was given the name 'Hazel', and was made to perform household cleaning duties for several of the members for a few weeks. Here again, the name of the subordinate male is female. But it also refers to a 1950s television show of the same name, about a character of the same name who is a domestic worker for a nuclear-family household. The men draw on the show and the larger cultural metaphor of women as domestic workers, to name a structurally subordinate position for 'Hazel'.

One of the most common examples of this kind of positioning is the use of *bitch* to insult another man. I collected several examples of this, and heard many more which I did not record or note down. In the next excerpt, Pete uses bitch in the prototypical way. It takes place during the chapter correspondent election. Like several other members (including Mack), Pete suggests three offices and the proper candidate for each. Mick reminds him not to argue for other offices and Pete then argues he can say whatever he wants when he has the floor.

Excerpt 6

```
01 Mick:    Pete
02 Pencil:  You're a moron ((to Mitty, who just spoke))
03 Pete:    Kurt for chapter correspondent,
04          [Ritchie for sch-olarship,
05 ?:       [no no:::::
06 Pete:    and Ernie for hi[storian.
07 ?:                       [Ritchie for chaplain.
08 Pete:    allright well Ritchie for historian,
09          and Ernie for scholarship.
10 Mick:    We're on one vote right now.
11 Pete:    Hey I get to say my piece I got the floor bitch.
12 Mick:    Darter.
```

Here we see Pete clearly in opposition to his addressee, here Mick. He finishes his statement by calling Mick 'bitch', normally a term used to refer derogatorily to a woman (or a female dog, from where the insult derives). This insults Mick both through the 'conventional' manner of calling him a dog, and by drawing on a social ideology of female as subordinate.

We have evidence that 'bitch' is associated with this subordinate role through another derogatory term used by the men: 'bitch boy'. This term is loaded with dominant-subordinate meaning: first through 'bitch', and second through the term 'boy', also used to refer to a servant. We have the story of the origin of the term from Mack:

Excerpt 7

01 Mack:	So bitch boy um
02	Chicken hawk and I don't know if you've ever met him KW um
03	one time was tellin a story
04	and I don't know if there were other people around
05	or if he's just told this story so many times
06	but um he apparently was at another school I think
07	maybe with his brother,
08	he was in a bar with his brother,
09	the details of it I'm not- I don't remember very well.
10	Anyway he was at this bar
11	and I think maybe he was talking to this- he was talking to a girl.
12	another guy some strange guy bigger than K though
13	um came over and started hassling him
14	either about the girl or he was standing in his place
15	you know the normal bar nonsense. and um
16	so K kinda left it be for a while and uh
17	he he I think he mentioned it to his brother
18	now they were there with a friend of his brother's
19	and apparently this friend of his brother's
20	they were at the bar
21	this friend of his brother's was quite a big man
22	very large you know
23	like six four you know like two hundred and fifty pounds or something
24	strong
25	big guy
26	and um so K went back over I think to talk to this girl
27	and uh apparently this same guy started giving him problems again
28	eh and this guy this big friend of Ks brother
29	comes up behind- behind this guy this guy that's bothering K,
30	and just puts his arm around him very gently
31	and kind of pulls him in close
32	and starts talking to him r:::eally kind of
33	y- you know I don't even wanna I don't even wanna try and do the voice
34	that K does you're gonna have to ask K for it.
35	but t- he starts really talkin to him
36	like he's pimpin this guy or somethin' you know

37   and he goes you know what we gon do?
38   You gon be my bitch boy fa the rest of the night
39   and then he just went down the list of things that he's gonna make=
40   this guy do for him an
41   it wasn't- it was demeaning things like
42   you know you gonna get me drinks
43   your gonna come in and wipe my ass and
44   you know nothing nothing like
45   I'm gonna kick your ass or anything like that.
46   he spoke real calmly and real coolly and
47   you know You gon be my bitch boy tonight, you know
48   and so that's where it came from and
49   bitch boy you know it's pretty self explanatory
50   you know it's just a little boy
51   who's gonna do all the bitch work for me I dunno

The bitch boy relationship is clearly one of dominance. Not a dominance of actual physical violence, but one of potential violence symbolized by the things the dominant male makes the subordinate do. But it also has an essential sexual component as well, one that on the surface looks to be homosexual. Under the surface, though, the relationship is a metaphorical male dominant-female subordinate metaphor. Notice in lines 35–6 that Mack says 'he starts talking to him like he's pimpin' this guy,' indicating he's treating him like a prostitute under his care. Here we see clearly Mack equate *bitch* with *woman*, stating that the relationship is metaphorically a heterosexual one, not homosexual. So in using one of the most overt named dominance relationships in the fraternity group, the men use a term that not only has a lexical association with women (*bitch*), but also draws on the metaphor of a woman as a (sexual) servant to a (physically) powerful, dominant man. Thus, the meaning of bitch boy, which Mack claims is 'pretty self explanatory' in line 49, is only self explanatory if you have access to this cultural script of heterosexual relationships of this type. Moreover, the use of the term presupposes an understanding of this relationship and through its repetition reifies the existence of the dominance heterosexual model. The 'male' half of the term (*boy*) also helps to create the subordinate position of the addressee through age and race hierarchies. *Boy* is clearly an address term used with a younger and less powerful person; a male who has not yet made it to his full dominant position. It also indexes a racial cultural model in which powerful White men address Black men with the term, such as in Ervin-Tripp's (1969) example of an exchange between a Black physician and a White police officer. The fraternity men, then, when they use *bitch boy*, are creating a number of different identities and relationships. Most immediately for the discourse, they are creating a relationship between who is the bitch boy and who is his dominator. However, they are also crucially drawing on a shared an ideology of gender relationships in which a woman is dominated by a man.

What about other address terms, especially those which are more clearly (heterosexual) male? Consider again the address terms in the monopoly game, where we saw Pete use 'Hi honey I'm home' to taunt Dave. Pete also uses the address term *dude*: in the Monopoly game he addresses another player as 'Dave, dude, dude Dave', clearly playing with language by using alliteration and chiasmus. Pete is here having fun with language given the resources of the game. But the relationship he has – and wants to construct – with Dave is quite different. In the *dude* situation, Pete is not clearly dominating Dave, but rather Dave has something Pete wants (the red property). So Pete is constructing a solidary and perhaps even a subordinate relationship with Dave. This is the way the two clear 'masculine' address terms are used in the fraternity (*dude* and *man*): as solidarity indexes to focus on cooperative actions, and even to diffuse tensions during confrontations. So the generic masculine address terms focus on equality and solidarity, whereas the female terms are terms of dominance and insult. Thus, not only are male and female separated, they are treated unequally. Moreover, through the term *bitch boy* (and similar creative terms such as 'Hazel') male and female are related metaphorically through an assumed heterosexual ideology.

The address terms I have considered thus do more than just position a man as a woman. They position a man as a woman *in a narrative* – a cultural script. This woman, moreover, is clearly in a subordinate position in the narrative: as a housewife, as a prostitute, as a domestic servant. Each use of the address term makes sense only if the interlocutors share access to the cultural script.

This has implications for the way we understand language to index social identity. The standard assumption is that a certain variant of a variable becomes associated with a recognized cultural group, and people who identify, with that cultural group are statistically more likely to use the variant. This is the 'acts of identity' model of language and identity (LePage and Tabouret-Keller 1985). It requires a knowledge of groups and the way they act, and a direct, one-to-one indexing of linguistic form to group identity. What we see here is that heterosexual identities and ideologies are being created in a much more complex way: there is really no separated group of heterosexuals in the dominant culture. This group, like men a few decades ago, is considered the norm, and is indeed hardly a coherent group. But as we have seen here that we can identify heterosexuality as part of these men's socially constructed identity. We must therefore have a model of language and identity that is itself much more complex than the acts of identity model, one that can take account of mocking and metaphorical positionings within a group that perpetuate its ideologies.

Such a model would recognize a multilayered social indexing of language, similar to Silverstein's (1996) orders of indexicality. The model would index at least four levels of social relationship: a local stance within an ongoing speech event, a position within an institution, a status in wider society, and, potentially at least, a place within a cultural model or script. And we have seen that there could be indexing within these levels as well, as local dominance relationships are indexed by a primary indexing of the cultural model.

Summary

We have seen how language is used by the men to reproduce a hegemonic heterosexuality which is embedded in the larger context of hegemonic masculinity. We saw that their society (greek-letter society) is organized around an ideology of difference and how the speech activities which make up this society – both mixed and single sex – are based on the notion of sexual difference and heterosexuality. There is an elaborate cultural script around different kinds of heterosexuality, and these have led to the naming of these scripts and speech activities: throwing raps, scamming, a drunk story, the commitment thing. One of the most secret and sacred genres of the fraternity is centred around narratives of heterosexuality: fuck stories. In interaction, men metaphorically represent other men as women in order to claim dominance over that man (even in play), as we saw for the 'Hi honey I'm home' line, as well as 'bitch'. The metaphorical assignment of homosexuality worked in a similar way. These two metaphors find a complex but telling synthesis in the term 'bitch boy'. Importantly, in all of these examples the men were performing relationships for the men. We thus see that heterosexuality is embedded in the more important relationships of male dominance hierarchies and homosociability.

Similar practices of cathexis have been discussed by ethnographers of other European cultures. For example, Almeida (1996) describes a variant of the 'fuck story' genre told by the men he studied in a Portuguese village. He also describes a similar dichotomy of heterosexuality focusing on women as sexual partners and women as marriage partners. The fraternity men and the Portuguese men show how much time and effort go into displaying these kinds of heterosexuality: For both groups of men, these stories are central to their socializing, and are something exalted and enjoyed, not merely expected.

Most importantly, these speech strategies of heterosexuality are how men in both cultures create status among their peers. Heterosexuality is thus not just about sexual object choice, but it also has a social construction that is primarily used by social actors to compete within same sex groups. This pattern suggests that patterns of male domination are not simply about men dominating women. Rather, in both cultures, male domination in heterosexual displays is about men displaying power *over* other men (and women) to other men. The stories and other forms of heterosexual display therefore represent same-sex status competition in which heterosexual gender differentiation and dominance is not the goal, but one strategy with which to construct a hegemonic masculinity. This finding suggests that in order to understand language and gender patterns, we need to understand how language is used to create difference and status within gender groups.

Transcription conventions

[ ]	Bounds simultaneous speech.
=	Connects two utterances produced with noticeably less transition time between them than usual.
(number)	Silences timed in tenths of seconds.
#	Bounds passage said very quickly.
^	Falsetto.
TEXT	Upper case letters indicate noticeably loud volume.
°	Indicates noticeably low volume, placed around the soft words.
Text	Italics indicates emphatic delivery (volume and/or pitch).
-	Indicates that the sound that precedes is stopped suddenly.

:	Indicates the sound that precedes it is prolonged.
,	Indicates a slight intonational rise.
?	Indicates a sharp intonational rise.
he, ha	Laughter.
(text)	Transcript enclosed in single parenthesis indicates uncertain hearing.
((comment))	Double parentheses enclose transcriber's comments.

Chapter 11

Hideko Abe

2004

LESBIAN BAR TALK
IN SHINJUKU, TOKYO

THIS CHAPTER FOCUSES ON the relationship between identity and language use observed among women at lesbian bars in Shinjuku, Tokyo. I chose lesbian bars as a setting for ethnographic linguistic study because lesbians, in contrast to gays, have been generally underrepresented in Japanese studies. Watanabe (1990) argues that lesbianism in Japan has historically been marginalized and is much less well documented than male homosexuality. As Moonwomon-Baird puts it, 'Lesbian practice is regarded as marked behavior, but goes unremarked much more than is true of gay male practice, even in this era of both friendly and hostile societal discourse on queers' (1997: 202).

This study discusses two issues: (1) naming and identity construction in discourse and (2) linguistic behaviour and interaction at lesbian bars. In the first part of this chapter, I examine how certain terms of social categorization are used to differentiate one individual's identity from others and how the social spaces of lesbian bars help individuals construct, renew, or vitalize their identities. Then I discuss how lesbian speech at bars tends to contain extensive use of masculine forms with wide contextual and individual variation. As I will discuss later, these two phenomena are crucial to understanding the relationship between Japanese lesbian identities and linguistic practice.

Method and data collection

Tokyo's Shinjuku Ni-choome 'the Second Block', an area as small as 300 meters by 400 meters, is often referred to as the world's largest gay town. It was formerly a district inhabited by Japanese female prostitutes who served American personnel during the Occupation after World War II. According to a recent gay travel guide, there are 217 gay bars in Ni-choome. By contrast, there are 12 lesbian bars in Ni-choome and one in Sanchoome 'the Third Block' in Tokyo, four in Osaka, and one each in Kyuushuu and Hokkaido.

The fieldwork for this study was conducted between September of 1999 and June of 2000 in the Shinjuku area of Tokyo. I visited lesbian bars almost every week, spending at least two to three hours as a customer and researcher at each bar. I also corresponded with employees via e-mail. In total, there are 13 lesbian bars in Shinjuku, and I visited 12 of them; I spent considerable time at some, and others I visited only once. Not all lesbian bars are the same; some target older middle-class professional women while others target younger nonprofessional women, both middle- and working-class. However, some bars have both types of women. All employees of the bars are lesbians.

Whenever I visited a bar for the first time, I arrived at opening time so that I could be the first customer and spend time alone with the owner or the manager of the bar to explain my research. This is when I asked for permission to take field notes. I was allowed to have a notebook in front of me and to make notes at any time. Often employees jokingly said to me, 'a *mata nan ka kaiteru*', 'she's writing something again' while they were serving other customers. I conducted interviews with owners and employees but also interacted with other customers, all of whom knew of my research project. I did not tape-record interactions at bars, nor did I conduct interviews outside the bars. There are two reasons for not recording the interactions. The first is that there was always loud music playing at the bars, which would have made recording almost impossible. Second, and more important, the bar owners and employees did not agree to recording. The reason was clear. In most bars, women are anonymous and it was important that they be allowed to remain so. My sources of data thus are (1) interviews, (2) field notes, (3) articles from magazines, and (4) e-mail messages.

Naming and identity construction in discourses at lesbian bars

The definition of the community served by lesbian bars turned out to be broader than I had expected. While some owners and employees described their businesses as places that catered only to a female clientele, some welcome *onabe* and *nyuu haafu* 'transsexual/transgendered people' and even gay male friends of customers or employees. Owners and employees generally assume that female clientele are homosexual or bisexual but welcome others. During my visit to one bar, I encountered a situation in which a *jooren*, 'regular customer' brought her friend and introduced her to the owner and employees as a *nonke*, 'straight'. It appears that a customer's sexuality has to be stated explicitly if she or he is straight.

I found it crucial to differentiate between a lesbian bar and an *onabe* bar. The word *onabe*, 'pan', which is parallel to *okama*, 'pot', meaning male homosexuals, is often used to refer to lesbians in a broad sense, but the two words, lesbian and *onabe*, are not the same (Valentine 1997), as is clearly demonstrated in example (1). In this example, the manager (A) of a lesbian bar is talking about her sexuality.

> (1)   *Yoosuru nijishoteki ni wa dooseeaisha tte koto ni narimasu ne. Onabe to chigau no wa, jibun no josee to yuu see o mitometa ue de, josee ga suki tte yuu.*

'Anyway, I am a homosexual by the dictionary definition. How I
am different from *onabe* is that I accept my sex as female and like
women'.

Another employee (B) at a different lesbian bar contends that a lesbian is a woman
who feels comfortable with her female body (in other words, with her biologically
female sex) and who chooses a woman as a partner. Unlike straight women, her
identity as a woman is constructed through a relationship with another woman.
However, according to this employee, an *onabe* loves women and chooses a
woman as a partner, but an *onabe's* social and emotional identity is male. Thus,
both the concept of *onabe* and that of lesbian challenge the conventional heterosexual gender arrangement, yet her explanation remains restricted within the binary
'woman'/'man'.

The same employee (A) explains the difference between *onabe* and *rezu* (or
rezubian), 'lesbians', in example (2).

(2)   *Chigaimasu ne. Ishikiteki ni mo. Kore wa yoku iwareru n desu kedo,*
      onabe san wa, rezu no ko to wa tsukiattari, anmari shinai n desu yo.
      Sore wa, onabe san wa jibun ga otoko to shite miraretai tte yuu no ga
      aru kara, onna o suki na rezu no ko to wa, tsukiaenai.

      'Yes, we are different. Consciously as well. People often say this
      – *onabe* do not date lesbians. Because they want to be seen as
      men, they cannot date a lesbian who likes women'.

It is significant that the speaker added *-san* 'Ms./Mr.' to *onabe* and *ko* 'child' to
rezu. The former emphasizes the distance between the speaker and the referent,
while the latter constructs an intimate or friendly relationship. This kind of identity construction through naming is also found in other interviews.

Onabe bars, then, are butch-type bars where staff members usually wear men's
clothes and work as hosts. There are three *onabe* bars in Tokyo (Valentine 1997).
Customers at *onabe* bars are usually half lesbians and half *nonke* 'straight women'.
According to many employees of *rezubian* bars, these bars are places where
customers, who may be *onabe* or lesbians, and employees are on equal terms,
whereas in *onabe* bars employees are there to serve customers. They also suggest
that customers who are tired of *onabe* bars may move on to host bars, where young
straight men serve women.

Nine of the 13 lesbian bars accept only women, including heterosexuals, *onabe*,
and *nyuu haafu*. In example (3), a manager (C) of another lesbian bar talks about
her clientele.

(3)   *Toriaezu, rezu no okyaku sama ga taihan nan desu kedo, rezu ja nai ko*
      mo iru n desu ne. Rezu wa rezu de kakusazu ni, soo ja nai ko mo
      tanoshiku. Betsu ni itsu mo rezu no wadai bakkari tte wake nai kara.
      Dansee wa ne, watashi no hontoo ni goku shitashii homo no kata to ka,
      soo yuu hito dake desu ne. Yappari onna no ko ga dansee no me o ki ni
      shinai de kiraku ni nomeru tte koto de, kihonteki ni dansee wa dame
      desu. Onabe no ko to ka nyuu haafu no ko to ka kiraku ni asobi ni kite

kureru shi, futsuu no onna no ko datte ii shi. Mattaku futsuu no otoko wa dame. Dono janru ga doo ka ja nakute, mainoritii de zenzen oorai. Soo soo, guroobaru na imi de nan de mo oorai.

'Anyway, the majority of our customers are lesbians, but there are some who aren't. For lesbians, they don't have to hide their identity. Nonlesbians can have a good time here too. We don't talk only about lesbianism, you know. As for male customers, only a few close homosexual friends of mine can come here. As a rule, we don't allow male customers because we want to provide a place where women feel comfortable drinking without worrying about men's eyes. People who are *onabe* or *nyuu haafu* come here as well. Ordinary [meaning heterosexual] women are also welcome. But ordinary men are not welcome here. I'm not categorizing people, but as long as they are a minority, they're totally welcome. Yes, anybody in a global sense is welcome'.

Whereas speaker (A) in example (2) added *-san* to *onabe*, speaker (C) uses the term *ko* 'child/young person' (instead of *hito* or *kata*, two terms for 'person'), as in *onabe no ko* 'a young *onabe*' and *nyuu-haafu no ko* 'a young *nyuu haafu*'. This shift indicates that onabe are here treated as in-group members (customers). This use of *ko* is a reflection of the fact that the majority of customers are in their twenties (younger than the owners or employees) and also that employees want to sound more inclusive and intimate. The alternative words, *hito* or *kata*, are more formal and distant. Interestingly, the women I interviewed never use *ko* to refer to men; instead they use *dansei* 'men' or *otoko* 'men' or even *homo no kata* 'homosexuals'. Otherness is emphasized by non-use of *ko*.

Linguistic behavior and interactions at bars

In this section, I discuss several linguistic features found in interactions at lesbian bars among employees as well as between employees and customers.

First-person pronouns

Previous studies have claimed that the use of first- and second-person pronouns exhibits the most gender-differentiated characteristics of the Japanese language. Ide (1979) asserts that the first-person pronouns *watakushi* and *watashi* are used by both sexes, the forms *boku* and *ore* (standard) as well as *wagahai* and *washi* (nonstandard) are used exclusively by men, and the forms *atakushi* and *atashi* (standard) as well as *atai* and *uchi* (non-standard) are used by women. Kanamaru (1997) claims that *jibun* is also a masculine form. *Jibun* is a reflexive pronoun; its use as a personal pronoun is relatively old-fashioned and is often associated with men in sports or in militaristic groups such as the *jieetai* 'self-defense army' or the police force. It is clear that these options for first-person pronouns reflect the strong sense of an idealized form of women's and men's speech. However, the choice of personal pronouns is not as categorical as was once believed. Women in different parts of

Japan may have different options and women in different parts of the age spectrum may use different forms.

An example from the bisexual and lesbian magazine *Anise* (Hagiwara 1997) gives some insight into the use of first-person pronouns among lesbians, *onabe*, and transsexuals. Examples (4)–(7) are drawn from the magazine transcript of a panel discussion among six people, two self-identified female-to-male transsexuals (T1 and T2), two self-identified *onabe* (O1 and O2), and two self-identified lesbians (Ll and L2). They are talking about their gender.

(4)   T1:   *Boku wa rezubian ga kirai nan ja nakute, rezu ikooru onna, jibun ga onna ni mirareru no ga iya datta.*
'It is not that I dislike lesbians, but lesbian means a woman. I didn't want to be perceived as a woman'.

O2:   *Jibun mo yoku rezu tte iwarete 'jibun wa otoko nan da' tte tomodachi to kenka shimashita.*
'I was also told that I'm a lesbian. I used to fight with my friends for saying that I'm a man'.

(5)   T2:   *Boku wa nenrei ga agareba penisu ga haete kuru mon da to omotte ita,n desu yo.*
'I believed that once I got older, I would grow a penis'.

(6)   L1:   *Watashi wa monogokoro tsuita toki kara, zutto onna no ko ga suki datta. Otoko to ka onabe ni naritai tte kimochi mo atta kedo, seken no hito wa otoko na no ka onna na no ka waketagaru n da yo ne. Ippan shakai de wa joshi toire ni wa hairenai shi.*
'Ever since I was a child, I always liked girls. There was a time when I wanted to be a man or *onabe*. People want to categorize themselves into men or women. In this society, I can't use a public women's bathroom'.

L2:   *Watashi wa joshi toire ni hairu yo.*
'I use a women's bathroom'.

(7)   O2:   *Jibun mo danjo to ka kangaenai hoo nan desu yo.*
'I tend not to think about if someone is a man or woman'.

The three groups of speakers use first-person pronouns distinctively; the transsexuals use *boku*, the *onabe* use *jibun*, and the lesbians use *watashi* almost uniformly. It is as if there is a rule for them to use a different personal pronoun depending on their own identity (at least in this context).

The use of first-person pronouns shown in examples (4)–(7), however, does not mean that each speaker uses the same pronoun no matter what context s/he is in. Further analysis suggests that speakers negotiate gendered speech norms in each context. This negotiation becomes more apparent if we examine examples in which a speaker shifts the use of pronoun forms, which is frequently observed at lesbian bars. In fact, one of the participants in the panel discussion (Ll) is an employee at a lesbian bar I often visited, where I observed her use of *jibun*. Moreover, I observed the use of several first-person pronouns at lesbian bars: *watashi*, *atashi*, *ore*, *washi*, and *jibun*, with the same speaker using multiple first-person pronouns depending on the context. One of the first questions I often asked at bars concerned the use of personal pronouns. Younger employees in their early twenties exclusively listed *jibun* 'oneself' (a form commonly considered masculine) as their favorite first-person pronoun. One employee explained that she uses the term because *watashi* and *atashi* exhibit too much femininity, but she does not want to use *boku* or other 'masculine' first-person pronouns because she is not a man. She said that she refuses to *dooitsuka-suru* 'merge and identify' with men. An employee at a different bar argued, 'Why do I need to use *boku*? I don't even like men'. Her use of *jibun* is illustrated in example (8).

(8)   *Kutte nee, jibun wa. Nan da, nan ni mo nee jan.*
       'I haven't eaten. What! There's nothing left'.

This employee was 21 years old and had been working at the bar for several months. Asked by her female supervisor if she had eaten something before coming to work, she replied, using *jibun*. During the course of the evening, this young employee maintained the use of *jibun* irrespective of whether she was talking to her coworkers or to customers. As she puts it, for her, *jibun* is the most neutral personal pronoun available. The use of *jibun* was observed at all the bars in my study.

However, at a bar down the street I observed a quite different interaction. The employee in example (9) was 20 years old and had been working almost a year. When I entered, there was nobody but her in the bar. We introduced ourselves and started talking about various things such as why she started working there and whether she enjoyed working at the bar. When I noticed her using *jibun* in our interaction, I asked the reason for her choice. Her answer was that she did not want to sound too feminine by using *watashi* or *atashi*. She added that *jibun* was her favorite term and that she did not use other 'masculine' personal pronouns, unlike her boss, who uses *washi*. It is interesting to note that *washi* presents a more 'masculine' nuance to her than *jibun*. However, her answer does not reflect her actual speaking practices. She and I had been talking alone for more than two hours when the telephone rang. The caller was a regular customer, whom this employee knew very well. The employee explained to me that there had been a party at the bar the night before during which this customer got drunk and did some crazy things that upset the employees and other customers, but the customer claimed that she did not remember anything. The employee did not believe she had forgotten. The employee's side of the conversation was as follows.

(9)   *Omee na, fuzaken na yo, ore oko-ru yo.*
       'Are you kidding? I'll get mad at you'.

       Jaa, A-san ni kiite mi na yo.
       'Then, ask A'.

       Anne, soo da yo, anta, minna ni meewaku kaketa n da kara.
       'You bothered everyone'.

> *Ore* sugee koshi itai man. Koshi ni kita yo.
> 'As for me, my lower back hurts. It really hurts'.

Here we see the employee's shift from *jibun* in her conversation with me to *ore* in her interaction with her customer. In the first instance of *ore*, the speaker is expressing her anger or frustration and thus is very emotionally involved. In the second instance, she is describing how much pain she has now thanks to the customer. The use of *ore* in this example as opposed to her previous use of *jibun* exhibits negotiation of multiple identity positions in relation to different contexts. For her, *jibun* is used in more formal settings of interaction, such as an interaction with a relatively new customer who is also a researcher, but *ore* is her preferred choice in more intimate and emotional contexts.

The use of *boku* is quite different. The speaker in example (10) is a lesbian customer in her mid thirties who works at a computer graphics company. She and I had been discussing the use of first-person pronouns for a while and I had noticed that she used *atashi* in our conversation. When I asked if she ever used different first-person pronouns, she answered by saying:

(10) *Atashi* wa kyosee o haru toki, '*boku*' o tsuka-u.
      'I (*atashi*) use I (*boku*) when [I] make a false show of power'.

She added that she uses *boku* in arguments at her workplace with her male boss, who may suspect that she is lesbian, and claims that this helps her situate herself at the boss's level. Here the speaker explicitly recognizes the forcefulness attached to 'masculine' forms. She also expressed the belief that the 'feminine' first-person pronoun, *atashi*, did not make her strong. However, in explaining the use of *boku* the speaker used the term *kyosee* 'false show of power', literally, *kyo* 'emptiness' + *see* 'power, force', which implies merely a superficial or even empty power.

Second-person pronouns

Second-person pronouns are also considered highly gendered, but to a lesser degree than first-person pronouns. Many researchers identify two forms (*anata* and *anta*) for women and five or more forms (*anata*, *anta*, *kimi*, *omae*., *kisama*, *otaku*, and *temee*) for men (Ide 1979; Kanamaru 1997). However, actual uses of second-person pronouns do not necessarily conform to these gender classifications.

I found two types of second-person pronouns at the bars I studied: *anta* and *omee*. The frequency of these two terms is not high, since speakers generally prefer to use nicknames or first names. *Anata* 'you', a more formal second-person pronoun, is almost never used. The use of *omee*, a very casual 'masculine' second-person pronoun, is found among close friends at bars, between employees and customers, and between customers. In example (9), the speaker used both *anta* and *omee* in criticizing one of her customers. *Omee* is used to express the employee's extreme rage toward the customer (*omee no, fuzaken na yo*), whereas *anta* accompanies an attempt at persuasion (*soo da yo, anta, minna ni meewaku kaketa n da kara*). Thus, the shift between the two pronouns reflects the change in her emotional state.

The customer (in 10) who uses *boku* in arguments with her boss also told me that she uses *omee* when she argues with close male friends, adding that *omee* has a certain forcefulness that cannot be expressed by *anta* or *omae*, a term that is stereo-typically associated with male speakers. The speakers in these examples both assert that *omee* helps them argue more persuasively. Both speakers are manipulating the pragmatic meaning (forcefulness) attached to the term *omee*.

Commands and requests

Other linguistic forms that are often associated with gender roles are found in commands and requests. For instance, the use of bald imperative verb forms, such as *tabero* 'eat', is generally considered to indicate that the interlocutor is not in a superior position and also that the speaker is a man. This type of imperative is traditionally categorized as a 'masculine' form (Martin 1975). Tohsaku (1999: 43) notes that this type of imperative form 'sounds very blunt and harsh' and says that female speakers should not use it at all.

Despite this prescription, example (9) includes strong imperative forms. The first negative imperative, *fuzaken na* 'don't mess with me', can be articulated differently in different contexts, from the most formal *fuzakenai de kudasai*, to *fuzakenai de*, to the very informal *fuzakeru na*. The assimilation and reduction of *-ru* (in *fuzakeru na*) to *-n* (in *fuzaken na*) indexes even stronger roughness or toughness. As noted earlier, the speaker in this example is extremely angry and emotionally involved.

Sentence-final particles

The last linguistic feature I discuss here is sentence-final particles. The functions of these forms have been identified as (1) indicating the speaker's emotions and attitudes such as doubt, caution, and confirmation (Martin 1975: 914, Makino and Tsutsui 1986: 45); (2) encouraging rapport between speech participants (Makino and Tsutsui 1986: 45); (3) achieving a close monitoring of the feelings between speech participants (Maynard 1987: 28); and (4) expressing one's own masculinity and/or femininity (Makino and Tsutsui 1986: 49). Traditional gender classification of sentence-final particles suggests three types: (1) feminine forms, which are said to be predominantly used by female speakers (e.g., *wa* with a rising intonation, *na no/na no ne, kashira*); (2) masculine forms, used by male speakers (e.g., *zo/za, da, da yo*); and (3) neutral forms, used by both women and men (e.g., *yo ne, ka no*). As Okamoto (2004) argues, the traditional classification should be understood as a reference point rather than a description of actual use.

The actual use of sentence-final particles at the lesbian bars bears this point out. The most frequently used sentence-final particles are *yo* and its variations such as *da yo* and *da yo ne*. For example, in (11) an employee and a few customers are chatting while looking at a magazine article, which describes an *onabe* bar.

(11) Customer: *Kore otoko <u>da yo</u>, hakkiri itte.*
      'This is a man, frankly speaking'.

   Employee: *Kurabete moraitaku nai ne.*
      'I don't want you to compare me with this guy'.

The customer points out that the figure in the picture in the magazine looks like a man. She uses *da yo* in this utterance. As mentioned earlier, in the conventional classification, *da yo* is regarded as a masculine form. Yet it seems that this form is used more commonly used by many women than it used to be (Abe 2000). Thus, it is possible that this form is neutral for this speaker.

Other conventional masculine forms are found in example (12). Here younger employees, who typically refer to themselves as *jibun*, are talking with some customers in their thirties. Two of them are trying to remove a spot from the surface of a toy.

(12) Employee: *Kosutte mo torenee n <u>da</u>.*
        'We can't get rid of it even by rubbing'.

      Customer: *Nani ka iro ga chiga-u <u>zo</u>.*
        'Hey, the color is somehow different!'

The employee uses *da*, a (moderately) masculine form, and the customer uses *zo*, which is often classified as strongly masculine. In addition, the 'rough' negative form, *nee*, is used instead of *nai*. Moreover, the speaker uses *kuu* 'to eat' instead of *taberu* 'to eat'. The latter is a standard form of the verb, while *kuu* suggests 'masculine' speech. This speaker elsewhere uses the plain interrogative form *ka* (verb + *ka*) in *Ureshii ka* 'are you happy?' and *Nomu ka* 'do you want to drink?' another construction associated with 'masculine' speech. This type of question form is usually considered too strong and rude for women to use.

In sum, these speakers are rejecting the forms that they feel are too feminine, while adopting masculine or neutral forms. Their use of masculine forms, however, does not mean that lesbians want to be identified as men, as the discussion on the difference between lesbian and *onabe* clearly demonstrates, nor is it simply a case of butch lesbians speaking like men. On the other hand, even though they may consider themselves women (also indicated earlier in their comparison of lesbians and *onabe*), they are not using stereotypical feminine forms. I argue, therefore, that their linguistic choices indicate that they are marking their difference in speech, which, they believe, supports their identities as lesbians. Speakers use masculine speech styles in a complex way in order to express a variety of context-dependent meanings related to their lesbian identities and relationships.

Chapter 12

Robert J. Podesva, Sarah J. Roberts and Kathryn Campbell-Kibler

2002

SHARING RESOURCES AND INDEXING MEANINGS IN THE PRODUCTION OF GAY STYLES

Introduction

IN RECENT YEARS AN INCREASING NUMBER of linguists have criticized sociolinguistic approaches to style limited to correlations between linguistic variation and pre-defined social categories. Instead, researchers such as Ochs (1991), Irvine (2001), and the California Style Collective (1993), have sought to highlight the ways in which linguistic practice produces and reproduces social meaning.

Drawing on this work, we propose a new approach to style, which centers around two important concepts. First of all, we distinguish between linguistically conveyed meanings relating directly to the immediate context of the discourse participants, and those involving the construction of personal or stylistic identities. Further, we argue that indexical relationships (in the sense developed in Ochs 1991) relate these different types of social meaning to each other, as well as to linguistic resources. Using this approach, we examine a gay activist's use of phonetic features in a radio interview to project a style which is markedly gay and yet differs from the style usually identified as gay by researchers and the culture at large.

Gay ways of speaking

Sociolinguistic research on the speaking styles of gay men has centered on identifying the features that constitute a monolithic speech variety, often referred to as Gay Speech or the Gay Accent. Scholars have argued that the speech of gay men, or alternatively gay-sounding speech, differentiates itself from other speaking styles on the lexical (e.g., Rodgers 1972), phonetic (e.g., Crist 1997), and discourse (e.g., Leap 1996) levels. Although we do not question that some segments of the gay male community may use the features discussed in these works, we take issue with the practice of labeling them as specifically gay male features. We argue that labeling a linguistic feature as gay is at once too general and too specific.

First, the assumption that there is a singular gay way of speaking homogenizes the diversity within the gay community, erasing or at least deeming unimportant to sociolinguistic inquiry the many subcultures comprising the community. Gay culture encompasses reified categories such as leather daddies, clones, drag queens, circuit boys, guppies (gay yuppies), gay prostitutes, and activists both mainstream and radical, as well as more local communities of practice which may not even have names. Membership in one of the subcultures often takes precedence over a more general affiliation with the gay community, and social activities – and hence opportunities for linguistic exchanges – are usually organized around membership not in the gay male community at large, but in its subcultures. The distinction between the subcultures constructed stylistically, through dress, use and choice of drugs, music preferences, and linguistic resources. The meanings of stylistic resources, linguistic or otherwise, are negotiated in these gay subcultures. Thus treating the meaning of a linguistic feature as generally as gay ignores the community that has worked to give the feature meaning.

Second, while labeling linguistic features as gay is too general, it also runs the risk of not being general enough. By simply assigning gay meanings to linguistic features, one reifies as gay certain linguistic features that are shared throughout society. For instance, Leap (1996) identifies cooperative discourse as a marker of 'Gay Men's English,' but Cameron (1998) points out that cooperative discourse also occurs among young heterosexual men. And then there are the original coop- erators: women, the subject of the first discussions of cooperative discourse in the language and gender literature (e.g., Coates 1998b; Tannen 1990). By labeling cooperative discourse as a specifically gay feature, one ignores its use by women and straight men. What is missing is an analysis that allows cooperative discourse to contribute to heterosexuality in some situations and to the construction of gay identities in others.

To avoid these two problems, we propose a framework for style in which linguistic features become associated with communities by indexing the stances, acts, and activities that characterize and constitute them. Such a framework moves beyond linguistic features that directly index gross demographic characteristics (e.g., gay), allowing for linguistic features that index social meaning on a micro-level. At the same time the framework enables linguistic resources to index identities through intermediary social meanings (e.g., stance of precision), and these social meanings may be shared across communities. In the following section we explicitly lay out our framework for style.

Style

We view style as the situational use of linguistic resources (including phonetic variables, syntactic constructions, lexicon, discourse markers) to negotiate one's place in the local communicative context as well as in society in general. Style permeates language not as a separate component or dimension but as a building block for creating and perpetuating social meaning. However since meaning is always somewhat in flux and dependent on the ever-changing contexts in which resources are used, style itself is always a work in progress.

This approach differs considerably from many contemporary approaches to style. In variationist sociolinguistics, style (intraspeaker variation) is usually treated as unidimensional and linked in some way to stable social categories. Labov (1966) and others regard style as a function of attention paid to speech, ranging from casual to highly monitored speech. Their methodology reveals the stratification of social categories such as class or 'sex' by correlating linguistic variation to stylistic variation. This approach shows that categories have empirical relevance to linguistic variation, but (as with any correlational approach) it does not reveal whether categories shape linguistic practice or are themselves derivative of language use. It also assumes the stability of both style and social categories; this methodology routinely elicits pre-defined 'styles' from speakers (such as Casual Style, Reading Style, etc.) and categories serve to locate a given speaker within a fixed social structure. Finally, this approach limits style to a single dimension and does not explain how situational and interactional factors, such as social power, mode of interaction, topic, setting, contribute to intraspeaker variation.

Bell (1984) proposed an alternative unidimensional approach that treats style as interpersonal audience accommodation. Drawing on accommodation theory (Coupland and Giles 1988), Bell proposed that style represents efforts by speakers to converge with or diverge from the speech of their addressee(s). As a result, style as intra-speaker variation is derivative of interspeaker variation (the style axiom). In a recent revision to his model (Bell 1997: 244) he highlights the role of identity and differentiation in the production of style. He characterizes the process along the following lines:

1.   Group has its own identity, evaluated by self and others.
2.   Group differentiates its language from others': 'social,' or inter-speaker variation.
3.   Group's language is evaluated by self and others: linguistic evaluation.
4.   Others shift relative to group's language: 'style,' or intra-speaker variation.

Identity therefore serves as the basis of social and linguistic differentiation, and evaluation links social attitudes towards groups to the groups' patterns of variation. These attitudes then filter down to the level of intraspeaker variation: 'Style derives its meaning from the association of linguistic features with particular social groups' (1997: 243).

Bell's model however takes as its starting point predefined 'groups' which already possess their own identities. It accepts uncritically the notion, questioned by Cameron (1998) and others, that identity is a predetermined and stable fact instead of a construct constituted through social and linguistic practice. As research in the field of language and gender has often shown, identity cannot be separated from the social performances that produce and perpetuate meaning. By making style a by-product of identity, Bell precludes the possibility of style as a means of constituting group identities.

Our approach to style, in accordance with recent research on identity and the role played by language in forming identity, assumes that identity and style are co-constructed. Instead of treating stylistic variation as merely reflective of one's social address or identity, we view style as the linguistic means through which identity is produced in discourse. A style may be viewed as a collage of co-occurring linguistic features which, while unfixed and variable, work together to constitute meaning in coherent and socially intelligible ways. Style simultaneously gives linguistic substance to a given identity and allows the identity to be socially meaningful.

Irvine (2001: 77) mentions that distinctiveness underlies both style and identity: 'Whatever "styles" are, in language and elsewhere, they are part of a system of distinction, in which a style contrasts with other possible styles, and the social meaning signified by the style contrasts with other social meanings.' Along these lines, we need to examine a style not just in relation to others it may draw on, but also in relation to those other styles to which it opposes itself – particularly in the local, situational contexts in which styles are produced. In the case of gay styles one would need to consider how a given style opposes itself to other perceived gay styles (such as those associated with the various subcultures mentioned in the previous section), in addition to the obvious opposition between gay and straight. An approach to gay speech that posits a single dimension of identity or 'gayness' independent of local context misses not only much of the diversity within the gay community but also ignores Zwicky's (1997: 31) observation that variables are employed by 'different speakers, in different places, on different occasions.'

Ochs (1991) proposes an explicit framework for understanding how linguistic resources are linked to abstract categories or groups. Most resources are not correlated directly to social categories. Rather they bear pragmatic information about particular situations. Certain resources may contribute to stances and acts that impact the immediate speech situation; for instance, 'tag questions may index a stance of uncertainty as well as the act of requesting confirmation/clarification/feedback' (Ochs 1991: 335). At the same time, speakers derive from past experiences an understanding that these resources are differently used across society and therefore develop 'norms, preferences, and expectations regarding the distribution of this work *vis-à-vis* particular social identities of speakers, referents, and addressees' (1991: 342). As a result, resources may indirectly index abstract social categories in a constitutive sense; for instance, one may lay claim to a female identity by using tag questions to produce a stance of hesitancy, which in some communities is normatively associated with female identity.

So while a few variables directly index a given category (such as the indexing of male gender by the pronoun *he* or the use of *gay* to index a putative gay category), most index categories only indirectly and function primarily to express pragmatic meanings relating to local context. The meanings that contribute to style may either derive directly from the use of linguistic resources or indirectly via the speech acts, activities (socially-defined speech events such as debate or prayer), or stances that speakers perform in the course of conversation.

For instance, /in/ vs. /iŋ/ variation (as in *workin'* vs. *working*) is a classic example of a variable which expresses a stance of informality, contributes to working class styles, and is meaningful ideologically in contrasting a friendly, close-knit working class group against a more institutionally-based middle class (Eckert 2000). This approach allows us to incorporate Labov's concern for formality/informality (which he characterized as attention paid to speech) while distancing variation from simple demographic characteristics. Conversely, styles that are legibly associated with certain social groups may be used to enact certain stances. Cheshire (1997) discusses the case of a teenaged boy increasing his use of vernacular markers in a school setting relative to his out-of-school speech, in contrast to his friends, who decrease their use of the variables at school. In this case he uses his vernacular style to display a stance of resistance against the authority of the school.

Our priorities, as set forth by this approach to style, would include the identification of linguistic resources that are used to constitute different gay styles, an analysis of how these resources are used to index different meanings, and speculation on how a particular style may index more than a single category at the same time – as one's identity as gay is hardly independent from other possible identities relevant to a given context. In the data presented below, we examine what might be termed 'mainstream gay activist style,' which is here constructed in the setting of a radio discussion, primarily in opposition to a straight audience, as well as to a more flamboyant gay style. Gay identity is highly salient for representatives of gay political organizations, especially in public discussions. But at the same time, participants are frequently warned against sounding 'too gay.' We suggest that the style displayed is an attempt to portray at once strong gay identity and professional competence – as evaluated by a mainstream, mostly straight audience.

The study

The radio discussion selected as a data source for this study occurred on a popular National Public Radio talk show and dealt with a politically sensitive gay issue: namely, whether private voluntary organizations reserve the right to ban gays from their membership. Our study focuses on the speech of Speaker A, an openly gay attorney and reasonably famous gay rights activist. We chose to examine his speech because it evoked a strong gay percept and because his contribution was of suitable length for phonetic analysis. When he appeared on the radio program, he was representing in court an individual who had been dismissed from such an organization. Although the host introduced issues directly bearing on gay identity at the outset of the program, the debate mainly revolved around an intricate discussion of anti-discrimination laws. Speaker A's contribution foregrounded his expertise in interpreting law and repeatedly named the ousted individual as his professional 'client.' For the most part, he was speaking more as an attorney than as a gay man.

We contrast Speaker A's speech with that of Speaker B, his opponent in the debate. Speaker B was a representative of a libertarian organization, and his speech did not evoke a gay percept. Their primary point of contestation did not revolve around gay rights but rather concerned the role of government in regulating the internal affairs of private organizations. Speaker B, in fact, made it clear that he

did not personally favor the discrimination. Since the issue structuring the opposition between the two speakers called on Speaker A's legal expertise instead of his
experience as a gay man, Speaker A's role as attorney was emphasized.

An acoustic analysis was conducted on the speech of Speakers A and B, concentrating on the following variables:

1.   Durations of /æ/, /eɪ/
2.   Durations of onset /s/, /l/
3.   Fundamental frequency (f0) properties (max. mm, range, and value at vowel
     midpoint) of stressed vowels
4.   Voice onset time (VOT) of voiceless aspirated stops
5.   Release of word-final stops

Though we have opted to call these phonetic features variables, we do not use
the term in the traditional sociolinguistic sense. Rather than coding data categori-
cally, we have quantified values acoustically. For example, the duration of a segment
is coded in milliseconds rather than with a perceptual label, such as short or long.
With the exception of word-final stop releases, all variables considered here are
continuous.

Following Crist (1997), who reported that for five out of six male speakers
the segments /s/ and /l/ were longer in gay stereotyped speech, we examined
the duration of /s/ and /l/ in onset position. Rogers, Smyth, and Jacobs (2000)
have since duplicated Crist's finding, showing that sibilants (both /s/ and /z/) and
the lateral approximant (/l/) exhibit greater duration in gay-sounding speech.

The pitch properties of Speakers A and B were also investigated, since high
pitch and wide pitch ranges are often anecdotally associated with gay styles of
speaking. Though Gaudio (1994) found that neither pitch range nor pitch variability
provided sufficient cues to yield a gay percept, Jacobs, Rogers, and Smyth (1999)
have recently found that listeners are more likely to identify speakers as gay if they
have large pitch ranges, regardless of whether the speakers are gay or straight. Four
measures of fundamental frequency (f0), the acoustic correlate of pitch, were taken
for each stressed vowel: maximum f0, minimum f0, f0 at vowel midpoint, and f0
range.

The variables discussed thus far – the durations of onset /s/ and /l/ and the
four measures of fundamental frequency – have been associated with stereotypically
gay speech, but Speaker A does not employ a flamboyantly gay style. We have
therefore identified a number of other variables that could potentially be used in
an activist style based on our impressionistic judgments from radio interviews
with six gay activists. These variables included the durations of the vowels /æ/
and /eɪ/, the duration of voice onset time (or aspiration) for voiceless stops,
and the release of word-final stops. Unlike the continuous variables discussed
above, the release of word-final stops was coded as a boolean: marked for the presence or absence of a burst. Long voice onset time (VOT) and the frequent release
of word-final stops exemplify hyperarticulation, a feature identified by Walters
(1981), as cited by Barrett (1997).

We now turn to a discussion of Speaker A's stylistic construction of identity
using the phonetic features reviewed in this section.

Results

The variables we examined fall into roughly three categories. We first discuss segment duration of onset /s/, onset /l/, /æ/, /eɪ/, and aspiration of voiceless stops. These variables group together naturally as the findings for any one segment cannot be analyzed without looking at the others, given the strong influence of overall speech rate. Next, we present the findings related to f0: the high and low for each vowel (stressed vowels in multisyllabic words), the range (difference between them), and the f0 at the midpoint of the vowel. Finally, we give the results for the frequency with which each speaker released final stops.

The duration variables do not lend themselves to straightforward analysis, due to the confounding factor of overall speech rate. Table 12.1 summarizes the results for the duration variables. Speaker A has a higher mean for three of these five variables: /æ/, /s/, and VOT. Given this trend, it would be inadvisable to interpret these specific duration variables as individually significant in this context. Instead we suggest that Speaker A merely has an overall slower rate of speaking than does Speaker B, and these variables are not being used independently of rate. Thus the vowel /eɪ/, which contradicts this trend, is being used as a meaningful variable, or correlates with a meaning distinct from overall speech rate. This correlation may indicate a relationship between words in which this vowel appears and topics which inspire emphatic stress or shifts in speed. Throughout the interview both speakers vary their speech rates to color their points. In addition, they both use repetition of particular key lexical items freely as a rhetorical device, and the selection of words to repeat (and stress) may influence these duration results.

Use of this strategy is evidenced in the duration of /eɪ/ in the word *gay*. Hypothesizing that this word could serve as a locus of performance or meaning, we looked at the duration values of Speaker A's tokens of /eɪ/ in *gay*, in all other words, and in other words in which it is the final segment. The results are shown in Table 12.2. Speaker A's tokens of /eɪ/ occurring in the word *gay* are significantly longer than those that do not, and have a higher mean than Speaker B's overall mean. A similar lexical analysis could not be conducted on Speaker B's speech, as he avoided the term *gay*, using it only twice during the hour-long program.

Table 12.1 Results for the duration variables (in ms)

	Mean		Standard deviation	
	A	*B*	*A*	*B*
/æ/	93*	76	44	39
/eɪ/	107	131*	46	53
/s/	111*	100	36	30
/l/	70	66	20	31
VOT	73*	59	25	23

* significantly longer (alpha level = 0.05)

Table 12.2 Speaker A's durations of /eɪ/ (in ms)

	Mean	Standard deviation
Tokens of *gay*	162.2	68.2
Other tokens of /eɪ/	102.4	39.8
Other tokens of word-final /eɪ/	101.5	50.3
All tokens of /eɪ/	107.8	46.2

As mentioned previously, the durations of /l/ and of /s/ have been linked to stereotypically gay performances (Crist 1997). We found no difference in the duration or the variance of /l/ between the two speakers. Speaker A does have a significantly longer mean for duration of /s/ than does Speaker B. This may indicate some stylistic use of this variable, or it may result from an overall speech rate difference, as discussed above.

Another commonly cited factor in establishing a gay percept is f0, the results for which are summarized in Table 12.3. Speaker B has higher average levels for maximum f0, minimum f0, and f0 at vowel midpoint, as well as a higher variance for all of these values. This suggests both that Speaker B has a generally higher voice than Speaker A (whether through biology or effort), and that his f0 is more variable across tokens.

The two speakers exhibit no difference in the f0 range, calculated as the difference between the maximum and minimum values within each vowel. This shows that neither speaker exceeds the other in use of 'swoopy voice,' a feature commonly associated with gay men.

Overall, Speaker A uses neither a higher pitch nor a wider f0 range relative to his counterpart to perform a gay identity. These results establish that Speaker A does not use pitch in ways usually attributed to gay-sounding men. Nonetheless, Speaker A is self-presenting as a gay man, and is immediately perceptible to listeners as such. We conclude that the type of gay style Speaker A is performing differs from the other styles that have been investigated. Further, the way that his style differs from this more recognized style is not merely idiosyncratic (or inexplicable) variation, but a deliberate and common response to the meanings associated with wide pitch

Table 12.3 Results for fundamental frequency (f0) variables (in Hz)

	Mean		Standard deviation	
	A	B	A	B
V midpoint	131	137*	31	39*
Max	142	152*	33	41
Min	122	130*	128	36*
Range	21	21	19	18

*significantly higher (alpha level = 0.05)

Table 12.4 Percent of released word-final stops

	A (N = 248)	B (N = 202)
Released	22.4%	12.9%
Unreleased	77.6%	87.1%

$\chi^2 = 7.04$, $df = 1$, $p = 0.004$

variation and especially its use by gay men. In particular, we propose that higher pitch and even more, wide pitch ranges, form part of a recognizably flamboyant gay style. We use flamboyant here, not to describe the intensity of the social meaning, but as an integral part of the meaning itself. It is frequently tempting to see broad demographic categories as essential basic meanings, and variation within them as aligned along a continuum. In this case, the continuum might place the stereotyp-ical 'queen' at the far extreme of gayness. Others who deviate from that image, either in terms of body-related characteristics such as race, disability status, weight, or linguistic performance, are then cast as less gay. We question this arrangement, and suggest that the speaker under investigation, while striving not to sound too gay, is not bound to the continuum, but is rather inhabiting a different space altogether. That is, using high f0 and wide f0 ranges is not simply a flamboyant way of being gay in the world, but rather a way of being flamboyantly gay. It is precisely this per-formance which Speaker A is avoiding, both as a result of his goals for the show (which include being non-threatening and competent) and the paths along which the discussion runs, focusing primarily on legal questions, and as a result, requiring him to speak with authority on serious topics.

In addition to duration and pitch, we investigated the release of word-final stops for both speakers. Speaker A has a significantly higher percentage of released stops than Speaker B, as shown in Table 12.4. This result does not mean, however, that this variable directly indexes gay for this speaker, as sexual orientation is hardly the only difference between the two speakers, or even the only difference made relevant by the context and topics of discussion. To look for the meaning of this variable in one context, it is useful to see where and how it is used by other people in other contexts. Bucholtz (1996) mentions this same feature as forming a part of a geek girl style, and that it has a particular link to education and literacy for these speakers. Ashburn (2000) discusses its use by members of the science fiction conven-tion community, as does Benor (in press) among Orthodox Jews, again with similar implications.

We propose that this variable has a culture-wide relationship to education or precision, and that Speaker A is using it for this purpose. This use accomplishes two goals. In the first place, as a lawyer he has an interest in establishing his identity as an educated and competent representative of the profession especially in a context where he is answering questions on specifically legal issues. And secondly he may be trying not to sound too gay, a goal often explicitly discussed by activists and speakers in the gay community as important when appearing before a mainstream, mostly straight audience. We posit that the phenomenon of not sounding too gay is not merely a function of dampening general features that say 'gay,' but a different performance entirely. 'Too gay' here is, in fact, a code. It is code for other social meanings associated with gay men and particular gay styles such as frivolity, promiscuity, and excitability. While speaking to potentially hostile audiences, activists often construct themselves in opposition to these images, as well as the other meanings populating the social space around them. Invoking cultural ideas concerning education and authority is one way to distance oneself from these qualities.

Conclusion

Our findings further problematize the notion of a singular gay way of speaking. First, we have demonstrated that Speaker A is not exploiting pitch or the duration of /l/ to produce a gay style, even though these phonetic features have been linked to stereotypically gay speech. We argue that Speaker A is performing an entirely different kind of gay identity, one which strongly contrasts with a stereotypically gay style. Although high pitch, wide pitch ranges, and prolonged /l/s index a gay style, they index only one of many gay styles. Speaker A is performing a non-stereotypical gay identity, and his performance illustrates that linguistic styles – including gay styles – are as diverse as the individuals and communities producing them. Second, Speaker A uses the release of final stops, a feature which also constitutes part of a geek girl style, in the production of his gay identity. This finding illustrates how a linguistic feature may be employed without evoking solely a gay meaning and also highlights the importance of contextualizing features that express social meaning.

We would like to emphasize that there is a need for additional studies investigating how sets of variables cluster together to form gay styles and all linguistically constructed styles. If we can demonstrate patterns similar to those observed in this study for a number of speakers, and in particular if we observe those speakers cross-situationally, we will be able to abstract over individual idiosyncrasies and arrive at a more complete understanding of how variables group together to index different kinds of identities. The overall picture would express much more complexity than an approach assuming simple oppositions, such as gay vs. straight. With a focus on style as an indexically constituted social meaning, we are better equipped to analyze how the individual negotiates identity across situations and how groups may co-vary in interesting and perhaps unexpected ways.

Chapter 13

Rusty Barrett

1995

SUPERMODELS OF THE WORLD, UNITE!

Political economy and the language of performance among African American drag queens

Introduction

THIS PAPER FOCUSES ON the use of language in performances by
African American drag queens (hereafter AADQs), specifically on the use of
a stereotyped variety of white women's speech. As such it examines one type of
language use among a subset of gay African American men; it is not meant to
provide a general description of the language of gay African American men, but
rather to consider the relationships between markers of gender and ethnicity in
drag performances specifically. I would like to argue that the use of stereotyped,
standard white women's language by AADQs presents a case in which the use of
a variety closely tied to the cultural authority of the dominant group (in this case
heterosexual European Americans) acts as a form of resistance against that authority.

The language considered here comes from public performances by practitioners
of 'glam' drag, or what Newton (1979 [1972]) calls 'high drag.' Glam drag performances typically involve gay men dressing as extremely 'sophisticated' and highly
feminine 'women.' These performances usually take place in gay bars and most
often involve lip-synching to popular music. With the exception of RuPaul, all of
the examples in this paper were collected during such performances in Texas during
the spring of 1993.

Ethnic and gender representations in drag

A number of scholars have argued that the representation of 'femininity' produced
by drag queens is essentially misogynistic and degrading to women (e.g. Ackroyd
1979; White 1980; Lurie 1981; Frye 1983; Williamson 1986; Tyler 1991).[1] Other

scholars have responded by arguing that drag is not 'about' women, but rather is about questioning of traditional gender roles or reclaiming stereotypes of gays as effeminate (e.g. Goodwin 1989; Dynes 1990; Butler 1990, 1993b). For example, Butler argues that drag highlights the fact that gender roles are a type of 'performance,' unrelated to biological sex. Thus drag performances question heterosexist assumptions about the relationship between biological sex and gender behavior.

These two arguments do not necessarily stand in direct opposition to one another, however, and it is possible that these scholars are arguing at cross purposes. While agreeing that gay drag performances are a means of undermining essentialist connections between sex and gender, I do not see that this function of drag necessarily prevents drag from sometimes producing misogynistic representations of women. Thus, it is possible to subvert homophobic assumptions concerning gender roles in a way that produces a hyperfeminine representation that many women find offensive (although drag as a phenomenon need not be inherently sexist).

In the case of AADQs, the representation of women usually involves questions of ethnicity as well as gender. For example, Jennie Livingston's 1991 film, *Paris is Burning*, a documentary about African American and Latino drag queens and transsexuals[2] in New York City, depicts the drag queens as imitators of white upper-class society. Much of the critical response to the film has focused on the fact that (as depicted in the film), the drag queens are desirous of the symbols of the White society that excludes them.

In a provocative review of *Paris is Burning*, bell hooks notes that the drag queens in the film present 'a sexist idealization of white womanhood' (1992: 145). Like other critics, hooks saw the drag queens in the film as 'wanting to be white.' Yet hooks' response is unique in its recognition of the power of this 'brutal imperial ruling-class capitalist partriarchal whiteness' (1992: 149):

> Significantly, the fixation on becoming as much like a white female as possible implictly evokes a connection to a figure never visible in this film: that of the white male patriarch. And yet if the class, race, and gender aspirations expressed by the drag queens who share their deepest dreams is always the longing to be in the position of the ruling-class woman then that means there is also the desire to act in partnership with the ruling-class male.
>
> (1992: 148)

While not negating the critique that *Paris is Burning* represents AADQs as 'wanting to be white,' it is important to recognize that this representation is built upon fairly common homophobic stereotypes about the social posturing of gay and lesbian African Americans. In some African American communities, expressions of homophobia frequently state that homosexuality among African American men is the result of 'emasculation of the black men by white oppression' or 'a sinister plot perpetuated by diabolical racists who want to destroy the black race' (Simmons 1991: 212). By focusing on the ways in which the drag queens in the film strive to achieve 'real' representations of wealthy white people, *Paris is Burning* perpetuates stereotypes that portray African American lesbians and gays as collaborating with the dominating white culture.

My own research on the use of language by African American drag queens in Texas would suggest that the assumption that AADQs want to 'be white' is not only overly simplistic, but almost entirely unfounded. Although AADQs may appropriate stereotyped white women's speech, they also deride other drag queens who lip-synch to the music of white singers (such as Liza Minelli or Sinead O'Connor) as 'wanting to be white,' a grave insult. Thus, rather than assume that *Paris is Burning* is an accurate representation of AADQs in general, I would like to entertain the possibility that the self-representations of the drag queens in the film might be influenced by Livingston's status as a white woman. In terms of language, some of the drag queens in *Paris is Burning* typically use standard (and feminized) white English (as opposed to language that would be classified as typical of 'African American English'[3]). Given the importance of immediate audience in determining the choice of language style (e.g. Bell 1984) and the problematic status of interviews as a means of capturing uninfluenced behavior (e.g. Briggs 1986), it is possible that the drag queens in *Paris is Burning* tuned their speech to Livingston, their interviewer. Indeed, during my own research I encountered drag queens who spoke to me (a white gay male) only in a white standard style. Livingston is usually absent from the film, however, and her absence has the effect of turning what were interviews into monologues. Thus, language intended for a specific audience is presented as a more general representation of 'truth.'

Thus, it was widely assumed that, because they strove to dress and act like wealthy white people, the drag queens in *Paris is Burning* accept the colonial authority of white society. This assumption parallels the assumption by sociolinguists that speakers attempting to speak the dominant standard variety (such as Labov's (1972) hypercorrecting lower middle classes) accept the authorial power of the hegemonic code. One would expect that the use of white women's speech by African Americn drag queens would thus be a collaborative move, reflecting an acceptance of white authority. Although this may be true in some instances, it is not absolute.

As Marjorie Garber (1992) has noted, the symbolic force of drag is built upon 'an exploitation of the opposition between construction and essence' (1992: 152). Just as drag may displace assumptions about gender (by juxtaposing female gender with male sex), it may displace assumptions about ethnicity (by juxtaposing white ethnicity with black race). Just as the representation of female gender in drag does not reflect a love of womanhood (and may even be misogynistic), the representation of white ethnicity is often highly critical of white society. As Judith Butler has argued about the drag queens in *Paris is Burning*, the appropriation of the symbols of the dominant culture can serve as a form of resistance to dominating authority:

> This is not an appropriation of dominant culture in order to remain subordinated by its terms, but an appropriation that seeks to make over the terms of domination, a making over which is itself a kind of agency, a power in and as discourse, in and as performance, which repeats in order to remake – and sometimes succeeds.
>
> (1993: 137)

In the remainder of this paper, I will focus on the use of a stereotyped form of white women's language by African American drag queens. I hope to demonstrate the ways in which this usage can be seen as a way of appropriating and redefining the symbols of white domination as a form of resistance. In this sense, the use of 'white' language by African American drag queens parallels some uses of 'feminine' language by gay men more generally.

White woman's language as used by AADQs

The 'white woman' style of language used by AADQs does not necessarily reflect the actual speech of any 'real' white women, but is a stereotyped representation of a wealthy, straight, European American form of femininity. It may function to distinguish drag queens from other African American gay men and can be an important factor in establishing credibility as a drag queen. For example, a friend of mine who produced drag shows once told me that he had instructed a man who was fairly new at drag to never speak on stage because she could not sound like a white woman.

The stereotyped form of 'white women's' speech used by AADQs is similar to Lakoff's description of 'woman's language' (WL). The characteristic features of WL are as follows (Lakoff 1975: 53–6):

- Women have a large stock of words related to their specific interests, generally relegated to them as 'woman's work': *dart* (in sewing) and specific color terms (*ecru*, *magenta*). 'Empty' adjectives like *divine*, *charming*, *cute* . . .
- Question intonation where we might expect declaratives: for instant tag questions ('It's so hot, isn't it?') and rising intonation in statement contexts ('What's your name, dear?' 'Mary Smith?').
- The use of hedges of various kinds. Women's speech seems in general to contain more instances of 'well,' 'y'know,' 'kinda,' and so forth . . .
- Related to this is the intensive use of 'so.' Again, this is more frequent in women's than men's language . . .
- Hypercorrect grammar: women are not supposed to talk rough.
- Superpolite forms . . . women don't use off-color or indelicate expressions; women are the experts at euphemism . . .
- Women don't tell jokes.
- Women speak in italics (i.e. betray the fear that little attention is being paid to what they say).

Some of these features, such as the use of specific color terms and empty adjectives, overlap with gay male speech more generally. A distinction between the two styles is often maintained, however, with specific empty adjectives serving as more salient markers of either gay male identity (e.g. 'flawless,' 'fierce,' 'fabulous') or femininity (e.g. 'cute,' 'darling'). In addition, AADQ's white woman style generally includes careful (often hypercorrected) 'standard' English phonology.

The use of white women's style by AADQs

These last three characteristics of WL (euphemism, not telling jokes, and speaking in italics) are vital to the maintenance of 'ladylike' behavior and serve to keep

women from becoming the center of attention during conversation. AADQs sometimes flaunt the fact that they do not meet the expectations of white middle-class
propriety by calling attention to violations of these characteristics, especially the
use of obscenities. In the following example, an AADQ is introducing a stripper.
She plays on the fact that as a 'lady' she is not supposed to use obscenities:

Example 1

1)   Are you ready to see some muscles? (audience yells) . . . Some dick?
2)   Excuse me I'm not supposed to say that, words like that in the microphone.
3)   Like 'shit,' 'fuck,' and all that, you know?
4)   I am a Christian woman.
5)   I go to church.
6)   I'm always on my knees.

In this example, the drag queen purposely contradicts herself by saying words like
'shit' and 'fuck' that she (as a 'lady') is 'not supposed to say.' The contradiction
is continued with the sentence, 'I'm always on my knees' which carries the double
meaning of 'always praying' and 'always performing fellatio.' In both cases the
surface image (of a good Christian woman) is undermined by inferences about the
'true' nature of the performer's persona.

This creation of an ambiguous relationship between the referential meaning of
an utterance and the intended or inferred meaning is a form of signifyin(g) (Mitchell-
Kernan 1971; Abrahams 1976; Smitherman 1977; Gates 1988, etc.). Signifyin(g)
is a rhetorical device in African American English (hereafter AAE) which Mitchell-
Kernan defines as follows:

> The Black concept of signifying incorporates essentially a folk notion
> that dictionary entries for words are not always sufficient for inter-
> preting meanings or messages, or that meaning goes beyond such
> interpretations. Complimentary remarks may be delivered in a left-
> handed fashion. A particular utterance may be an insult in one context
> and not another . . . The hearer is thus constrained to attend to all
> potential meaning carrying symbolic systems in speech events – the total
> universe of discourse. The context embeddedness of meaning is attested
> to by both our reliance on the given context and, most importantly, by
> our inclination to construct additional context from our background
> knowledge of the world . . . we seem to process all manner of informa-
> tion against a background of assumptions and expectations.
>
> (1971: 92–3)

The very nature of drag restructures heterosexist hegemonic 'assumptions and
expectations' about the form of gender norms and the relationship between gender
and sex. Drag performances demonstrate that the (normative) indexical meaning
of (linguistic and extra-linguistic) signs related to femininity is insufficient for interpreting the full meaning conveyed by the speech events of the performance. Speech
events such as that in example 1 force the listener to construct meaning based on

background knowledge of what assumptions and expectations about gender and ethnicity are being questioned. Although the white woman style is used, the utterances produce inferences that violate the expected behavioral norms associated with the style itself. Thus, one of the ways in which AADQ performances operate as a form of resistance to the cultural authority of white English is to use signifyin(g) to produce inferences about the potential range of interpretation conveyed by a given speech-event. An understanding of such inferences leaves the status of the dominant code (white English) in a state of ambiguity in which the code itself is used to undermine the cultural authority it represents.

Code-switching (the alternation between two languages or two varieties of the same language) represents another process by which the language of AADQ serves to challenge linguistic hegemony. In addition to using the white woman style, AADQs use African American English and gay English in their performances. Code-switching between African American English and standard varieties may be seen as a form of resistance to the authority represented by the dominant code. One way in which this form of resistance takes place is through what Carol Myers-Scotton (1993: 131–42) has termed 'code-switching as a marked choice.' Myers-Scotton defines this type of code-switching as a move away from the language variety dictated by social expectations of what is the proper form for a given interaction. As such marked code-switches represent a desire to replace the set of 'rights and obligations' (Myers-Scotton 1993) between the participants in the interaction. Switches between the white woman style (or gay English[4]) and AAE can thus be used to define (or redefine) the relationship between the performer and audience members. In example 2, an AADQ is introducing a white stripper in a gay bar with a predominantly white clientele.[5] By switching to a low pitched voice and addressing an African American audience member (saying, 'Hey what's up, home boy?' – line 7), the AADQ creates a momentary solidarity with the African American audience member by using a marked switch to the code that indexes African American identity.

Example 2

1) Please welcome to the stage, our next dancer,
2) He is a butt-fucking tea, honey.[6]
3) He is hot.
4) Masculine, muscled, and ready to put it to ya, baby.
5) Anybody in here (.) hot (.) as (.) fish (.) grease?
6) That's pretty hot, idn't it?
7) (Switch to low pitch) Hey what's up, home boy? (Switches back)
8) I'm sorry that fucking creole always come around when I don't need it.
9) Please, welcome,
10) hot, gorgeous, sexy, very romantic,
11) and he'd like to bend you over and turn you every which way but loose.

The potential power of the code-switch is evident from the fact that she apologizes for speaking 'that fucking creole.' Yet the apology itself is not entirely in standard white English. For example, the word 'come' does not have the standard English

[+s] suffix. This mix of nonstandard and standard English creates an ambiguity as to the sincerity of the apology. Thus, the apology is a type of signifying by creating the possibility that the referential meaning of the statement might not represent the totality of meaning that is actually intended.

In example 3, an AADQ interrupts a performance in a bar with primarily African American patrons to address a table of white audience members. Before this exchange, the AADQ has been speaking primarily in AAE. When she turns to address the white audience members, she switches to a 'white woman' style. The word 'doing' is pronounced with the final-rising intonation (the L*H described by McLemore 1991) stereotypical of younger white middle-class women (especially sorority women) in Texas.

Example 3

1)   Oh, hi, how are you doing?
2)   White people. Love it.
3)   I, I'm not being racial cause I'm White.
4)   I just have a <obscured> I can afford more sun tan.

In this case, the white woman style serves to distance the white audience members, implying that, as whites, they must be, spoken to in white English. This switch indirectly indexes the issues of power created by the presence of the white audience members in a bar that where African Americans constitute the vast majority of patrons. In addition to pointing out the social difference of the white spectators, the AADQ jokingly states that this switch in styles is not racist, because she is 'also white' and only has a better sun tan. The focus on ethnic difference created by a switch in language varieties is used to point out the irony of the fact that many whites place great value on darkening their skin while maintaining racist attitudes towards Blackness. By placing the issue of race in a performance context (and bringing up the issue primarily through the use of language style), the performer is able to indirectly bring up issues that would be 'taboo,' in another context. This makes it possible for the AADQ to produce humor at the expense of whites in their presence without being overtly confrontational.

In addition to marked code-switching such as in examples 2 and 3, AADQs often exhibit what Myers-Scotton (1993: 117–31) calls 'code-switching as the unmarked norm.' This type of code-switching occurs when the alternation between two languages or language varieties is the basic method of communication between bilingual or bidialectal peers. In code-switching as the unmarked norm, the symbolic meaning or indexical force of the code-switches is not found within a given switch from one variety to another, but in the overall pattern of alternations between more than one form. Among AADQs, alternations between AAE, gay English, and a white woman style are common for situations that do not carry corresponding social expectations for a given style (such as ingroup communication between AADQs). The use of AAE and gay English indexes AADQs' identities as African Americans and gay men, respectively, while the use of the white woman style indexes their identity as drag queens. In terms of political economy, the white woman style carries the symbolic force of the dominant code in addition to indexing the stereotyped form of white femininity produced by drag queens. Among AADQs, code-switching as the unmarked norm often results in cases where styles overlap with one another. For example, syntax typical of AAE may be pronounced with standard English phonology and vice versa. In addition, lexical items associated with a given style may occur in utterances that are primarily in a different style. For example, during an appearance on the Arsenio Hall show, RuPaul (an AADQ whose single 'Supermodel' was a major dance hit of 1993) often used AAE syntax with a stereotypically 'white woman' phonology, as in example 4:

Example 4

You know, in my mind's eye I always been a superstar, you know.
And nobody couldn't tell me no different.

In this example, all of the words are pronounced with standard English phonology, except for the final word 'different,' which occurs without the final [t], as one might expect from a speaker of AAE. Although the phonology is in the white woman style, the syntax of the utterance is typical of AAE. Thus, two different styles (with very different symbolic associations) occur simultaneously.

Consider the following speech given by RuPaul at the 1993, March on Washington for Gay, Lesbian, and Bisexual Rights:

Example 5

1) Hello America
2) my name's Ru Paul,
3) supermodel of the world
4) (starts a chant) Hey Ho Hey Ho Hey Ho
5) where I see myself in ten years.
6) And I say I see myself in the White House, baby!
7) Miss Thing goes to Washington
8) Can you see it? Wha-we gonna paint the mother pink, OK?
9) We put one president in the White House, I figure you can do it again.
10) Everybody say love! (audience responds, 'love!')
11) Everybody say love! (audience responds again, 'love!')
12) Now drive that down Pennsylvania Avenue!
13) Peace, love and hairgrease!
14) I love you!

The speech begins with typical feminized standard English pronunciation, yet the phrase 'supermodel of the world' is pronounced without a final [d] on 'world,' a form characteristic of AAE. After initiating the chant, RuPaul returns to a white woman style up until line 6, where the intonation moves toward gay speech on the phrase 'in the White House, baby.' For example, the word 'baby' is spoken with a long falling intonation such as that of the stereotypical pronunciation of the word 'FAABulous.' In line 7, RuPaul refers to herself as 'Miss Thang,' a term that may serve to index both gay identity and African American identity. The word 'thang' is pronounced with the standard [ɪ] (as in 'sit'), rather than the [ei] (as in 'late') or [æ] (as in 'pack'), forms more typical of AAE (and some varieties of Southern white English). Thus, the term 'Miss Thang' is actually pronounced as 'Miss Thing,' so that a lexical item closely tied to AAE is produced with standard white phonology. Line 8 begins with a white woman style. However, the word 'mother' is pronounced without a final [r] as in AAE and the word 'OK?' is produced with a stereotypically gay exaggerated intonation. Lines 9 and 10 are both primarily in the white woman style, although line 10 begins a call-response routine, a speech act typically associated with African Americans (especially African American preachers). The intonation of lines 11 and 12 (the second 'Everybody say love!'), however, is more typical of the intonational patterns found in African American preaching.

Thus, the presence of the standard white variety of English co-occurs with other varieties that symbolize identity in marginalized groups. This type of code-switching diminishes the force of the hegemonic code by suggesting that, although the speaker is competent in the dominant variety, she or he maintains his or her identity as a member of dominated groups. The symbolic status of standard English is accompanied by solidarity with groups (African Americans and gays) that are oppressed by the authority symbolized by the standard.

Another way in which AADQs manipulate the white woman style is by using the style to produce a voice that consciously represents a white woman. This use of the white woman style is particular to performances and is often used to convey some critical response to the domination by white society. Often, the voice of the 'white woman' is introduced either through direct reference (such as 'I'm a white woman' or 'This is how white women are . . .') or through some stereotypical white remark ('Look! Black people!').

Examples 6 and 7 were performed by a Texas AADQ in a gay bar with almost exclusively African American patrons. Example 6 consists of a monologue about selling rat traps for use in various neighborhoods in a city in Texas. At the beginning of the monologue, the AADQ takes on the voice of a white woman who is shocked by the number of African Americans in the bar (lines 1–2). As she moves from rat traps for white neighborhoods to those for African American neighborhoods, her speech switches from the white woman style to AAE.

Example 6

1) I don't wanna take up all your time
2) I know y'all wanna disco, ooh – all these Black people.
3) OK! What we're gonna talk about is, um, rat traps, um. [speaker pulls a small mouse trap out of a bag]
4) This is a rat trap from {name of wealthy white neighborhood}
5) It's made by BMW. It's real compact.
6) It's, thank you <obscured> it's really good.
7) It's very convenient and there's insurance on it.
8) And this is from {name of same wealthy white neighborhood (line 4)}. [speaker pulls a large rat trap out of the bag]

9) OK, now for {name of a housing project with primarily African American residents}.

10) This rat trap is made by Cadillac. It's a big mother fucker, [speaker pulls a gun out of the bag]

11) Now for the {name of inner city area with primarily African American residents} you just don't need no rat trap,

12) cause those mother fuckers look like dogs out there.

13) Shit!

14) I put in a piece of cheese, the mother fucker told me,

15) 'Next time put in some dog food.'

As the monologue begins, the 'white woman' realizes that she shouldn't talk for too long, as the 'black people' probably want to 'disco.' Here, the white woman style is used to ridicule white stereotypes of African Americans as being obsessed with dancing. It also presents a stereotype of white conceptions, of politeness, especially the hesitation of whites to enter into linguistic interactions with African Americans. The monologue switches to AAE in line 9, at the beginning of the discussion about the rat trap for residents of the housing project. The descriptions of the rat traps contrast the current living conditions of whites (5–8) and African Americans (9–15). The different voices created through dialect opposition serve to produce a critique of the inequality in existing social conditions of whites and African Americans. In this case, the linguistic variety of the dominant group (whites) is used to point out the oppressive nature of their domination.

In example 7, an AADQ uses the white woman style and AAE to mock white stereotypes about African American men. Although this example is not necessarily typical, I include it here because it demonstrates the way in which language style can serve to create a sophisticated critique of social stereotypes, in this case white stereotypes of African Americans. In this example, performed in a gay bar for an audience that was predominantly African American, an AADQ uses the white woman style in acting out an attack on a rich white woman by an African American man. Although simulating the rape of any woman is misogynistic, it is important to note that this performance is primarily a response to the white myth of the African American rapist. As Angela Davis (1983) has pointed out, fraudulent charges of rape have historically been used as excuses for the murder (lynching) of African American men.

Because it is based on the racist stereotype of African Americans as having voracious sexual appetites, the myth of the African American rapist operates under the false assumption that rape is a primarily sexual act (and not primarily an act of violence). The myth assumes that all African American males are desirous of white women and are willing to commit acts of violence in order to feed this desire. This fabricated desire for white women is then used as justification for senseless acts of violence on African American men. For African American gay men, who may not be sexually desirous of any women, the ludicrous foundation of this myth is heightened. Nevertheless, African American gay men (including most of patrons of the bar where this performance took place) must continuously deal with the ramifications of the myth of the black rapist, including unfounded white fears of violence. Lines 1–21 present the attack on the white woman in which the

AADQ uses primarily the white woman style, mixed with AAE. At the beginning of the sequence, the AADQ calls up a male audience member to participate in the performance and hands him a toy gun.

Example 7

1) I'm a rich White woman in {name of wealthy White neighborhood}
2) And you're going to try to come after me, OK?
3) And I want you to just . . .
4) I'm going to be running, OK?
5) And I'm gonna fall down, OK? OK?
6) And I'm just gonna . . . look at you . . .
7) And you don't do anything.
8) You hold the gun . . .
9) Goddamn – he got practice. [audience laughter] <obscured>
10) I can tell you're experienced. [He holds the gun, but so that it faces down, not as if he were aiming it]
11) OK hold it.
12) You know you know how to hold it, don't play it off . . .
13) Hold that gun . . . Shit . . . Goddamn . . .
14) [Female audience member]: Hold that gun!
15) That's right fish! Hold that gun! Shit!
16) OK now, y'all, I'm fish, y'all, White fish witch!
17) And I'm gonna be running cause three Black men with big dicks chasing me!
18) [Points to audience member] He's the leader, OK?
19) Now you know I gotta fall, I want y'all to say 'Fall bitch!'
20) [Audience]: Fall bitch! [The AADQ falls, then rises, makes gasping sounds, alternating with 'bum-biddy-bum' imitations of the type of music used in suspense scenes in movies/TV]
21) Now show me the gun! [The audience member holds up the gun and the AADQ performs an exaggerated faint]

Upon giving the gun to the audience member, the AADQ instructs him not to do anything other than hold the gun (lines 7–8). The 'white woman' is just going to look at him (line 6). Despite the AADQs insinuation that he is 'experienced' with guns (line 10), the audience member fails to hold the gun correctly until a woman in the audience yells at him (line 14). The white woman assumes that 'Black men with big dicks' are chasing her through the park (line 17) and faints upon seeing the man with the gun (line 21). Thus, the African American man is basically passive throughout the exchange and the 'White woman' reacts primarily based on fear fed by racism.

In the remainder of the performance, the corollary to the myth of the African American rapist is presented, the myth of the promiscuity of the African American woman. In lines 22–5, the same scene is acted out with an 'African American woman' (speaking AAE) rather than a 'white woman.' The African American woman, upon seeing the large feet of the man with the gun, informs him that she will have sex with him and that the gun is unnecessary (line 25–6).

Example 7 continued

22)   Now this Black fish . . .
23)   <obscured> Black men's running after her..
24)   I ain't no boy! Fuck y'all! Fuck y'all mother fuckers! [AADQ looks at the gun]
25)   You don't have to use that baby, I see them size feet.
26)   Come on! Come on!

The performance thus contrasts stereotypes about African American and white attitudes toward sexuality. While the white woman is overcome with fear and faints, the African American woman is willing to engage in sex because of her assumptions about the size of the man's penis. The performance touches on numerous aspects of the myth of the African American rapist, both the sexist assumptions concerning the pure and fragile nature of white women and the racist assumptions concerning the sexual prowess and endowment of African American men, the sexual voracity of African Americans generally, and the 'violent' nature of African American men.

Here, the linguistic variety of the dominant group is used to create a voice that is confronted with the possibility of violence from a member of the dominated group. The insecurity of the authority symbolized by white English is demonstrated by the fear of the white voice. At the same time, however, the white woman style represents a form of womanhood. This representation of womanhood is, however, highly stereotyped and potentially derogatory hyperfemininity. The white woman style is used in a misogynistic attempt to draw laughter about rape. The use of the white woman style thus criticizes white racism while simultaneously producing a misogynistic representation of women (both African American and white).

Conclusion

The use of the white woman style by AADQs suggests that the symbolic power of a language variety is highly context dependent. In some cases, the use of the white woman code may symbolize the position of relative power held by white women in American society. As Hall (1995) has argued for women who work in the phone sex fantasy industry, women's language may be a powerful commodity in some interactions in specific communities. Because of the potential power of white women's language as a symbol of white domination, it is possible for the white woman style to symbolize the collaborative consciousness that hooks finds so offensive in *Paris is Burning*. Most often, however, the status of the white linguistic variety is accompanied by code-switching that may symbolize solidarity with African Americans and/or gay men. Code-switching provides a means of simultaneously employing the dominant standard variety for the status that it symbolizes and maintaining symbolic solidarity with groups that are dominated by the authority symbolized by the standard variety.

In response to *Paris is Burning* most critics readily accepted the collaborative stance of AADQs as desirous of the symbols of power held by white society. This acceptance parallels the general assumption by sociolinguists that the use of the standard variety reflects acceptance of the authority symbolized by the standard. The use of the white woman style by AADQs suggests, as Judith Butler argues for *Paris is Burning*, the symbols of domination may be appropriated as a means of resistance. Such an appropriation represents a rather pervasive and decidedly queer form of resistance. The reclaiming of symbols of domination as a means of diffusing the power they carry is a means of 'queering' conceptions of normative behavior. It constitutes one aspect of the highly political force of camp (Meyer 1994). For example, the use of the word 'queer' as a self-categorization diffuses the pejorative power carried by straight usage. The lesbian butch-femme aesthetic (Case 1993 [1989]; Nestle 1981) represents a reworking of traditional gender roles that calls their status into question. The conscious production of stereotyped effeminacy by gay men diffuses the derogatory power of heterosexist assumptions about queer behavior. Thus, lesbian and gay uses of language may appropriate and rework the symbols of domination, including the symbolic force of a linguistic variety.

These appropriations of the symbols of straight domination, including the use of a white woman style of speaking by AADQs, suggest that the assumptions of many sociolinguists concerning the symbolic force of linguistic varieties may be overly simplistic. The presence of a dominant hegemonic variety may not always represent collaboration with the dominating social group, or even accomodation to or coercion by the dominant group. The appropriation of a dominant linguistic variety may actually serve as a means of resisting the domination symbolized by the variety. Because lesbian and gay uses of language might not be easily understood within current sociolinguistic models, a deeper understanding of such language uses is crucial to developing a richer understanding of the relationship between language and society.

Heteronorms

THIS SECTION OF THE READER looks at the part played by language and language-use in sustaining heteronormative social arrangements. As we explained in our general introduction, the term 'heteronormativity' encapsulates the insight that sexuality is organized and regulated in accordance with certain societal beliefs about what is normal, natural and desirable. One basic norm privileges heterosexuality by comparison with other sexual preferences: indeed, 'privileges' is an understatement, for there is considerable pressure on people to make the supposedly 'natural' choice, and not to do so can incur severe social sanctions – from fairly subtle discrimination to outright and even murderous physical violence. However, there is more to heteronormativity than the normalization of heterosexuality. Some expressions of heterosexuality are more equal than others: in the heteronormative hierarchy the most favoured form of sexuality is monogamous (involving marriage or quasi-marital relationships), reproductive (with intercourse – penetration of a vagina by a penis – being the preferred sexual practice) and conventional in terms of gender roles (which is to say, based on a norm of men as sexually active/dominant and women as sexually passive/subordinate). All these aspects of heteronormativity have reflexes in everyday linguistic practice.

The first two pieces we reproduce, by the conversation analyst Celia Kitzinger and the variationist sociolinguist Penelope Eckert, deal with heterosexuality as an identity that is manifested in everyday talk. In 'Speaking as a heterosexual', Kitzinger (Chapter 14) makes the point that we do not generally find people prefacing utterances with the words 'Speaking as a heterosexual . . .': heterosexual identity can be taken for granted unless and until it is specifically disclaimed. Yet Kitzinger shows that everyday conversations – her many examples come from corpora collected and used by conversation analysts since the 1960s – are full of instances where speakers display their heterosexuality. That display is not ostentatious, but a matter of conversationalists 'giving off' heterosexuality in the course of going about their ordinary interactional business, for instance by routinely referring to their and other people's spouses and 'in-laws', and by treating heterosexual relationships or rituals as 'natural' subjects of conversation. These absolutely unremarkable ways of talking function, Kitzinger argues, as a resource for 'doing being ordinary', which is not available in the same way to lesbians and gay men. Just as heterosexual couples can hold hands or kiss in public without attracting negative sanctions, whereas same-sex couples risk stares, abuse and even assault, so casual verbal references to a same-sex relationship are not typically treated as marks of the speaker's ordinariness, but rather as a provocative flaunting of his or her deviance. Consequently, one of the things that is accomplished in mundane social interaction is the construction of 'a normative taken-for-granted heterosexual world'.

Penelope Eckert's 'Vowels and nail polish' (Chapter 15) is concerned with the emergence of a 'heterosexual market' among preadolescents, and the effects that has on girls in particular. To demonstrate maturity and maximize their value in the emerging market, girls such as Trudy, whose linguistic and other behaviour is the focus of Eckert's discussion here, engage in intensive self-styling using every symbolic resource at their disposal: clothes, make-up, hair-styling, ways of walking and ways of using language. Though the resulting linguistic style may index other dimensions of identity (e.g. ethnicity and social class) more directly than gender and sexuality, Eckert shows that its production is linked to the preadolescent girl's investment in heterosexual femininity – an investment that, she argues, initially promises the girls excitement and a certain kind of power, but then 'gradually transforms into a discourse of female objectification and subordination'.

The next two pieces deal with an aspect of heteronormativity that has been a long-standing concern for feminist activists and scholars: the definition of sexual consent. The orthodox heteronormative assumption is that men are active initiators of sex, while women's role is to accept or reject their advances; but in addition, women are expected to guard their reputations by not 'giving in' too easily. Consequently, their saying 'no', or otherwise signalling a lack of interest, is not necessarily to be taken at face value (for a more detailed discussion of the semiotics of 'no' in sexual situations, see Kulick, Chapter 23).

Both Susan Ehrlich's 'The discursive reconstruction of sexual consent' (Chapter 16) and Deborah Cameron's 'Degrees of consent' (Chapter 17) examine the sexual politics of consent in a particular context: that of North American university campus life in the 1990s. By the early 1990s, the prevalence of rape and other sexual misconduct in campus communities had become a serious public concern – one that many universities felt impelled to address by instituting complaint procedures and codes of conduct. At the same time, there was a surge of interest in the alleged phenomenon of 'male–female miscommunication', as discussed in bestselling books such as Deborah Tannen's *You Just Don't Understand* (1990) and John Gray's *Men are from Mars, Women are from Venus* (1992). Though not directly related to it, this discourse on gender and communication came to influence the debate about sexual misconduct on campus, giving rise to the belief that 'date rape' (i.e. forced sex occurring in the course of an originally consensual romantic encounter between already-acquainted parties) might in many cases be a consequence of men and women 'misreading each other's signals'.

Ehrlich's chapter analyses the way the 'miscommunication' account is mobilized in judicial proceedings following a complaint of sexual assault. She shows how in practice it can become an exercise in victim-blaming: women are criticized for not communicating clearly enough to men, whereas men are not held equally accountable for their failure to interpret what women say and do (for another thought-provoking discussion of this point, see Kitzinger and Frith 1999). The asymmetry here is related to heteronormative beliefs about what is 'natural' in sexual encounters between men and women: for instance, that it is a man's job to overcome a woman's 'natural' resistance, and a woman's responsibility to contain, if she cannot or will not satisfy, a man's 'natural' sexual urges. In that framework, it becomes 'natural' to see 'miscommunication' in sexual situations as essentially the woman's failure to exert control verbally.

Cameron's chapter discusses, and reprints extracts from, a policy that was formulated by Antioch College in Ohio in an effort to pre-empt misunderstandings by requiring people of both sexes to communicate in specific ways about – and during – sex. The Antioch policy defines 'consent' as the explicit utterance of 'yes' (rather than the absence of 'no'), and says that the 'yes' must be elicited in advance for each separate act. That of course entails that the parties to a sexual encounter must describe in words every action they propose to perform. When the policy came to the attention of the media, this aspect of it was consistently ridiculed. Did Antioch really expect sex-crazed adolescents to interrupt the spontaneous flow with a lot of unnecessary verbiage? Yet some of the students Cameron interviewed claimed that the requirement to verbalize about sex actually heightened rather than diminishing their enjoyment.

This section concludes with two chapters exploring the meanings of English 'keywords' belonging to the semantic field of sexuality: *sex* (in the sense of 'sexual activity') and *marriage*. Stephanie A. Sanders and June Machover Reinisch's 'Would you say you "had sex" if . . .?' (Chapter 18), a study of what English-speakers (in this case, a sample of 600 US college students) understand the expression *have sex* to refer to, was originally published in the wake of the political controversy regarding the then US President Bill Clinton's relationship with White House intern Monica Lewinsky. Clinton had both admitted that Lewinsky performed fellatio on him and denied that he 'had sexual relations' with her. This apparent contradiction would have made sense to many of the informants in Sanders and Reinisch's sample, who reported that they would not use the word 'sex' to describe oral–genital contact. Prototypically, this study suggests, 'sex' means the penetration of a vagina by a penis – the heteronormative sex act par excellence, since, unlike oral or anal sex, it is heterosexual by definition, and has the potential to lead to conception.

In Sally McConnell-Ginet's piece on the word *marriage* (Chapter 19), the contested issue is, precisely, whether the term by definition must refer to a heterosexual union. In many societies currently, including the US, which is the main focus of McConnell-Ginet's discussion, gay and lesbian activists are campaigning for the status of marriage to be extended to same-sex relationships. McConnell-Ginet considers to what extent, if any, this is a question about semantics – about what the word *marriage* means. Her own approach treats language-use and other social practices as interconnected and mutually influencing one another: while on one hand she both notes and shows that 'the institution [of marriage] itself keeps changing' (a fact that has clearly affected the definition of the word *marriage* over time), on the other hand she argues that 'words do not just label pre-existing determinate concepts: they often play a role in shaping concepts and in channeling thoughts and actions'.

Language, then, does not only reflect the heteronormative order in which it is used. As all the chapters in this section suggest, it is actively involved in reproducing that order; and as some of them show, it may also be one instrument for challenging, subverting or changing it.

Chapter 14

Celia Kitzinger

2005

'SPEAKING AS A HETEROSEXUAL'

(How) does sexuality matter for talk-in-interaction?

Introduction

COMPARED WITH THE ACCUMULATION of research on the speech and language of lesbian, gay, bisexual and transgendered (henceforth LGBT) people (e.g. Livia and Hall 1997; Chesebro 1981; Jacobs 1996; Kulick 1998, 2000; Leap 1996), the talk of heterosexuals *qua* heterosexuals has been much less studied. As Cameron and Kulick (2003: 153) point out, 'one of the privileges enjoyed by dominant groups in general is that their identities and modes of behaviour are rarely scrutinized in the same way as the identities and behaviours of subordinated groups'. Animated in part by the analytic interest in how dominant groups construct the social world, this article draws on a series of conversations accumulated by conversation analysts over the course of a couple of decades of data collection and inspects them for the varying ways in which the co-conversationalists display their heterosexuality to one another, and, thereby, to us as analysts.

As I will show, virtually all the talk upon which the classic findings of conversation analysis (CA) are based is produced by heterosexuals, who reproduce, in their talk, a normative taken-for-granted heterosexual world. Whatever their 'internal' sexual desires and fantasies, however they might 'privately' describe their own sexual orientations, the 'public' identities they display in interaction are insistently heterosexual – and over the course of the interactions in which they are engaged, these co-conversationalists reflect and reproduce a profoundly hetero-normative social order. Nowhere in the data sets on which CA is founded does anyone announce that they (or anyone else they know) is 'heterosexual' or preface a turn with 'Speaking as a heterosexual . . .', yet the heterosexuality of the inter-actants is continually made apparent.

In drawing attention to the displayed *heterosexuality* of the speakers in the classic CA data sets, it is not my intention either to advance the claim that nonhetero-sexuals speak differently from heterosexuals, or to mount a challenge to the general applicability of classic CA findings. Rather, by analysing these data sets for what they reveal about how heterosexuality is produced in talk, my intention is to open up further the analytic opportunities within CA for studying the taken-for-granted. These classic data sets may well reflect the social worlds of many ordinary hetero-sexual British and American people in the 1960s to 1980s at the times these data were collected. It was – and maybe still is – possible to treat heterosexuality as universal, to display one's own and other people's heterosexuality without being heard thereby as doing anything special, and to display an assumption of living in a world apparently almost entirely devoid of LGBT people.

As I will show, a distinctive feature of these 'displays' of heterosexuality is that they are not usually oriented to as such by either speaker or recipient(s). Rather, heterosexuality is taken for granted as an unquestioned and unnoticed part of their life worlds. Unlike those performances of gendered or racialized identities which are actively 'worked up' – such as Agnes's self-presentation as female (Garfinkel 1967), or telephone sex workers' constructions of varying racial identities in conformity with the sexual preferences of their clients (Hall 1995) – these co-interactants are generally 'giving off' rather than actively displaying their heterosexual identities. They are simply allowing their heterosexuality to be inferred in the course of some activity in which they are otherwise engaged. I suggest that this very inattentiveness to heterosexuality as a possible identity category, and the ease with which inter-actants make heterosexuality apparent without being thereby being heard as 'talking about' heterosexuality, both reflects and constructs heteronormativity.

The data

In this article, I draw on data sets collected and analysed by the founders of CA (Sacks, Schegloff and Jefferson) and by other leading conversation analysts (notably Drew, Goodwin, Heritage, Lerner, Maynard, Pomerantz and Zimmerman) to show how co-conversationalists routinely produce themselves (and each other) as hetero-sexual. Data sets widely used in CA publications include conversations between friends and colleagues (e.g. HGII, TG, SN-4, Upholstery Shop), telephone calls to and from private homes (e.g. the Rahman, Heritage, Holt, SBL and NB corpora), dinner time conversations (Virginia, Automobile Discussion, Chicken Dinner) and institutional data such as the group therapy session (GTS, Sacks 1995a,b), suicide prevention center calls (Sacks 1972, 1995a,b), and 911 emergency calls (Zimmerman 1992). In researching this article I have drawn on the original record-ings and existing transcripts of them when I have access to these, and on the published versions of the data when I do not. (See the end of this chapter for transcription conventions.) Most of these data sets are in the form of audio rather than video recordings (and most are telephone conversations): hence my analysis focuses on audible rather than visually accessible heterosexual displays – on how people talk heterosexuality into being rather than on how heterosexuality is displayed visually or through body deployment. In most of these data, the members of heterosexual couples are neither jointly present, nor in interaction with each other. This means that individuals are presenting themselves as heterosexual without the assistance of a co-present heterosexual partner – and I have limited my analysis in this paper to such displays.

In presenting this analysis, I also speculate as to how interactions do – or might – run off differently when speakers display not *hetero-* but *homo*sexuality, and what this tells us about the social world. In so doing, I draw on published self-report data from LGBT people, from the rare instances in which an LGBT identity is made available or discussed in the classic CA corpora, and on a limited amount of my own data featuring lesbians in interaction with heterosexuals (see also Land and Kitzinger 2005).

Speaking as heterosexuals: co-constituting a heteronormative world

The question I am using the data sets to address is how people produce themselves and others as heterosexual and – in so doing – co-constitute a normative hetero-sexual world. I begin by considering those occasions on which heterosexuality is displayed through talk that is explicitly oriented to (hetero)sex or to (hetero)-relationships.

The most explicit (hetero)sexual references in these conversations are in the form of sexual joking, banter, reports of (hetero)sexual activity and innuendo. Paul Drew's (1987) classic analysis of 'po-faced receipts of teases' includes data in which a sister teases her brother by alleging (in the presence of their parents) that he spent the night with his girlfriend (Drew 1987: 228); a young woman being teased about her supposed sexual interest in a (male) member of a rock band (Drew 1987: 228); and a newly married heterosexual couple whose complaint about the apparent structural deterioration of their new home is met with a teasing suggestion that this is attributable to their 'bumping around' ('that is, in bed', Drew 1987: 229). The 'dirty joke' that forms the centrepiece of one of Sacks' most celebrated lectures (Sacks 1995b: Lecture 9) begins 'there was these three girls and they just got married?' and employs the taken-for-granted cultural commonplace of a 'honey-moon' – with all its sexual implications – in developing a joke about fellatio between the bride and her new husband (see also Sacks 1974). Overall, the data support the (previously undocumented) claim that 'talk about sexuality is often about hetero-sexual desires and activities, again reinforcing the presumption of universal heterosexuality' (Eckert and McConnell-Ginet 2003: 207).

A second fairly explicit way in which heterosexuality is displayed in these conversations is through topic talk about heterosexual relationships – typically marriage or marriage-related topics such as engagements, weddings, marital trou-bles, etc. The civil institution of marriage is available in the UK and the USA to two persons over the age of consent irrespective of their 'race'/ethnicity, religion, nationality or class – subject only to the constraint that they must be of different sexes. In both countries there was – and in some social contexts still is – social disapproval of 'inter-racial' marriages, or of marriages between couples of (say) different religious backgrounds or social classes (Romano 2003) but in neither country – during the years in which these data were collected – was that social opprobrium formally encoded in laws banning such marriages as was then (and still is) the case for same-sex couples. No country in the modern history of the world permitted same-sex marriage until 2001 and hence all references in the data sets to marriage (and to associated institutions such as engagements, weddings, honeymoons, divorces etc.) index different-sex couples and, thereby, heterosexuality. In indexing heterosexuality in this way, speakers treat it as the taken-for-granted normative default way to be – and do so independently of whether or not they 'approve' of the particular heterosexual relationship they are talking about.

In Fragment 1 (below), Ron tells family news, displaying the heterosexuality of his two sons, each of whom is located with reference to his place of residence, his marriage, and (at least by implication in Shawn's case) his job. The 'news' about Shawn is his geographical relocation, to which mention of his 'wife' is subordinated; the 'news' about Michael is his one-year old marriage.

Fragment 1

```
[Holt SO88(II)-2-2]
    01 Ron: .hhh Just to bring you up to date with our
    02          family uh:m: .t.hh our eldest son u: Shawn
    03          u-who lives with iz wife in Taunton, ih he
    04          now practices in Bridgewa↑ter?
    05          (.)
    06 Les: eeYe:s,?
    07 Ron: .t He transferred from Newt'n Abbott to r-.hhh=
    08 Les: =[Oh lovely. ]
    09 Ron: =[(Tauntonn )]so th[(at he c'n be )         ]=
    10 Les:                    [Nice an' handy for you.]=
    11 Les: =[  ↑ Y e : s ?]
    12 Ron: =[  So that's very  ]u-That's very[good,?
    13 Les:                                   [.hhhheeyah
    14 Ron: Uh:m: Michael is still: soldiering on very
    15          happily as uh::um (.) policeman (.) in:
    16          ee[Yeovil. ]
    17 Les:       [Yeo↑vil?]
    18          (0.2)
    19 Les: Good,?
    20          (.)
    21 Ron: And has: uhm: uh seems to be quite happy
    22          [an-n(.)d he'n Ginny've just been married=
    23 Les: [.p.t.khhhhh
    24 Ron: twelve ↑months =
    25          (.)
    26 Les: eeYes,
    27          (0.2)
```

Across the data sets, there is a fair amount of talk that takes a negative or critical stance towards particular (past, current or possible future) marriages: Nancy berates her estranged husband (NB.II calls, see Drew 1987: 238–9; Jefferson 1984:

95); Emma – whose husband has just left her – confides her marital problems to her daughter and sister (NB.IV.4, see Drew and Holt 1988: 408–410); Billy and his girlfriend Gail are 'definitely not married' ('They have a prob'm [. . .] Definite pro:b'm,' TG); the early warning signs that might have led to the separation of Jean Claude's parents are reported ('you know the mum did an awful lot independently' (Holt: J86:1:4); and a complaint about a mother-in-law criticizes her as a wife (she 'nagged- (1.0) uhr 'er own husband' Holt: 2.9).

Clearly it is not the case that all heterosexual relationships are treated as acceptable, good or desirable ones: negative representations derive from considerations of recipient design and local interactional concerns, such as building a complaint about a mother-in-law (Holt 2.9). But nowhere in the data is heterosexuality itself treated as problematic: instead, even in the course of complaining about it, the different-sex definition of marriage is underwritten and reinscribed simply through being treated as taken-for-granted.

Although sexually explicit jokes and topic talk about heterosexual relationships and rituals constitute the most overt ways in which these people reveal their own (and others') heterosexuality, these are perhaps the least analytically interesting, precisely because of their explicitness. As Schegloff (2000: 718) has said, the relevances that shape the formulated experience exhibited in talk-in-interaction are made apparent 'not only in what persons choose overtly to talk about; perhaps least of all'. In the remainder of this article, I move from talk 'about' heterosexual sex and heterosexual relationships to show the extent to which heterosexuality forms a taken-for-granted backdrop that shapes talk in which people are explicitly oriented to other topics and actions entirely. I suggest that it is in and through *this* talk, far more than in talk 'about' (hetero)sex and (hetero)relations, that we can gain an analytic purchase on the mundane ways through which heteronormativity is produced and reproduced in ordinary talk-in-interaction.

It is common for speakers to mention their heterosexual involvements (dates, engagements, weddings, marriages) without being thereby engaged in topic talk about them. In Fragment 2 the caller is clearly making available a hearing of herself as heterosexual: she has a date with a male and is concerned about whether or not he really 'wants' her. She is not, however, 'announcing' her heterosexuality, nor is the information about her date tonight conveyed as simply 'news' or topic talk. Rather she makes available the information that she is heterosexual as part of the main action she is engaged in – describing her feelings of being 'nothing', and (despite her date tonight) like someone 'no man' would want. Her heterosexuality is a taken-for-granted background resource she draws on in displaying the suicidal feelings that have led her to make this call.

Fragment 2

```
[from Sacks 1995a: 66]
    01 Cal: I'm a grown woman an attractive woman I have a
    02 Clt: [Do you have any]
    03 Cal: [real nice date ] good looking guy for a date
    04      tonight and and I somehow I'm feeling that
    05      I'm nothing ((smiling sigh))
```

```
06 Cal: And I know nobody's a nothing But I am. It's
07      like everybody else is somebody and somewhere
08      along the line I muffed up.
//      ((possible break))
09 Cal: And I do think what man wants a neurotic
10      childless forty year old woman. No man.
```

One interactional problem for LGBT people in heteronormative contexts may be a difficulty in making apparent their homosexuality in the service of some action in which they are engaged without having the revelation of their sexual identity treated by the recipient as the main action. It may well be harder for someone with a same sex 'date' to deploy it, as the speaker does in Fragment 2, as evidence for the depth of her depression without having the thereby-revealed fact of her homosexuality topicalized as possibly related to her suicidal feelings. It may be harder for someone with a same-sex partner to refer to events (such as a geographical relocation) with reference to her relationship with that partner, not just because she lacks a straightforward term ('married') to describe the role of that relationship in her life, but also because she runs the risk of being heard to have made a gratuitous reference to her counter-normative sexuality. Fragment 3 comes not from the main data corpus but from a field observation of my own: it is a conversation (as it turns out, the *entire* conversation) between two women encountering each other for the first time during lunch at an academic conference:

Fragment 3

```
[Author: FN: 2003]
    01 Ali: How long have you been vegetarian?
    02 May: Since I met my partner. She's vegetarian.
    03 Ali: Oh. ((turns to person seated other side of her and
            doesn't address May again over the course of nearly
            an hour))
```

Ali's question to May was prompted by Ali's request to the serving person for the vegetarian option and is hearable as a topic proffer. May's response answers the question first with a formulation of duration that makes her couple relationship available, and then with an account for the relevance of that formulation that (via the proterm) makes her lesbianism available. Ali receipts the answer as news – but that is *all* she does: having initiated the interaction and launched vegetarianism as a topic for discussion with May, she now abandons it, and the conversation with May, altogether without providing any account for her withdrawal from the conversation. The absence of any rationale from Ali for failing to follow up on her question (e.g. 'let me just say hi to X . . .') leaves May to surmise the likely reason for the shift in attention – and that may be sufficient to convey to May that the reason lies in her having incidentally made available her lesbian identity.

The single most common way in which speakers display both their own and others' heterosexuality is (as May displays her lesbianism in Fragment 3) via person reference forms – especially non-recognitional ones. How to refer to a person unknown to another (i.e. the deployment of non-recognitional person reference forms) has been described as 'a central problem of sociology' (Sacks 1995a: 41). In the rest of this section I show how non-recognitional person reference often deploys terms from the heterosexual kinship system (e.g. 'husband', 'mother in law'), thereby locating the speaker, or those about whom s/he is speaking, as heterosexual. Widespread use of heterosexual kinship terminology displays the extent to which 'how the society and the world works' is organized with reference to heterosexual marriage.

(i) 'Husband' and 'wife'

By referring to their 'husbands', female callers position themselves as 'wives'; by referring to their 'wives', male callers position themselves as husbands, thereby displaying, incidentally, in the course of the action in which they are otherwise engaged, their location within heterosexual marital units. Whether or not these people are 'really' heterosexual (whatever that means exactly), the speakers' selection of person reference terms like 'husband' or 'wife' makes that inference available to their recipient – and people who identify themselves as lesbian or gay (or who have same sex sexual partners) are commonly described as 'passing for straight' if they remain within heterosexual marriages.

The data set includes many instances of people refering to their 'husband' or 'wife' without being oriented thereby to 'speaking as a heterosexual' – especially (but far from exclusively) in interactions with strangers. In data from suicide counselling calls reported by Sacks (1972; 1995a), the terms 'husband' and 'wife' are frequently used, as in Fragment 4 below, in which the loss of a 'wife' is provided as an instance of a 'personal problem' that has caused the caller to feel suicidal. The reference term 'wife' here evokes the culturally-understood inferences of an intimate and caring relationship, such that the loss of such a category member renders understandable the caller's depression.

Fragment 4

```
[From Sacks 1972: 50]
     01 A: Has there been some personal problem or difficulty
     02    that you're experiencing?
     03 B: Yes. I just lost my wife and I feel awfully
     04    depressed.
```

In Fragments 5 (also from the suicide prevention calls) and 6 (to emergency police) the callers refer to their 'husband' – thereby rendering 'ordinary' and 'natural' the action they are performing, as callers, in contacting the call-takers for help on behalf of this other person.

Fragment 5

```
[From Sacks 1995a: 73]
     01 A: Hello this is Mr Smith
     02 B: Say, my husband is suicidal and, I mean,
     03    he's attempted it about half a dozen times.
```

Fragment 6

```
[IND PD 59, in Schegloff 1996: 525)
    01 Pol: What's the trouble lady,
    02 Cal: I don't know my husband's sitting in his chair
    03      I don't know what's wrong with him he can't talk
    04      or move or anything.
```

The use of the kinship categories 'husband' and 'wife' mobilizes the inferences which attach to such relationships, obviating the need for the caller to account for the other's depression, or her concern on behalf of the other. Whatever other interactional hurdles these speakers encounter, their invocation of a different-sex spouse is *not* problematic. Rather, the sheer ordinariness of one spouse calling on behalf of another, makes the use of these kinship terms a powerful resource for 'doing being ordinary' (Sacks 1984), with all the interactional benefits (of not having to provide accounts, explanations, justifications, etc.) that attach to being an 'ordinary' person doing a 'natural' activity. By contrast, in Fragment 7, someone calling for help on behalf of 'a friend' presents an epistemically down-graded version of the 'history' of the person she calls about ('I believe . . . line 2) and finds herself giving an account as to why it is she, rather than a 'family' member, who is calling:

Fragment 7

```
[From Sacks 1972: 69]
    01 Cal: ... I'm calling for a friend who's had a history of
    02      mental disturbance; I believe attempted suicides
    03      were involved at that time ...
    04 Clt: ... What is your relationship to her?
    05 Cal: Just a friend.
    06 Clt: Just a friend. I see.
    07 Cal: Her family moved out about a year ago.
    08 Clt: No family. I see.
    09 Cal: Not in this part of the country.
```

Relational categories (e.g. husband-wife, neighbor-neighbor, friend-friend) 'constitute loci for rights and obligations' (Sacks 1972: 40), with spouses (and parents-children) treated as pre-eminent among these (see also Kitzinger 2005). For lesbians and gay men calling about a suicidal partner or depressed by a partner's death, there is no readily available and taken-for-granted term comparable to 'my husband' or 'my wife' upon which to draw. Lesbians and gay men do not have easy access to a person reference term like 'husband' or 'wife' that renders no longer appropriate the need for an account (Sacks 1995a: 23–4) as to why they are the person calling, or why that, in itself constitutes an unremarkable account as to why they might be depressed.

In Fragment 8, Mrs Mears has telephoned the owner of a house she would like to rent: the house has been advertised in the newspaper and the owner is unknown to her. When the owner asks for her name (line 3), she gives both her own name – using the title 'Mrs' which identifies her as a married woman – and the name of her husband, whose title implies his membership in the medical profession. In this instance, her heterosexual marital status provides her with a resource to lay claim to (as Sacks says) 'a possible extra qualifier for renting a house' (Sacks 1995a: 758).

Fragment 8

```
[SBL 1.3; see Sacks 1995a: 757]
    01 Own: I'll continue to try to get the: tenant: and see:
    02       'n let her know that someone wants to see it.
    03       .hhh Do you mind giving me you:r na:me.
    04 Mea: mm We:ll my na:me is Missus Mears. My husband
    05       is Doctor Mears
    06 Own: Uh tha- How do you spell that.
```

References to husbands and wives have the effect (neither intended nor oriented to in any of these calls) of displaying the caller's heterosexuality, and their location within the 'legitimate' and socially sanctioned legal status of marriage. These invocations of spouses are designed to achieve interactional goals related to the immediate sequential contexts in which they occur. There is no sense that these are contrived self presentations of heterosexuality: what the speakers are working up is an account for depression, or their eligibility as tenants. Their conformity with heteronormative expectations makes available to them resources for engaging in these other activities – resources not available to LGBT interactants.[1] Any attempt to deploy parallel terms invoking a same-sex partner is (even in the twenty-first century) likely seriously to derail the interaction by displaying the speaker's counter-normative lesbian or gay identity (see Land and Kitzinger 2005).

Finally, it is worth noticing that there are very few instances in these data corpora in which one spouse refers to the other using a person reference form *other than* one of the following four: 'my husband/wife'; the person's name; 'Mum'/'Dad' – or variants thereof – when talking to their children (e.g. Schegloff 1992: 1323, Excerpt 22); or the relevant proterm ('he' or 'she'). The massive numerical predominance of these four reference forms reflects a socially normative practice, such that when reference forms *other than* these are deployed, something special is being done interactionally – as, for example, when the non-normative formulation is employed in the service of a request to the co-interactant. So, a truck driver produces a locally initial reference to his wife as 'the lady that answers the door' – a formulation that is recipient designed for the police dispatcher in the service of the request he is making for a message to be delivered [IPD ND 1]. However, the 'unmarked' non-recognitional reference form for married different-sex partners is 'wife' or 'husband' – meaning that the (legally imposed) absence of these terms for same-sex partners often presents a significant interactional hurdle in terms of forwarding the action(s) in which they are engaged.

(ii) 'In law' terminology

American and European kinship terminology includes the concept of 'in law' in consideration of family composition, and its use constitutes either the speaker, or one of the speaker's relatives, as located within a marital heterosexual relationship. In Fragment 9, Lesley has called a plumber and, having made contact with someone she takes to be his wife, she formulates her request so as to display both her recipient's presumed heterosexual marital status, and her own, via her selection of 'mother-in-law' as a person reference form for the person subsequently referred to as 'Mrs Nan Field' (a husband is a prerequisite for a mother in law). The person reference form is not of course selected *in order* to display Lesley's marital status, but in order to render unnecessary an account as to why it is she who is calling on behalf of this person.

Fragment 9

```
[Holt:1:6]
    01 Les: Could you:r husband call on my mother in law please
    02        (0.4)
    03 Les: a:nd uh have a look at he:r um: (1.0) .h uh her
    04        bathroo:m,
```

In Fragment 10, Emma is offering an account as to why her daughter may not be able to visit her for Thanksgiving.

Fragment 10

```
[NB.4.9]
    01 Emm: .hh Her hu- u-her father in la:w's in the ho:spit'l
```

Emma launches her turn with what sounds as though it is probably headed for 'her husband's father' and repairs it to 'her father in law' – thereby perhaps rendering the relationship between the sick man and her daughter more 'personal' and immediate (and hence more compelling as a reason for her daughter not to visit her). In any event, either version refers to the same role-occupant in a kinship system that is organized around marriage. Without having designed her turn to achieve this, Emma is displaying that she has a married heterosexual daughter. Likewise, in the course of a reporting designed as a prelude to inviting the recipient to co-participate in the event (see Drew 1984: 139–40), Guy displays that he has a heterosexual daughter (married to his 'son in law').

Fragment 11

```
[NB:1:1:2]
    01 G: .hhhhhh Hey uh, hh My son'n law's down,
    02    'nd uh thought w'might play a little golf
    03    either this afternoon er tomorrow. Wouldju
    04    like tuh (0.9) hh get out? hh
```

People in same sex couples (and unmarried different sex partners) do not have unproblematic access to terminology that would locate their partner's parents and siblings in relation to them (as 'mother/father in law' and 'brother/sister in law' do for married heterosexuals). Nor, of course, do the parents and siblings of people in same sex couples have access to the terminology of 'son/daughter in law' or 'brother/sister in law' to refer to their relative's same-sex partner. Creative solutions may include using these terms anyway despite their 'factual' inaccuracy; deploying various circumlocutions (e.g. 'my daughter's friend/ partner/girlfriend' for the person who might otherwise be a 'daughter in law') and inventing variants that signal same-sex couples' exclusion from equal marriage rights (e.g. my own parents used 'daughter out-of-law' as a non-recognitional referent for my partner; a lesbian author refers to her lover's brother as 'my brother-if-there-were-a-law', MacLean 1995).

(iii) Identification of other with reference to their spouse

In Fragments 12 and 13 speakers use a person reference form that identifies the person they are speaking about as some other person's spouse: 'Mr Quinn's wife' and 'Mittie's husband'. The speakers are recipient-designing the turns with reference to how they figure their interactant knows this person, and they display an analysis that Mr Quinn and Mittie are the people clearly known to recipient, such that the talked-about people can be located with reference to them.

Fragment 12

```
[H:088:1:8:5]
 01 Leslie: Well a'course um:: Mister Quinn's wife has had lumps
 02          removed fr'm 'er neck hasn't she
```

Fragment 13

```
[Schenkein, in Schegloff 1996: 519]
   01 Joe: Oh you know, Mittie- Gordon, eh- Mittie's
   02      husban' died.
```

In Fragment 14 the speaker is engaged in a search for the name of 'that guy' and is producing 'clues' for his recipients: he first attempts an identification of him with reference to his workplace and then with reference to his wife.

Fragment 14

```
[AutoDiscussion (transcription simplified)]
   01 Cur: Didju know that guy up there et-oh. What the'hell
   02      is's name usetuh work up't (Steeldinner) garage did
   03      their body work. for 'em.
   04      (2.0)
   05 Cur: Oh:: he meh- uh,
   06      (0.5)
   07 Cur: His wife ra[n off] with Bill McCa:nn.
```

Schegloff (1996) has pointed out that person reference provides 'the terms through which people are observed, noticed and experienced' – and what we see in each of Fragments 12–14 is that those terms are formulated with reference to the hetero-sexual marital relationship, and hence reproduce heteronormativity.

(iv) The production of (heterosexual) couples

When speakers refer to two persons in a 'couple' relationship, such references are generally done so as to display the couple relationship. This is most explicit when terms like 'boyfriend' or 'husband' are used, as in Fragments 15 and 16:

Fragment 15

```
[Terasaki 1976: 53, in Levinson 1983: 351]
    01 D: Y'wanna know who I got stoned with a
    02     few w(hh)eeks ago? hh!
    03 R: Who.
    04 D: Mary Carter'n her boy(hh)frie(hhh)nd.hh
```

Fragment 16

```
[Rahman.B.2.14]
    01 Ver: .h 'R yih[go]in yih won't be goin t'th'town
    02       tomorrow will you.
    03 Jen: .h Well ah hahftih go ah:'m ah'v got s'm::
    04       eh:: Liz en uhr husb'n coming foh:: (0.7)
    05       e s- uh s- |supper
```

The use of two first names conjoined by an 'and' may convey 'heterosexual coupledom' when one name is 'male' and the other 'female' and when the activ-ities in which these two people are engaged (for example visiting or eating out with friends) is culturally understood to be a 'coupled' activity:

Fragment 17

```
[NB.II.5]
    01 Emm: .t.hh Uh Kay en Errol w'r s'pozetuh come ↓DO:WN
    02       uh: la:s' ni:ght,
```

Fragment 18

```
[NB.IV.4]
    01 Emm: .hhh ↑We were spoze tih gone ou'tuh dinner with
    02       Bill'n Gladys
```

List formulations typically use prosody and tempo to produce people in pairs of (heterosexual) couples as in Fragment 19:

Fragment 19

```
[Holt X(C)-2-1-4]
    01 Kat: I [thought maybe we c'd g- have a get together of,=
    02 Les:   [.hh
    03 Kat: =Melissa 'n Brian: 'n (0.5) Sarah 'n that bloke,
    04       (.) oh: uh Cli[ve?
```

By pairing together the (identifiably different-sex) names of the four people (with a pause between the two pairings) Katherine's talk produces them as two heterosexual couples. (An LGBT version might have been 'Melissa 'n Sarah 'n (0.5) Brian 'n that bloke, (.) oh: uh Clive'.)

Heterosexual couples are also produced by referring to them by a shared surname:

Fragment 20

```
[SBL.3.2]
    01 Cla: So anywa:y she: cancelled'er cla:ss out but (.)
    02       a:n:' (.) the Gra:hams c'dn come on Tue:sdee
    03       [so:]it's] [too ba::d,
```

Many of these methods of producing the heterosexual couple are surely also available to and about same-sex couples (and unmarried couples): references to 'Jenny and her girlfriend', to visiting 'Maria and Alice', or to a guest list including 'Margaret and Sophie, and Bill and Mark' must be commonplace in the non-heteronormative contexts they reflect and constitute. Thus far, at least, I am not suggesting that the practices available to do person reference are distinctively different for same-sex and different-sex couples – only that they may be deployed differently in the heterosexist contexts they thereby reveal themselves to be oriented to.

(v) Pronominal heterosexuality: the use of locally initial proterms

Another method through which (heterosexual) couples are produced in the classic CA data sets is through speakers' use of pronouns – in particular, first person plural proterms ('we', 'us', 'our'). Across the (non-institutional) data sets, use of a locally initial and unspecified 'we' is normatively treated by co-interactants as meaning the speaker and his/her spouse. In Fragment 21, Lesley moves from the first person singular ('I'm teaching tomorrow, line 1) to the first person plural ('we'll be up . . .' and 'we'll be able to lie in . . .') without specifically naming who else is included in her 'we' – though this person (Mark, who is of course known by Mum to be Lesley's husband) is finally named at line 19.

Fragment 21

```
[Holt X(C)1-1-1]
 01 Les: Well I'm teaching tomorrow so:,
 02 Mum: Oh: goody:.[hee!
 03 Les:             [we:'ll be up[e- aa-
 04 Mum:                          [heh heh eh-eh h=
 05 Les: We'll be able to LIE: I:N:. Becuz U:SUALLY WE'RE UP
 06      at SIX 'n toMORROW is eh we'll be able t' l get up at
 07      six thirty.
 08      (0.6)
 09 Mum: Oh. u-Why:::,
 10      (.)
 11 Mum: he he hn-[Why are]you why: six thirty.
 12 Les:          [ Becuz ]
 13 Les: Becuz I always ↑do when I'm teaching.
 14      (0.3)
 15 Mum: Oh I see:,
 16      (0.4)
 17 Mum: An' you usually get up at si:x.
 18      (0.7)
 19 Les: Well ye:s, cz Mark has: (.) does 'n (.) hour's overtime
 20      befo:re sk- work starts.
 21      (1.0)
 22 Mum: Oh:-:.
```

In Fragment 22, a locally initial 'we' is used by Emma (line 8); however, the other person who constitutes the speaker's 'we' is never named. This causes no apparent difficulty for her co-interactant, who seems to be assuming that 'we' invokes the husband with whom — it is evident from other calls in the corpus — Emma is co-constituted as a couple.

Fragment 22

```
[NB.II.3]
    01 Lot: ...lo:,
    02 Emm: £G'morning Letitia£=
    03 Lot: =u.-hHow'r YOU:.=
    04 Emm: =FI:NE HOW'R [YOU:.
    05 Lot:             [eh he:h heh WUDIYIH kno:w.=
    06 Emm: =.hhh Jis got down last ni:ght.eh
    07 Lot: OH YOU DI[:D?
    08 Emm:          ['hhh We BEEN tuh PA:LM SPRI:NGS.
    09      (0.2)
    10 Lot: Oh: God ah be't it's [ho:[:t
```

As elsewhere in the analyses advanced in this article, I am pointing to the *absence* of trouble in the co-conversationalists' talk: the ease with which an unspecified locally initial 'we' is managed and deployed reflects 'how the society and the world work' (Schegloff 1996: 465) in relation to heterosexual married couples. The locally initial use of 'we' in these instances seems to rely in part on (and to reproduce) the overarching primacy of the couple as a collectivity in relation to which Anglo-Americans locate themselves, and in part on the kinds of activities in which the collectivity indexed as 'we' is reportedly engaged: sleeping and rising together (Fragment 21) and vacations (Fragment 22) are culturally understood to be the kinds of activities in which couples engage (although of course others may also do so); the combination of an unspecified 'we' engaged in activities culturally understood as 'the sorts of things couples do together' makes available – indeed, may in some circumstances mandate – the hearing of 'we' as 'the couple of which I am a part'.

It is also common practice for speakers to use the pronoun 'he' or 'she' as a method for referring to just one member of a couple and for distinguishing the one from the other – a practice that is, of course, possible only when the members of the couple can be differentiated by sex. In deploying a proterm as an unproblematic person reference for one member of a couple unknown to the cointeractant, a speaker also thereby conveys that the couple is composed of people of different sexes. In Fragment 23, Lesley is offering some assistance to someone whose husband – encountered recently at a party political meeting – has apparently lost his job, and whom she knows vaguely but has not seen (as transpires later in the call) for many months. She gives as the reason for the call the offer of possible help from 'friends in Bristol' (clearly treated as unknown to her recipient – both through her use of a non-recognitional reference and, of course, because the purpose of her call is to put the recipient and her husband in touch with them). It is worth looking in some detail at how these 'friends in Bristol' are produced as a couple, and as a *heterosexual* couple.

Fragment 23: Three heterosexual couples

```
[Holt:2:3]
01 Mar: One three five?
02        (.)
03 Les: Oh hello, it's um: Leslie Field he:re,
04 Mar: Oh ↑hello:,
05 Les: Hello, .tch.h I ↑hope you don't mind me getting
06        in touch but uh- we metchor husband little while
07        ago at a Liberal meeting.
08        (0.3)
09 Mar: Ye:[s?
10 Les:    [.hh And he wz: (0.3) i-he told us something of
11        what'd happen:ed,
12        (0.5)
13 Les: to him .hh An:' I wondered haa- (0.2) i-he said he
14        m::ight have another position in vie:[w,
```

```
15 Mar:                                           [Mmhm,
16 Les:  .hh (.) Uhm (0.3) .tch Well I don't know how that
17       went, .h uh (.) It's just thet I wondered if he
18       hasn:'t (0.3) uh we have friends in: Bristol
19 Mar:  Ye:s?
20 Les:  who:-(.) uh: thet u-had the same experience.
21 Mar:  Oh↑:.
22 Les:  And they uhm: .t (0.2) .hh He worked f'r a printing
23       an:' paper (0.9) uh firm[u-
24 Mar:                          [Ye:s,
25 Les:  uh[:- which ih puh- uh: part'v the Paige Group.
26 Mar:    [Yeh,
27       (.)
28 Les:  .hh And he now has: u-a:: um (1.1) I don't think eez
29       called it consultancy (0.2) They find positions for
30       people: in the printing'n paper (0.4) indus[try:,
31 Mar:                                             [Oh I see:[:.
32 Les:                                                       [hh
33       An:d if: i-your husband would li:ke their addre[ss.
34 Mar:                                                 [Y e :[: s,
35 Les:                                                       [<As
36       they're specialists,
37 Mar:  Ye::s?
38       (.)
39 Les:  Uhm: my husband w'd gladly give it [t o  h i m .]
```

First, the relevance of hearing the 'friends in Bristol' as a couple is supplied by a local context in which 'couples' (specifically, married heterosexual couples) are indexed in the preceding talk. At line 6, Lesley's 'we' (rather than, say, 'I') produces her as a member of some unspecified collectivity on whose behalf she is 'getting in touch' (see likewise her 'us', line 10 and 'we', line 18) – and hence, as proposed in my analysis of 'we' above, is likely to be heard as invoking her marital unit. Lesley also references the marital relationship of her co-interactant ('your husband', line 6) – such that the relevant interactional units are constituted as two married couples. The 'friends in Bristol' are first hearable as a married couple, then, in the context of the two other married couple relationships already indexed in this talk. The subsequent pronoun repair from 'they' to 'he' (at line 22) extracts one member of the couple from the collectivity and is performed because, although the 'experience' (line 20) of unemployment, and its consequences on their lives, was presumably a shared event for both members of the couple already indexed in the plural (with 'friends', line 18), it was only one member of the couple who lost a job – the one who 'worked for a printing and paper firm' (lines 22–3), and for whom the proterm 'he' is appropriate. Notice that 'he' is treated as serving to differentiate the member of the couple who was employed (and subsequently lost employment) from the other, and hence produces the other as female. If both members had been male, 'he' would not have been usable in differentiating the two members of the couple from one another and a different formulation – for example, 'one of them', 'the employed one', etc. – would have been necessary to do so.

Fragment 24 is quoted by Sacks (1995a: 762–3) and (with reference to Sacks's earlier argument) by Schegloff (1996: 475, footnote 19) – both of whom point to the use of a locally initial 'he' at line 6, which 'it appears clear' (Schegloff), is 'obviously' (Sacks), a reference to Mr Hooper:

Fragment 24

```
[From Sacks 1995a: 762–3]
   01 A: How is Missuz Hooper.
   02 B: Uh oh, about the same.
   03 A: mm, mm mm mm. Have they uh th-uh
   04    Then she's still continuing in the same way.
   05 B: Yes, mm hm.
   06 A: Well I hope uh he can con- uh can, carry on
   07    that way, be[cause-
   08 B:              [Well he wants to make a chay- a change,
```

As Sacks (1995a: 763) says:

> Focussing on 'I hope he can carry on,' there's no 'he' being talked about; no person that could be referred to via 'he' has been introduced. Who's 'he'? Obviously in this case 'he' is Mr Hooper. The topic is Mrs Hooper's illness. The introduction of him in such a way as requires the use of Mrs Hooper to find who 'he' is, may be one way that, that Mr Hooper is being talked of 'subtopically' is done.

What makes it 'obviously' (Sacks 1995a: 763) the case that 'he' indexes the husband? First the use of the title 'Mrs' (line 1) indexes the existence of a husband (at least at some point), whereas the use of a first and last name would not, and 'Miss' would be counter-indicative – but in any event, the interactants seem to share some information about Mrs Hooper and presumably both know of the husband's existence (part of what Schegloff [1996: 457] means, perhaps, when he says that the 'he' reference 'invoke[es] recipient's (B's) knowledge of the matters being talked about to solve what – that is relevant to this topic – this person reference could be referring to'). The plural proterm 'they' at line 3 is hearable as possibly inviting the recipient to understand Mrs Hooper as part of an (unspecified) collectivity. The invocation of another as part of a collective 'they' may, like the invocation of oneself as part of a collective 'we', produce the heterosexual (married) unit as the collectivity generally understood as thereby referenced. The subsequent production of a locally initial 'he' (line 6) (possibly hearable as extracting a male from the 'they' at line 3) produces a male person as needing to 'carry on' in the context of Mrs Hooper's illness. The apparent ease with which the speakers produce and understand this locally initial 'he' as Mrs Hooper's husband displays (for us as analysts) the extent to which coping with a wife's illness is an activity category-bound to 'husband', and that this category boundedness is a *resource* that is relied upon by the speaker who deploys – and the recipient who makes sense of – the locally initial proterm. The 'knowledge of the matters being talked about' (Schegloff 1996: 457) is not merely knowledge specific to the individual circumstances of Mrs Hooper (in Fragment 24) or the 'friends in Bristol' (in Fragment 23, about whom the recipient in fact has no prior knowledge): it rests also on cultural knowledge about what categories of person care about and for each other, and possibly share a single family income – categories produced here in terms of the heterosexual married couple.

Through the invocation of husbands and wives with locally initial proterms ('we', 'he', 'she'), speakers treat the existence of such persons as a taken-forgranted feature of their social worlds. Across these conversations, then, a 'couple' is understood as composed not just of two people, but specifically of two people of different sexes.

Speaking as a homosexual

There is only one identifiably homosexual speaker in the data sets reviewed here: a caller to the suicide prevention center in the data collected by Sacks (see Sacks 1972, 1995a). Although many of the suicide calls involve problems in heterosexual relationships (spousal deaths, divorces or abandonments, see Sacks 1972: 52, 56), and although many callers make apparent that they *are* heterosexual (e.g. calls 9, 14, 16, 17, 19, 23, 24 in Sacks 1972), nobody calls the suicide line *because* they are heterosexual. Rather heterosexuality in these calls, as elsewhere in the data corpora collectively, is a taken-for-granted backdrop. By contrast with these suicidal heterosexuals, the one suicidal homosexual caller presents his sexual orientation as the reason for the call (Sacks 1972: 65–6, 1995a: 46–7). This speaker is alone in these data corpora in orienting to his talk as conveying information about his sexual orientation. That is, he is 'speaking as a homosexual' in a way that no heterosexual in these data is ever 'speaking as a heterosexual'[2].

Fragment 25

```
[from Sacks 1995a: 46]
    01 Clt: Is there anything you can stay interested in?
    02 Cal: No, not really.
    03 Clt: What interests did you have before?
    04 Cal: I was a hair stylist at one time, I did some
    05      fashions now and then, things like that.
    //      ((lines omitted))
    70 Clt: Have you been having some sexual problems?
    71 Cal: All my life.
    72 Clt: Uh huh. Yeah.
    73 Cal: Naturally. You probably suspect, as far as the
    74      hair stylist and, uh, either one way or the
    75      other, they're straight or homosexual, something
    76       like that.
```

Sacks comments that:

> In this case, while it might not be proper for this man to say about himself that he's troubled by possible homosexual tendencies, he finds a way to invoke a subset of occupational categories, 'hair stylist . . . fashions . . . and things like that,' which constitutes an adequate basis for inferring homosexuality. And in his subsequent talk he proposes that such an inference has 'probably' been made by the other.
>
> (Sacks 1995a: 47)

By contrast, the inference of *hetero*sexuality (made on the basis of different-sex partners and spouses) is never oriented to as such by interactants. These casual and un-oriented to displays of heterosexuality in the service of local interactional goals constitute a mundane instance of heterosexual privilege by those who take for granted, as others cannot, their access to the culture's kinship terminology and their own conformity with a heteronormative social order.

Conclusion

The field sometimes known as 'queer linguistics' (Kulick 2002) has focused overwhelmingly on 'deviant' groups. As Cameron and Kulick (2003: 149) point out, 'understanding the processes that maintain the hegemony of heterosexuality requires attention to be given not only to the cases in which bodies/relations/desires "deviate" from the norm, but also to those cases in which they do not'. I have focused in this article on instances in which apparently non-deviant heterosexuals produce themselves as such, and I have drawn attention to the utterly banal and commonplace nature of these heterosexual performances. I have shown various ways in which, without any orientation to so doing, speakers 'give off' their heterosexuality, and I have argued that the co-interactants in these data sets are not actively 'doing being heterosexual' or 'flaunting' their heterosexuality – but are simply getting on with the business of their lives, treating their own and others' heterosexuality as entirely unremarkable, ordinary, taken-for-granted and displaying it incidentally in the course of some other action in which they are engaged. For the 'normal' heterosexual participant, nothing special is happening. For any 'deviant' LGBT participant in (or eavesdropper on) the conversations in the data corpora from which these fragments have been extracted, a clamorous heterosexuality is everywhere apparent.

This analysis offers evidence to counter a common criticism of LGBT activists: the charge that we 'flaunt' our sexuality (e.g. '. . . do you have to let everyone know? Why flaunt it?' Manahan 1982: 68). One response is to draw attention to the many ways in which *heterosexuals* display their heterosexuality in ordinary everyday interaction. This study documents some of those displays, and shows how in the everyday talk analysed here, heterosexuality is 'naturalized' – constructed as an invisible (un-oriented to) category. This research, then, lays some empirical groundwork for using CA to explore the relationship between the casual disclosure of sexual identity by heterosexual people who are doing 'nothing special' and the management issues attendant upon disclosing a lesbian or gay identity.

Transcription conventions

Aspects of the relative timing of utterances

[ ]	square brackets	overlapping talk
=	equals sign	no discernible interval between turns (also used to show that the same person continues speaking across an intervening line displaying overlapping talk)
<	less than sign	'jump started' talk with loud onset
(0.5)	time in parentheses	intervals within or between talk (measured in tenths of a second)
(.)	period in parentheses	discernable pause or gap, too short to measure

Characteristics of speech delivery

.	period	closing intonation
,	comma	slightly upward 'continuing' intonation
?	question mark	rising intonation question
¿	inverted question mark	rising intonation weaker than that indicated by a question mark
!	exclamation mark	animated tone
-	hyphen/dash	abrupt cut off of sound
:	colon	extension of preceding sound – the more colons the greater the extension
↑↓	up or down arrow	marked rise or fall in intonation immediately following the arrow
here	underlining	emphasized relative to surrounding talk
HERE	upper case	louder relative to surrounding talk
°here°	degree signs	softer relative to surrounding talk
>this<		speeded up or compressed relative to surrounding talk
<this>		slower or elongated relative to surrounding talk
hhh		audible outbreath (no. of 'h's indicates length)
.hhh		audible inbreath (no. of 'h's indicates length)
(h)		audible aspirations in speech (e.g., laughter particles)
hah/heh/hih/hoh/huh		all variants of laughter
( )	empty single parentheses	transcriber unable to hear word
(bring)	word(s) in parentheses	transcriber uncertain of hearing
((coughs))	double parentheses	transcriber's comments on, or description of, sound: other audible sounds are represented as closely as possible in standard orthography, e.g., 'tcht' for tongue click; 'mcht' for a lip parting sound

Chapter 15

Penelope Eckert

1996

VOWELS AND NAIL POLISH

The emergence of linguistic style in the preadolescent heterosexual marketplace

THE CHALLENGE OF A THEORY of linguistic practice is to locate the speaking subject within a social unit in which meaning is being actively constructed, and to investigate the relation between the construction of meaning in that unit and the larger social structure with which it engages. It is for this reason that Sally McConnell-Ginet and I (Eckert and McConnell-Ginet 1992) have called for using the community of practice as the site for the study of language and gender. A community of practice, as defined by its originators, Jean Lave and Etienne Wenger (1991), is an aggregate of people who, through engagement in a common enterprise, come to develop and share ways of doing things, ways of talking, beliefs, values – in short, practices. For the sociolinguist, the value of the construct 'community of practice' resides in the focus it affords on the mutually constitutive nature of individual, community, activity, and linguistic practice. For the student of language and gender, it offers the possibility to focus on the local construction of gender – to see how gender is co-constructed with other aspects of identity, and to identify what one might abstract from this as gender.

In the following pages, I will briefly sketch a series of events and developments, as a community of practice within a cohort of preadolescents moves through fifth and sixth grades. Originating in a loosely assembled collection of childhood playmates and classmates, this community of practice develops in the form of a heterosexual crowd. The crowd's membership and practices are in continual and rapid flux as its members jointly move towards adult social heterosexuality. I will focus on the emergence of a local style among the female participants in this crowd – a style that they see as 'teen' style but that others, depending on their point of view, might see as reflecting gender, ethnicity, class, attitude. Through an account of some day-to-day events, I hope to describe the nature of stylistic development, the interconnection of language with style in action and appearance, and its role in the co-construction of gender, class, age, ethnicity, and a number of interrelated terms of identity. These events take place at Hines Elementary School, a school in Northern California serving a low income, ethnically heterogeneous student population composed primarily of Mexican Americans, Asian Americans, particularly Vietnamese, and smaller numbers of African Americans, South Islanders, white Anglo Americans and other groups.

The passage from childhood to adolescence brings the emergence of a peer dominated social order. In the process, the very meaning of gender is transformed since it brings, most saliently, a transition from a normatively asexual social order to a normatively heterosexual one, transforming relations among and between boys and girls. While heterosexuality is quite commonly viewed as an individual development, observing preadolescence makes it quite clear that heterosexuality is above all a social imperative (Rich 1980), and changes in individual relations between boys and girls are mediated by a cohort-based heterosexual market. In *Gender Play* (1993), Barrie Thorne documents the beginnings of the heterosexual market in elementary school. She notes the frenetic engagement in pairing up, fixing up, and breaking up; and girls' engagement with the technology of femininity – coloring nails and lips, frequently with age-appropriate semi-pretend cosmetics such as lip gloss and felt-tip pens; and the rejection of childish games.

The transition into a heterosexual social order brings girls and boys into mutual and conscious engagement in gender differentiation, in the course of which boys appropriate arenas for the production of accomplishment, and girls move into the elaboration of stylized selves. Both boys and girls come to view themselves as commodities on the heterosexual market, but while boys' value on the market is tied to the kinds of accomplishment that they have been cultivating throughout childhood, the girls' value is tied to the abandonment of boys' accomplishment, and the production of style and interpersonal drama. Girls become engaged in the technology of beauty and personality, learning to use a range of resources in which language use is elaborated along with the adoption of other resources such as nail polish, lip gloss, hair style, clothing, and new walks. It is not uncommon in fifth grade to see girls and boys running around, making sudden movements, rolling on the floor or throwing themselves to the ground, using their bodies in much the same way. Increasingly in sixth grade, girls stop running and start monitoring their facial expressions, striking feminine and dramatic poses, adorning and inspecting their hands in a disembodied manner, arranging their breasts. And boys begin to subdue their facial expressions, control their hair, spread out their shoulders, develop deliberate tough or athletic walks and flamboyant moves on the athletic field or court, consciously deepen their voices. The process of objectification affects both boys and girls, as they work to produce value as complementary commodities on the market. But the nature of this complementarity is not neutral but involves qualitative changes in girls' place in the world. As boys take over casual playground sports, girls replace vigorous physical playground activity with observing, heckling, and occasionally disrupting boys' games, and with sitting or walking around in small and large groups. The practice of walking around has in itself symbolic significance. Moving away from the crowd and walking around slowly, intensely engaged in conversation draws attention to those who do it, by contrasting with the fast movements of their peers, with play, with the larger groups engaged in games, and with the louder tone of children's talk. This walking, furthermore, is a visible occasion on which girls engage in intense social affiliation activities, negotiating heterosexual pairings and realigning friendships.

Not everyone is engaged in the heterosexual market. Indeed, the market is located locally within particular communities of practice – heterosexual 'crowds'. While any dyad or triad of girls can walk around and talk, only certain girls' walking and talking will carry status. The crucial ingredient is the public knowledge that they have something important to talk about – that the social relations they are exercising in their talk are important social relations – those of the emerging heterosexual crowd. The boundaries of the crowd are quite fluid, and part of community practice is the management of participation, marginality, and multiple membership. In particular, since among the girls much of the activity has to do with realignments, the management of fluidity is central to community practice. Thus it is not simple engagement in heterosexual social practice that signals the entrance into adolescence, but the cohort-wide co-construction of social status and heterosexual practice. Furthermore, the development of a 'popular crowd' that is by definition heterosexual brings the cohort, simultaneously, into engagement with the world beyond the age cohort. Participation in the heterosexual market offers new possibilities for the construction of a public persona. The crowd dominates the public sphere, partially by inserting the private sphere into it. Heightened activity and style draw attention to those who are engaged in it, and make their private affairs public events. In this way, they take on status as public people. This 'going public' is a crucial component of the process of maturation taking place in this age group. Such things as girls' trips to the mall, and gang-oriented territoriality, are primarily about inserting and viewing the self as an independent agent in the public domain.

Both the negotiation of heterosexuality and relationships in general, and the technology of beauty and personality, become professional areas, in which girls are recognized as more knowledgeable than boys. Since it is still new and mysterious, this knowledge is respected and a source of status and admiration from both boys and girls. Heterosexuality is, in some important sense, a girls' pastime, engaging girls more among themselves than with boys. Boys play a more passive role in the process, leaving the girls to do much of the initiating, and frequently passively participating in girls' strategies. One boy, for example, broke up with his girlfriend of six months at the request of her friends, who wanted to punish her for being 'a bitch'. There is an excitement about all this realignment, about venturing into the unknown. Seeking legitimate agency, girls opt for power and excitement in the heterosexual market. Seeing that they won't gain recognition for the pursuits that boys are taking over, girls choose to call the shots, and to become experts, in a whole new arena. Girls become heighteners of the social, breathing excitement into heretofore normal everyday people and situations, producing desire where none was before. The direction of all this energy to the sphere of social relations throws girls into a conscious process of stylistic production as they jointly construct group and individual styles, and in the process propel themselves into the public arena. This stylistic production brings together resources from a broad marketplace of identities, merging aspects of gender, ethnicity, age-appropriateness, heterosexuality, class, immigration status, etc., into one highly meaningful local style.

Linguistic style is a way of speaking that is peculiar to a community of practice – its linguistic identity (California Style Collective 1993). Briefly put, style is a clustering of linguistic resources that has social meaning. The construction of a style is a process of bricolage: a stylistic agent appropriates resources from a broad sociolinguistic landscape, recombining them to make a distinctive style. In this way, the new style has a clear individual identification, but an identification that owes its existence to its life in a broader landscape of meaning. Above all, that style is not simply a product of community practice — it is not just a way of displaying identification — it is the vehicle for the construction of this identification. It is precisely the process of bricolage that allows us to put together meanings to construct new things that are us and that place us in relation to the rest of the world. This process of bricolage takes place within communities of practice, and to a great extent is the joint work of the community and of the tensions between individual and community identities.

I relate the following series of vignettes in order to illustrate the emergence of a complex style as the age cohort moves into heterosexual social practice. This emergence of style is accomplished in a complex interplay between group and individual identity and style (see Wenger 1998). In the following account, I focus on the interaction between Trudy, a stylistic icon, and the home girls, the community of practice that is most prominent in her school-based activities.

In February of fifth grade, as I walked out of the lunchroom onto the playground, Trudy and Katya, who normally played Chinese jumprope at recess, rushed over and invited me to come with them. They told me that they no longer always played at lunchtime — sometimes they just talked instead. Katya said 'just talk' with a hunch of her shoulders, wide eyes, and a conspiratorial grin. They led me over to some picnic tables, telling me behind their hands that what they talk about is boys, and that Trudy is 'with' someone. Once we were seated on the picnic tables, Trudy and Katya hesitated, giggled, and looked around conspiratorially. Trudy then whispered behind her hands, informing me that it was Carlos that she was with, and then told us both that he had kissed her. Katya 'ooooo'ed and looked wise. I asked where he'd kissed her and she laughed uproariously and pointed to her cheek. We sat for a few more moments, and then went off to play hopscotch.

A few weeks later, as I was playing Chinese jumprope with Alice and two other girls, Trudy, Katya and Erica came along and tried to join in. Alice, whose rope we were using, said they couldn't join. In a fashion reminiscent of the way in which boys occasionally disrupt girls' games, Trudy and Erica jumped into the circle both at once, taking giant leaps onto the rope, creating chaos and laughter, simultaneously outjumping Alice and dismissing the game. Alice got upset and folded up the rope. This was the last time I ever saw Trudy play a 'child's game'. This is not to suggest that the transition away from kid stuff is abrupt — Trudy may well have played Chinese jumprope at home some more, as adolescent behavior is slowly incorporated into day-to-day practice. A year later, for example, Trudy reached into her low-slung baggy jeans to show me her new sexy lace underpants, saying, 'Yesterday I wore kid pants' (meaning cotton pants).

Trudy moved quickly into the world of teen behavior, of heterosexuality, flamboyance, and toughness. She took to walking around the playground with a group of girls, talking and heckling a group of boys as they played football. Together, this group of girls and of boys came to constitute a highly visible, predominantly Mexican American, heterosexual crowd. Trudy became a key player in this crowd, flamboyant in her style and highly active in pursuing relationships among both girls and boys. As fifth grade drew to a close and sixth grade took off, crowd activity progressed fast and furiously, as male and female pairings were made and broken, as girls' friendships shifted, and as drama built with girls accusing each other – or girls outside the group – of 'talking shit', and kissing or trying to steal their boyfriends. Trudy emerged as a stylistic icon: she had more boyfriends (serially) than anyone else, she was more overt in her relations with her boyfriends, she dressed with greater flair, she was sexier, tougher, louder, more outgoing, more innovatively dressed, and generally more outrageous than any of her peers. The highly prominent style that became Trudy's hallmark was simultaneously an individual and a group construction. The heterosexual crowd supported Trudy's activities, providing the social landscape, the visibility, and the participation necessary to make them meaningful. At the same time, Trudy made meaning for the crowd and for its members individually and severally, her actions drawing others into the adolescent world, taking risks in their name.

After school one day, a small group of girls fussed over Trudy, who was crying because her boyfriend had told someone that he wanted her to break up with him. 'He won't do it himself, he wants me to do it', she sniffed. The assembled group of admiring and sympathetic girls criticized the boyfriend. 'That's what he always does', said Carol. Sherry said 'He just uses girls'. Trudy sniffled, 'I like him so: much'. In her heartbreak, Trudy established herself as way ahead in the heterosexual world – as having feelings, knowledge and daring as yet unknown to most of her peers. At the same time, she gave Carol and Sherry the opportunity to comfort her, to talk knowingly about her boyfriend's perfidy – to participate in the culture of heterosexuality. In this way, her flamboyance propelled Trudy and those who engaged with her into a new, older, sphere.

After the breakup, Trudy 'got with' Dan. 'I love Daːn', she kept saying in my ear, the vowel nice and backed, 'I love Daːn'. During hands-on science, my tape recorder sat turning in the middle of the table. Every once in a while Trudy leaned forward to the microphone and whispered, 'I love Daːn'. Her group asked me later if I'd listened to the tape – they asked, with a frisson, if I'd heard what she was whispering. Her pronunciation of the vowel in Dan has special significance. In Northern California Anglo speech, /æ/ is splitting into two variants, raising before nasals and backing elsewhere. Latino speech is set apart from other local dialects with the lack of such a split – all occurrences of /æ/ are pronounced low and back, and this pronunciation is commonly foregrounded as a stylistic device.

One day, a group of girls sat at the edge of the playground complaining that there weren't any cute boys (i.e. the boys in their class hadn't become cute over the summer). As they talked, they kept their collective eye on the boys who were goofing around nearby. One of them pointed out that there was one cute boy, at which point they all called out in unison, 'Saːm!' As they intoned his name, pronouncing the vowel long and low, the girls attracted Sam's attention as well as that of the group of boys. They moved on to make humorous observations about other boys, and about each other's activities with boys, hooting loudly after each observation in a kind of call and response. The boys began to get agitated, and Jorge yelled something at them. Trudy stood up, stuck out her butt at him and called, 'Kiss my ass, Jorge, you get on my nerves!' Linguistic devices, such as the pronunciation of /æ/, the meat of studies of variation, take on their social meaning in use – in the occasions on which they are given prominence in connection with social action. Trudy's use of language, like her use of other aspects of style, has a special status. Her flamboyance is a platform for the construction of meaning of all sorts. As other girls report her actions to each other, as they take on bits of her style, they are propagating sound change (the backing of /æ/) along with the meaning that Trudy and her community of practice have imbued it with. This meaning, though, is constructed not for the vowel in isolation, but for the larger style.

As sixth grade got under way, the girls' crowd expanded, and dubbed itself the 'home girls'. They took to greeting each other with a hug – in the morning as they arrived at school, and as they emerged from their different classrooms at recess, as they split up at the end of recess, and before they went home at the end of the day. At first awkward and self-conscious gestures among Trudy and a small handful of friends, the hugs spread and became stylized – a brief one-armed hug became the favorite. This greeting clearly indicated who was part of the crowd and who was not, at the same time that it endowed the crowd with an air of maturity. Fortuitously, in an attempt to regulate unwanted physical contact among students, teachers and administrators 'outlawed' hugging when it began to spread. Hugging, therefore, had additional value as an act of defiance – particularly as the girls, on the way to the playground at recess, took to stopping by one classroom to give a quick hug to other home girls who were being kept in from recess because of unfinished work or misbehavior.

Girls' open defiance towards teachers was incorporated into home girl style in the course of sixth grade. But most girls found it difficult to display defiance in the classroom, and once again Trudy stepped in for them. Her defiance, however, only verged on being openly rude, and aimed to be an entertaining stylistic display. One day, for example, the teacher went around the class asking students how they rated a report they had just heard. Trudy was inspecting her long red fingernails, and clicking them loudly on her desk to the admiration of many in the room. The teacher called out, 'Trudy?' Trudy answered, 'What'. The teacher, mishearing, said, 'Did you say "two"'? Trudy said, 'No. I'm all "what"'.

Trudy sprawled across her table, squirming and calling out unwanted answers and comments to the teacher. She told me she had had too much chocolate at lunch and she was feeling 'hyperactive'. When PE finally arrived, she burst onto the playground, jumping on and off a picnic table shouting 'whassup? whassup? whassup?' She climbed on the table, struck a pose with hips out, told me she'd beaten up Sylvia 'because she's a bitch', and gave me a blow-by-blow story of the fight that would have put any tough guy to shame. One day, Alicia entered the classroom, standing unusually tall. She strolled over and rested her fingertips on my table, tilted her head back, hand on hips, and said, 'Whassup?' In this way she signaled to me that she was now hanging with the home girls.

All of these – the ritual hugs, the greetings, the songs, the accusations, the fight stories – are part of an emerging style. The transition into a heterosexual social order brings boys and girls into mutual and conscious engagement in gender differentiation, in the course of which girls move into the elaboration of flamboyantly stylized selves. The development of flamboyant linguistic style is a key part of this elaboration, and inseparable from the emerging use of other aspects of gendered style such as nail polish, lip gloss, hair style, clothing, and new walks. These stylistic endeavors are inseparable from the construction of meaning for the community of practice, and from the construction of an identity for the individual as a participant in that community. At the same time, they are what provide the emergence of the adult from the child – and for girls, the transfer of meaning and excitement from the physical to the social. What is particularly important about this entire process is that what will later be adult endeavors with grave consequences, are initially engaged in for a kind of childish excitement and then for a sense of power in the heterosexual market, with no clear view of the subordination that lies around the corner. The development of an adolescent persona is a gradual process that begins with playing with small stylistic components – nail polish, a watch, a hair arrangement, a pose, a dance step, a facial expression, a phrase, a pronunciation, a song. It begins with the development of 'attitude' toward boys, transforming them into objects, in relation to which one can display new styles of behavior, and play out scenarios. Initially a terrain for the development of new initiative, it gradually transforms into a discourse of female objectification and subordination.

Chapter 16

Susan Ehrlich

1998

THE DISCURSIVE
RECONSTRUCTION
OF SEXUAL CONSENT

UNTIL THE 1950S AND 1960S in Canada and the US, the requirement of utmost resistance was a necessary criterion for the crime of rape (Estrich 1987); that is, if a woman did not resist a man's sexual advances to the utmost, then rape was considered not to have occurred. While the criterion of utmost resistance is not currently encoded in criminal definitions of rape in Canada and the US, Crenshaw (1992: 409) notes that a similar concept is operative in the adjudication of rape and sexual harassment cases to the extent that the interpretation and characterization of events in such cases is 'overwhelmingly directed toward interrogating and discrediting the woman's character on behalf of maintaining a considerable range of sexual prerogatives for men'. Here I expose a new manifestation of the utmost resistance standard – one that relies on a model of miscommunication between women and men. I demonstrate how a 'deficiency model' of miscommunication between women and men (Crawford 1995) informs, indeed dominates, this sexual assault tribunal. I argue that the general framing of these proceedings in terms of a deficiency model of miscommunication between women and men succeeds in characterizing the complainants' behaviour as 'inaction' or lacking in appropriate or utmost resistance, thereby affirming the 'sexual prerogative' of the defendant.

The university disciplinary tribunal

The data presented here were transcribed from audiotape recordings of a York University (Canada) disciplinary tribunal dealing with sexual harassment. York University disciplinary tribunals are university trials that operate outside of the provincial or federal legal system. Members of the university community can be tried for various kinds of misconduct, including unauthorized entry or access, theft or destruction of property, assault or threat of assault and harassment, and discrimination that contravenes the provincial Human Rights Code or the Canadian Charter of Rights and Freedoms. Each case is heard by three tribunal members who are drawn from a larger pool consisting of university faculty members and students.[1] Penalties range from public admonition to expulsion from the university. Normally, these tribunals are open to the public. In the case described here, two charges of sexual harassment had been brought against a male student (the defendant) by two female students (the complainants), all undergraduates at York University. The tribunal members hearing the case consisted of a man who was a faculty member in the Law Faculty (the tribunal's chair), a woman who was a faculty member in the Faculty of Arts, and a woman who was a graduate student in the Faculty of Arts. The case against the defendant was presented by the university's legal counsel. According to the regulations of York University, *sexual harassment* is defined as 'the unwanted attention of a sexually oriented nature made by a person who knows or ought reasonably to know that such attention is unwanted'. The defendant was charged by the same plaintiffs under the Ontario Criminal Code on two counts of *sexual assault*.[2] While the defendant's behaviour fell under the category of sexual assault under the Ontario criminal code, York University's rules and regulations do not include sexual assault as a possible offence. Thus, within the context of York University the defendant was charged with *sexual harassment*.

In colloquial terms, the defendant has been accused of two instances of 'acquaintance' or 'date' rape. These instances occurred in the women's dormitory rooms two nights apart. Each woman had invited the defendant to her room and, in both cases he allegedly persisted in unwanted sexual behaviour. Both women reported that they were quite clear and insistent that he stop, but their demands were ignored. In one case, another man and woman were in the room while the unwanted sexual behaviour took place; the woman served as a witness for the prosecution's case. The two complainants were casual acquaintances prior to the alleged instances of sexual harassment. They met coincidentally a short time after the incidents, discovered each other's experience with the defendant, and together each lodged a complaint of sexual harassment.

While not technically a criminal court of law, the York University disciplinary tribunal functions like one to the extent that each side, the prosecution and the defence, presents its version of the events at issue to the members of the disciplinary tribunal. As others have noted, courtroom talk assigns differential participation rights to individuals depending on their institutional role: questioners in legal contexts have the power to allocate turns, to frame the topic of questions and even to restrict the nature of responses through the syntactic manipulation of questions. In the case described here, the complainants, defendant and their witnesses testified under questioning by their own representatives (the defendant was represented by his mother, a family friend, and himself) and by the tribunal members. All participants were also cross-examined by representatives from the other side. Thus, unlike jury trials, the 'talk' of this disciplinary tribunal was not designed for an overhearing, *non-speaking* audience – the jury – but rather for members of the disciplinary tribunal who themselves had the right to ask questions of the defendant, complainants and witnesses.

Analysis

(Re)definition of consent[3]

Examples (1)–(5) demonstrate how the defendant constructs himself as innocent by redefining what constitutes consent on the part of the complainant, Marg.[4] According to the defendant, unless the complainant showed strong resistance after each sexual advance, his sexual aggression was welcome. In other words, if the complainant did not resist each of the defendant's advances as soon as it was initiated and if these signals of resistance did not take particular (strong) forms, the defendant interpreted the complainant's behaviour as conveying consent. Consider the following example (1), in which the defendant (Matt, MA) is questioned by the university counsel (Hilda, HL).[5]

(1)

> MA: Uhm she was just reciprocating and we were fooling we were
>   fooling around. This wasn't . . . heh this wasn't something that
>   she didn't want to do.
> HL: How did you know?
> MA: How did I know?
> HL: Yeah.
> MA: Because she never said 'no', she never said 'stop' and when I was
>   kissing her she was kissing me back . . . and when I touched her
>   breasts she didn't say no.

This example shows the defendant explaining how he knew when the complainant was expressing consent – because she didn't say 'no' and didn't say 'stop' in response to each of his sexual advances ('when I was kissing her', 'when I touched her breasts'). Examples (2)–(5) are further expansions on this theme. Especially noteworthy in examples (2)–(5) is how temporality becomes crucial to the defendant's notion of consent. In each example, there is explicit acknowledgement on the part of the defendant that the complainant has expressed lack of consent at some previous point in the interaction; however, because she did not communicate her protests in the wake of each of his acts of sexual aggression, he understood her to be 'consenting'. In example (2), the university counsel questions the defendant about events that took place after Marg left the dormitory room (to tell Bob, the other man present, that Matt was taking advantage of her). The university lawyer is trying to determine why the defendant continued with his sexual advances after hearing of the complainant's feelings.

(2)

```
 1   MA: I still wanted to clarify this because this was I felt that this was
 2        really abnormal. So I asked her I said ['do you']
 3   HL: [What was abnormal?]
 4   MA: Well that she goes and tells Bob that I'm taking advantage of her
 5        and then she comes =
 6   HL: = Did you ever think for a moment that she that she felt you
 7        were?
 8   MA: Well at that point for her to say to say that I was taking
 9        advantage of her when she let me kiss uh kiss her, when she
10        never said 'no', when she never said 'stop', when she never got
11        up out of the bed and said 'Bob and Melinda, Matt is taking
12        advantage of me. Help me'. Uh for her to go for her just to say
13        uh you know 'I couldn't do anything and I was just lying there'
14        and uh, and then sort of like she can't do anything and then she
15        escapes and then goes to Bob and says 'Matt took advantage of
16        me' uh, and then and then after saying that, she gets back into
17        bed with me.
18   HL: But it was her bed.
19   MA: Yeah but if somebody takes advantage, if I was if I was a
20        woman =
21   HL: =Yeah =
22   MA: =Okay? And I was in bed with somebody =
23   HL: = Right =
24   MA: = And this person and two other people were next to me, okay?
25        And this person started to take advantage of me and was doing
26        things I didn't want to do, okay? I would get up out of bed,
27        I would ask this person to leave, I would tell the two other
28        people and I would deal with it then.
29   HL: Right
30   MA: I don't understand the logic of . . . no I'm sorry. I do not think
31        that it's appropriate to get back into a bed with somebody who
32        you claim was taking advantage of you.
33   HL: So you felt when she got back into bed that that was a consent to
34        other activities?
35   MA: At that point when she comes back to bed, at that point I wasn't
36        even looking for consent. ((defendant's representative
37        interrupts))
38   HL: You at that point you didn't believe that she didn't want you to
39        do this?
40   MA: Of course not.
```

While Matt acknowledges that Marg felt he was taking advantage of her, he attempts to discredit and undermine this charge by pointing out in lines 10–12 that 'she never said no' ('when she let me kiss her'), 'she never said stop', 'she never said Matt is taking advantage of me' at previous points in the encounter. We see here how the timing of acts of resistance is an integral part of Matt's definition of consent: only if Marg were to protest *then*, at the very moment Matt initiated a sexual advance, would he hear her as expressing a lack of consent. The question of timing is also operative in Matt's response to questions about why he resumed sexual activity after Marg's comments to Bob. Matt focuses on Marg's subsequent act, that is, 'getting back into bed', in justifying his interpretation of consent. Indeed, Matt's repeated use of temporal expressions referring to previous points in the interaction (e.g. *then, at that point* in lines 5, 8, 14, 16, 28, 35) indicates the importance of temporality to his definition of consent. It seems that every new point in the interaction provides a new opportunity for Matt to ascribe consent or lack of consent to the complainant's behaviour.[6]

Examples (3) and (4) contain further questioning of the defendant by the university's counsel. Example (3) shows Matt claiming that, at some point during the night, Marg indicated that under different circumstances she might willingly engage in sexual activity.

(3)

    HL: Yeah so she told you under different circumstances [she]
    MA: [Yeah]
    HL: might be willing to engage in sexual activity with you.
    MA: Under the circumstances which she explained to me =
    HL: = Right with everyone in the room.
    MA: Well yeah I mean the =
    HL: = So she did tell you at some point that she didn't want to have sexual activity with you with everyone in the room. Am I right?
    MA: At that point she did.

Like example (2), example (3) demonstrates the importance of each of Marg's responses to Matt's successive acts of aggression in his determination of consent. When confronted with evidence of Marg's non-consent, Matt again invokes the issue of timing: from his perspective, Marg's expressed lack of consent at one point in this encounter does not preclude her consenting to his advances at a subsequent point. Example (4) describes events that occurred after those represented in example (3).

(4)

    MA: She was like caressing and like we were fooling around and I was caressing her and everything.
    HL: She already told you that under different circumstances she might do it. Right?
    MA: She had said earlier in the washroom =
    HL: =Yeah. So this is after =

MA: =Yeah but the thing, I knew, I know what you're saying but the thing is this, whenever I was engaged with sexual activity with Marg, okay? If Marg or anybody for that matter, if if that person at that time when I'm doing something, say if I'm lying in bed with them and reach over and grab their breast and, I had already done something with this person and they consented with it and, they did not move my hand away or anything and didn't say 'no', didn't say 'stop', didn't say uh uh uh, jump up and say 'No I want you to leave', I am assuming, okay? uhm that if a person does not resist to anything when they, that that that is consent.

HL: Okay.

MA: I never heard and I don't . . . I never heard from uh this instance you're referring to. I never uh: heard at that time her refuse to engage in whatever we were engaged in.

In this example, the defendant is quite explicit about his definition of consent: 'If Marg or anybody for that matter, if if that person at that time that I'm doing something [. . .] didn't say "no", didn't say "stop", didn't [. . .] jump up and say "No I want you to leave", I am assuming, okay? [. . .] that is consent'. In short, Matt seems to be saying that since Marg did not express resistance in response to each of his advances, she 'consented' to his sexual aggression.

Whereas examples (1)–(4) have illustrated the temporal aspect of Matt's definition of consent, example (5) shows that his understanding of consent rests also on the strength of expressions of resistance.

(5)

((From the tribunal member's questioning of the defendant))

GK: One last question, if Marg was asleep and there's testimony that says that she's asleep and we have testimony that says it's debatable whether she was asleep =

MA: = Mhmm =

GK: = Uh why do you continue caressing her?

MA: Well as I said last week what occurred was that we had gotten back into bed and we started kissing and she said that she was tired, you know, she never said like 'no', 'stop', 'don't', you know, 'don't do this' uhm 'get out of bed'.

Matt acknowledges that Marg has said that she is tired; he does not construe this as resistance – she did not say 'no' 'stop' 'don't', etc. We see almost identical comments by the defendant about the strength of signals of resistance in examples (1) and (2), for example, 'she never said no', 'she never said stop' (in line 10 of example (2)). In sum, examples (2)–(5) all contain Matt's acknowledgments that Marg has expressed lack of consent at some point during the course of their encounter. However, because Matt defines 'consent' as the absence of vehement expressions of resistance in the wake of every sexual advance, he contends that his escalating sexual aggression is justified.

'No' means 'No' and hegemonic masculinities

One way of understanding Matt's (re)definition of consent is in terms of the socially conditioned process by which linguistic forms are endowed with meaning. According to McConnell-Ginet (1989: 50) 'meanings are produced and reproduced within the political structures that condition discourse' with the result that 'a sexual politics may have helped some men to "steal the power of naming"'. Because linguistic forms depend for their full interpretation or meaning on social context, including mutually accessible cultural knowledge, the question of whose beliefs and values inform this cultural background knowledge is crucial to understanding how linguistic forms come to 'mean'. McConnell-Ginet (1988: 91) argues that the cultural knowledge forming the background for the interpretation of linguistic utterances is not neutral:

> The point is . . . that men (and dominant groups generally) can be expected to have made disproportionately large contributions to the generally available background beliefs and values on which speakers and writers rely in their attempts to mean.

For example, the utterance 'You think like a woman' functions as an insult in most public contexts in North American culture, not because all listeners adhere to the proposition that women have questionable intellectual abilities, but rather because listeners are aware that such a proposition is prevalent and pervasive within the speech community; i.e. it is part of a set of mutually accessible cultural beliefs. Likewise, a woman will say 'no' with sincerity to a man's sexual advances, but the 'no' gets filtered through a series of cultural beliefs and attitudes that transform the woman's direct negative into an indirect affirmative: 'She is playing hard to get, but of course she really means yes' (McConnell-Ginet 1989: 47). (Or in Matt's case, 'no' means 'yes' in the absence of aggressive and frequent expressions of resistance.) Because linguistic meanings are, to a large extent, determined by the dominant culture's social values and attitudes, they may lose their intended meanings in the context of a sexist speech community.

A feature of hegemonic masculinity (Connell 1987) perhaps relevant to Matt's (re)construction of 'consent' (out of the absence of strong and frequent enough expressions of resistance) is what Hyden and McCarthy (1994: 548) have termed the 'male sexual drive' discourse. Hyden and McCarthy note that one of the public 'discourses' surrounding victims of rape in the West concerns their naiveté about men's socially acceptable 'compelling' and 'uncontrollable' sexual impulses. Indeed, Estrich (1987: 101) refers to American sex manuals that 'laud[ed] male sexual responses as automatic and uncontrollable' (although also comments on newer ones that 'no longer see men as machines and even advocate sensitivity as seductive'). That Matt himself invokes this 'male sexual drive' discourse is shown in example

(6): here the university counsel, HL, is asking him why he continued with his sexual advances towards CD, the other complainant, when earlier he had indicated that he was not interested in her sexually.

(6)

> HL: Okay . . . Then you – she said you said 'I changed my mind about not wanting to sleep with you'.
> MA: Okay, there was a point . . . and this is the, I believe second time in the evening that she said she did not want to have sex. Uhm we were fooling around and then I stopped and I said I wanted to discuss something with her, but I was very reserved. Then I told her, well . . . cause we were fooling around I had become aroused and that . . . uhm: uh: that I was . . . yeah that I was sexually aroused and that I had desires to want to have sex. And I had expressed to her earlier that I . . . didn't want to and . . . it was more because we were involved in such . . . heavy sexual activity that I changed my mind.

Given that Matt's sexual advances towards the two complainants seem to depend on whether he is sexually aroused from one moment to the next, it is perhaps not surprising that he claims to interpret Marg's expressions of resistance as also variable from moment to moment. Put another way, Matt's interpretation of 'consent' relies on culturally dominant values and beliefs (or discourses) that form the background for the interpretation of linguistic utterances. Changing one's mind about wanting sex is completely consistent with the 'male sexual drive discourse' which says that once aroused, men's sexual urges are 'compelling' and 'uncontrollable'. And I am suggesting that Matt's interpretation of Marg's expressions of resistance as variable and as not definitive relies on such views of hegemonic masculinity.

Ideological frames: miscommunication and the utmost resistance standard

Henley and Kramarae (1994) and Crawford (1995) have pointed to the cultural pervasiveness of models of miscommunication between women and men in accounting for 'many sites of gender struggle including sexual violence and aggression' (Crawford 1995: 108). One version of such a model, the *difference* or *dual-cultures* model (associated most notably with Maltz and Borker (1982) and Tannen (1990)), suggests that women and men learn different communicative styles because of the segregated girls' and boys' peer groups they played in as children, resulting in inadequate or incomplete knowledge of the other group's communicative norms. In this view, miscommunication is the by-product of women and men growing up in different sub-cultures. While critiques of the difference model of miscommunication are numerous in the language and gender literature, Eckert and McConnell-Ginet (1994: 437) are particularly critical of the passive role it ascribes to women and men in the construction of gendered identities: 'the emphasis on separation and resulting ignorance misses people's *active engagement* in the reproduction of or resistance to gender arrangements in their communities' (emphasis mine). Citing the example of a man interpreting a woman's 'no' to mean 'yes' in the context of potential sexual relations, Eckert and McConnell-Ginet argue that this 'reading' is possible not because of the man's mistaken belief in shared communicative norms (e.g. because he mistakenly believes that the woman's expressions of resistance may change from moment to moment), but rather because he is actively exploiting ideas about gender differences in communication. In a similar way, I am arguing here that the defendant's discursive (re)definition of consent strategically invokes notions about 'gendered' speech styles and miscommunication in his justification of sexual assault. Moreover, the defendant's characterization of the events in question as consensual sex is legitimized by the general 'framing' of these proceedings in terms of a difference or dual-cultural model of miscommunication.

In examples (2) and (4), we see that Matt makes reference to his interpretation of Marg's behaviour, specifying the particulars necessary for him to understand her as refusing his advances. If he were a woman, he says (in example (2), lines 15–22), his resistance would be vehement and unequivocal, occurring precisely after a sexual advance. Two of the tribunal members were even more explicit than Matt in articulating the idea that miscommunication was operative on the night of the alleged sexual assault. For example, in questioning Marg and her co-complainant at the closing of the tribunal, the male faculty member, BW, raised the possibility that Matt perceived the events differently than the complainants did. This is illustrated in example (7).

(7)

> BW: All that we were trying to flush out is for you to comment on
> . . . Are we talking here about a situation in which you basically
> are saying that Matt is not telling the truth about these things, or
> is there a possibility that two people could have had different
> perceptions about what was going on? Sort of a vague question,
> but what we're trying to understand is whether you're telling
> the tribunal that in your mind Matt is lying to us, or in your
> mind you could actually say maybe he could understand this a
> certain way.
> CD: I . . . I honestly don't know what's going on in his mind. I don't
> know if he's making it up. I don't know if he just doesn't
> understand what happened. I I don't know =
> BW: = We know that you don't know but is it possible I guess is the
> question. Is it possible that he . . . saw the events differently than
> you perceived them?
> CD: I suppose it's possible.

Notice in example (7) that the tribunal member does not accept 'I don't know' as an appropriate response to his questions about the defendant perceiving the events differently than the complainants. Instead, the complainant is enjoined to acknowledge that misperception and miscommunication were possible ways of understanding the unwanted sexual aggression. To some extent, then, the tribunal member's questioning had the effect of restructuring the propositional content of the complainant's responses (i.e. from 'I don't know' to 'I suppose it's [miscommunication] possible'). Even more insistent about this particular characterization of events is the female faculty member, GK, when questioning Marg:

(8)

1	MB:	I kept saying 'let's just go to sleep'. I didn't honestly know what
2		else in my mind to do at that time. For me that was all I could
3		do to tell him I didn't want to do anything.
4	GK:	And did it occur to you through the persistent behaviour that
5		maybe your signals were not coming across loud and clear, that
6		'I'm not getting through what I want and what I don't want?'
7		Does it occur to you I need to stand up and say something'.
8		'I need to move him to the floor?' This is the whole thing about
9		getting signals mixed up. We all socialize in one way or the
10		other to read signals and to give signals. In that particular
11		context, were you *at all* concerned your signals were not being
12		read exactly and did you think since signals were not being read
13		correctly for you, 'should I do something different with my
14		signals?'
15	MB:	I did. He made me feel like I wasn't saying anything, that I
16		wasn't saying 'no' and that's *why* I asked to talk to Bob, thinking
17		if I couldn't tell him maybe Bob could tell him. Bob came in the
18		room and said everything was okay just to forget about it and go
19		back to sleep. I tried that. I told Matt, I said if the circumstances
20		would have been different, maybe. It was a lie but I mean it was
21		another way for me to try to tell him 'no'. I mean obviously I
22		just wanted to go to sleep. It wasn't getting through so I tried
23		different approaches. And in my mind I hoped that they were
24		getting through. I mean. I was making it as clear as I could. I'm
25		not sure if that answers your question or not but . . .
26	GK:	No. it's because right from there to the end you, you had felt
27		that you hadn't made it clear because at the end you said you
28		were willing to lie and give him this phone number and get rid
29		of him. So all along the way you felt your signals were not read
30		correctly. But the whole thing is, you know, that concerns all of
31		us is that the signals of, you know, between men and women are
32		just, are not being read correctly and I'm not debating who's
33		lying and who's telling the truth because it's not mine to say
34		that. The substance is why, that signals, do you feel at that time
35		your signals were not being read correctly?

Note that, in lines 9–10, GK contends that signals are bound to get mixed up because 'we all [are] socialize[d] in one way or the other to read and give signals'. Furthermore, lines 31–2 show GK invoking gender socialization as an explanation for this differential interpretation of 'signals': 'the signals [. . .] between men and women [. . .] are not being read correctly'. This tribunal member seems to subscribe to a 'different-but-equal' model of miscommunication on lines 32–3: 'I'm not debating who's lying and who's telling the truth'. In other words, it is not a question of one person lying and the other telling the truth; rather, 'signals' are interpreted differently by these individuals. On lines 4–14 and 26–30, however, she seems to subscribe to a 'deficiency' model of miscommunication (Crawford 1995) – one in which the complainant is represented as deficient in her attempts to communicate lack of consent. For example, she first asks on lines 9–12 whether Marg was concerned about the interpretation of her 'signals': 'In that particular context, were you at all concerned your signals were not being read exactly?' and then assumes (or presupposes) in line 12 (in the clause introduced by since) that the 'signals' were not being read correctly: 'did you think since signals were not being read correctly for you, "should I do something different with my signals?"' Moreover, on lines 26–30 the tribunal member asserts that Marg must have known her signals were not being read correctly 'all along'; otherwise, she would not have lied to the defendant. Implicit in the tribunal member's questions, then, is the claim that Marg was responsible for 'do[ing] something different with [her] signals', given that she knew Matt wasn't interpreting them correctly.

In example (9), GK continues to be preoccupied with the inappropriateness of the complainant's signals.

(9)

```
36    GK:   What I'm trying to say and I I realize what I'm saying is not
37          going . . . You never make an attempt to put him on the floor or
38          when he leaves the room, to close the door behind him or you
39          know you have several occasions to to lock the door. You only
40          have to cross the room. Or to move him to the floor, but these
41          things are offensive to you?
42    MB:   I was afraid. No one can understand that except for the people
43          that were there. I was extremely afraid of being hurt. Uhm: as
44          for signals, they were being ignored. I tried I mean maybe they
45          weren't being ignored I don't know why he didn't listen to
46          them. I shouldn't say they were being ignored but he wasn't
47          listening. And I kept telling him. I kept telling him, I was afraid
48          to ask him to sleep on the floor. It crossed my mind but I didn't
49          want to get hurt. I didn't want to get into a big fight. I just
50          wanted to go to sleep and forget about the whole entire night.
```

In this example, GK again suggests that Marg has not been clear enough with her 'signals' of resistance. On lines 36–41, GK lists a series of actions that were not pursued by Marg, 'You never make an attempt to put him on the floor . . . to close the door behind him or . . . to lock the door', and then asks whether these were offensive to Marg. Indeed, while GK's comments sometimes take the form of interrogatives, they often have the illocutionary force of assertions, for example, You should have put him on the floor, You should have closed the door, You should have locked the door. By continuing to focus on 'options' not acted upon by Marg, this tribunal member raises the possibility that Marg has not 'chosen' (i.e. 'options' imply 'choices') the best means of resistance or, put another way, that she has not resisted to the utmost.

Though GK asks Marg repeatedly about the inappropriateness of Marg's 'signals' in examples (8)–(9), she does not generally focus on questions of appropriateness when she asks Matt about his interpretations. In examples (10) and (11), we see GK questioning the defendant, Matt.

(10)

51	GK:	You said often that it was important to you that Marg had never
52		said 'no' to you or that 'she didn't like you', but you read into
53		her actions, but you were always looking at non-verbal signs
54		from her to understand that it was consensual. The fact that she
55		invites you into into her bed, well maybe that may be verbal, the
56		fact that she stays in bed with you, the fact that she doesn't leave
57		and so on, uh some of them were not, most, a lot of them I see
58		as non-verbal signals.

(11)

59	GK:	I'm trying to gather from this is that you read more verbal
50		signals than non-verbal signals [and I'm trying and I'm trying to]
61	MA:	[that she likes me?]
62	GK:	Yes so that your paying attention to her, according to your
63		testimony, to her non-verbal signals. It is really hard you see,
64		the point is when when the idea 'no means no' when when when
65		people are- tend to give people signals in different ways and I'm
66		just trying to interpret for [myself these signals.]
67	MA:	[Yeah I know there's there's a
68		communication thing.]

Here, we see the tribunal member expressing her understanding of the events in terms of a 'difference' model of miscommunication: she asserts, on line 65, that 'people [. . .] tend to give people signals in different ways' and wonders, on line 59–60, whether Matt 'read more verbal signals than non-verbal signals'. Not surprisingly, the defendant echoes her characterization of the events: 'Yeah I know there's there's a communication thing'. In contrast to GK's questioning of Marg, however, there is no suggestion in her questioning of Matt that he had other 'options' or ways of interpreting Marg's 'signals': the tribunal member is 'just trying to interpret these signals [for herself]'. Like example (11), example (12) shows GK concerned with Matt's verbal and non-verbal 'signals'.

(12)

```
69    GK:  Uh and you say 'I can't read her mind' at some times. Now I'm
70         concerned that there's certain verbal signals you pick up and
71         certain non-verbal signals you pick up =
72    MA:  = Mhmm =
73    GK:  = Uh and then there's certain very clear verbal signals and non-
74         verbal signal that you choose not to pick up or you don't pick up
75         and it's really hard for me to know.
```

While GK does focus on 'signals' from Marg that Matt did not 'pick up', there are no direct assertions in example (12) about Matt knowing that his interpretations were faulty. (Consider, by contrast, GK's assertion to Marg on lines 29–30 of example (8): 'So all along the way you felt your signals were not read correctly'.) Nor does GK assert what other 'options' Matt could have or should have pursued. (Again, compare example (12) to GK's questioning of Marg in example (9), lines 37–8: 'You never make an attempt to put him on the floor or when he leaves the room, to close the door behind him'.) Thus, although the complainant was repeatedly criticized for not making her signals clearer and not changing her signals, Matt is not generally criticized for what might be faulty or inaccurate interpretation of signals. Indeed, when GK questions Matt about 'mixed signals' in (10)–(12) it seems to be her assessment of the situation that is at issue. For example, as already noted, on lines 65–6, she is 'just trying to interpret for [herself] these signals' and on line 75 'it's very hard for [her] to know' about the signals that Matt does or does not 'pick up' on.

In addition to the types of questions found in examples (10)–(12), GK's questioning of Matt also focused on Marg's behaviour, specifically, the 'options' that she did not 'choose'. That is, in the following examples (13) and (14), we do not see GK questioning Matt about his behaviour or interpretations; rather, GK is attempting to confirm that Marg did not pursue avenues of resistance that GK seems to regard as appropriate. Beyond GK's noting 'the fact that [Marg didn't] leave' on line 56 of example (10), consider her comments in examples (13) and (14):

(13)

```
GK:  Uh when you left the room, as you left the room several times,
     was the lock ever used?
MA:  The lock was never used =
GK:  = Was the lock ever used when you were inside the room?
MA:  The lock was never used.
```

(14)

> GK: Okay. And as you said earlier and I want to make sure that
> I understand correctly, at no point were you asked to go on
> the floor?
> MA: No.

The idea that women, and not men, are deficient communicators in the context of potential sexual relations has been characterized previously as a *deficiency model* of miscommunication between women and men (Crawford 1995). Such a model does not assume separate-but-equal communicative styles; rather, women are blamed or held responsible for failing to signal their lack of consent clearly and unambiguously. Crucially, such an interpretive or ideological perspective functions to deflect men's responsibility for rape; instead the victim is held responsible for being deficient in her attempts to communicate. GK's continued emphasis on the 'options' or 'signals' not chosen by the complainant, I would suggest, has the effect of characterizing the complainant's signals of resistance as weak, infrequent and inappropriate and her behaviour as lacking in resistance. I noted earlier that the criterion of utmost resistance is not currently encoded in criminal definitions of rape; however, it seems to be operating in the way Matt construes 'consent' from Marg's presumed lack of strong enough resistance. The criterion of utmost resistance is given further legitimacy when a tribunal member asks questions (and makes assertions) that presuppose the inadequacy of the complainant's communication of resistance. In the preceding examples, we have seen that a 'different-but-equal' model of miscommunication is quickly replaced by one in which the woman is held responsible for miscommunication. That is, talk about 'difference' only thinly conceals the assumptions that truly underlie the tribunal member's questions – androcentric assumptions that legitimize the defendant's defence of weak and equivocal 'signals' on the part of the complainant. In characterizing the complainants' signals as inadequate, the tribunal members affirm the defendant's definition of the situation, and in particular, a ('masculine') code of behaviour in which 'real' resistance is expressed aggressively and directly. If, indeed, GK subscribes to a 'difference' model of miscommunication (as her comments would suggest), then one might expect her to apply different interpretive standards to the defendant's and the complainants' testimony. Repeated reference to 'options' the complainants could have or should have chosen, however, suggests that GK views the complainants' communication of resistance as 'deficient', in line with Matt's assessment of their behaviour as indirect and equivocal. (See, in particular, lines 24–7 in example (2).) These observations are consistent with Henley and Kramarae's (1994: 401–2) comments regarding the '*metastructure* of interpretation' in the context of men's dominance and women's subordination: 'the accepted interpretation of an interaction (e.g., refusal versus teasing, seduction versus rape, difference versus inequality) is generally that of the more powerful person, therefore [the man's interpretation] tends to prevail'.

Outcome of the tribunal proceedings

The tribunal found the defendant's behaviour to have fallen substantially below university standards. More specifically, their decision stated that both complainants were unresponsive to the defendant's sexual advances, that the defendant demonstrated an indifference to the complainants' wishes, and that the defendant's actions were disrespectful and insensitive. In spite of the university counsel's recommendation that the defendant be expelled, the tribunal members decided only to bar him from domitories on campus. They argued that the defendant did not pose a threat to the university community and that the university setting was a good place for him to become 'sensitized to the need for respecting the sexual autonomy of women' (In the Matter of M.A. p. 37). I would suggest that such a penalty is lenient for two convictions of acquaintance rape but, at the same time, is entirely consistent with the assumptions underlying this adjudication process. Indeed, comments in the tribunal members' written decision were consistent with the defendant's definition of consent and the 'deficiency' model of miscommunication that dominated and structured the proceedings:

> At the outset of their interaction with Mr. A., both complainants were very clear as to their intentions. They clearly set the limits at the very beginning but their resolve became somewhat ambiguous as the night progressed. Did their actions leave Mr. A. with the impression that they had changed their minds later in the evening? There is little doubt that both complainants did not expressly object to some of the activity that took place that evening. It is also clear that their actions at times did not unequivocally indicate a lack of willing participation. For example, the actions of Ms B. [Marg] in constantly returning to bed may have left Mr. A. with the impression that she was interested in continuing the sexual touching. Further, much was made of the fact that Ms D. [the other complainant] voluntarily attended a pub with Mr. A. the very evening after the incident, and that she even slow danced with Mr. A.
>
> (In the Matter of M.A. Reasons for Judgement of the
> University Discipline Tribunal, p. 9)

The written decision thus underscores the notion that the complainants' protests were too infrequent, unclear, weak and equivocal to send the message to the defendant – who may understand 'signals' differently – that the complainants were consenting to sexual activity. Of particular interest is the tribunal members' characterization of Marg's behaviour: she is described as 'constantly returning to bed' which 'may have left Mr. A. with the impression that she was interested in continuing the sexual touching'. Not only does this statement reiterate the 'deficiency' of Marg's communications of resistance, it also endorses the temporal aspect of Matt's definition of 'consent'. Because every new point in the interaction provides a new opportunity for Matt to ascribe 'consent' or lack of consent to Marg's behaviour, Marg's returning to bed constantly would undoubtedly, according to Matt's definition of 'consent', negate other expressions of resistance.

Alternative ideological frames

Sanday (1996: 237) argues that justice will only prevail in acquaintance rape trials once 'the scrutiny shifts from, the complainant . . . to the defendant's behavior. Did the defendant obtain consent? Did the defendant know whether the complainant consented? These are the questions to be answered in determining whether a crime was committed'. Up to this point, I have argued that notions of inaccurate 'signalling' and miscommunication between women and men, invoked in the 'talk' of this tribunal, create the ideological space in which the defendant's characterization of events receives some legitimacy: the complainants are described as not expressing resistance strongly enough and frequently enough. Consistent with Sanday's remarks, it was the complainants' behaviour that was generally interrogated as to its appropriateness, not the defendant's. How, then, might an alternative ideological perspective inform acquaintance rape tribunals and trials, so that women's communications would not be regarded as deficient and their behaviour would not be characterized as lacking in resistance? Such an ideological perspective would need to acknowledge the power dynamics that shape the behaviour of women and men in the context of potential sexual relations. Especially relevant, in this regard, are the complainants' own explanations of their actions in the face of sexual violence. Consider Marg's comments in the second part of example (9) and in example (15).

(15)

> HL: Do you have anything more that or specific to say to the panel about the evidence that you've heard and uh that Matt has given?
>
> MB: The truth? I mean I don't know what else to reply to. You think, at least I do, that you know you're walking down the street and someone grabs you. I was prepared for that I thought, but you don't expect someone that you know to do that and when it's happening, I mean, you do whatever you have to to survive. ((crying)) I mean I was just thinking how to survive that second. I mean I didn't care if that meant getting back into bed with him. If he didn't hurt me I didn't care at that second. I mean I didn't want to do the things I did and looking back on them I shouldn't have gotten back into bed, I should have yelled, I should have done something, but, I was in a room full of people that weren't helping me and somebody was trying to hurt me. I did whatever I could to get by. I don't know what else to tell you.

In response to many questions throughout the tribunal about their 'deficient' attempts to communicate, Marg and her co-complainant typically pointed to their intense and extreme feelings of fear. Indeed, on lines 47–9 of example (9), Marg explains her failure to pursue an 'option' suggested by GK in terms of her fear: 'I was afraid to ask him to sleep on the floor. It crossed my mind but I didn't want to get hurt'. Similarly, in example (15), Marg cites the need to survive (without getting hurt) as motivation for 'getting back into bed with [Matt]': 'I was just thinking how to survive that second. . . . I didn't care if that meant getting back into bed with him. If he didn't hurt me I didn't care at that second'.

These examples show very clearly the complainant's fear, confusion and paralysis when confronted with the threat of unwanted sexual aggression. Although the defendant and complainants in this case, may, indeed, communicate resistance in different ways, what 'difference' models of communication (both deficiency and separate-but-equal) fail to capture are the structural and systemic inequalities (alluded to in Marg's quoted comments) that engender 'difference'. As Henley and Kramarae (1994: 400–1) argue, 'cultural difference does not exist in a political vacuum . . . [it is] shaped by the context of [men's] supremacy and [women's] subordination'. More specifically, women's submission to men's sexual advances often (if not always) occurs in situations where physical injury is a threat to women and where physical resistance can escalate the possibility of violence. British and American research on violence against women shows that, in general, women who are being assaulted remain physically passive because, they believe, this will prevent a more serious or prolonged attack (Dobash and Dobash 1992).

Marg's comments on lines 42–50 of example (9) and in example (15) illustrate this phenomenon – Marg contends that she did not pursue certain of GK's 'options' because she feared that they would only increase the severity of an attack. In addition, the circumstances surrounding the events described in this tribunal held their own particular dangers. Escaping to a deserted campus at 4 am (an option that the tribunal member, GK, suggested as viable for the complainant) could hardly be considered safe. Seen in this light, Marg acted in ways that (she believed) would minimize her risk of physical violence and injury. Thus, it is not that her behaviour is lacking in resistance; rather she can be seen as considering possibilities for action given the restricted options available to her, and as actively negotiating relations with the defendant in order to prevent further and more extreme instances of violence – from the defendant or from someone else.

Since the early 20th century, courts in Canada and the US have found it useful to invoke the notion of a *reasonable person* in considering whether certain kinds of behaviour should be deemed as harmful or offensive and thus punishable. The reasonable person is supposed to represent community norms; thus, whatever would offend or harm a reasonable person is said to be more generally offensive or harmful. Feminist legal scholars (e.g. Abrams 1989) have recently challenged the generalizability of a reasonable person's experiences, arguing that men and women may experience sexual advances or sexual harassment differently. Indeed, some state courts and lower federal courts in the US have modified the reasonable person standard and introduced a *reasonable woman* standard for evaluating charges of sexual harassment. One such US court (Ellison v. Brady 1991) justifies introducing the reasonable women standard in the following way:

> We realize that there is a broad range of viewpoints among women as a group, but we believe that many women share common concerns which men do not necessarily share. For example, because women are disproportionately victims of rape and sexual assault, women have a stronger incentive to be concerned with sexual behavior. . . . We adopt the perspective of a reasonable woman primarily because we believe

that a sex-blind reasonable person standard tends to be male-biased and tends to systematically ignore the experiences of women.

(Ellison v. Brady, 924 F.2d 872, 878–81 (9th Cir. 1991))

Other feminist scholars have attempted to transform notions of reasonableness such that gender-differentiated responses to sexual harassment are accounted for. Drawing on Gricean concepts of conversational cooperativeness and implicature, McConnell-Ginet (1995) demonstrates the value of linguistics to these legal issues. She argues that the contextual information that interlocutors rely on in successfully interpreting utterances often includes knowlege about others' experiences and perspectives, even if these are different from one's own. Thus, McConnell-Ginet proposes defining reasonableness in terms of an interlocutor's 'access to certain socially available knowledge, e.g., on recognizing and taking account of socially structured differences among people that affect whether or not a person is substantially harmed by particular actions' (McConnell-Ginet 1995: 4). For example, because women, as a group, are more likely than heterosexual men to be victims of men's sexual violence, women *may* be more threatened by sexual banter than men. However, a *reasonable* (as McConnell-Ginet conceives of reasonableness) man would be able to recognize the potential harm of sexual banter for a woman, even if he himself would not experience the same bad effect. That is, determining whether certain actions are offensive to a reasonable person may require looking beyond a reasonable person's own experiences and perceptions (i.e. beyond questions such as 'what effect would an action like this have on me?') to the socially structured differences among people that may affect perceptions of harm and offensiveness.

Conclusions

In this paper, I have argued that the ideological frame of the tribunal proceedings analysed here failed to acknowledge the particularities of women's responses to the threat of sexual violence. By characterizing the complainants' expressions of resistance as 'deficient' and their behaviour as 'inaction', it seems to me that two of the tribunal members (GK and BW) did not look beyond a reasonable *man's* own experiences and perceptions to the 'socially structured differences' between women and men that may 'affect whether or not a person [woman] is substantially harmed by particular actions'. Despite much talk about 'difference' and miscommunication, the tribunal members' focus on the so-called lack of resistance exhibited by the complainants did not take seriously the complainants' frequent expressions of fear, paralysis, and humiliation in the face of unwanted sexual aggression.

In a provocative discussion of sex discrimination law and policy in the US, MacKinnon (1987) talks about the way that ideas about sex 'difference' often derive from inequality, rather than the other way around. It is not that dominance relations are simply mapped onto a pre-existing difference between the sexes; rather the power asymmetry between women and men 'succeeds in constructing social perception and social reality' such that sex differences are exaggerated 'in perception and in fact'. Indeed, for MacKinnon (1987: 40) 'gender might not even code as difference, might not mean distinction epistemologically, were it not for the consequences of social power'. Within the context of these tribunal proceedings, I am arguing that the consistent reference to gender *differences* and miscommunication between the complainants and the defendant had the effect of obscuring and neutralizing the power dynamics between women and men that undoubtedly shaped the complainants' responses to Matt's sexual aggression. We thus see the social and political effects of discourse *about* gender differences in deflecting a defendant's accountability for sexual assault.

Deborah Cameron

1994

DEGREES OF CONSENT

The Antioch College Sexual Offense Policy

SINCE 1991, ANTIOCH COLLEGE, a small, educationally 'progressive' undergraduate institution in the US state of Ohio, has had a Sexual Offense Policy (see the appendix below) which states that any act of sex must be prefaced by requesting, and receiving, explicit verbal consent. The policy further states that obtaining consent is an ongoing process: 'Asking "do you want to have sex with me?" is not enough. The request for consent must be specific to each act'. As a spokeswoman explained:

> If you want to take her blouse off, you have to ask. If you want to touch her breast, you have to ask. If you want to move your hand down to her genitals, you have to ask. If you want to put your fingers inside her, you have to ask.

Not only does no mean no under this policy; anything less than a clear 'yes' means no as well. The policy also rejects the common idea that in sex, one thing 'naturally' leads to another. And if either party is under the influence of drugs or alcohol, their consent is null and void. Thus if a complaint is made, none of the familiar excuses – she led me on, I didn't understand her signals, I was too drunk to know what I was doing – will be accepted. The policy is binding on all members of the Antioch community (employees as well as students) and violations can result in expulsion or sacking. It is also gender-neutral, giving the same rights and obligations to all individuals – male and female, straight or lesbian/gay.

The introduction of the policy coincided with the early 1990s media furore about 'political correctness' and 'date rape' on college campuses. Consequently Antioch's approach attracted international media attention. Many commentators branded it extreme and puritanical – even now it is still cited as a case of 'political correctness gone mad'.

In December 1993 I went to Antioch College and talked to people involved with the policy, including the Dean of Students, 'peer advocates' (students who educate and support other students), and campus feminists. The first point everyone wanted to stress was that the policy had been initiated by students themselves because of their dissatisfaction with the way the college had handled incidents in the past. A group of about 30 students had gone to the administration and demanded change. Those who drafted the policy included students, faculty and administrators. All were irritated by suggestions that 'PC' college authorities were high-handedly interfering in students' sex lives.

It was also pointed out that compliance with the policy is largely self-imposed. No one is spying on couples' behaviour. People can choose not to comply, so long as they understand the risk. If a complaint is made and they cannot say consent was obtained they will be found to be in breach of the policy and treated accordingly.

That being so, I was surprised how many students told me that they routinely chose to comply, even in situations where a complaint was very unlikely. Media coverage had focused on how unrealistic it was to expect young people to engage in the kinds of conversations the policy prescribed during sexual encounters. Yet the students I spoke to did not seem to have a problem. Peer advocate Kate Bates was typical in commenting: 'When I first came to Antioch I thought "this is stupid", but by my third year I supported it completely, I could really see the benefits'. Kate thought the policy made it easier to say no to unwanted sex and to speak up and be heard if your wishes were ignored. Sierra Levy, a lesbian feminist, observed that the policy validates people who actively want to interact in a sexually egalitarian way. As she put it, having to negotiate everything makes sex 'subject to subject, not subject to object'.

Dean of Students Marian Jensen emphasized that the policy is not just a disciplinary measure but an 'educational tool', intended to raise the level of discussion about sexuality generally. 'You see these kids walking out of their orientation sessions and saying "Gosh, I'm 18 years old and I've never thought about this stuff before"'. Dean Jensen feels strongly that students want to discuss the issues and they want to be given guidelines. Asked about media coverage which scoffed at the idea that college students need 'lessons in having sex', she replied: 'Americans are in a state of denial about the need young people have for guidance about sexuality'.

Kate Bates agrees. She finds that many students initially feel unable to talk about sex: in the workshops new students are required to attend they ask to have terms like 'fellatio' or 'cunnilingus' explained to them, and often they have given no thought to how to communicate what they do and don't want. Both sexes often subscribe to stereotypical ideas – for instance that men should want sex all the time and that women have no automatic right to refuse. The policy is intended to challenge these myths, making both men and women feel able to say no, but also making them think about what they really want to say yes to. A number of students mentioned an unexpected side-effect. By introducing a more elaborate language for talking and thinking about sex, the policy appears to have improved some students' sex lives – they report that they are actually having more pleasurable sex. This might surprise the media pundits who have harped on the policy's 'puritanical' quality.

Women I spoke to generally felt it was better to have the policy than not to. But some had criticisms too – particularly those who defined themselves as radical feminists. When I asked Sierra Levy if she thought the policy was feminist, she answered: 'it's more of a humanist policy'. Essentially, its goal is to ensure respectful and responsible behaviour between individuals. The assumption is that anyone can behave sexually in an abusive way, and that every case of abusive behaviour is in principle the same as every other. Without denying that, say, lesbians can behave abusively (and should be held accountable if they do), this arguably overlooks the structures of power built into heterosexual relationships and the way these can blur the line between consent and coercion, making even Antioch's strong definition of consent less effective in practice than in theory. Since 1991 the ultimate sanction of expulsion has been used only once: it is difficult to believe that in a community of several hundred there has only been one rape in three years.

Kate Bates believes many women are still having sex they do not want, because refusing and complaining go against peer group norms that ultimately have to do with compulsory heterosexuality. There is still enormous pressure on women to go on dates with men and to have sex with the men they date. Refusing isn't 'cool': it isn't compatible with being attractive or popular. Thus women may consent to sex for reasons other than actively wanting to have sex with a particular man in a particular situation. They are not necessarily under immediate duress, but the norms of the culture are coercive for these women.

The relatively high number of complaints made by men against women, and by lesbians, may reflect the fact that these groups experience less routine coercion, so are more likely to notice and be outraged when it does happen. But this deflects attention from the much greater incidence of men coercing women, and the way that reinforces existing power relations between the sexes. Apart from radical feminists, few people I spoke to made direct links between sexual violence and wider power structures. Forced and unwanted sex were more usually represented as the product of a situation in which large numbers of young people, unused to independence and confused about sex, experiment with adult ways of living and sometimes make mistakes. Many people also invoked a 'socialization' model in which both sexes are oppressed by stereotypical expectations, and there is systematic 'miscommunication' between women and men. I asked Kate Bates if she thought some men were not just unclear whether women were consenting to sex, but indifferent as to whether they consented. She replied: 'I don't know what you do about that'.

Considering the struggle feminists have had, and are still having, to make people accept that 'no means no', Antioch's insistence that consent depends on saying 'yes' is radical. Like all measures intended to reduce the incidence of sexual violence and coercion, it has limitations in practice; but unlike a lot of policies with similar aims, this one also has value as a 'thought experiment', obliging people at least to think – and if they actively comply with the policy, to talk – about sex, gender and power in ways that challenge what passes elsewhere for common sense.

Appendix: extracts from the Antioch College Sexual Offense Policy (1991)

[*Editors' note:* These extracts are from the 1991 version of the Policy (i.e. the one Cameron's interviewees were talking about), and it has been edited to retain only those parts which are of general interest, omitting procedural details.]

All sexual contact and conduct on the Antioch College campus and/or occurring with an Antioch community member must be consensual. When a sexual offense, as defined herein, is committed by a community member, such action will not be tolerated. Antioch College provides and maintains educational programs for all community members, some aspects of which are required. The educational aspects of this policy are intended to prevent sexual offenses and ultimately to heighten community awareness.

Consent

1. For the purpose of this policy, 'consent' shall be defined as follows: the act of willingly and verbally agreeing to engage in specific sexual contact or conduct.
2. If sexual contact and/or conduct is not mutually and simultaneously initiated, then the person who initiates sexual contact/conduct is responsible for getting the verbal consent of the other individual(s) involved.
3. Obtaining consent is an on-going process in any sexual interaction. Verbal consent should be obtained with each new level of physical and/or sexual contact/conduct in any given interaction, regardless of who initiates it. Asking 'Do you want to have sex with me?' is not enough. The request for consent must be specific to each act.
4. The person with whom sexual contact/conduct is initiated is responsible to express verbally and or physically her/his willingness or lack of willingness when reasonably possible.
5. If someone has initially consented but then stops consenting during a sexual interaction, she/he should communicate withdrawal verbally and/or through physical resistance. The other individual(s) must stop immediately.
6. To knowingly take advantage of someone who is under the influence of alcohol, drugs and/or prescribed medication is not acceptable behavior.
7. If someone verbally agrees to engage in specific contact or conduct, but it is not of her/his own free will due to any of the circumstances stated below, then the person initiating shall be considered in violation of this policy:

    a)   the person submitting is under the influence of alcohol or other substances supplied to her/him by the person initiating;
    b)   the person submitting is incapacitated by alcohol, drugs, and/or prescribed medication;
    c)   the person submitting is asleep or unconscious;
    d)   the person initiating has forced, threatened, coerced, or intimidated the other individual(s) into engaging in sexual contact and/or sexual conduct.

Offenses defined

The following sexual contact/conduct is prohibited and, in addition to possible criminal prosecution, may result in sanctions up to and including expulsion or termination of employment.

Rape: Non-consensual penetration, however slight, of the vagina or anus; non-consensual fellatio or cunnilingus.

Sexual Assault: Non-consensual sexual conduct exclusive of vaginal and anal penetration, fellatio and cunnilingus. This includes, but is not limited to, attempted non-consensual penetration, fellatio, or cunnilingus; the respondent coercing or forcing the primary witness to engage in non-consensual sexual contact with the respondent or another.

Sexual Imposition: Non-consensual sexual contact. 'Sexual contact' includes the touching of thighs, genitals, buttocks, the pubic region or the breast/chest area.

Insistent and/or Persistent Sexual Harassment: Any insistent and/or persistent emotional, verbal or mental intimidation or abuse found to be sexually threatening or offensive. This includes, but is not limited to, unwelcome and irrelevant comments, references, gestures or other forms of personal attention which are inappropriate and which may be perceived as persistent sexual overtones or denigration.

Non-Disclosure of a Known Positive HIV Status: Failure to inform one's sexual partner of one's known positive HIV status prior to engaging in high risk sexual conduct.

Non-Disclosure of a Known Sexually Transmitted Disease: Failure to inform one's sexual partner of one's known infection with a sexually transmitted disease (other than HIV) prior to engaging in high risk sexual conduct.

Procedures

1. To maintain the safety of all community members, community members who are suspected of violating this policy should be made aware of the concern about their behavior. Sometimes people are not aware that their behavior is sexually offensive, threatening, or hurtful. Educating them about the effects of their behavior may cause them to change their behavior. It is strongly encouraged that suspected violations be reported, and that they be reported as soon as is reasonable after a suspected violation has occurred. Where criminal misconduct is involved, reporting the misconduct to the local law enforcement agency is also strongly encouraged.

[§§2–7 omitted]

8. The Hearing Board and any appellate body which hears a case under this policy shall administer its proceedings according to these fundamental assumptions:

    A. There will be no reference to the past consensual, nonviolent sexual contact and/or conduct of either the primary witness or the respondent.

    B.   No physical evidence of a sexual offense is necessary to determine that one has occurred, nor is a visit to the hospital or the administration of a rape kit required.

    C.   The fact that a respondent was under the influence of drugs or alcohol or mental dysfunction at the time of the sexual offense will not excuse or justify the commission of any sexual offense as defined herein, and shall not be used as a defense.

Remedies

1.   When a policy violation by a student is found by the Hearing Board, the Hearing Board shall also determine a remedy which is commensurate with the offense, except in those cases where mandatory remedies are prescribed in this policy.

2.   For Rape: . . . the respondent must be expelled immediately.

3.   For Sexual Assault: . . . the respondent must: a) be suspended immediately for a period of no less than six months; b) successfully complete a treatment program for sexual offenders before returning to campus; and c) upon return to campus, be subject to mandatory class and co-op scheduling so that the respondent and primary witness avoid, to the greatest extent possible, all contact, unless the primary witness agrees otherwise. In the event that the Hearing Board determines that a second violation has occurred, with the same respondent, then the respondent must be expelled immediately.

4.   For Sexual Imposition: . . . the recommended remedy is that the respondent: a) be suspended immediately for a period of no less than three months; b) and c) as for Sexual Assault.

5.   For Insistent and/or Persistent Sexual Harassment: . . . the recommended remedy is that the respondent: a) be suspended immediately for a period of no less than six months; b) and c) as for Sexual Assault.

6.   For Non-Disclosure of a Known Positive HIV Status: . . . the recommended remedy is that the respondent be expelled immediately.

7.   For Non-Disclosure of a Known Sexually Transmitted Disease: . . . the recommended remedy is that the respondent be suspended immediately for a period of no less than thee months.

8.   In all cases, a second offense under this policy, regardless of category, must receive a more severe consequence than did the first offense if the second offense occurred after the Hearing Board's first finding.

9.   The remedy for a third offense, regardless of category, must be expulsion.

Confidentiality

1.   All of the proceedings of the Hearing Board, and all testimony given, shall be kept confidential.

2.   For the duration of the Hearing process and any appeals process, the primary witness, the respondent, and any witnesses coming forward shall have the right to determine when and if their names are publicly released. No one shall make a public release of a name not their own while the process is underway.

Educational and support procedures

1. A minimum of one educational workshop about sexual offenses, consent, and the nature of sexual offenses as they pertain to this policy will be incorporated into each quarterly orientation program for new students. Attendance shall be required of all students new to the Antioch community.

2. Workshops on sexual offense issues will also be offered during all study quarters. Each student shall be required to attend at least one workshop each academic year for which she/he is on campus for one or more study quarters.

3. A one-credit PE self-defense course with an emphasis on women's self-defense will be offered each quarter.

4. Permanent support groups for female and male survivors of sexual offenses will be established and maintained.

5. A Peer Advocacy Program will be maintained that shall consist of both female and male community members. The Peer Advocates shall provide information and emotional support for sexual offense victims/survivors and primary witnesses.

6. A support network for students who are on Co-op will be maintained, with trained crisis contact people available.

Chapter 18

Stephanie A. Sanders and June Machover Reinisch

1999

WOULD YOU SAY YOU 'HAD SEX' IF ...?

T HE DEGREE TO WHICH INDIVIDUALS VARY with respect to the behavioral criteria involved in labeling an interaction as having 'had sex' has implications for both clinical and research purposes. Recent public discourse regarding whether oral-genital contact constitutes having 'had sex' highlights the importance of explicit criteria in contrast with implicit assumptions in this area. Unfortunately, a review of the literature demonstrates that, empirical exploration of what is included in definitions of having 'had sex' for the general public in the United States remains scant. Social and legal definitions of 'sex,' 'sex act,' 'having sex with,' 'sexual relations,' and various crimes related to having 'had sex,' including adultery, rape, and statutory rape, vary depending on the source but often refer to sexual intercourse, which, in turn, is often defined as 'coitus' or 'copulation' (*Random House Unabridged Dictionary* 1993; *Black's Law Dictionary* 1990; *Oxford English Dictionary* 1989; *Webster's Third New International Dictionary of the English Language* 1993; Kim *et al.* 1998). Not surprisingly, engaging in behaviors other than penile-vaginal intercourse is a strategy used by some to preserve 'technical virginity' (Klein and Petersen 1996; Chillman 1983; Herold and Way 1983; Sheeran *et al.* 1993; Feldman *et al.* 1997; Mahoney 1980). In keeping with such views, a 1996 convenience sample of college students found that almost 3 out of 4 students reported that they would not include in a list of their sexual partners those with whom they only had oral sex (Klein and Petersen 1996). In concert with that perspective, when asked, 'Is oral sex 'real' sex?' only 52% of men and 46% of women said yes. However, this suggests that for some, engaging in an act they define as 'sex' does not necessitate defining the other person as a 'sexual partner' and, hence, does not inevitably lead to labeling the interaction as a sexual relationship.

The current public debate [i.e. following the Bill Clinton/Monica Lewinsky affair of the late 1990s – Eds] regarding whether oral sex constitutes having 'had sex' or sexual relations has suffered from a lack of empirical data on how Americans as a population define these terms (The Starr Report 1998; Baker and Marcus 1998).

The data reported here were originally collected in 1991 for their relevance to sexual history information gathering and to specifically examine the need for behavioral specificity to avoid possible confusion (Reinisch *et al.* 1988). These findings also serve as an indication of attitudes regarding definitions of having 'had sex' among college students assessed prior to current media publicity about this issue. The respondents today range in age from late 20s to early 30s.

Methods

The data were collected in 1991 as part of a survey containing 102 items addressing the prevalence and interrelationships among behaviors associated with sexually transmitted disease risk from a randomly selected, stratified undergraduate sample. Participants were students at one of the largest Midwest state universities, originating from 29 states (10 in the Midwest, 11 in the South, 5 in the Northeast, and 3 in the West). The majority of participants were from the Midwest. Potential participants were first contacted by a letter informing them that they had been chosen at random, explaining that The Kinsey Institute for Research in Sex, Gender, and Reproduction Studies was conducting a large survey of college student sexual behavior, and describing the procedures for data collection and insurance of confidentiality. Letters were followed by telephone contact to enlist participation. Of the 1029 students contacted who were eligible and potentially available, 599 undergraduates (58%) met the requirements of completing the questionnaire in 13 supervised group sessions during the 36-day study period and matched the racial demographics of the university population. Those who did not participate either declined because of lack of interest (23%) or did not show up for their scheduled appointments (19%). Mean (SD) age was 20.7 (3.1) years, with 96% of the sample falling between ages 18 and 25 years. The sample was 59% female. Matched to university demographics, 92% were white, 4% were black, and 4% identified themselves as a race/ethnicity other than black or white. Ninety-six percent identified themselves as heterosexual. When queried about their political position, 78.5% classified themselves as moderate to conservative. Although 42% were not registered to vote, there were more registered Republicans (32%) than Democrats (19%), while 7% identified themselves as independent. Additional details regarding the methods, sample demographics, and behavioral data are presented elsewhere (Reinisch *et al.* 1995).

The behaviors relating to having 'had sex' were arranged in random order to prevent the conveyance of a preconceived hierarchy. For each behavior, valid percentages (including only those who answered yes or no) and 95% confidence intervals (CIs) were determined for women, men, and the overall sample. The item read, 'Would you say you "had sex" with someone if the most intimate behavior you engaged in was . . . (mark yes or no for each behavior):

(a) a person had oral (mouth) contact with your breasts or nipples?
(b) you touched, fondled, or manually stimulated a person's genitals?
(c) you had oral (mouth) contact with a person's breasts or nipples?
(d) penile-vaginal intercourse (penis in vagina)?

(e)   you touched, fondled, or manually stimulated a person's breasts or nipples?
(f)   a person had oral (mouth) contact with your genitals?
(g)   you had oral (mouth) contact with a person's genitals?
(h)   deep kissing (French or tongue kissing)?
(i)   penile-anal intercourse [penis in anus (rectum)]?
(j)   a person touched, fondled, or manually stimulated your breasts or nipples?
(k)   a person touched, fondled, or manually stimulated your genitals?'

Results are presented with 95% CIs and χ^2 analyses corrected for continuity were used for specific group comparisons.

Table 18.1 Percentages for participants answering yes to the question, 'Would you say you "had sex" with someone if the most intimate behavior you engaged in was . . . ?'

Behaviors	Percentage indicating 'had sex' (95% confidence interval)		
	Women	Men	Overall
Deep kissing	1.4 (0.2–2.6) (n = 353)	2.9 (0.8–5.0) (n = 245)	2.0 (0.9–3.1) (n = 598)
Oral contact on your breasts/nipples	2.3 (0.7–3.9) (n = 352)	4.1 (1.6–6.6) (n = 245)	3.0 (1.6–4.4) (n = 597)
Person touches your breasts/nipples	2.0 (0.5–3.5) (n = 353)	4.5 (1.9–7.1) (n = 244)	3.0 (1.6–4.4) (n = 597)
You touch other's breasts/nipples[†]	1.7 (0.3–3.1) (n = 348)	5.7 (2.8–8.6) (n = 244)	3.4 (1.9–4.9) (n = 592)
Oral contact on other's breasts/nipples[‡]	1.4 (0.2–2.6) (n = 352)	6.1 (3.1–9.1) (n = 245)	3.4 (1.9–4.9) (n = 597)
You touch other's genitals	11.6 (8.3–14.9) (n = 354)	17.1 (12.4–21.8) (n = 245)	13.9 (11.1–16.7) (n = 599)
Person touches your genitals[§]	12.2 (8.8–15.6) (n = 353)	19.2 (14.3–24.1) (n = 245)	15.1 (12.2–18.0) (n = 598)
Oral contact with other's genitals	37.3 (32.3–42.3) (n = 354)	43.7 (37.5–49.9) (n = 245)	39.9 (36.0–43.8) (n = 599)
Oral contact with your genitals	37.7 (32.6–42.8) (n = 353)	43.9 (37.7–50.1) (n = 244)	40.2 (36.3–44.1) (n = 597)
Penile-anal intercourse	82.3 (78.3–86.3) (n = 350)	79.1 (73.9–84.3) (n = 239)	81.0 (77.8–84.2) (n = 589)
Penile-vaginal intercourse	99.7 (99.1–100) (n = 354)	99.2 (98.1–100.3) (n = 245)	99.5 (98.9–100) (n = 599)

n is the total number of respondents in each category for each behavior

[†] Data are significant at $P = .01$; $\chi^2_1 = 5.90$; [‡] Data are significant at $P = .004$; $\chi^2_1 = 8.46$; [§] Data are significant at $P = .02$; $\chi^2_1 = 5.01$

Results

As can be seen in Table 18.1, almost everyone agreed that penile-vaginal intercourse would qualify as having 'had sex.' Approaching this level of common perspective and yet importantly different is the fact that while 81% of participants counted penile-anal intercourse as having 'had sex,' 19% did not. In contrast, few individuals considered deep kissing (nearly 2%) or breast contact (nearly 3%) as having 'had sex' with a partner. Answers to the breast contact items (a, c, e, and j) did not vary substantially regardless of the directionality of behaviors or whether contact was manual or oral. Approximately 14% to 15% indicated that manual stimulation of the genitals (either given or received) would constitute having 'had sex.' Only 40% indicated that they would say they had 'had sex' if oral-genital contact was the most intimate behavior in which they engaged (60% would not). For the behaviors less frequently included as having 'had sex,' men were slightly more likely to incorporate them into the 'had sex' category.

Seventy-four percent (95% CI, 69%–79%) of women and 80% (95% CI, 74%–85%) of men had penile-vaginal intercourse experience. Eighty-two percent (95% CI, 78%–87%) of women and 84% (95% CI, 79%-89%) of men had oral-genital experience. Responses to the 'had sex' question did not differ in general based on these experiences with the following exception: of those who had experienced (1) both oral-genital contact and penile-vaginal intercourse, (2) neither of these behaviors, or (3) only penile-vaginal intercourse, 59% said that oral-genital contact did not constitute having 'had sex' (95% CI, 54%–63%). In comparison, those whose most intimate sexual experience was limited to oral-genital contact (8%; 95% CI, 6%–11%) were significantly even more likely (75%; 95% CI, 62%-87%; $\chi^2_1 = 4.37$; $P = .04$) to rate this form of contact as not meeting their criteria for having 'had sex.'

Comment

These data make it clear that general agreement regarding what constitutes having 'had sex' and how sexual partners are counted cannot be taken for granted. Among the behaviors assessed, oral-genital contact had the most ambivalent status. Overall, 60% reported that they would not say they 'had sex' with someone if the most intimate behavior engaged in was oral-genital contact. Additionally, we found evidence of belief in 'technical virginity.' Compared with others, those who had experienced oral-genital contact but had never engaged in penile-vaginal intercourse were less likely to consider oral-genital contact as having 'had sex.' These findings are consistent with other reports indicating that oral sex is not consistently defined as having 'had sex' and seem relevant to the issue of 'technical fidelity' as well.

One out of five indicated they would not count penile-anal intercourse as having 'had sex.' This finding has implications for sexual history taking and prevention education, given that the study was conducted during the era of widespread public information and education campaigns regarding the association of risk of human immunodeficiency virus infection and unprotected anal intercourse.

Future investigations should examine such variables as the relational context of the behavior (eg, was it within an established relationship? Was it extramarital or extra relational?), the relevance of orgasm (some consider behaviors less intimate if no orgasm occurs), issues of consent, the relevance of cohort and socioeconomic status to definitions of what constitutes sex, and the potential costs/benefits of labeling a behavior as having 'had sex' (eg, in cases of extramarital behavior, discrepancies between partners are likely).

The virtually universal endorsement of penile-vaginal intercourse as having 'had sex' in contrast with the diverse opinions for other behaviors highlights the primacy of penile-vaginal intercourse in American definitions of having 'had sex.' The lack of consensus with respect to what constitutes having 'had sex' across the sexual behaviors examined herein provides empirical evidence of the need for behavioral specificity when collecting data on sexual histories and identifying sexual partners. These data indicate that prior to the current public discourse, a majority of college students attending a major midwestern state university, most of whom identified themselves as politically moderate to conservative, with more registered Republicans than Democrats, did not define oral sex as having 'had sex.'

Chapter 19

Sally McConnell-Ginet

2006

WHY DEFINING IS SELDOM 'JUST SEMANTICS'

Marriage and *marriage*

Setting the stage

SHOULD *MARRIAGE* BE DEFINED to exclude or include same-sex unions? Legislatively, the US Congress has answered 'to exclude' (italics in this and the two following examples indicate the principal 'defining portions'):

> *Defense of Marriage Act* (DOMA) HR 3396 (passed 342–67, July 12, 1996);
> S 1740 (passed 85–14 September 10, 1996); signed by President William J. Clinton, September 21, 1996.
> a.   No State, territory, or possession of the United States, or Indian tribe, shall be required to give effect to any public act, record, or judicial proceeding of any other State, territory, possession, or tribe respecting a relationship between persons of the same sex that is treated as a marriage under the laws of such other State, territory, possession, or tribe, or a right or claim arising from such relationship.
> b.   In determining the meaning of any Act of Congress, or of any ruling, regulation, or interpretation of the various administrative bureaus and agencies of the United States, *the word 'marriage' means only a legal union between one man and one woman as husband and wife, and the word 'spouse' refers only to a person of the opposite sex who is a husband or a wife.*

But Congress has remained neutral in refusing to endorse the proposed amendment to the US Constitution restricting marriage to opposite-sex couples.

> Proposed federal marriage amendment (FMA) (SJR30 defeated 50–48, July 14, 2004; HR256 defeated September 30, 2004; 227 for, 186 against with 290 needed for passage)

Marriage in the United States shall consist only of the union of a man and a woman. Neither this Constitution, nor the constitution of any State, shall be construed to require that marriage or the legal incidents thereof be conferred upon any union other than the union of a man and a woman.

On the other hand, the Supreme Judicial Court of the Commonwealth of Massachusetts has resoundingly answered 'to include,' arguing in the majority opinion that to do otherwise is inconsistent with that state's provision of equal rights for all its citizenry.

Extract from decision of Supreme Judicial Court (4–3), Commonwealth of Massachusetts, *Goodridge*, November 18, 2003.
We construe civil marriage to mean the voluntary union of two persons as spouses, to the exclusion of all others.

It is not only legislators, judges, and politicians offering opinions: many ordinary folk are also weighing in on defining marriage. Some say definitional debates are 'just semantics,' therefore trivial. Others, on both sides, argue that it matters considerably whether the word *marriage* shall be construed as including or excluding same-sex unions.

Linguist Geoffrey K. Pullum in a posting to Language Log on February 25, 2004 disapproves:

I twitch a little each time I hear someone talking about . . . pass[ing] a law, or a constitutional amendment, that **defines** marriage as being a man and a woman, as if something lexicographical was at issue . . . This issue is being represented as **linguistic**, relating to a democratic right of the people to stipulate definitions, when it's nothing of the kind. . . . Don't let them tell me they are revising a **definition**. It's nothing to do with defining the word 'marriage'. *Webster's* has done that perfectly well. It's about a denial of rights.

[boldface in original]

In this paper, I will argue that the recent debates are, contra Pullum, about both definition and language (specifically, about regulating uses of the word *marriage*). I will agree with him, however, that they are also about rights and other substantive matters of public policy.

What we linguists and many others often fail to appreciate is that defining words is not just something lexicographers do: defining is a metalinguistic practice that plays an important role in intellectual inquiry as well as in social and political life. Why? Defining matters because words do not just label preexisting determinate concepts: they often play a role in shaping concepts and in channeling thoughts and actions. Philosophers have traditionally distinguished nominal from real definitions, the nominal being about language and the real about concepts and reality. The marriage controversy makes clear that nominal definitions often have import that goes far beyond language.

Even what lexicographers do is less definitive than we might want to believe. As Pullum notes, citing *Webster*'s, current lexicographers seem to recognize both exclusive and inclusive construals as widespread and include each as a separate sense in their entries. (In this example italics pick out both the exclusionary meaning encoded in (1), DOMA, and pushed by supporters of (2), FMA – sense 1a – and the inclusionary construal – sense 1d – endorsed by the Massachusetts court.)

> Entry from American Heritage Dictionary, 4th ed., 2000.
> Marriage 1a. The legal union of a man and woman as husband and wife. b. The state of being married; wedlock. c. A common-law marriage. d. A union between two persons having the customary but usually not the legal force of marriage: a same-sex marriage. 2. A wedding. 3. A close union: 'the most successful marriage of beauty and blood in mainstream comics' (Lloyd Rose). 4. Games. The combination of the king and queen of the same suit, as in pinochle.

The current conflict is over whether sense 1a or 1d is to be deployed in certain significant contexts. How will *marriage* and related words be interpreted at passport control points? On tax forms? In settling disputes over inheritance? By hospitals granting visitation rights or recognizing medical powers of attorney? By those trying to protect their children or themselves in the face of difficulties developing in a union with another person? And contexts like these, where legal arrangements might have force, do not exhaust those where definitions of marriage matter. What interpretations are in force when parents are talking about adult offspring's life choices? When family reunions or memorial services are being planned? When a parent of a young child dies? Finding that *Webster's* and the *American Heritage Dictionary* recognize that some sizeable group of people do apply the word *marriage* to some same-sex relationships does not answer questions like these.

What definitions do

Defining canonically associates a linguistic expression to be defined – the DEFINIENDUM – with something indicating a meaning for that expression, the DEFINIENS. The definiens is often indicated linguistically although nonlinguistic means – pictures or pointing or other demonstrations – can also direct attention to the concept the definer offers as the meaning of the definiendum. In this paper, methods for defining are not at issue. What is at issue are the purposes of definition and, related to these purposes, the grounds on which definitions are or should be appraised.

Most readers of the *American Heritage Dictionary* definition, above, will already have *marriage* entered in their mental lexicons with something like the proffered definiens for the main 'senses' that the lexicographers have identified. (Actually, only card players are likely to recognize sense 4, and sense 3 reports on the apparent conventionalization of what began as a metaphorical extension, conveyed by pragmatic principles rather than by semantic conventions.) Even those who oppose the idea that same-sex marriage should be countenanced typically are familiar with and reliably interpret *marriage* as it occurs in *same-sex marriage*, roughly along the lines indicated in sense 1d.

Nonetheless some of these folks may hold that a relationship's being a same-sex marriage would not entail that it is a marriage, just as something's being an artificial flower does not entail that it is a flower. And there are many others, holding that a same-sex marriage would indeed have to be a marriage, who on those grounds reject the very possibility of same-sex marriages. They claim that having spouses of different sexes is an essential feature of 'real' marriage. Rev. Vernon C. Lyons, pastor of the Ashburn Baptist Church in Orland Park, IL represents the sentiments of a large group:

> Same-sex marriage is an oxymoron. If we accept same-sex marriage, we may as well discard our rationality and accept square circles, dry rain, loud silence, low skyscrapers, pure adultery, honest lying, and good murder.
>
> (Quoted in *Chicago Tribune*, May 18, 2004, sec. 1, p. 20)

Lyons is applying the contradiction test that introductory semantics texts offer students for identifying which parts of what is conveyed by the use of an expression are due to what it means, i.e. which are semantically significant. He is unlikely to be impressed by Pullum's claim that the existence of an entry in *Webster's* for one sense of *marriage* that is gender-neutral means that *same-sex marriage* is not a contradiction. The same *Webster's* entry, just like 4 from *AHD*, also identifies a distinct (and first mentioned) sense of *marriage* that is restricted to man-woman unions. For that mixed-sex sense of *marriage*, then *same-sex marriage* is contradictory. Lyons and others on his side in the debate are clinging to sense 1a and refusing to join the community of users for whom 1d has become unexceptional.

Both sides have ignored the fact that what is held to be 'essential' to the concept associated with a word can (and does) change through time. For example, American courts during much of the 20th century specified that a rape victim had to be a woman other than the legal wife of the perpetrator, making both marital rape and rape with a male victim contradictory. Their refusal to see marital rape as semantically possible relied on the following doctrine formulated in mid-17th century England by Chief Justice Sir Matthew Hale:

> The husband cannot be guilty of a rape committed by himself upon his lawful wife, for by their mutual matrimonial consent and contract, the wife hath given up herself in this kind unto her husband, which she cannot retract.

The contradiction test gives conflicting answers precisely where there is disagreement over which conventions members of the speech community should follow, where there are competing possibilities.

Scholars in the behavioral and social sciences certainly have wrestled with how most fruitfully to define [marriage] for their purposes. I will illustrate by pointing to a debate begun in the mid-1950s and persisting into the 1970s on how to define marriage, given institutionalized arrangements anthropologists were encountering in various parts of the world that seemed like marriage in many ways but did not fit the one woman-one man or many women-one man models most familiar to them. Eileen Jensen Krige reviews a number of these discussions and gives the following examples of earlier definitions of marriage (all sources cited by Krige 1974):

a. Marriage and family may be defined as a culturally approved relationship of one man and one woman (monogamy), of one man and two or more women (polygyny) or one woman and two or more men (polyandry), in which there is cultural endorsement of sexual inter-course between the marital partners of opposite sex and, generally the expectation that children will be born of the relationship [Robert F. Winch, 1968 edn. of *Encylopedia of the Social Sciences*].

b. A union between a man and a woman such that children born to the woman are recognized, legitimate offspring of both partners. [*Notes and Queries in Anthropology*, 1951].

c. The constituent units of marriage are men and women and this seems to be marriage's single, universal feature. [P.G. Rivière 1971].

During this same period, Sir Edmund Leach, reviewing a number of different kinds of marital arrangements and paying special attention to a polyandric case among the Sinhalese, concluded that marriage cannot be defined in terms of necessary and sufficient conditions but is more like what Wittgenstein called a 'family-resemblance' concept. Leach (1955: 183) offered a list of rights, some subset of which he took to be present in all the different arrangements to which anthropolo-gists had applied the term *marriage*.

[A] marriage may serve: A. to establish the legal father of a woman's chil-dren, B. To establish the legal mother of a man's children, C. To give the husband a monopoly in the wife's sexuality, D. To give the wife a monopoly in the husband's sexuality, E. To give the husband partial or monopolistic rights to the wife's domestic and other labour services, F. To give the wife partial or monopolistic rights to the husband's labour services, G. To give the husband partial or total rights over property belonging or potentially accruing to the wife, H. To give the wife partial or total rights over property belonging or potentially accruing to the husband, I. To establish a joint fund of property – a partnership – for the benefit of the children of the marriage, J. To establish a socially significant 'relationship of affinity' between the husband and his wife's brother . . .[I]n no single society can marriage serve to establish all these types of rights simultaneously; nor is there any one of these rights which is invariably established by marriage in every known society.

All of the definitions cited by Krige and most of the rights Leach lists assume sex-differentiated marital roles: man/husband/father and woman/wife/mother. But Edward E. Evans-Pritchard had earlier coined the term *woman-marriage* because he observed among the Nuer of Sudan an institutionalized relation of one woman to another that seemed otherwise exactly like the more conventional two-sex marriages he also observed. Rivière claims that woman-marriage, reported in a variety of forms from different parts of Africa, involves one woman's assuming the 'conceptual role of male,' and Evans-Pritchard sometimes implies such an analysis. Krige argues, however, that Rivière's ploy of saying that there is always 'conceptually' a different-sex pairing fails to acknowledge that practices she observed among the Lovedu in southern Africa allow considerable scope for social roles to be filled by either sex, 'buying' a bride being one such potentially gender-neutral role. Krige does not cite Kathleen Gough on the definition of marriage, which offers the following:

> Marriage is a relationship established between a woman and one or more other persons, which provides that a child born to the woman under circumstances not prohibited by the rule of the relationship, is accorded full birth-status rights common to normal members of his [or her] society or social stratum.
>
> (Gough 1959: 39)

Gough developed this definition especially to encompass the marriage of a woman to a 'collectivity of men,' which is how she characterizes certain arrangements among the Nayar of Kerala (India). She draws attention to her choice of *persons* rather than *men*, however, as extending the definition's scope to cases of woman-marriage. Gough's definition singles out one of the women involved in a marriage; it is any children she might bear whose status is central to the purposes of the marriage, and it is she who defines marriage. For Krige too, marriage revolves around a woman whose (potential) children are at issue.

> The only constituent element that would appear to be indispensable in a marriage is the bride. Without a bride, there could be no marriage.
>
> (Krige 1974: 32–3)

As Krige notes, the role of genitor is not only conceptually but practically distinct from that of husband even in different-sex marriages among the Lovedu. More generally, she argues that 'the sexual relationship between the parties concerned in a marriage is not, as is commonly believed, central to the institution. Marriage may be entered upon by people of the same sex in capacities that have no sexual connotation' (1974: 34).

Both Gough and Krige assume two distinct roles in marriage, which could be called *husband* and *wife*. They also both assume that a woman always fills the *wife* role but allow for the possibility that a woman may also assume the *husband* role. Their conceptions might allow for (some) contemporary marriages of two women though not for marriages of two men. They were writing before the recent movement for rights for sexual minorities had gotten widespread recognition, before advances in reproductive technologies, before adoption rights got extended beyond legally married heterosexual couples. Even so they may have overlooked some cases of their own era or earlier that would have challenged the assumption of sharply differentiated roles or their conviction that a marriage must involve a woman.

Recent anthropologists and other scholars have, not surprisingly, taken a fresh look at marriage and the related concept of family. I focus instead on this snapshot of earlier anthropological debates over defining marriage because these discussions can be more easily separated from the contemporary social situation in the US than more recent feminist scholarship. These mid-century anthropologists were clearly grappling primarily with the question of which definition of marriage, if any, would prove most fruitful for scholars to use in exploring the wide range of social and cultural arrangements found around the world that regulate certain kinds of mutual dependence of adults and also rights and status of (potential) children born to or adopted by one or more of the adults. Their own cultural backgrounds certainly affected how they engaged in these definitional projects, but they were not participating in our current controversy over same-sex marriage.

Evaluation and values: persuasive definitions

Philosopher Charles L. Stevenson introduced the notion of a PERSUASIVE DEFINITION:

> [T]he term defined is a familiar one, whose meaning is both descriptive and strongly emotive . . . [T]he definition [aims] to alter the descriptive meaning of the term . . . but . . . does not make any substantial change in the term's emotive meaning . . . [T]he definition is used [to try] to secure, by this interplay between emotive and descriptive meaning, a redirection of people's attitudes.
>
> (Stevenson 1944: 210)

In this passage he illustrates the notion by discussing a literary definitional debate:

> Our language abounds with words which . . . have both a vague [i.e., underspecified] descriptive meaning and a rich emotive meaning. The descriptive meaning of them all is subject to constant redefinition . The words are prizes which each man seeks to bestow on the qualities of his own choice. Many literary critics, for instance, have debated whether Alexander Pope was or was not 'a poet'. The foolish retort would be, 'It's a mere matter of definition'. . . . [I]mportant matters . . . lie behind the acceptance or rejectance of the tacitly proposed, narrow [descriptive] definition of 'poet'. It is not a matter of 'merely arbitrary' definition, then, nor is any persuasive definition 'merely arbitrary', if that phrase is taken to imply 'suitably decided by a flip of a coin'.
>
> (1944: 213)

What does not emerge as clearly as it might from this is that the 'important matters' lying behind whether or not the word *poet* should be applied to particular creators of texts go far beyond whether we ought to view the creator so tagged in a positive light. Should this person's works be included on the syllabus for a poetry course? Is the person a potential candidate for a poetry prize? Should aspiring poets look to this person as a possible role model? And of course once certain kinds of texts are generally classified as poetic, people need not evaluate them all positively. Still Stevenson's insight that it is often value considerations that lead to a push to extend, contract, or shift the extensional boundaries of a particular expression is important.

Much of the controversy over marriage arises from the social values associated with the institution and a host of moral and religious judgments about practices associated with it, perhaps especially sexuality and child-rearing but also such matters as long-term commitment, affectionate intimacy, and mutual dependence. Some critics of the historically inequitable institution of marriage have offered persuasive definitions that do not so much shift the informational content of the word, what it denotes, as try to encourage others to examine it critically by offering negatively charged descriptions of it. The samples below come from *A Feminist Dictionary*, edited by Cheris Kramarae and Paula A. Treichler (1985):

> Marriage is
> 'an institution which robs a woman of her individuality and reduces her to the level of a prostitute' (Mrs. Flora Macdonald Denison, 1914)
> 'slavery' (Nelly Ptaschkina 1918)
> 'a labor relationship [with parallels to indentured labor or slavery, but] the terms of the marriage contract are never spelled out' (Diana Leonard 1982)
> 'a relation of economic dependence [of women upon men]' (Charlotte Perkins Gilman 1899)

The same source also offers considerably more positive persuasive definitions:

> Marriage is
> 'a total relationship of human closeness which begins with the head and involves a mutual drowning in each other's depths' (Ghadah al-Samman 1970)
> a lasting relationship in which another person helps meet needs, including those for 'sex, love, companionship, shared experence, being comfortable with someone, being important to someone, trust, approval, moral support, help, emotional security, cooperation in attaining a common goal, closeness, affection, touching, feedback, understanding, feeling like a part of something, the need to do for others, the need for personal growth' (Naomi Quinn 1984)

Persuasive definitions try to shift or influence attitudes and values, either by shifting or specially highlighting some portion of what the definiendum designates or by redescribing what is designated.

Legal definitions

Legal theorist Michael Bayles argues that judges should offer 'instrumentalist definitions'[1] to be evaluated by how well they serve to produce a 'justifiable legal system' (1991: 263). Whether or not those definitions happen to be ones that square with established linguistic conventions or whether they would be optimal for non-legal purposes (for the ethicist or the scientist, for example) does not decide the question of whether or not they work well for the law. Practical, scientific, and ethical considerations can, of course, be relevant to establishing what definition might work best in a particular case.

Certainly, some of the recent discussion of defining marriage has addressed questions of implications for the overall justice and workability of the legal system. For example, the Supreme Judicial Court of the Commonwealth of Massachusetts offered equal rights, social stability and children's welfare considerations to support its gender-neutral definition of marriage. This brief extract gives some of the flavor of that attention to general consequences.

> [B]arring an individual from the protections, benefits, and obligations of civil marriage solely because that person would marry a person of the same sex violates the Massachusetts Constitution . . . Marriage is a vital social institution . . . The exclusive commitment of two individuals to each other nurtures love and mutual support; it brings stability to our society. For those who choose to marry, and for their children, marriage provides an abundance of legal, financial, and social benefits [and] imposes weighty legal, financial, and social obligations . . . [The] marriage ban [prevents same-sex families] from enjoying the immeasurable advantages that flow from the assurance of a stable family structure in which children will be reared, educated, and socialized. . . . It is the exclusive and permanent commitment of the marriage partners to one another, not the begetting of children, that is the sine qua non of marriage . . . [The decision] does not disturb the fundamental value of marriage in our society . . .That same-sex couples are willing to embrace marriage's solemn obligations of exclusivity, mutual support, and commitment to one another is a testament to the enduring place of marriage in our laws and in the human spirit.
>
> [Extract from majority decision in Goodridge, written
> by Chief Justice Margaret H. Marshall]

As we will see later, those favoring retention of exclusive definitions of marriage generally agree that promoting social stability and children's welfare are appropriate goals for the legal system: they reject the Massachusetts' court's assessment of which definition might best promote such goals.

But it is not just consequences for the legal system deriving from the content of definitions of marriage that matter. It also matters just how these definitions enter into the overall legal system. There are some who support an exclusive definition at state levels or even at the federal level as in DOMA, but argue against FMA on the grounds that the US constitution is not the place to define marriage. Legal scholar Joanna Grossman of Hofstra University provides some historical background on amending the constitution to regulate marriage:

> [S]eventy-seven other constitutional amendments have been proposed
> that would have given Congress the power to regulate marriage and

divorce at the national level. Three would have enshrined the once commonplace ban on interracial marriage in the constitution. But none ever
made it to a vote . . . The Constitution has always served to guarantee
minimum rights and liberties. It has almost never been used to rein in
individual rights. The only exception is the Eighteenth Amendment
– which established Prohibition – and its repeal only 14 years after rat-
ification speaks for itself . . . There is [only] one limit on states' power
to regulate marriage and divorce . . . the federal constitution's minimum
guarantees of equality . . . [On this basis], in Loving v. Virginia, the
Supreme Court [in 1967] held Virginia's ban on interracial marriage
unconstitutional.

(http://writ.findlaw.com/grossman/20040715.html)

The Supreme Court could, on a similar basis, strike down DOMA or the state laws
now being adopted that impose exclusive definitions of those who can marry.

The extralegal M-web

Outside legal contexts, the M-web extends not only to moral and religious discourse
but to more mundane social talk: I will consider examples of both.

Marriage is 'sacred'

The sacredness or 'sanctity' of marriage is often cited by those who want to keep
an exclusive (mixed-sex only) interpretation:

> I feel like it dilutes the sacredness of my marriage with my wife. It
> cheapens it and turns it into something of less value. . . . I don't see why
> we have to change the rules to satisfy that tiny group of people.
>> (Kevin Salts, quoted in the *Honolulu Advertiser* in opposition
>> not only to same-sex marriage but to any legal recognition
>> of same-sex unions, fearing that such recognition paves the
>> way for extending marriage itself)

Those expressing sentiments like these do not explain how the existence of
same-sex marriage would diminish the sacredness they attach to different-sex
marriage. Churches would still be free if same-sex marriage is legalized to refuse
to marry same-sex couples just as the Catholic church refuses to marry those who
have been divorced. But the real issue probably has little to do with the church.
Perhaps it's like a band that starts admitting folks to play without requiring them
to audition so that the oldtimers who competed to join the band now complain that
playing in the band no longer 'means' anything: even gay men and lesbians, grumble
these heterosexuals, now are admitted to what was once our club. Or perhaps
it is because these folks find distasteful the very idea of a homosexual relationship, something they see as sinful, being compared to their 'sanctified' heterosexual
relationship. Such an explanation probably applies particularly well to those who

believe that all sexual encounters, hetero- or otherwise, are wrong outside marriage, perhaps even that they are suspect if not aimed at reproduction.

For some, marriage is considered sacred because it is considered a life-time exclusive commitment to someone one loves deeply. It is on grounds like these that the 'sanctity' of marriage is also cited by some supporting the inclusive interpretation (extending to same- as well as different-sex unions):

> Especially for religious people, marriage makes a statement that 'this is someone I love and will grow old with'. When you're just 'partners' or 'living together' they think . . . you know, every day a new lover'. With marriage, the commitment is real, and they believe it.
> (Quote from Anne-Marie Thus of the Netherlands, who in 2001 married Helene Faasen, her long-time partner and co-parent; note that theirs is a civil and not actually a church-sanctioned marriage; www.cbsnews.com/stories/2004/03/04/ world/printable604084.shtml)

But the 'sanctity' area of the M-web is a messy one. Its secular interpretation as a matter of long-term commitment and the only site for 'legitimate' sexual activity is threatened by the relatively high rates of divorce now current as well as by widespread extramarital, including premarital, sexual activity. And its religious interpretation as deriving from the status of marriage as a religious 'sacrament' lacks the long pedigree that many assume. Historically, marriage in Europe is first primarily economic and only after many centuries 'sanctified' officially by Christian churches:

> The Church struggles throughout to induce people to solemnize their unions in church or in the presence of priests, 'in the face of the church', as they put it. But before the Council of Trent, c. 1570 in the full force of Counter-Reformation, they never managed to make it required by law. Prior to that date, you can say that marriages were independent contracts, often followed by church ceremonies and often taking place just outside (significantly) the church door. Church porches, some think, burgeoned to accomodate endowment ceremonies in rainy countries. Property matters outside, souls (if desired) within. . . . Of course, to lay people marriage was largely a business matter at all social levels. It can be analyzed in terms of the question: watch the money. See in what direction dowries, bride-prices etc. moved, and then think marriage market.
> (Personal communication, Paul Hyams, professor of history, Cornell University)

Marriage is about family and children

Although there are many heterosexual marriages without children (often as a matter of choice) and many in which there are no connections to the natal families of either spouse, marriage is strongly associated with expectations of children. Those supporting heterosexual exclusivity often speak of children's interests.

[If same-sex marriages are allowed, then m]arriage will no longer be a carrier of the message that children need mothers and fathers. Instead the law will legitimate the principles of family diversity: that adults get to form the families they choose and children will resiliently adjust. Or not, but who cares?

> (Maggie Gallagher, cited http://www.leaderu.com/focus/
> redefining_marriage.html, March 22, 2004)

Ages of experience have taught humanity that the commitment of a husband and wife to love and to serve one another promotes the welfare of children and the stability of society.

> (President George W. Bush, February 24, 2004,
> statement supporting DOMA and FMA)

But the other side is also concerned for children's welfare. Perhaps most notably, the Goodridge decision, summarized above, argued that forbidding same-sex marriage

works a deep and scarring hardship [on same-sex families] for no rational reason. [It prevents children of same-sex couples] from enjoying the immeasurable advantages that flow from the assurance of a stable family structure in which children will be reared, educated, and socialized . . . It cannot be rational under our laws to penalize children by depriving them of State benefits because of their parents' sexual orientation.

And conservative columnist Andrew Sullivan argued in 2004 that children growing up in families with heterosexual parents may also benefit from the more inclusive concept:

[My Catholic family taught me that what] really mattered was family and the love you had for one another. . . . The most important day of your life was when you got married. It was on that day that all your friends and all your family got together to celebrate the most important thing in life: your happiness – your ability to make a new home, to form a new but connected family, to find love that put everything else into perspective. . . . This isn't about gay marriage. It's about marriage. It's about family. It's about love . . . These family values are not options for a happy and stable life. They are necessities. *Putting gay relationships in some other category – civil unions, domestic partnerships, whatever – may alleviate real human needs, but by their very euphemism, by their very separateness, they actually build a wall between gay people and their families* (emphasis added). They put back the barrier many of us have spent a lifetime trying to erase . . . I want [a kid like me] to know that his love has dignity, that he does indeed have a future as a full and equal part of the human race. Only marriage will do that. Only marriage can bring him home.

Where the M-word has been

Some oppose making marriage more inclusive on the grounds that it is an inherently unchanging institution, the same in different cultures and throughout history:

> The union of a man and woman is the most enduring human institu-
> tion, honoring – honored and encouraged in all cultures and by every
> religious faith.
>
> [President George W. Bush, February 24, 2004]

We have already seen that marriage is diverse across cultures and that it has changed
through time. But given the frequent references to the bible in these debates, it is
instructive to consider how the FMA, quoted earlier, might need to be reworded
if historical precedents recorded biblically were followed:

> A. Marriage in the United States shall consist of a union between one
> man and one or more women. (Gen 29:17–28; II Sam 3:2–5.) B.
> Marriage shall not impede a man's right to take concubines in addition
> to his wife or wives. (II Sam 5:13; I Kings 11:3; II Chron 11:21) C. A
> marriage shall be considered valid only if the wife is a virgin. If the wife
> is not a virgin, she shall be executed. (Deut 22:13–21) D. Marriage
> between a believer and a nonbeliever shall be forbidden. (Gen 24:3;
> Num 25:1–9; Ezra 9:12; Neh 10:30) E. Since marriage is for life, neither
> this Constitution nor the constitution of any State, nor any state or
> federal law, shall be construed to permit divorce. (Deut 22:19; Mark
> 10:9) F. If a married man dies without children, his brother shall marry
> the widow. If he refuses to marry his brother's widow or deliberately
> does not give her children, he shall pay a fine of one shoe and be other-
> wise punished in a manner to be determined by law. (Gen. 38:6–10;
> Deut 25:5–10)

And it is probably useful to remind non-historians of the profoundly gender-
asymmetric nature of marriage in many places until relatively recently. English legal
scholar Sir William Blackstone's doctrine of femme couverture enunciated in his
commentaries said that 'the very being or legal existence of the woman is suspended
during the marriage, or at least is incorporated' into that of the husband.

   Contemporary marriage in the US has only a few legal vestiges remaining of
this profoundly patriarchal past,[2] although the social and cultural traces of it have
by no means vanished. It is also instructive to remember the racism operative in
the history of marriage in the US. Though unenforceable since the 1967 decision
in Gooding v. Virginia, Alabama did not repeal its law against interracial marriage
until November 2000.

   The bottom line is that conceptions of marriage have changed significantly over
time, especially in the direction of increased gender equity. Although most people
in Anglo-American culture have indeed assumed historically that marriage unites
one woman and one man, definitions of marriage and the institution itself keep

changing: most people under 30 see no problem with same-sex marriage and fewer people overall oppose it now than opposed interracial marriage in 1967. Although the M-word has been places that many do not want it to revisit, its future could potentially be open to less problematic understandings.

The semiotics of sex
and the discourse
of desire

THE FINAL SECTION OF THIS BOOK contains some very recent work on language and sexuality. Its four chapters, all written since 2000, are linked by the attention they give to the semiotic resources that both enable and constrain individuals when they communicate *desire*.

Though some linguists had previously addressed questions about the verbal encoding of erotic desire (see e.g. Harvey and Shalom 1998), the place of desire in language and sexuality research became a more overt subject of debate following the publication of a review article in which Don Kulick (2000) surveyed the literature on gay and lesbian language. Kulick argued that while this literature offered a number of valuable insights, it was concerned mainly with issues of sexual identity, and seldom referred to any overall theory of sexuality. Consequently, a number of phenomena that figured prominently in theoretical discussions, such as fantasy, desire, repression, pleasure, fear and the unconscious, had rarely been investigated in linguistic research. Kulick concluded his review by suggesting that issues of desire should be brought more explicitly within the scope of the field.

This was and is a challenging proposal in several respects. One challenge is *defining* desire: as we have noted elsewhere (Cameron and Kulick 2003: 106–32), theorists have conceptualized it in a number of different ways. There are psychoanalytic accounts (such as Lacan's) that theorize it as a lack that originates with the loss of pre-Oedipal connection to the mother; in contrast there are antipsychoanalytic approaches (such as that of Deleuze and Guattari) that treat it as a kind of energy or force sustaining or blocking social relationships. However desire is defined, though, a focus upon it implicitly challenges the identity-based model that has dominated most thinking about language and sexuality, by suggesting that the notion of identity explains only part of what is relevant to the linguistic construction of sexual meaning. Theorists of desire stress that individuals are not fully in control of the meaning and effects of what they do, and that language can always say more than speakers intend, or mean something different from what they intended. So the idea of language as a resource speakers use to construct a coherent self or perform a certain kind of identity, while not invalid, is not the whole story either; language can also disrupt or undermine its users' efforts to present themselves in particular ways.

This observation suggests a further challenge for empirical researchers: to move beyond the abstraction of theoretical accounts and locate the workings of desire in the real language used in real situations by real people. Some discourse and conversation analysts (e.g. Billig 1999) have tried to do this by analysing the way silences, fears and affective stances are collaboratively constructed in situated interactions. Other, anthropological and historical, approaches are exemplified by the four chapters we have included in this section. Using desire as a lens through which to examine particular linguistic performances, the four authors whose work appears here explore the semiotic codes through which sexual meanings and desires become (or fail to become) intelligible.

David Valentine (Chapter 20) addresses an anxiety that students of language may feel when they begin to think about desire. 'One of the problems in "talking about desire"', he writes, 'is defining what "desire" might mean; indeed there is great difficulty in defining such an object, particularly for anthropologists, leery of psychological and individualistic explanations for human action'. But this difficulty need not lead to paralysis. Valentine proposes an uncomplicated solution: 'one approach may be to simply listen to what people have to say about their desires without trying to account for them in terms of identity categories'. His article focuses on an individual known as Miss Angel, who is a participant in a New York City 'alternative lifestyles' support group. In a single encounter, Angel declares herself to be a pre-op transsexual, a woman, a former drug addict, HIV-positive, gay and 'a woman with a large clit' – in addition to at one point saying 'I dunno *what* I am' and later asserting 'I know what I am'. When Angel remarks, 'I went to bed with my own kind once', the facilitator's efforts to establish what she means by 'my own kind' (a woman? A gay man? A transsexual? Some entirely different category of person?) do not ultimately bring clarification, but only frustration for all concerned. Valentine analyses this frustration as illustrative of how erotic desires do not align neatly with identity categories, and he sees it as symptomatic of the way that 'particular kinds of identity categories disable certain kinds of desires from being validated'. If we explore these kinds of disjunctions and document the ways that erotic desire exceeds identity categories, Valentine suggests, then we can better understand not only the processes through which different kinds of desires are deemed intelligible or unintelligible, but also the political consequences of categorizing some experiences as 'sexual' and others as 'gendered'.

Laura M. Ahearn's chapter is about love letters written by women and men in a Nepalese village. She explains that during the 1990s, romantic love was redefined in this region in such a way that 'desire itself came to be seen as desirable'. From having been previously seen as a destructive and shameful emotion, desire – in the sense of sexual attraction and emotional connection – was re-imagined as a positive motivation for marriage between a man and a woman. Ahearn's article addresses the much-debated issue of whether love in its contemporary Western sense is universal. She shows that it is not: in Nepal, romantic love in this sense is new. It was facilitated by – and remains tightly linked to – recent historical develop-ments that include formal education, literacy, the consumption of commodities and the development of a sense of self grounded in individualism. Although Ahearn doesn't use the term, the villagers' love letters exemplify what theorists have called 'self-fashioning' or 'the technology of the self'. Desire here (and, we would argue, everywhere else) constitutes a means through which individuals in particular historical and social circumstances fashion themselves as particular kinds of people, who feel particular kinds of emotions and want particular kinds of relationships with others.

Momoko Nakamura's article (Chapter 22), published here for the first time, discusses the semiotic process of *indexicalization* – how particular linguistic features come to 'index' (point to) particular groups of language-users. In much of the liter-ature on language and sexuality, and certainly in the popular imagination, there is a usually unstated assumption that certain linguistic features come to signify a particular group because the features are in common use among members of that group. Thus if, for instance, gender inversion and 'swoopy' intonation are associ-ated with homosexuals, it is taken to be because homosexuals habitually exhibit those traits in their speech. Nakamura, however, argues against this commonsense idea. She makes the obvious but not always fully appreciated point that in any social group, linguistic usage will vary: members of a given group do not all talk the same way. The question then arises: how and why do some features of language-use – but not others – acquire a strong indexical link to particular groups? That question becomes even more complicated when we consider that the group a certain feature indexes may not even exist in the real social world. Nakamura observes that Japanese speakers can tell you exactly how Martians talk (they are supposed to say – in Japanese – 'we are aliens from outer space', with flat intonation in a shrill, mechanical voice). The group that is her subject, 'schoolgirls' in the nine-teenth and early twentieth centuries, is a somewhat similar case. Though female students, unlike Martians, did exist in Meiji Japan, 'schoolgirls' became a distinc-tive social category only *after* the language that supposedly belonged to them was already appearing in novels and other publications. Just as 'Martian speech' was not created by Martians, 'schoolgirl speech' was not created by actual schoolgirls, but by fiction writers and social commentators.

Of particular relevance for our thinking about language and sexuality is the process through which this constructed schoolgirl language came to be *sexualized*. Writers of stories about school-age girls used certain features to mark out 'bad girl' characters – those who were uninterested in being 'good wives and wise mothers' – from 'good girls', who accepted their prescribed role. The features signified one of the main faults ascribed to the 'bad girls', namely frivolity. As the forms then began appearing in pornographic texts, they acquired a more explicitly erotic meaning. So what began as a literary convention for representing the speech of rebellious female students (though at the time female students generally did *not* speak in that way) came over time to signify 'schoolgirl' – a sexualized female position indexed by a certain way of talking. This way of talking in principle became available to anyone (that is, not just 'real' schoolgirls) who wanted to produce the erotic meaning associated with it – a combination of sexiness and youthful innocence that some men found particularly appealing. The process of indexicalization Nakamura describes here might equally be called 'insexualization'. Her approach, looking at the history of a form's uses in different representational genres, might be a fruitful one for exploring the sexualization of other linguistic forms – for example how the use of deictic terms in athletic or military commands, such as 'Suck in that gut!' or 'Lift those legs!' came to be recast as self-referential sex-talk in gay pornography, as in 'Suck that dick!' or 'Fuck that ass!' (where 'that' in both cases means 'my').

The final piece is Don Kulick's (2003) examination of the word 'No' (Chapter 23). The focus of the discussion is the word itself, rather than who utters it. This is important, and relates to the distinction discussed in the text between performance ('something a subject does') and performativity ('the process through which the subject emerges'). By focusing not primarily on who utters the word but on what its utterance or non-utterance *does* in particular interactions (the ones discussed are concerned with rape, the Homosexual Panic Defense, and sadomasochistic sexual scenes), the article shows how the presence or absence of 'no' in a variety of situations performatively produces those situations as sexual, even as it positions speakers differently in relation to structures of gender, erotics and power.

Though our selection from the literature ends with these chapters, the debates they contribute to are still very much ongoing. Language and sexuality is not only a diverse field of enquiry but also a rapidly developing one. Here we will not speculate on its future, but we hope this compilation of past and present research will help readers to engage with whatever comes next.

Chapter 20

David Valentine

2003

'I WENT TO BED WITH
MY OWN KIND ONCE'

The erasure of desire in the
name of identity

Introduction

WHAT DOES IT MEAN to talk about erotic desire? By this, I mean two
interrelated things: what does it mean to talk about desire in a scholarly
context; and what does it mean to talk about one's own desires? In the contemporary USA, popular discussions of erotic desire are drawn inevitably into a discussion of 'sexuality,' one which again, inevitably occurs against and invokes the binary
of hetero/homosexual identity (troubled perhaps by the evidence of bisexuality,
though even with bisexuality, desire is seen to lie discretely within the bounds of an
identity category, namely 'bisexual'). Within queer, feminist, and anthropological
scholarship, Foucault's famous point that sexual identity has come to stand as the
truth of who we are (Foucault 1981 [1980]: 51–73) has been utilized to show
how, since the late nineteenth century in the West, the erotic is not expressed as
particular *desires* but, rather, as discrete *identities*. Foucault and others (e.g. Weeks
1981; Katz 1995) have pointed to the power of identity categories to both
proliferate discourses about, and simultaneously restrain, talk of erotic desire as an
experience which bears the name 'sexuality.' Erotic desires which fall outside the
trinary of heterosexuality, homosexuality (either/or) and bisexuality (both/and), or
which fail to make sense in terms of their basic logic of binary gender, are rendered
unintelligible. Such 'unintelligible' desires present a unique opportunity for scholars
to investigate the complexity of erotic desire, its expression in practice (linguistic
and otherwise), and its relationship to identity categories.

Yet, despite the influence of Foucault, the troubling nature of desire-beyond-
sexual identity has received relatively little attention. Since the early 1990s, many
anthropologists have indeed pointed out that Western sexual identities and identity labels cannot make sense of and indeed, are complicated by non-Western
sexual practices and desires (e.g. Blackwood 1995; Donham 1998; Johnson 1997;
Kulick 1998). However, there has been little corresponding work which looks

explicitly at the erratic connections between erotic desire and identity in US settings outside of immigrant communities (e.g. Manalansan 1997). Most anthropologists of sexuality in the USA have tended to follow the basic anthropological tenet of using one's informants' categories to describe them. Consequently, gay men and lesbians the usual subjects of discussions of 'sexuality' in the anthropological liter- ature are usually discussed in terms of those categories of identity which are meaningful to informants. As a result, the ontological assumptions which underpin these emic categories are left unexamined (e.g. Lewin 1993; Shokeid 1995; Weston 1991). While attention to study subjects' self-categorization is clearly central to the anthropological enterprise, critical analyses of those categorizations is also vital to analysis.

If anthropology (and other social sciences) has neglected the ontological under- pinnings of desire, there has been even less work in linguistics and linguistic anthropology which takes up the deeper implications of considering language and desire. As Kulick (2000) points out, much of the work that takes on the relation- ship between language and erotic desire has coalesced around a discussion of 'sexuality,' usually focusing on gay- and lesbian-identified (and occasionally trans- gender-identified) subjects. As with the studies I mentioned above, this work similarly depends for its analysis on a close identification with study participants' self-identity as gay and lesbian. But, as Kulick points out, there is a central flaw in much of this work, drawing as it does on a tautology: people who are lesbian and gay speak in a way that is defined as 'gay language'; and people who talk a 'gay language' are, thus, gay. Kulick argues that such studies continuously capitulate, to a sexuality = identity formula. To move beyond this dynamic, Kulick proposes a reorientation of 'language and sexuality' studies from a focus on sexual identity to a focus on desire. He argues that a focus on desire will both complicate under- standings of what 'sexuality' is and enable an examination of the relationship between linguistic practices and sexuality that is not constrained by identity categories.

Central to Kulick's argument is a critique of the essentialism implicit in much of the work on language and sexuality. This critique draws on a central tenet of contemporary social theory: that essentialized categories of identity obscure the cross-cutting nature of social experience and identification. Being 'gay' or 'lesbian' for example, is experienced by different people in radically different ways depending on their racial identification, location, age, social class, personal history, and so forth. What is less clear, though, is that such categories of identity achieve a density of meaning through their reiteration, even in scholarly work that attempts to disrupt that meaning. By this I mean that even scholars who take a critical approach to essentialized identities require some baseline understandings about bodies and practices, about the relationship between signifier and signified, in order to mount a critique in the first place.

To take the examples of 'gay' and 'lesbian' once more, while we might accept that very different kinds of people may use these categories in identifying them- selves, there are also some basic assumptions that flow from the organization of the categories themselves. Primary among these is that people who identify as 'gay' or 'lesbian' are understood as unambiguously men or women, and that they direct their desire to others who are, respectively, unambiguously men or women. That is, these categories rest implicitly on the logic of binary gender which underpins the homo/hetero identity structure, a structure which requires clearly gendered men and women to desire one another (or each other).

For those people who are not unambiguously gendered, the category 'transgender' has, since the early 1990s, become ubiquitous (by people so identified and in scholarly texts) to encapsulate this experience. 'Transgender' has become both a powerful tool of activism and a convenient label for social scientific research in bringing together a range of social and medicalized identities formerly seen as separate including, but not limited to, transexuals, cross-dressers, drag queens,[1] and intersex people. Indeed, the power of the category is that it is actively seen as a *collective* term to gather in all non-normative expressions of gender, no matter how they are labeled. Another central element of contemporary discourses of 'transgender' is that transgender identities are seen to emanate from the experience of 'gender,' not 'sexuality.' In other words, transgender identities are conceptualized as quite distinct from homosexual identities, which are seen to have their source in 'sexuality.'

At the same time, it is important to note that even in discussions of transgender-identified[2] people, sexual desire is still generally encoded as either heterosexual or homosexual (or, indeed, bisexual). That is, sexual identity is usually claimed by transgender-identified people in accordance with their gender of identity. While most transgender-identified people insist on the differences between homosexuality and transgender identity (a significant point I will return to), many *also* identify as homosexual, based on their erotic and affective attraction to people who share the same gender category with which they identify. However, to reiterate, in contemporary scholarship and activism these identities are seen to flow from distinct kinds of ontological sources transgender identity from 'gender,' and homosexual or heterosexual identity from 'sexuality.'

As such, this seems like a very neat system, which accounts both for gender identification and erotic desire within a double binary of homosexual/heterosexual and masculinity/femininity, with their roots respectively in yet another binary: that of sexuality and gender. But things are not always so clear cut, for frequently, as I will show, erotic desires expressed in speech can conflate, confuse, and contradict this neatness.

Language and desire

As I noted above, 'talking about desire' in this paper refers not only to scholarly discussions of desire, but also points to the place where such an investigation might begin. One of the problems in 'talking about desire' (in a scholarly sense) is defining what 'desire' might mean; indeed there is a great difficulty in defining such an object, particularly for anthropologists, leery of psychological and individualistic explanations for human action (see Kulick 2000, 2003). Here, however, I propose that one approach may be to simply listen to what people have to say about their desires without trying to account for them only in terms of identity categories. Indeed, my suggestion is to listen to talk-about-desire to see what that talk can tell us *about* identity categories. In paying attention to expressed erotic desire whether in the intimacy of a particular encounter, reports of past experiences, or fantasies spoken out loud the contradictions produced by categories of self-identity can become evident. By so doing, we may expose the complicated politics of the double binary (that is, homosexual/heterosexual and masculinity/femininity), enable a critical approach to the relationship between identity and desire, and a richer analysis of the binary of gender/sexuality that underpins them.

In what follows I will examine: (a) the way erotic desire is expressed in speech, in this case, reports of past experiences; (b) the ways that different kinds of desires are differently adjudicated as valid or invalid; and (c) the historical and cultural conditions that allow such adjudication to take place. Paying attention to what people *say* about their desire and the ways such assertions are accepted or rejected enables us to investigate the power of identity categories to obscure particular desires both in people's lives and in scholarly discussion of them. Moreover, this focus also points to a deeper epistemological issue, one which underpins both the question of language and desire but also much contemporary social theory: the relationship between gender and sexuality. In the data I present here, I want to show first that the use of particular kinds of identity categories disable certain kinds of desires from being validated. But second, I want to show that this process rests upon and reproduces a central analytic and political proposition in contemporary queer and feminist anthropology, as well as studies of language and sexuality: that those human experiences we call 'gender' and 'sexuality' are distinct arenas of social practice, experience, and analysis (see Rubin 1984). While the separation of gender and sexuality has been a theoretically productive tool, I will argue here that ironically this separation implicitly underpins the identity labels that feminist and queer scholars are at pains to deconstruct. Further, this theoretical framework, in which a gender and sexuality are seen as separable human experiences, has implications beyond the study of gender and sexuality. My argument is that a progressive political and theoretical move to make a space for 'sexuality' as a field of investigation and activism has unwittingly produced a system whereby those who are already disenfranchised through poverty and racism cannot be fully accounted for contemporary theorizations about gender and sexuality.

A focus on 'desire' in the form of its expression through speech enables us consider the politics of categorizing certain experiences as 'sexual' and others as 'gendered.' To do so, I focus on two aspects of talk: first, the use of identity categories themselves; but second, and equally importantly, what people say about their erotic desires in ways that cannot be accounted for by these categories. The broader question is, therefore: what does the expression and adjudication of desire in talk tell us about the politics of sexual and gender identity in the contemporary USA?

The alternative lifestyles group: 'someone like me'

The data I will discuss are drawn from an 'alternative lifestyles' support group at a Lower East Side community project in New York City in the Fall of 1996. I attended this group over the course of that Fall, and on one occasion I was able to tape record the proceedings. The participants were a group of friends and acquaintance who came to the group weekly to talk about their experiences. As a group, they were united primarily by the fact that they all were tenants in low-income housing, for which this organization was a resource and gathering place. However, the core group consisted of mostly young African American or Latina/o people who could be described, or would describe themselves during the meeting as gay, lesbian, bisexual and transgender (among other categories), even though, as I will show, these identifications were far from stable for all participants. Others came in and out over the weeks I was able to attend this group, and the one I describe here also included a young African American woman whose brother had come out to her as gay (and who was struggling to understand what this meant), as well as Sylvia, a very old white woman in a wheelchair who appeared to attend every group meeting at the center, whatever its topic.

The only outsiders in this group were myself a white, gay-identified man and Nora. Nora is Latina, a self-identified heterosexual transexual woman, a former drug user, and now a peer educator for several NYC social service agencies. In conversation, Nora is explicit about her transexual history, but refuses to accept that this makes her less of a woman. She has been in recovery from drug addiction since the early 1990s, and part of that recovery and personal growth has been working for social service agencies in New York. Through this experience, Nora has developed an understanding of 'transgender' which has been shaped in contexts of political and social service advocacy since the 1990s: that of a collective category which gathers into it any kind of non-normative gender expression, and which is distinct from homosexuality. This is evident from her explanation of what 'transgender' means to one of the group members early on in the meeting. Transgender, she said, is an

> umbrella term which includes [. . .] transexuals, pre-op, post-op, uh, transvestites, drag queens, female impersonators [. . .] you know, it makes it much easier to define [. . .], a person or group or whatever.

Though Nora and the group participants shared common life experiences of poverty, racism, drug addiction, and non-normative gender or sexual identity, the way they talked about themselves in this group was quite divergent, a difference underpinned precisely by Nora's experience in social service settings both as a client and as a counselor where she has learnt this usage of 'transgender.' It is this difference, in particular, the escalation of Nora's attempts to get one of the group members to identify as *either* transgender *or* gay that I will focus on in the analysis below.

At the beginning of this meeting, as we sat gathered around a conference table in an untidy meeting room, Nora introduced herself as follows: 'I'm Nora, I'm transexual and I'm a woman and transexual is my alternative lifestyle.' I introduced myself as 'a non-transgender gay man' which got a conversation going about what 'transgender' means (from which I have excerpted Nora's explanation, above). However, not everyone in the room professed such stable identities as Nora and I did. For example, when Ben, another core group member introduced himself, he said: 'I'm Ben, I'm just a male who enjoys . . . male companionship as well as female companionship.' Note that Ben did not refer to himself as 'bisexual' in this statement, though other group members did take on particular identity categories in talking about themselves.

One of them was Miss Angel. We had not been talking long when she entered the room, late as usual. Miss Angel — African American, a former drug user and sex worker — was one of the central participants in the group, the acknowledged linchpin of the core group of friends, who also worked as a chef at the community center. Upon her arrival, everything stopped and we waited as she took her place, made her observations, and came to rest. As she came in, so too did another participant, a woman I had not met before. As such, I introduced myself and explained my presence (and my tape recorder). Ben took this as a sign that I hadn't met Angel before, and he told her to introduce herself to me.

Excerpt A

1	Angel:	Introduce ourselves? To whom?
2	Ben:	Do you all know each other? [i.e. do Angel and I know each other]
3	A:	Yes! These homosexuals know each other up in here! They better!

This brief excerpt is significant, particularly for what follows. In noting that we have met before, Angel grouped herself and me (identified to the group in this and earlier meetings as a gay man), as 'homosexuals.' While Ben's earlier cited statement to the group is interesting because he avoided identity categories in talking about himself, Angel's talk is notable because she did not: indeed during the rest of the meeting, she used a plethora of identity categories about herself, 'homosexual' being only the first. When Angel finally sat down and took command of the meeting (as she was wont to do), the following exchange took place:

Excerpt B

1	Angel:	My name is Angel, I'm a pre-op transexual. I dunno *what* I am, I'm a woman, simply . . ., OK? I'm HIV positive.
2	Nora:	A genetic woman?
3	A:	I'm a drug addict woman.
4	Interjection:	Was!
5	Nora:	Was or still are
6	Int:	I hope!
7	A:	No I was but I'm still, you know, they say you still supposed to say you're a drug addict.
8	Int:	Well.
9	A:	OK, still a drug addict.
10	N:	It's up to you if you want to say that, you know, if you don't want to I mean [you don't have to].
11	A:	Well whatever, look I'm telling the story right? Thank you. And I'm 31 years old and I'm a woman.

In this exchange, Angel makes several claims about herself that she is a pre-operative transexual, a woman, a (former) drug addict, HIV positive and, moreover, that 'I dunno *what* I am.' In this support group, as indeed in many of this kind, the divulging of personal information such as HIV status or substance abuse history is not uncommon. Nora's question (Excerpt B, line 2), which is meant as a joke, leads Angel to provide another qualifier for 'woman,': 'drug addict' (Excerpt B, line 3). This results in a discussion of Angel's history of drug addiction, and a discussion of what you are 'supposed' or 'don't have to' divulge about such details. In the end, Angel asserts her right to say who she is, and says simply: 'I'm 31 years old and I'm a woman.'

Given the distinction made in most contemporary theory and activism between homosexual and transgender/transexual identity, Angel's claims to be (implicitly) homosexual (Excerpt A, line 3) and a transexual woman (Excerpt B, line 1) are somewhat confusing; certainly they were confusing to Nora (and to myself), as is evident from an exchange that happened a few minutes later:

Excerpt C

1	Angel:	I had to get to know new friends when I turned gay and it's not easy being gay.
2	Nora:	How was your experience when you became a woman, a transexual woman?
3	A:	I was 13 years old when I did everything.
4	N:	Was it even harder?
5	A:	Was it harder? No.
6	N:	Did it go from bad to worse?
7	A:	No . . . Um, when I was 13. It was hard, I went to school –
8	Ben:	With breasts.
9	A:	The breasts.

This excerpt marks the first point in the conversation in which Nora attempts to disaggregate Angel's different self-identifications: as homosexual and as trans-gender/transexual. Nora's questions to Angel above (Excerpt C, lines 2, 4, 6) are significant because Nora is implicitly proposing to Angel two different states of coming out: as 'gay' when she was 13, and as a 'transexual woman' at a later date. Angel, however, does not make this distinction: she was 13 when she did 'everything.'

To return to the conceptualization of desire and identity in the contemporary USA, the reason for this misunderstanding is, I would argue, based on different conceptual notions of personhood and identity: Nora, schooled in the language of 'transgender' through her work in social service agencies, sees a necessary division between experiences of being gay (the realm of 'sexuality') and experiences of being transgender (the realm of 'gender': 'how was your experience when you became a woman, a transexual woman?'). Angel does not ('I was 13 years old when I did everything.').

This divergence in understandings became clearer still in a later exchange between them, as they discussed Angel's sexual history. Angel had informed us that she had had sex with straight and gay men, and with women (with one of whom she had had a child). However, all of Nora's questions her implicit attempts, as in Excerpt C above, to elicit a stable identity from Angel failed. A crucial point in the conversation occurred when Nora tried to pin Angel down on precisely how she labels herself after Angel made a seemingly oblique statement:

Excerpt D

1	Angel:	I went to bed with my own kind. I tried it once.
2	Ben:	How was it?
3	A:	How was it?
4	B:	Uh huh.
5	Nora:	Now what is your own kind mean by definition, because you're always telling us-
6	A:	I'm a woman, well you know.
7	N:	You're a woman, transexual, you're gay, you're homosexual.
8	B:	A man.
9	A:	Look, me, like me, someone like me. Someone like me . . . Someone like me.
10	N:	[who] changes sexuality[3], uh huh
11	B:	With breasts.
12	A:	With breasts.
13	N:	OK.
14	A:	I went out with someone like me. Her name was Billie Jean, she lives in Coney Island.

Here Nora finally tried to get Angel to define what her 'own kind' is. She listed the identity categories that Angel had used about herself in this meeting (woman, gay, homosexual, transexual) implying that she cannot be all of these things. To this, Angel insisted: 'look, me, like me, someone like me. Someone like me . . . Someone like me.' In the end Ben offered: 'with breasts' to which Angel affirmed 'with breasts,' and Nora left it there: 'OK.' However, while Nora's 'OK' indicates she was not willing to draw Angel any further on the topic, the import of her questions in excerpts C and D is that she was attempting to get Angel to channel her expressions (and experiences) of erotic desire be it her desire for a woman, a man, or for 'someone like her' through identity categories that cannot, in the end, account for them.

Both in excerpts C and D, Ben offers 'with breasts' by way of explanation of Angel's being, which Angel affirms (in Excerpt D, line 12). This reference to Angel's breasts – the result of hormone therapy – is the final word in both cases. The reference to her body is particularly instructive, for Angel's changing body shifts her in contemporary progressive understandings into the category of 'transgender' or more specifically, 'transexual,' a category she indeed uses to describe herself. Yet, as is clear from the preceding conversation, Angel does not always stick to this definition of self. Indeed, Nora's attempts to pin her down on this point relates directly to the double binary I invoked earlier Angel is conflating gendered and sexual identities, recounting desires which cannot be accounted for in a system which sees gender and sexuality as distinct.

Perhaps in response to this questioning, Angel tried to summarize her theory of sexuality and desire shortly after this exchange. She said:

> When it comes down to sex, I don't think . . . it's two men going to bed with each other, a man and a woman going to bed with it or pre-op or nothing like that. I just think it's just two people having sex, making love to each other, enjoying each other's company, enjoying each other's time, when we're together.

Here Angel is proposing a fluidity to sexual identity that neatly encapsulates a non-identitarian politics of sexual desire. A short while later, Nora made the following comment, which seems to support Angel's theory of desire:

> You label yourself what you want to label yourself. Other people don't label you, I mean unless you want to be labeled yourself, you know.

Yet Nora's questioning throughout this meeting points to the ways that such desires and passions are subject, always, to a rigorous system of labeling, whether or not someone wants to be labeled. Those desires that cannot be labeled or which require different kinds of labels at different times are produced as incoherent, or, at the very least, the product of confusion.

Later in the group, Nora tells of her days of sex work when non-transgender men who were her clients would ask her what their desire for her meant for their own sexual identity:

Excerpt E

1   Nora: And they're attracted to that [a feminine person with a penis] So they would tell me, 'well what am I?' I said 'well I can't tell you what you are unless you know and I can't not tell you this is what you are and this is what you're gonna be, you know, because it's not my life.' My life, I know what I am.
2   Angel: I'm a woman with a large clit.
3   Nora: I know what I am.

In this excerpt, Nora states 'I know what I am' and her statements of self never vary: she is a heterosexual transexual woman. Nora's claim overlaps yet another assertion by Miss Angel this time that she is 'a woman with a large clit' which joins the other categories she has taken on during the meeting: gay, homosexual, and transexual. In contrast to Nora's clear sense of knowing 'what I am' above, Angel claims 'I dunno *what* I am' (Excerpt B, line 1), an observation that Nora implicitly draws on in asking Angel to adhere to one of them.

I would argue that Nora's attempts to get Angel to pick just one of the definitions of self that she has used during the meeting fail not because Angel cannot account for 'what she is,' but rather because she can account for herself in many different ways. Nora, as I have noted, shares much of Angel's history and experience as a former drug user, sex worker, and person of color. However, Nora differs from Angel in that she has an understanding of gender and sexual identity gained through her contact with the social service agencies she works for, and defined by a distinct split between gay identities on the one hand and transgender identities on the other. Angel has no such model of personhood, and these distinctions do not seem to signify much to her. All she can say when Nora requests a definition of what 'my own kind' might mean is: 'someone like me.'

At the end of the group, Nora said: 'In the long run, as long as you know the truth that's really all that matters.' But what is the truth? And what operations of power and requirements for asserting identity to make sense of one's desire make some kinds of desires more true and more coherent than others? The ways these different kinds of knowledge are assessed, within this group and within a broader system of identity, complicates how such assertions of self and expressions of desire which are expected to be congruent with such identities are seen as being 'truthful.' Nora's inability to tell her former clients or to ascertain about Angel 'what' they are points to the place where desires escape identity and become unnameable and, consequently, unrepresentable.

Gender, sexuality, and the naming of desire

The interactions that occurred at the Alternative Lifestyles group and the conceptual mismatches they illustrate only make sense if one considers the history of the last quarter of the twentieth century, in which gay and lesbian (and later, bisexual and transgender) people made their mark in American society. By the end of the 1960s, when the now almost-mythical Stonewall rebellion was about to take place, homosexuality had long been pathologized. But it was also differently conceptualized than it was in the late 1990s when this group meeting took place. Homosexuality was seen in medical and popular understandings as a failure of *gendered* identity and desire, a phenomenon which produced homosexual men as feminine and homosexual women as masculine. That is, in the pre-Stonewall era, the dominant understanding of homosexuality was that it was caused by and was manifested in gender variance. In 1972, Esther Newton, could write that '[d]rag and camp are the most representative and widely used symbols of homosexuality in the English speaking world' (Newton 1979 [1972]: 100).

Thirty years later, it would be harder to make such an argument. It is interesting to note that Nora, in her description of 'transgender,' includes drag queens in her list of identities that are captured by 'transgender' (as do I in my own list; see note 1). While images of drag still figure large in media representations of male homosexuality, nowadays it is far more likely to see both gay men and lesbians in both news and entertainment media as gender-normative professionals and citizens: lawyers, teachers, and even parents. These images are the result of decades of gay and lesbian activism in which the link between homosexuality and gender variance have been at least partly replaced by the image of gay men and lesbians who adhere to time-honored white, middle-class American values. This activism has gone hand-in-glove with a call for gay and lesbian civil rights, based on the claim that gay and lesbian Americans are responsible citizens whose sexuality – coded as private in American culture – should not be the purview of public scrutiny or regulation. This schema opposes a still-powerful US American folk model of homosexuality which sees it as a gendered inversion, and, in Urvashi Vaid's words, works to make a claim that 'homosexual sexuality is merely the queer version of heterosexuality' (Vaid 1995: 44). In particular, accommodationist gay and lesbian politics has increasingly worked with a model of 'gay' which implicitly foregrounds the *similarity* of gay and lesbian people to heterosexual people (and, implicitly, an adherence to white middle class American-ness) while, at the same time, highlighting its *difference* from gender variance. This accommodationist politics took the forefront in many public campaigns for civil rights in the late 1980s and 1990s, and was articulated in high profile debates about homosexuals in the military, adoption, and marriage rights (for the purest examples of this kind of accommodationist politics, see the work of neo-conservative gay scholars and writers such as Andrew Sullivan 1995, and Bruce Bawer 1993).

During the same period, from the early 1990s, 'transgender' emerged in contexts of activism and social service provision as a collective category to provide a voice for those who were no longer capable of being accounted for in terms of 'homosexuality.' To be sure, the differences between gender-normative gay men and lesbians and those with variant expressions of gender are not new, and the connection between gender variance and homosexual desire has been contested for almost as long as homosexuality has existed as a category (see Chauncey 1994; Meyerowitz 2002). However, the advent of gay and lesbian activism in the 1970s resulted in a radical shift in medical and popular understandings of homosexuality, bringing the gender-normative model of homosexuality to the fore. These understandings rest, implicitly, on a theory of gender and sexuality that sees these two experiences as distinct in the sense that one does not have to be – indeed, in the language of much post-Stonewall gay activism, one *is not* – gender variant just because one diverges from the heterosexual norm. This insistence on distinguishing between gender and sexuality allowed for the emergence of a new category, 'transgender,' in the 1990s which rests precisely on this assumed distinction.[4]

So, in the past 30 years in the USA a newly emerging model of gender and sexuality as distinct arenas of social experience and analysis has resulted in the inability of Nora (representative here of larger institutional discourses and practices) to make sense of Miss Angel's expressed desires, because of the requirement that erotic desire be made sense of through sexual identity categories that are distinct from gendered identity categories.

This is not to say that this system is absolute. For one, the folk model of gender and sexuality which see gender and sexuality as intrinsically linked is far from dead. Moreover, activists and scholars have challenged the politics of neo-conservative writers and groups (e.g. Vaid 1995; Warner 1999); and feminist and queer scholars continue to query the relationships between 'gender' and 'sexuality' (e.g. Wieringa and Blackwood 1999; Jolly and Manderson 1997). Yet at the same time, the explanatory force of this heuristic separation has gained institutional force in the very use of identity category labels underpinned by that separation to talk about sexual desire. That is, as 'transgender' becomes a category of personhood but also of activism, politics, and in academic debates, the theoretical distinction between gender and sexuality becomes solidified as fact in every iteration of that category (and the category to which it is opposed: homosexuality). And as such, Miss Angel's voice and her desires are rendered as nonsensical.

Miss Angel's claim to be 'gay,' 'transexual,' and 'transvestite' may be seen, by people like Nora and others (e.g. see Plummer 1992) to hark back to an earlier (and implicitly, outmoded and false) model of homosexuality which conflated sexuality and gender. Yet, Angel's professions of identity and desire are not unique. Among many African American and Latino communities in NYC, such claims are frequently made. In the communities in which I did fieldwork where primarily young, poor, people of color predominated – drag balls, bars, sex work, strolls – the category of 'transgender' is rarely used. Rather, categories such as 'fem queen' (another category Angel sometimes used about herself), 'butch queen' (a category that I as a non-transgender identified gay man was frequently classed under), and 'butches' (masculine female-bodied people), as well as a range of others, were all seen as united by the overarching category of 'gay.' While the borders between these identity categories were strictly monitored in these communities, as categories generally are, the source of their commonality was never denied, and was seen to flow from a complex nexus between those experiences which, in contemporary social theory, we call 'gender and sexuality.'

In other words, to be 'gay' in these contexts is not necessarily marked by gender normativity. Rather, in those communities, it is the difference *from* heteronormativity rather than the difference between 'gay' and 'transgender' which underpins the organization of gender and sexuality. Yet, their unity as 'gay' people, defined by another set of characteristics the conjunction of their disenfranchisement in terms of both class and racial memberships and their non-normative genders/sexualities precludes them from membership in the contemporary mainstream understanding of 'gay.'

As such, these desires and senses of self which cannot be made to fit into certain identity categories are confusing. Early on in the meeting, Angel had demanded her right to tell her own story ('look I'm telling the story right?' Excerpt B, line 11), but she also recognized the power of institutions to form what one should say about oneself ('they say you still supposed to say you're a drug addict.' Excerpt B, line 7). In the end, Nora cannot push Angel to use a unitary category that makes sense in Nora's conceptualization of gendered and sexual identity, so Angel does get to tell her own story in her own words. But Angel's words, like many of her peers', are also subject to discourses and practices which produce those stories as incoherent. In a conversation with one social worker to whom I related the conversation I discuss here, she argued that Angel was a victim of 'false consciousness' and that she should be educated into a more enlightened understanding of identity. In other words, to paraphrase Miss Angel, 'they say you supposed to say you're transgender.'

For this social worker, and for many other social service providers, activists, and scholars, a model of gender and sexuality as separate experiences underpinning discrete identities is implicitly a truth, and no longer simply an analytic or an activist move. Yet ironically, as I have tried to show here, the practices and politics that have resulted from this shift have, in part, reproduced a set of social relationships whereby those who arguably have the most need for a progressive politics of sexuality and gender are excluded from its explanatory purview by being made to seem confusing and confused.

There are two related theoretical points which can be drawn from this analysis, which map onto the questions I asked at the outset: what does it mean to talk about desire, both in scholarly contexts and in talking about one's own desire? First, I have suggested that the use of identity labels, conceptualized through a binary understanding of 'sexuality' and 'gender,' reproduce a system where desires that span these experiences and are narrated as such are difficult to make sense of, or can be dismissed as a kind of 'false consciousness.' Secondly, though, paying attention to such desires, rather than dismissing them, gives us a way of focusing on the practices and desires which underpin the complex lives of human beings, unrestrained as they are experientially by how such desires come to be accounted for. As such, a focus on desire expressed in talk enables a complication of the categories that have gained such force and power in academic, activist, and increasingly, popular understandings of what counts as 'sexuality.'

Looking at what people say about what they desire, who they desire, and how they act upon those desires can highlight for us the political nature of desire and the ways such yearnings are shaped by the identity categories through which they are forced to speak if they wish to get a hearing. Such a focus can enable us to look more closely at the seemingly neutral categories of 'gender' and 'sexuality,' and complicate the relationship between them. And, most usefully, it requires us to not simply assume that desire is self-evidently explained by the categories 'gender' and 'sexuality' in using them to talk about the complexity of erotic lives.

Chapter 21

Laura M. Ahearn

2003

WRITING DESIRE IN
NEPALI LOVE LETTERS

Even though we keep meeting in person, I like to write you letters because I like to say that you are my life friend. To my dear, my life's dearest, dearest love: from your lover who is always, always drowning in your love and remembrances, I send love and remembrances forever that, like a river, can never dry up or break.

(From a letter written by Vajra to Shila in 1990[1])

DURING THE 1990S, the residents of Junigau, Nepal, dramatically redefined the emotion of romantic love. In a departure from previous cultural norms and practices, desire itself came to be seen as desirable. Young villagers became increasingly eager to experience romantic love, and new types of individuals and relationships were sought after (Ahearn 2001a; cf. Collier 1997). Junigau residents such as Vajra, who wrote the letter excerpted above, and his sweetheart, Shila, both contributed to, and were swept along by, currents of social change that affected all segments of Nepali society.

In this article, I focus on the ways in which romantic love was experienced, discussed, and written about by villagers in the 1990s. I also examine the impact (sometimes significant, sometimes negligible) of the acquisition of literacy skills on gender hierarchies and intimate relationships. I maintain that a close analysis of literacy practices in a setting such as Junigau can improve our understanding of how desire is discursively constructed in particular social and linguistic contexts (Besnier 1995; Abu-Lughod and Lutz 1990).

Desiring development, and the development of desire

The love letter correspondence of Shila and Vajra illustrates many of these themes. I met Shila on the very first day I arrived in Junigau in 1982 as a Peace Corps teacher. At that time she was a lively, skinny, mischievous little girl of 12 or so who had long since been pulled out of school in order to help her widowed mother with domestic and agricultural chores. From time to time Shila would attend evening female literacy classes, but often she was kept busy at home or in the fields. I met Vajra a few days after my arrival in Junigau when I started teaching at the village school. He was one of my brightest students in seventh grade English, and he eventually went on to study at the campus in Tansen, the district center. In those years I never imagined that the studious, painfully shy Vajra and the vivacious, popular Shila would ever be attracted to each other. Nevertheless, by the summer of 1990, when they were both in their early twenties, it was clear to everyone, including me, that they were courting.

Vajra and Shila had known each other their whole lives, but both say that it was only after they worked together on the construction of a youth club building in 1990 that they began to notice each other. The youth club building was only one of many development projects undertaken in the village in the 1990s. 'Development' (bikās) was the watchword of the decade. Especially after a democratic government was instituted in 1990, radio programs, textbooks, and government officials all urged villagers to help develop Nepal. During these years, in addition to the youth club Vajra and Shila helped to put up, the following buildings were also constructed in the village of Junigau: a health clinic, six tea shops, a building for Village Development Council meetings, and an English-medium primary school. Villagers also dug out a jeep road to Tansen, previously a three-hour walk away, and began sending their daughters to school, either in Junigau or in Tansen, at a rate almost equal to that of their sons.

Higher rates of school attendance and frequent evening female literacy classes led to increasing literacy rates in Junigau, especially among young women in the village, and the ability of more villagers to read and write contributed to social changes in the areas of both love and development. School textbooks and female literacy workbooks in the 1980s and 1990s were saturated with 'development discourse' that emphasized the importance of individual agency (Ahearn 2001b) and the fulfillment of individuals' desires. The ability of young Junigau women to read and write also led to an unexpected application of their newly acquired literacy skills: the writing of love letters, a practice which was previously impossible because of very low literacy rates among girls and women. Once the extraordinarily rapid shift away from arranged marriage and capture marriage toward elopement or 'love marriage' began to occur young villagers were able to draw upon their new literacy skills to conduct illicit love letter correspondences. Since it remained culturally inappropriate for young villagers to court in any public setting, love letters were often the only way for Junigau residents to communicate their romantic feelings to their sweethearts. But Junigau love letters written in the 1990s did more than merely facilitate elopements. The letters also provided an opportunity for young villagers to talk about what love meant to them, what they desired from a love relationship, and what kinds of people they wanted to become. For these reasons, the literacy practice of love letter writing both reflected and helped to shape the significant social changes that were occurring in the village during this time period.

Such was the case with the love letter correspondence of Vajra and Shila. Even though they lived within shouting distance of each other, there was no culturally sanctioned way for them to 'date.' Although they occasionally had the opportunity to sneak away together while working in the fields or going to the village tap to get water, most of their courting took place through letters. This suited Vajra just fine, as he was extremely shy, especially around members of the opposite sex. In a December 1992 interview, Vajra described how afraid he used to be of girls and women; if one accidentally brushed against him, he said, he felt a current (*karant*) of electricity. Eventually, however, as his parents increased their pressure on him to marry, Vajra started thinking of what kind of person he would like his 'life friend' (*lāiph phrend*) to be. New cultural expectations surrounding marriage had emerged in the 1980s and 1990s in Junigau, and Vajra longed for a marriage that was very different from what his parents and other older villagers had had. Rather than acceding to his parents' wishes when it came to the choice of a bride for him, Vajra desired a companionate marriage with a woman of his own choosing. Because of the kind of person he hoped to become – a 'developed,' educated person – Vajra wanted to be able to choose a similar type of person to be his wife. He hoped to find someone to whom he felt both sexually attracted and emotionally connected – in other words, he desired *desire* in his marriage.

In explaining how his courtship with Shila got started, however, Vajra did not make himself out to be an active agent in search of the perfect 'life friend.' Instead, echoing he ideology of romantic love that became popular in Junigau in the 1990s, he eschewed agency, claiming that love 'just happens' to people. Vajra described a phenomenon I have heard echoed in many villagers' accounts of how they started their courtships: infatuation starts with a '*dekhā dekh*' – an exchange of glances, what we might call in English 'love at first sight.' According to this ideology of love, no one has to *do* anything. Thus, the village agentive theory regarding romantic love that emerged in the 1990s was that love is something that happens to people rather than something for which they themselves are responsible. Love, like other types of emotion, 'befalls' or 'is felt by' people. In the following account of the picnic at which Shila and Vajra first exchanged glances, note the use of intransitive verbs and impersonal phrasings as Vajra describes how their courtship progressed (in the following transcriptions, words in quotation marks were spoken in English):

VB: We went on a picnic there, and on the way to the picnic, at that time our courtship started, let's say, you know! [laughs] A little bit, umm, what should I say, now? At that time our courtship had its 'start.'

LMA: Did you talk . . .?

VB: No, we didn't talk. There was just an exchange of glances, one to the other, the other back – like that, see? Then later, well, well, it didn't become unbounded in any kind of direct manner. Umm, slowly, slowly, little by little, writing one or two words to each other, like that – yes, like that. I'd come and meet her, and doing so, it happened like that.

LMA: And you exchanged letters . . .?

VB: Yes, gradually we began to exchange letters, little by little. Later on it became extremely profound, it became very deep. [laughs briefly]

From these remarks, it can be seen that Vajra's notion of love, like all other emotions, derives from specific socio-cultural interactions, places, and moments in history (cf. Seidman 1991: 2–3). Junigau love letters of the 1990s both shaped and reflected changing notions of romantic love, thereby demonstrating that there is no universal, ahistorical experience of romantic love that all humans share. Context is absolutely crucial. While every human being might possess the capacity for romantic love, emotions do not exist as fully formed feelings, identical across all cultures and time periods.

Rather, emotions are constructed in and through linguistic and social inter-actions. Discourse is therefore central to any understanding of emotions. As Abu-Lughod and Lutz argue, 'the most productive analytical approach to the cross-cultural study of emotion is to examine discourses on emotion and emotional discourses as social practices within diverse ethnographic contexts' (Abu-Lughod and Lutz 1990: 1). Similarly, Jankowiak, a strong believer in the universality of romantic love, nevertheless notes that

> The relative frequency with which members of a community experi-ence romantic love may very well depend upon that culture's social organization and ideological orientation. What is obviously needed are many more close, fine-tuned analyses of the phenomenon of love as it is experienced and expressed in a variety of social settings, as well as ethnographic and historical contexts.
>
> (1995: 13)

Just such a close, fine-tuned analysis of the changing meanings surrounding romantic love in Junigau reveals that young villagers constructed romantic love in a culturally and historically specific way in the 1990s. They came to perceive love as happening to them; it afflicts and torments them, they said. It catches them in a web, makes them feel like they're going crazy. Vajra explained this to me in an interview in 1996:

> There's a song in Hindi, see? What it says is in relation to 'love,' see, is, *pyār nahī kiyā; pyār ho jātā hai*' ['Love is not created; love just is.'] This means that affection, love, can't be created. Love can't be created, see? It happens by itself, it is said. In an 'automatic' way, love settles in, one to the other. Now, really, that's how it happened with me.

Despite Vajra's increasingly desperate attempts to find an appropriate bride before his parents forced him into an arranged marriage, he still described his love as not having been a product of his own agency (cf. McCollum 1998; Quinn 1982, 1996). This concept of love as being beyond one's control is not new in Junigau. When I asked older people if they loved their spouses, they would often answer with a shrug and a sheepish smile that, yes, they did. Even in cases where a husband might gamble, be verbally abusive, or take another wife, the first wife would frequently tell me that she couldn't help it; she still loved him. There is a differ-ence, however, between this older idea of love befalling someone and more recent conceptions of the emotion. In earlier times villagers had viewed romantic love with a good deal of shame, or at least embarrassment. Love had no positive aspects to it; in fact, it primarily brought pain and trouble. Several older women shared a saying with me that conveyed their philosophy of love: *naso pasyo, māyā basyo* — 'the vein/hose [i.e., penis] entered, and love followed.' One would come to love one's husband, in other words, after having sex with him. This saying is interesting not only because of the causal theory for love it espouses but also because it was almost always said to me in the context of a woman explaining why she stayed with a husband who treated her poorly. This kind of love was far from the empowering kind of love Junigau villagers in the 1990s came to believe in; this kind of love was to be avoided, disavowed, or, if all else failed, reluctantly tolerated.

In the 1990s Junigau young people came to view romantic love as empowering them in other realms of their lives — an emotion of which to be proud, for it was associated with development and success. They continued to consider romantic love to be beyond their control, but they also began to see it as something that linked them with 'development discourse' and Western, commodified notions of 'success.'

Ideas about love are tied up not only with economic practices in any given society, but also with other social institutions and everyday practices, such as political movements, educational opportunities, gender ideologies, and kinship-based activities. Many Westerners automatically associate romantic love with sexual desire and marriage, and yet these connections are neither inevitable nor necessarily desirable to many Nepalis (cf. Lindholm 1995; de Munck 1998).

These interconnections can be seen in many of the 200-plus love letters Junigau residents generously shared with me. In the summer of 1990, for example, Vajra wrote the following words to Shila, with whom he had been corresponding at that point for about 6 months:

> There's nothing special [to write about], except that memories of you keep torturing me so much that I'm scratching a few words onto this page in order to give my heart some peace . . . Come today, and let's create an understanding that will make our love successful and that will make us never be separated.

In this letter and in many others, it can be seen that young correspondents conceive of love as something that happens to people, torturing them and giving them no peace. And yet, at the same time, love also empowers them, giving them a sense of agency in other parts of their lives aside from romance. In an example from another love letter correspondence, a young man named Bir Bahadur wrote the following in his first letter to his eventual wife, Sarita:

> In the whole 'world' there must be few individuals who do not bow down to love . . . In which case, Sarita, I'll let you know by a 'short cut' what I want to say: Love is the union of two souls. The 'main' meaning of love is 'life success.'

Along the same lines, in two later letters, Bir Bahadur writes,

> When love and affection have become steady, one will certainly be able to obtain the things one has thought and worried about. (. . .)
> May our love reach a place where we can in our lives overthrow any difficulties that arrive and obtain success.

Thus, in Junigau love letters from the 1990s, love is portrayed as empowering even as it makes people 'bow down.' Junigau love letter writers believe that love enables them to achieve 'life success,' which they define as carving out lives for themselves that mirror the images they see and hear about in a diverse array of media, from textbooks and magazines to Hindi and Nepali films to Radio Nepal development programs. These images promote a lifestyle based on formal education, knowledge of English, lucrative employment, the consumption of commodities, and a sense of self founded on individualism. Furthermore, when 'success' is mentioned in reference to romantic love, Junigau letter writers reveal their assumption, or at least hope, that 'successful' romantic love will result in marriage, and that marriage will be idyllic in nature. Even as romantic love is portrayed as being beyond letter writers' control, therefore, it nevertheless is linked with a sense of agency in other realms of their lives. The same paradoxical qualities of love can be seen in these excerpts from a letter written by Vajra to Shila:

> What on earth is this thing called love? Once one falls into its web, one is ready to do anything at the invitation of one's beloved. Why, oh why, is it that what you say, memories of you, and affection for you are always tormenting me?

And yet a few paragraphs later, Vajra writes:

> These days nothing is impossible in this world. A person can do anything.

Shila responded with the following:

> Mother's Brother's Son, what is there left [to write about]? . . . May we be successful, I say. What is your wish . . . . ?[2] Of course, even when there are wishes and desires, no one knows anything about the time and circumstances under which they will be fulfilled.
>
> Some people say that if it's their lot in life, [whatever it is] they'll do it. But it seems to me that it's up to each person's own wishes . . . . Even without my telling you this, you would be knowledgeable about it.

Thus, love is increasingly associated in Junigau with being 'developed' and 'successful,' and it is more and more associated with independence and the ability to overcome all obstacles in life. Love has become an agent, and it has made Junigau villagers feel like agents in all realms of their lives but one: love.

Genres, genders, and practices

Although Junigau love letters constitute a unique new genre associated with its own set of literacy practices, there are nevertheless many intertextual linkages with other genres and practices in the village. Because Junigau men have been Gurkha soldiers in the British and Indian Armies for many generations, letter writing has long been viewed in the village as a way of staying in touch with male relatives.

All letters written in the village are likely to contain some of the same formulaic aspects, such as the date, time, and place of writing; mentions of kinship terms and Hindu gods, such as, 'Mother's Brother's Son. I'm in good health, and I pray to Pashupatinath for your good health, too'; and standard opening sentences such as, 'There's really nothing special that must be written; this is only for remembrance's sake.'

And yet, there are many characteristics of Junigau love letters that set them apart from other letters written in the village. The language of the love letters is often flowery, full of passages like the following: 'Dear, so dearer than dear, beloved Father's Sister's Daughter, with love that is more numerous than the stars in the sky, that is longer than a river, and that, like a river, never dries up, and with such delicious remembrances, from your beloved . . . . I love you from head to toe!' Also present in many love letters but virtually absent in other letter genres is the use of ellipses, which appear when letter writers want to avoid making statements that are too embarrassing to admit or too compromising to the writer should the letter be intercepted. Sometimes it is very obvious to both the writer and recipient what is intended, while at other times the writer leaves her/his meanings intentionally vague so as to invite the recipient to co-construct possible interpretations. In the passage just quoted, for example, the ellipses clearly refer to an omitted name ['from your beloved (Name)'], which is left out to protect the writer's identity should the letter fall into the wrong hands. In other cases, there is more ambiguity, as in the following statement: 'But even if, like an elephant, you don't speak, still, if you're going to beg forgiveness, then . . . . you'll have no other choice but to . . . .' (cf. Ahearn 2001a: 124ff.). Since young women have more at stake than young men (i.e., the complete ruin of their reputations) if their love letters are discovered, ellipses appear more often in their letters than in those of their male suitors.

In addition to ornate language, formulaic features, and ellipses, Junigau love letters in the 1990s also contained a great deal of development discourse emphasizing 'progress,' 'success,' and individual agency. Such development discourse was ubiquitous in the village at the time, saturating female literacy textbooks, primary school textbooks, magazines, novels, Radio Nepal development programs and soap operas, Hindi movies in the district center, politicians' speeches, and everyday conversations. Young villagers yearned to become 'developed' (bikāsī), and these sentiments were often expressed in love letters in ways that clearly echoed the written and verbal discourses prevalent in the community at the time. This was especially true of the letters written by young men, who tended to have more formal education than the young women. In addition to incorporating development discourse into their letters, many young men also incorporated English (or what they thought was English), since according to their language ideologies, English was associated with the 'developed' status they hoped to achieve.

Junigau love letters also echo the love letter guidebooks on sale in the bookstores in the district center (Bright n.d.; Manohar n.d.; Movsesian 1993).[3] While all the letter writers with whom I spoke claimed that they did not consult such guidebooks, the rhetoric, formats, and sentiments of the guidebooks are clearly influential, especially in cases where love letters are written with the assistance of close friends and/or relatives. Although such joint letter writing sessions are reportedly rare, all instances of reading and writing love letters are intrinsically social, as they involve individuals in literacy events that are shaped by socioculturally and historically specific norms and practices.

The gendered nature of these norms and practices is evident. It can be seen not only in the content and style of the love letters, with women's letters containing more ellipses, less English, and more references to the importance of trust in a relationship, but also in the ways in which love letter writing articulates with other literacy practices in Junigau. Young village men in the 1990s all attended either the local high school or a private high school in the district center, and they often used the literacy skills they acquired as part of their formal education to read magazines or novels in their ample leisure time, and to write other genres besides letters, such as lists of attendees at wedding feasts, proclamations of the village development council to be posted on the school bulletin board, or calculations for purchases at local tea shops. Most Junigau women, on the other hand, learned to read and write in evening female literacy classes, and their daily work at home or out in the fields often prevented them from applying their skills to other reading or writing tasks aside from love letters.

Risky writing

The emergence of a new ideology of love in Junigau in the 1990s both encouraged and was facilitated by the growth of love letter writing, which itself was made possible by increased rates of female literacy. Literacy and love are therefore integrally interwoven in the village. And yet, for newly literate women, neither the new ideas about love nor their nascent reading and writing skills have been unambiguously beneficial. Because women continue for the most part to move into the extended households of their husbands' kin upon marriage, they then come under the authority of their mothers-in-law, as is customary in Hindu families throughout Nepal and India. A woman who elopes after engaging in a love letter correspondence risks forfeiting her natal family's support should her husband turn out to be abusive, her mother-in-law cruel, or the marriage untenable. Many times have I heard Junigau parents warn their daughters that they should not expect to be able to run home to mommy and daddy if things go wrong after they elope. Indeed, there are cases in which a love letter correspondence is followed by an extremely unhappy marriage. And because of a continuing double standard when it comes to gender, the consequences of these infelicitous matches fall more heavily on the women, who must live with their husbands' extended families, than with the men, who can marry another wife or simply have extramarital affairs.

And yet, although gender and age hierarchies often continue to be enforced in Junigau, the close emotional ties that develop over the course of a love letter correspondence sometimes lead to conflicts resulting in reconfigurations of power dynamics within joint families that benefit recently married daughters-in-law. A new husband's loyalties, previously assumed to remain with his parents (who in the past were the ones who obtained a wife for him) are nowadays sometimes transferred from his parents to his wife because of the strong emotions engendered by a love letter correspondence.

The following case study illustrates how one Junigau couple utilized their literacy skills to express their desires and embark upon particular life paths, sometimes challenging and sometimes reinforcing (wittingly or unwittingly) existing gender hierarchies in the process.

Durga Kumari's two love letter correspondences

It was not the sort of wedding gift Mirgun Dev had expected: a pillowcase full of incriminating letters that his new bride, Durga Kumari, had written to another man. The three youths who delivered it were relatives of the jilted former boyfriend, and they insisted on presenting their 'gift' to Mirgun Dev in person. It was the eve of the post-wedding *dhobhet* feast in the summer of 1995, and the courtyard at Mirgun Dev's house was full of people preparing food and alcohol to take to Durga Kumari's parents' house for the blessing ceremony the next day. Upon looking inside the pillowcase and realizing what it contained, Mirgun Dev flew into a rage, storming up to the attic to escape the prying eyes of neighbors and family. Once there, he quickly downed two bottles of *raksī*, the rice alcohol that the women of his family had distilled to take to the feast. Thus fortified, he returned to the courtyard and searched out Durga Kumari, threatening within earshot of everyone to kick her out of his house because of her correspondence with another man prior to her marriage. Following her into the tiny room they had occupied during the two weeks since their elopement, Mirgun Dev accused her of not being a virgin when he married her and, half-crying and half-shouting, he shoved her against the wall. I was worried that the violence would escalate, but, fortunately, Mirgun Dev's sister and mother were able to calm him down. 'This is your wife!' they reminded him. 'She's yours now, no matter what happened in the past! Just forget it!' The scene ended with Mirgun Dev sobbing himself to sleep.

As shocked as Mirgun Dev appeared to be when he discovered what the pillowcase contained, he had received a hint of Durga Kumari's previous relationship from Durga Kumari herself, though he may not have realized it at the time. Mirgun Dev and Durga Kumari had had a very brief courtship consisting of an exchange of several love letters and a single meeting in person. The brevity of the courtship was atypical for the 1990s in the village of Junigau, but Mirgun Dev was under extreme pressure from his elders to find a wife during his two-month leave from the Indian Army. They were so desperate for the labor of a daughter-in-law that they were prepared to arrange a marriage for Mirgun Dev if he failed to bring home a bride himself.

Mirgun Dev had to act quickly, therefore, but his shyness put him at a disadvantage. Unlike other young men in Junigau who had started relationships before enlisting as Gurkha soldiers in the Nepali, Indian, or British Army, Mirgun Dev had been too shy to initiate a correspondence with anyone, and so he had had to start a relationship from scratch when he arrived home on leave. Another villager's wedding feast provided Mirgun Dev with the opportunity to meet unmarried young women, and Durga Kumari, a pretty, vivacious high school student from the other side of the village, caught his eye. Emboldened by their brief conversation at the wedding feast, Mirgun Dev wrote Durga Kumari a letter. He asked one of his male relatives to act as a go-between and deliver his declaration of lifelong love to Durga Kumari.

Durga Kumari's response was heartening. She spoke of her happiness at having received Mirgun Dev's letter and hinted that his feelings of love were reciprocated. She ended the letter, however, with a stern warning to Mirgun Dev not to back out of the relationship before marriage; after all, such a break-up would carry heavy consequences for Durga Kumari's reputation. A woman who carries on a relationship with one man before marrying another — even if the relationship takes place solely in writing and not in person — risks being labeled a *rādā* (literally, a widow, but when used as a term of abuse, it means 'slut'). So, Durga Kumari made the following appeal to Mirgun Dev at the end of her first letter to him:

> One thing that I hope you will promise is that you will love me truly, and that when you think about the future you will continue to want to do so and won't break up with me in the middle of our relationship. Okay?
>
> I do not want to go against your happiness; your happiness alone is my happiness.
>
> If you think that loving me will bring happiness into your life, then I will certainly accept your happy words. Not just in this life but in hundreds of lifetimes will I accept and love you.
>
> Later on in the middle of our relationship you are not to do anything [i.e., break up] — understand?
>
> I want you to love me without causing me suffering, okay?
>
> Finally, if you love me, send a 'reply' to this letter, okay?
>
> For now farewell,
>> Your
>>> Durga Kumari

Moving quickly to reassure her, Mirgun Dev responded in his next letter that his intentions were honorable. Indeed, he wanted to elope with her as soon as possible — ideally, he would bring her home to his house as his bride in the next couple of weeks. In Durga Kumari's second letter to Mirgun Dev, she states that he has completely won her over. She agrees to elope with him, but tells him that they cannot elope until after she has finished her final exams. Her education is important to her, she writes, but she just as clearly declares her eternal love for Mirgun Dev in passages such as the following:

> Mirgun Dev, to find a husband like you would be my good fortune. In this world thousands of people love, but many do so for 'fashion' and change their love as love were a thing to be auctioned off. But I consider my love to be like clear water, as pure, immovable, and immortal as the Himalayas.

It is in this second (and final) letter from Durga Kumari to Mirgun Dev that the incident with the pillowcase full of letters from Durga Kumari to another man is foreshadowed. Durga Kumari guesses that Mirgun Dev has been hearing rumors about her involvement in another love letter correspondence – and indeed such rumors were swirling about the village at the time, for I heard them from at least two sources. In the following passage, Durga Kumari urges Mirgun Dev to ignore such gossip:

> Mirgun Dev, it seems that I have become caught up with you in a web of pure love. I don't want to give you any hopes based on lies. There are thousands of people who will speak ill of me. In this world people are prepared to do anything for selfish reasons. They don't do anything else but speak ill of others. The world is like this. Villagers or your friends may speak ill of me to you, but please don't believe such talk, okay? Between us there should only be honesty in this life. There may have been many other men who wrote me letters – this is true, but I hate all of them and don't accept any of them – and never have.
>
> I haven't loved any man because I've stayed at home respectfully living with my mother and father. But today I love you because I see that your love is boundless. And I accept your proposal.

Mirgun Dev believed Durga Kumari's assertion that she had never loved another man, and so with great happiness he went forward with the elopement, bringing Durga Kumari home to live with him and his extended family. A Brahman priest was brought in from a neighboring village to conduct a short Hindu wedding ceremony, and all of Mirgun Dev's relatives welcomed their new daughter- or sister-in-law.

It was two weeks later, just before the newlyweds were to return to Durga Kumari's parents' home for the first time since the elopement for the *dhobhet* blessing ceremony, that Mirgun Dev received the pillowcase full of letters in which Durga Kurnari declared her love for another man. After his rage was spent, Mirgun Dev reluctantly went forward with the ceremony, and gradually the relationship between the spouses regained its warmth. By the time Mirgun Dev had to return to the Indian Army, they had put the incident behind them.

Six months or so later, after Mirgun Dev had returned to India, Durga Kumari found herself miserable in her marital home. The stigma of her previous love letter correspondence had not disappeared, and she felt mistreated by her husband's relatives, especially his mother. She had not been allowed to continue her schooling, as she had been promised, and she was being given all the most arduous tasks in the fields and in the house. Once again she resorted to letter writing, this time to complain to Mirgun Dev about her treatment and to urge him to return home and intervene on her behalf with his mother. Such letters from newly married women to their distant husbands are becoming more common in Junigau. In several recent cases among villagers, including Mirgun Dev's and Durga Kumari's, the men have indeed come home and have taken their wives' sides in the disputes. Life improved for Durga Kumari after that, but Mirgun Dev's mother felt betrayed when her son accused her of mistreating his wife. Such an act represented further proof, she claimed (as if any were needed!) that the *chhucho jovāna*, a selfish, mean, or backbiting time period, had arrived. For Durga Kumari and other new daughters-in-law, however, their use of their literacy skills in this manner gives them an advantage over their mothers-in-law, who are members of a generation of females who were rarely taught to read or write. Still, certain gendered notions, such as the importance of a bride's virginity and the assumption that men are more capable than women of taking effective action, persist even as literacy practices surrounding love and marriage change in Junigau.

Conclusion

The acquisition of literacy skills by women in Junigau has thus led both to radical social transformations and to a reinforcement of certain gender hierarchies. For any given woman, the use of her reading and writing skills entails risks, especially since a love letter correspondence leaves behind material traces that can be used as evidence against a woman, thereby ruining her reputation and most likely her chances of marrying anyone. Nepali men face no such risks.

In the case of Junigau, literacy has exposed villagers to new discourses of development and love, as expressed in textbooks, magazines, and other reading materials. The ability to read and write has also provided individuals with new opportunities – even as it has reinforced some of the gendered inequalities in the village. While the ability to engage in love letter correspondences has provided many young villagers with the chance to conduct courtships, many of which have resulted in elopements, there are also risks involved, especially for Junigau women. Because of a persistent double standard, women have much more to lose if their love letters are discovered, either before they marry, or, as in Durga Kumari's case, even after they marry. Literacy in Junigau has therefore been far from a neutral technology. Nor, however, has it been the unmitigated asset some would like to believe it to be. Instead, literacy, love, and social change have interacted in Junigau in complex ways that have only begun to manifest themselves.

During the 1990s in Junigau, young villagers used their new literacy skills to help them significantly reconceptualize the notion of romantic love, making it into a desirable emotion to experience and linking it up with other desired achievements, such as success, development, and education. Individuals' own desires also have begun to take precedence over those of their families, at least in some instances. As Sarita, the young woman who eventually married Bir Bahadur, exclaimed to me as she was trying to decide whether or not to elope, 'It's up to one's *own* wishes, it is! You should wear the flower you like, you know. You should wear the flower that *you yourself* like.' In a complex series of social transformations that are still underway, Junigau residents are redefining what love means in the context of marriage and are re-evaluating what it means to desire someone or something.

Chapter 22

Momoko Nakamura

2006

CREATING INDEXICALITY

Schoolgirl speech in Meiji Japan

Introduction

INDEXICALIZATION, A SEMIOTIC PROCESS whereby one entity becomes a pointer to another, is assumed to account for associations between linguistic features and social identities. The process in which a particular indexicality is created in a specific historical time and space, however, has not been extensively studied, because many assume that indexicality is constructed by repeated use in individual interaction. (I call such individual interaction in a specific context 'local practice.') Elinor Ochs (1991), for instance, accounts for indexicality as the process in which some linguistic features directly index affective meanings, through which they indirectly associate with social identities. The Japanese sentence-final particle *wa* directly indexes delicate intensity, which is the preferred image of Japanese women, so women are motivated to use it. The repeated use of *wa* by women reinforces the indirect association between *wa* and femininity. Here, the indexicality between *wa* and feminine identity is assumed to be constructed by repeated local practice.

The logic of indexicality formation by repeated use, however, contradicts the recent argument that the notion of 'Japanese women's language' is not naturally formed by the repeated local practices of women, but a language ideology historically constructed by discourses. The indexicality between feminine identity and linguistic features, such as sentence-final particles exemplified in Ochs's argument, constitutes the Japanese notion of women's language. If we assume that indexicality is constructed by repeated use, we should conclude that 'Japanese women's language' is also constructed by the repeated local practice of women.

Evolutionary-essentialist vs. constructive-ideological approaches

Studies of Japanese women's language can be divided into two approaches, which I refer to as the evolutionary-essentialist approach and the constructive-ideological approach. The evolutionary-essentialist approach assumes that 'women's language' has naturally evolved because Japanese women have always spoken differently from men. Women's linguistic practice is directly related to the notion of 'women's language.'

This approach is characterized by two further arguments. First, the origin of 'women's language' is discussed under the assumption that women's practice in the past has naturally resulted in the present notion of 'women's language' (Ide and Terada 1998; Ide 2003). They consider the origins to be *nyooboo kotoba* 'court-lady speech' used by women working in the imperial court in the fourteenth century and *yuujo kotoba* 'play-woman speech' used by professional prostitutes in the seventeenth century. They claim that these spread among ordinary women, evolving into 'women's language.' (Nakamura (2003a) shows, however, that not only women but also men started using court-lady speech on the one hand, and some women, especially merchants and servants, hated using it.)

Second, this approach considers linguistic sex differences to be the fact observed in practice. The accumulation of sex differences ultimately delineates the whole picture of 'women's language.' Such a view of sex differences is easily connected to the essentialist view that they are 'rooted in the women's common sensitivity based on their physiological nature' (Horii 1993: 101). Studies of practice have revealed, however, that women's (and men's) speech constantly changes and varies, according to age, family relation and generation, education, occupation and region of residence, and sexual orientation. Homogeneous 'linguistic sex differences' cannot be extracted from heterogeneous linguistic practice. It is impossible to assume that the diverse practices of women have naturally formed a single category of 'women's language.'

The constructive-ideological approach, on the other hand, considers 'Japanese women's language' to be a language ideology, 'the cultural (or subcultural) system of ideas about social and linguistic relationships, together with their loading of moral and political interests' (Irvine 1989: 255). This approach first claims to distinguish practice from ideology, that is, to distinguish women's speech from the notion of 'women's language' (Nakamura 2001; Inoue 2002; Okamoto 2004). Just like standard language, 'Japanese women's language' is 'a set of abstract norms to which actual usage may conform to a greater or lesser extent' (Milroy and Milroy 1985: 23). This approach denies essentialism in claiming that women (and men) have always spoken in a variety of ways considering many factors as well as gender. It denies the view that indexicality is constructed by repeated use and proposes to analyze the historical, political formation of a particular indexicality which constitutes the ideological construct of 'women's language.' According to this approach, 'Japanese women's language' is a language ideology, which has an indexical relation with a gender ideology of Japanese feminine identity.

This approach is characterized by two further arguments. First, this approach assumes that the ideology of 'women's language' has been historically constructed by discourse rather than through repeated use by women. Two types of discourse play major roles in its construction: language usage in fiction and explicit commentary on women's speech produced mainly by intellectuals. The former category includes novels, movies, TV dramas, comics, and TV games. As the use of particular features by female characters in fiction is repeatedly reproduced and widely consumed by a large audience, those features become associated with feminine identities.[1] The latter category includes etiquette books, school textbooks, dictionaries, grammar books, and commentaries by intellectuals. By evaluating, criticizing, and giving norms for women's speech, they associate particular features with femininity and label them as 'women's language.'

Second, it proposes to investigate the relationship between once-separated practice and ideology (Nakamura 2002). For instance, the ideology of 'women's language' is assumed to provide resources enabling practice as well as restricting it. The conception of 'women's language' as ideology liberates 'women's language' from women's 'essential' nature and redefines it as a linguistic resource which both women and men can use in their practices. At the same time, this approach redefines 'women's language' as an ideological construct with normative force. The diversity of practices can be reinterpreted as diverse responses of speakers to the norm of 'women's language' as well as to many other factors. Some, by simply using it as resource, reproduce the hegemonic femininity. Others may refuse to use it, trying to resist constructing such an identity. According to this approach, the analysis of the construction of a particular indexical relation through fiction and metalinguistic commentary in a particular historical time and space will clarify the historical formation of 'Japanese women's language.'

The present paper focuses on the process of creating indexicality between the linguistic category of 'schoolgirl speech' and the identity of schoolgirls during the early twentieth century in Japan. 'Schoolgirl speech' provides an insightful case in point because: 1) It has been shown that sentence-final particles, one class of features associated with social identities in Japanese, used in fiction were sex-differentiated during the early twentieth century (Komatsu 1988), 2) Sentence-final particles included in 'schoolgirl speech' are assumed to constitute what we now call 'Japanese women's language,' and 3) The emergence, formation, and establishment of schoolgirl identity and 'schoolgirl speech' are historically clear.

The first section discusses the sex-differentiated nationalization and the gendered construction of national language in Japanese modernization and traces the transformation of female students into schoolgirls by their costumes. The second section, by analyzing fiction and metalinguistic commentary, demonstrates that female students were speaking in a variety of ways but their diverse practices were categorized into a single notion of 'schoolgirl speech' by the four processes of sex-differentiation, selection, derogation, and sexualization. The third section shows that the construction of schoolgirls and 'schoolgirl speech' was a process politically synchronized with the sex-differentiated nationalization and the construction of the gendered national language. The fourth section traces the way female students imitated 'schoolgirl speech' and argues that the process of indexicalization simultaneously constructed both the language ideology of 'schoolgirl speech' and the gender ideology of schoolgirl identity.

In the following discussion, I use the two terms 'female students' (*joshi gakusei*) and 'schoolgirls' (*jogakusei*) distinctively. 'Female students' simply refers to students who were women. 'Schoolgirls' refers to the concept discursively created during the early twentieth century. The differences between them will be clarified in the following sections.

Female students in Japanese modernization

Sex-differentiated nationalization and gendered national language

In 1868, after almost three hundred years of seclusion, the Meiji government opened the country and faced the need to modernize it. As pre-modern Japan had been composed of relatively autonomous regional clans, it was necessary to synthesize people as 'citizens' of the country who would be workers and soldiers of the state. That process of building the inhabitants of the archipelago into a group of citizens of a single country has been termed 'nationalization.' Two gender-related factors which promoted nationalization were sex-differentiated nationalization and the construction of the gendered ideology of national language.

The process of nationalization was completely sex-differentiated, i.e., women and men were constructed into two different categories of citizens. Male citizens were expected to play the roles of workers and soldiers. To guarantee the reproduction of workers and soldiers, on the other hand, the roles of female citizens had to be confined to those of wife and mother, the one supporting the male citizenry and the other reproducing the next generation of male citizens (Wakakuwa 2001: 67). It was a process of separating women, the secondary citizenry, from men, the primary citizens.

The process of nationalization was also enhanced by the construction of *hyoojun go* 'standard Japanese,' that is, *kokugo* 'Japanese national language' (Lee 1996; Yasuda 1997; Osa 1998). At the end of the nineteenth century, there were several writing styles and various spoken styles in different regions of Japan. To import and spread Western knowledge and to promote national integrity, it was considered necessary to create standard Japanese by unifying speech and writing. The argument for *genbun itchi* 'the unification of speech and writing' emerged as a way to promote the modernization of Japan by creating a common colloquial style of writing.

The ideology of 'national language (standard Japanese)' was also a sex-exclusive notion. It was conceptualized as 'men's national language' established by unifying middle-class men's speech and writing. Japanese national language was conceptualized as 'the language of men in the middle society' (Okano 1964 [1902]: 510). Otsuki (1905: 17) claims the Tokyo variant to be the base of standard Japanese rather than the Kyoto variant because 'The language of Kyoto, though good for women, can sound weak coming from men.' Nakamura (2005) demonstrates that national-language textbooks and grammar books incorporated linguistic features associated with men in their descriptions of standard Japanese, while they excluded features associated with women. The ideology of national language was established by excluding linguistic features associated with women, as well as those of regional varieties and lower social classes. It was under the processes of sex-differentiated nationalization and the construction of gendered national language where female students emerged.

Transformation of female students into schoolgirls, observed in costumes

Japanese women officially became students for the first time in 1872 when the Japanese government issued *Gaku sei* 'The School System Law,' which declared the importance of education for everybody including women. At the beginning, there was no specific identity of a female student distinct from a male student. By the beginning of the twentieth century, however, they were transformed into a category called 'schoolgirls.' The identity of schoolgirl was constructed by symbolic systems such as costume (*ebicha-bakama* 'maroon trouser skirt'), hairstyle (*tabane gami* 'tied-up hair'), and language (*jogakusei kotoba* 'schoolgirl speech') (Honda 1990: 133).

From 1872 to 1879 female students wore *hakama*, the trouser-style kimono worn by male students. Pictures from the time show girls sitting just like boys, with their legs apart and their arms crossed in front of them. Even after The School System Law, few parents considered sending their daughters to school. In 1876, only 21% of girls attended school, and some girls were learning alongside their male counterparts (Fukaya 1966, 1998: 58). Those early female students were described as 'walking up and down the streets in *hakama* and wooden clogs, their sleeves rolled up and foreign books in their arms' (Karasawa 1958: 40).

In 1879, however, the Meiji emperor issued *Kyoogaku seishi* 'The Imperial Rescript on Education,' which remonstrated against too much Westernization and declared the start of ethical education based on Confucianism. Coeducation in secondary schools was prohibited in the same year. In 1881, sewing and domestic science became compulsory subjects for female students. 'From 1879 to 1882, *hakama* for women were prohibited' (Honda 1990: 71). Instead female students wore *kimono*, the traditional women's costume, which entailed that they were differentiated from male students.

In 1883, the Meiji government built *Rokumei-kan,* a Western-style dance hall, as a diplomatic space for foreign policy. Female students were expected to contribute to Japanese diplomacy as dancers. In 1896, the Women's Normal School asked their students to wear Western dress and they started teaching dancing.

After the Sino-Japanese war (1894–5), many intellectuals began to recognize female education as an indispensable factor to reinforce national power. Women's schools were expected to produce 'good wives' with high domestic abilities and 'wise mothers' who would efficiently bring up the next generation. The Education Minister made it explicit that the goal of women's high school education was 'to teach the knowledge to become a wise-mother-good-wife' (Fukaya 1966, 1998: 155). Male school, an object of public expenditure, was clearly distinguished from female school.[2] Instead of an obedient but incompetent woman bundled in *kimono*, therefore, *ebicha-bakama*, 'maroon trouser skirt' was chosen as the uniform of a future good-wife-wise-mother. This new uniform distinguished female from male students by the color of the uniform and from other women by its form. At the same time, the trouser skirt liberated these students from both the wide belt of a *kimono* and the tight corset of a Western dress, and they were able to ride bicycles and play tennis. A puff of wind would occasionally expose parts of their active bodies, and because of this they were eventually perceived as 'destroyers of the social order and deviators of sexual morals' (Honda 1990: 89).

Construction of 'schoolgirl speech'

Language also played an important role in the construction of schoolgirl identity. The creation of indexicality between particular linguistic features and schoolgirl identity can be divided into four processes: sex-differentiation, selection, derogation, and sexualization.

Sex-differentiation: denial of 'schoolboy speech'

Female students in *hakama* were described as speaking just like male students. A letter to the *Yomiuri* Newspaper in 1875 delineates a conversation between two female students, who want to become teachers and make their own money, rather than getting married, so that they can freely go to the theater and keep a gigolo (Soga 1875).[3]

(a) *kore wa* **boku** *no   oji   ga   **shoohoo** o   hajime*
     this TOP my GEN uncle NOM business OBJ start

     *mashite senjitsu   ittan **boku** ni hakama   ni*
     SFX   the other day a roll me to trouser-style kimono GOAL

     *itase   to   itte **tooyo** sare   mashita-yo*
     make QUOT say give do-HON SFX-PAST-SFP

     'My uncle started a business and gave me a roll of cloth the other day saying I should have a *hakama* [made out of it].'

(b) **kimi** *kitto* **hokudoo** *e kotowari* **tamae**
     you must mother to refuse   SFP

     'You must tell your mother that you will not marry.'

     eesu, eesu, eesu, eesu
     yes, yes, yes, yes

     'Yes, yes, yes, yes.'

The students use *boku,* the male first-person pronoun, Chinese words such as *shoohoo* 'business,' *tooyo* 'give,' *hokudoo* 'mother,' *kimi,* 'male second-person pronoun,' *tamae* 'sentence-final particle,' and the foreign word 'yes.' Komatsu (1974: 26) claims that 'schoolboy speech' is characterized by the use of 1) Chinese loan-words, 2) foreign words, 3) the first person pronouns *boku* and *wagahai,* 4) the second person pronoun *kimi,* 5) sentence-final particles such as *tamae* and *beshi,* and 6) *shikkei,* 'excuse me.'[4] The speech of female students in the above letter

Table 22.1 Use of schoolboy features by the female students of *Baika joshi no den*
         [*The Story of Miss Apricot Scent*] (1885)

Male student features	Sawayama	Tanaka	Ume
Address form *kun* (last name + *kun*)	○	○	×
First-person pronoun, *boku*	○	×	×
Second-person pronoun, *kimi*	×	○	×
Sentence-final particle, *tamae*	○	○	×

contains many of these characteristics. The conversation between two depraved
students was carried out in 'schoolboy speech.' Not only in clothes but also in
language, then, some female students behaved just like male students.

In novels as well, depraved female student characters spoke like male students.
In *Baika joshi no den* [*The Story of Miss Apricot Scent*] (Iwamoto 1885), the heroine
Ume, a good woman, stands by a tree while the other girls, Sawayama and Tanaka,
are running in the schoolyard. They do not behave in a feminine manner and they
have lost interest in their studies. There is a stark contrast between a good female
character who follows the norm of good-wife-wise-mother and bad characters who
refuse it. Table 22.1 shows their use of language. Both of the bad girls, Sawayama
and Tanaka, use many schoolboy features. On the other hand, the heroine Ume
never uses them. Depraved characters use schoolboy features, while good female
students do not.

USE OF SCHOOLBOY FEATURES BY FEMALE STUDENTS
(IWAMOTO 1885: 69)

Sawayama:	**boku**-*ra, iya, shoo-ra wa kore o michibikite toosee fuu ni suru gimu ga arimasu ze.*
	'We have a responsibility to lead them and liberalize them'
Tanaka:	*Sawayama-***kun**, *sonnani shiranu fuu o shi-***tamau** *na.*
	'Mr. *Sawayama*, do not pretend not to know so much.'
Ume:	*Sawayama-san, sakujitsu wa makoto ni arigatoo gozai mashita*
	'Miss *Sawayama*, thank you very much for yesterday.'

Selection: choosing 'teyo dawa speech' and Western words

Around 1879, some female students started using new sentence-final particles, such
as *teyo, dawa,* and *noyo.* Ozaki (1994 [1888]: 4) states: 'Eight or nine years ago
[1879–80], elementary female students began to use a strange form of language in
their conversation with intimate friends.'

Why did they begin to use such speech? Two facts imply that one major function of the speech was to resist good-wife-wise-mother education. First, they started
this speech when Confucianism and the sex-segregated educational system were
institutionalized. As we have seen, 1879 was the year when Confucian education
was revived after several years of relative freedom during which female students

enjoyed true equality of dressing, speaking and behaving just like their male counter-parts. Second, women's disciplinary books and ethical textbooks used in good-wife-wise-mother education required strict norms for women's speech (Nakamura 2003b). Honda (1990: 134) notes: 'They [female students] filled the closed space of "girl's school" with "foreign fashion" and "*teyo dawa* speech" and nonchalantly neutralized the image of a good-wife-wise-mother forced on them from outside that space.'

The society also considered the use of these sentence-final particles to signify resistance to good-wife-wise-mother education. First, this speech was considered to have a negative effect on good-wife-wise-mother education. An article, *Hagaki shuu* [Collection of Postcards] (1902) laments: 'obscene language such as *koto-yo* and *teyo* has an awful effect on the future wise-mother-good-wife.' Second, it was severely criticized as originating from the lower social classes. Ozaki (1994 [1888]: 5) assumes: 'The daughters of the low-grade vassals in Aoyama' began to use them. An article, *Reijo saikun no kotoba* [Language of Daughters and Wives] (1896), argues: 'It spread from lower society to the mansion world.' As more daughters from lower-class society began to go to girls' schools, 'schoolgirls have begun to speak the language of merchant's children.' (*Jogakusei to gengo* 1905). Takeuchi (1907: 24) decided that '*teyo dawa* speech' was originally spoken by *geisha*. The persistent crit-icism testifies to the power of the speech to resist the good-wife-wise-mother edu-cation. To clarify that this usage emerged in resistance to good-wife-wise-mother education, I will call it '*teyo dawa* speech' until we reach the stage when it is trans-formed into 'schoolgirl speech.'

In spite of the criticism, novel writers chose these new sentence-final particles to index the identity of a female student. The writers of novels, striving for the unification of speech and writing, proposed to write conversations in spoken language for a realistic effect (Tsubouchi 1969 [1886]: 34). Different sentence-final particles became a useful resource to describe different characters.[5] Nakamura (2004: 55–7) shows that, from the end of the nineteenth century to the beginning of the twentieth century, numerous novels used them for their female student characters. People started to call it '*teyo dawa* speech.'[6]

It is worth noting here that actual female students were speaking in a variety of ways. Some spoke like male students, others used '*teyo dawa* speech,' and some others spoke politely. Female students were always criticized for speaking like male students and using '*teyo dawa* speech' throughout the Meiji period. Iwamoto (1890) criticizes the use of impolite language, '*teyo dawa* speech,' and 'schoolboy speech' by female students. An article, *Jogakusei no heifuu* (1891), also criticizes their use of '*teyo dawa* speech' and 'schoolboy speech.' Another article, *Jogakusei to gengo* (1905), continues its criticism of '*teyo dawa* speech,' 'schoolboy speech,' and English. Okada (1957: 45), a writer, also testifies that female students around 1910 used the 'impolite' language of male students. These documents paradoxically prove that female students spoke a variety of styles, including 'schoolboy speech,' '*teyo dawa* speech,' as well as Chinese loan-words and English. Not all or most female students always and repeatedly used '*teyo dawa* speech.'

The creation of '*teyo dawa* speech,' therefore, was not the natural outcome of the repeated use by actual female students. Some of the female students did actu-ally use *teyo*, *dawa*, and *noyo*, but this simple fact did not make it a linguistic index of female students. It was the novel writers who selected 'teyo dawa speech' and foreign words as the index of female students. By having female student characters speak them in fiction, they turned these features into linguistic indexes of female students.

Derogation: frivolous students

Being used in novels, 'teyo dawa speech' was assigned more meanings than simple sex difference. These additional meanings transformed 'teyo dawa speech' into 'schoolgirl speech.' One of those meanings was frivolity. In a 1906 comic titled *Teyo dawa monogatari* [*The Story of* teyo dawa], female students fight and complain using *teyo* and *dawa* when they play a New Year's card game:

FRIVOLOUS FEMALE STUDENTS SPEAKING *TEYO DAWA* LANGUAGE
(*TEYO DAWA MONOGATARI* 1906)

(1)   *watashi ga saki **dawa**. watashi ga hayakut-**teyo**.*
      'I took [the card] first.' 'I was faster.'

(2)   *watashi **dawa**. iie, watashi **dawa**. aa, ude ga nuke **teyo**. moo, koo nare ba kenka **dawa**.*
      'I [took the card].' 'No, I took it.' 'Oh no, [someone is] pulling my arm.' 'Now, I will fight.'

(3)   *ara, kutsushita no kakato kara tsuki ga moreide **teyo**.*
      'Oh, [I can see] the moon [the heel] coming out of someone's sock.'

(4)   *goran nasai. konnani watashi no te ni kuitsui **teyo**. ara, yokut-**teyo**. watashi ja nakut-**teyo**. uso **dawa**.*
      'Look at this. You bite me on my hand.' 'Oh, I don't know. It's not me. You are lying.'

In novels as well, frivolity was associated with the use of 'teyo dawa speech.' One example is *Yabu no uguisu* [*Bush Warbler*] (Miyake 1888). There are four female student characters. Hattori is a normative girl who follows Confucian female virtue. Aizawa and Saito are frivolous girls and behave in an unwomanly fashion. Miyazaki wants to get married after graduation. Table 22.2 shows that their use of *teyo*, *dawa*, and *noyo* perfectly corresponds with their attitudes. The most frivolous girl, Saito, uses all of them. Aizawa uses *dawa* and Miyazaki uses *noyo*. The most normative,

Table 22.2 Use of *teyo*, *dawa*, and *noyo* by the four female students of *Yabu no uguisu* [*Bush Warbler*] (1888)

	Hattori	Miyazaki	Aizawa	Saito
Teyo	✕	✕	✕	○
Dawa	✕	✕	○	○
Noyo	✕	○	✕	○

Hattori, never uses them. Such usage made '*teyo dawa* speech' a linguistic index of frivolous female students.

USES OF '*TEYO-DAWA*' SPEECH BY FEMALE CHARACTERS IN *YABU NO UGUISU* [*BUSH WARBLER*] (MIYAKE 1971 [1888]: 133–5)

Hattori: *saa, saa, o-machi asobase . . . maa, itte, meshi agatte, irasshaina.*
             'OK, OK, please wait . . . well, come in and have some please.'
Miyazaki: *naichi zakkyo ni naruto dooda no kooda no to ossharu* **noyo**.
             '[He was talking about] what happens if people from other countries live inside of Japan.'
Aizawa: *honto* **dawa**.
             'That's true'.
Saito: *watashi wa kyoo wa nemukutte shooga nai noyo . . . yokut-***teyo** . . . tanso o oidashite yarun* **dawa**.
             'I am very sleepy today . . . I don't care . . . I'll let carbon dioxide out of here.'

As '*teyo dawa* speech' became associated with frivolity, serious knowledge spoken in '*teyo dawa* speech' was funny in its own distinctive way. *Jibore musume sakka* [*Conceited Woman Writers*] (Iwaya 1889) is a conversation between two female writers. As the title shows, it aims to ridicule them. They use many difficult Chinese-loan words with *teyo* and *dawa*. The discrepancy between the knowledgeable content and frivolous language successfully illustrates the foolishness of the so-called intelligent women.

Another feature of 'schoolgirl speech,' the use of Western language, was also used to symbolize the speaker's frivolity. *Shoobi no kaori* [*The Scent of Rose*] is a story of Eiwa Joko 'English Women's School,' where 'students do not use Japanese language from good morning to good night' (Iwamoto 1887: 79). The writer describes those students gossiping in English and criticizes them as 'They carry on their everyday conversation just like Westerners, so that . . . they talk about things [Japanese] shy daughters would blush over' (Iwamoto 1887: 79). *Momiji* [*Maple*] (Aeba 1888–9) is a story about two schoolgirl sisters. Osetsu, the elder sister, is 'elegant but not gaily dressed' and believes that 'to become a wife and a mother is a woman's destiny.' Although she studies English, she does not like Western dress. Okine, the frivolous younger sister, on the other hand, behaves in an unfeminine manner and often uses French words. Her first appearance in the novel symbolizes her frivolity, in which she comes into the room in a Western dress saying, '"Bonjour" in a shrill voice' and loudly discusses her superficial understanding of women's rights (Aeba 1988 [1888–9] (5): 13). The use of foreign words and '*teyo dawa* speech,' characteristic of the speech of modern Japanese educated women, therefore, was turned into the linguistic index of frivolous girls.

Sexualization: 'schoolgirl speech'

After the Women's High School Act (1899) stipulated at least one public women's normal school be established in each prefecture, schools were flooded with female applicants. The increase of female students brought two major changes to the way they were described in the novels. First, more female characters, not only students but also women in general, began to speak *'teyo dawa* speech' in novels and the labels 'schoolgirl' and 'schoolgirl speech' were widely recognized.

This wider use is observed in *katei shoosetsu,* 'family novels.' Family novels were healthy stories written for family readers based on Confucian or Christian ethics. In *Hamako* (Kusamura 1902), a young wife uses *teyo* and *dawa.* In *Chi kyoodai* [*Bosom Sisters*] (Kikuchi 1903), both a young mother and 19 to 20-year-old women use *teyo* and *noyo.* In *Meoto nami* [*Husband and Wife Wave*] (Taguchi 1904), a 21 to 22-year-old wife uses *dawa* and *noyo* (Nakamura 2004). Interestingly, *'teyo dawa* speech' in family novels does not function to distinguish normative girls from frivolous girls. For example, *Chi kyoodai* is the story of two 19 to 20-year-old sisters, Kimie and Fusae. Kimie is a bad girl who 'is controlled by a woman's vanity.' Fusae is a good girl who is 'kind and affectionate.' Both of them use *'teyo dawa* speech' (Kikuchi 1969 [1903]: 104–5]. Young women of high social class, whether normative or not, began to use it in novels.

The establishment of *'teyo dawa* speech' as an index of female sex, as well as youth and high social class, is most clearly shown in *Wagahai wa neko de aru* [*I Am a Cat*], in which a high-class, young, female cat speaks with *teyo, dawa,* and *noyo,* as in *Anata taihen iro ga warukut-***teyo** 'You look pale,' *Ara goshujin datte, myoo nano ne. Oshishoo-san* **dawa** 'Oh, [you call your master] *goshujin.* That's strange. [I call my master] *oshishoo-san,*' and *Ara iyada, minna bura sageru* **noyo** 'Oh, no. Everybody will hang up' (Natsume 1961 [1905]: 19). Natsume could describe not only the sex but also the age and status of a cat – which never spoke at all – by using different linguistic features. *'Teyo dawa* speech,' thus, had become the index of female sex, youth, and high social class.

The second change after the Women's High School Act (1899) was a sexualization of female student characters. Many novels described them as sex objects. The sexualization of female students accompanied the sexualization of their language, *'teyo dawa* speech.' And the association with sexuality completed the transformation of *'teyo dawa* speech' into 'schoolgirl speech.'

The sexualization of *'teyo dawa* speech' is most evident in the fact that female student characters began to play major roles in pornographic novels and they spoke *'teyo dawa* speech' when they had sexual intercourse. In a pornographic story *Sode to sode* [*Sleeve to Sleeve*] (Oguri 1907–11), three female student characters have sex among themselves and with men as well.[7] They always use 'schoolgirl speech.' Another woman, Oteru, who came to Tokyo from the countryside, never uses it. The contrast becomes even clearer if we compare the two scenes in which Oteru and Kimiko, one of the female students, both 22 years old, are having sex with the same man, Yoonosuke. While Kimiko uses *teyo* and *noyo,* Oteru uses *masu* instead.

> *Kimiko* (student): *watashi mo it-***teyo** *moo   it-***teyo**
> I   too come now come
>
> *aa kokoro ga . . . nukecchimaisoo . . . aa ii-***noyo**
> oh mind TOP   go out   oh good

'I'm coming, too. I'm coming now. Oh, my mind is going crazy. Oh, it is good.'

(Oguri 1998 [1907–11]: 54)

Oteru (non-student):   *i ii yoo, yoono . . . suke . . . sama*
              good   Yoonosuke   dear

         watashi . . . moo ikimasu aa . . . ikimasu
         I   now come oh   come

'Good, good, *Yoo, yoono, suke*, dear. I'm coming now. Oh, I'm coming.'

(Oguri 1998 [1907–11]: 33)

The strong link between 'schoolgirl speech' and higher social class and youth distinguished the sexuality emitted by 'schoolgirl speech' from other female sexualities. Women in this period were ideologically classified into three groups according to their sexuality and speech. The first group, explicitly sexual women, were professional prostitutes, who were associated with special styles of language used in their quarters. The second, also sexual women were those referred to by the sexist terms, 'widow, stepmother, and maid,' and they were indexed by non-standard Japanese. The last and the least sexual women were wives and mothers of high-class families, who were indexed by standard Japanese. The sexuality emitted by 'schoolgirl speech' is characterized by the innocence and high social class of female students, distinct from the sexuality of prostitutes and non-standard speakers. Ozaki (1994 [1888]: 4) notes that 'some men are happy hearing the speech because of its ring of innocence.'

That explains why older women characters of high class in novels use 'schoolgirl speech' in scenes in which they express their love to men. In *Yabu no uguisu* [*Bush Warbler*], a 27 or 28-year-old woman uses *dawa* when she is talking to her lover. Her way of speaking is described as 'sounding innocent in spite of her age' (Miyake 1971 [1888]: 127). *Hamako* (1902) is the story of the 23-year-old daughter of a rich family. The daughter, Hamako, uses *teyo* only in the scenes where she and her lover confess their love to each other. The narrator comments: 'Her way of speaking became as innocent and naïve as a child' (Kusamura 1969 [1902]: 63). In *Sono omokage* [*Her Silhouette*] (1906), Sayoko falls in love with her brother-in-law, Tetsuya, a 35 or 36-year-old lawyer, after her husband dies. She uses *teyo* only when they are confessing their love to each other (Futabatei 1962 [1906]: 349). These examples demonstrate that 'schoolgirl speech' became the linguistic resource to express sexuality in standard Japanese.

By the late-Meiji years, therefore, the sex-differentiated special identity of 'schoolgirls' was constructed. 'Schoolgirl speech,' mainly consisting of the use of Western words and the new particles such as *teyo, dawa,* and *noyo,* constructed the identity of schoolgirl from the aspect of language. One major difference between 'female students' and 'schoolgirls' was, while the former were regarded simply as students who happened to be women, the latter were characterized by a feminine sexuality distinct from that of older women, maids, and prostitutes. While the former category was contrasted with male students, the latter category was contrasted to other women.

'Schoolgirl speech' in sex-differentiated nationalization

The construction of schoolgirls and 'schoolgirl speech' was a process specific to the political situation of the early twentieth century Japan. First, the transformation of female students into schoolgirls was inevitable in accomplishing sex-differentiated nationalization. In nationalizing women into efficient wives and mothers, the improvement of women's education was vital. If women received education and become independent, however, they might refuse to fulfill these roles. The emergence of female students could be a threat to the nationalization of women. Thus, it was necessary to distinguish them from male students. The construction of schoolgirls transformed female students from dangerous women, who might attempt to become citizens equal to men, into sexual objects for men.

The formation of 'schoolgirl speech' and the sex-differentiated nationalization reinforced each other. By not choosing 'schoolboy speech,' novel writers first differentiated female students from male students, the direction which corresponded with the sex-differentiated nationalization. By not choosing 'polite language,' they excluded their subjects from the category of normative female students, the future good-wife-wise-mothers. The sexual and social deviance of female students was emphasized. The use of '*teyo dawa* speech' and Western words by frivolous characters further derogated the style. By using them for feminine sexuality, they successfully transformed female students into sex objects. As a result, '*teyo dawa* speech,' which had once functioned to resist the good-wife-wise-mother education, was redefined as 'schoolgirl speech,' which served to reinforce the educational policy and, hence, the nationalization of women. '*Teyo dawa* speech,' redefined as 'schoolgirl speech,' therefore, was no longer a threat to the sex-differentiated nationalization. In fact, Ozaki, who had criticized '*teyo dawa* speech' as strange in 1888, used a good deal of it in *Konjiki yasha* [*Gilded Demoness*] (Ozaki (1965 [1897]: 133).

The reproduction of 'schoolgirl speech' by female students

Actual female students enthusiastically read the novels discussed above and imitated 'schoolgirl speech.' 'Recent female students are wholly addicted to the *yokut-teyo* novels which they read when their teachers aren't watching' (Uchida 1986 [1894]: 179). An article, *Jogakusei to gengo* (1905), testifies that 'schoolgirl speech' in novels had a great effect on the way actual students spoke: 'Some of them [female students] began using English and Chinese loan-words as a result of reading novels. It was not that the writers of novels adopted female student's speech. Rather that the writers had an effect on the speech of female students.' Sato (1999 [1941]: 173) also argues that the spread of '*teyo dawa* speech' was motivated by the readers imitating the speech in fiction: 'The words used in woman's everyday conversation such as *teyo* and *dawa* are the result of the work of novelists. . . . In the beginning, female student readers imitated conversation in the novels and, now these words are used by women in general.'[7]

Some women continued to use 'schoolgirl speech' even after they had graduated from school. Their use of 'schoolgirl speech,' however, was closely tied to the narcissistic self-image of schoolgirls floating in their memories of schooldays, separated from their real lives. Kawamura (1993) analyzes readers' letters to *Jogaku zasshi* [*Women's Studies Magazine*] in 1916 and shows that those letters contain the 'schoolgirl speech' features, such as *(no)yo, te(yo),* and *(da)wa.* Many of the letters are from women who, after graduating from schools, moved back to their home-towns in Japan or to Japanese colonies. Since their everyday conversation 'must have been carried out in regional varieties specific to each area' (Kawamura 1993: 103), writing those letters was one of the few occasions they used 'schoolgirl speech.' Thus, their use of 'schoolgirl speech' in the letters, Kawamura (1993: 108) concludes, 'orients to construct a specific world of images, *an imagined community*, through "fictional" communication by the use of the common speech.' 'Schoolgirl speech' functioned to index the imagined identity of a schoolgirl.

Both the identity of 'schoolgirl' and the category of 'schoolgirl speech' are abstract ideologies loaded with political interests. Schoolgirls were not real people but the gender ideology of schoolgirl identity was created by several symbolic systems such as costume and language. Similarly, no actual woman always spoke 'schoolgirl speech.' It was a language ideology created by fiction and metalinguistic commentary. The abstract gender ideology of schoolgirl was given the means to be reproduced in linguistic practice by being associated with entities such as Western words and sentence-final particles. The process of indexicalization, therefore, simul-taneously constructed both the language ideology of 'schoolgirl speech' and the gender ideology of schoolgirls.

Relationships between practice and ideology

This analysis has demonstrated that indexicality is not naturally constructed by repeated use in local practice. The speech of female students in the early twentieth century ranged from 'schoolboy speech' and '*teyo dawa* speech' to polite speech. Local practices are too diverse to construct indexicality. Indexicalization is not the process which associates linguistic features with the identity of people already there. It is a political process in which both social identity and language ideology are simul-taneously constructed. The schoolgirl identity did not exist before 'schoolgirl speech,' but was created by being associated with the use of particular features.

The crucial role of fiction and metalinguistic commentary in constructing language ideology implies the importance of locating them in a specific political process. If we locate the acts of writing fiction and commenting on women's speech in a specific context, we can redefine them as practice. Although the term 'prac-tice' commonly refers to an interaction in a specific context, typically a face-to-face local interaction, both fiction and commentary are produced in a specific historical and political situation by a particular group of people. Investigations into who conducted particular practices in what political process enables us to clarify the political function of a particular language ideology.

By redefining fiction and commentary as practice, in addition to local practice, my analysis identifies two-way interactions between practice and ideology. First, practice *produces*, *reproduces*, and *resists* both language ideology and gender ideology. Fictional and metalinguistic practices selected '*teyo dawa* speech' and produced the language ideology of 'schoolgirl speech' and the gender ideology of schoolgirl identity. The local practice of some female students reproduced them by imitating 'schoolgirl speech.' Further use in novels and meta-comments also kept reproducing them. We have seen, on the other hand, that some female students continued to use 'schoolboy speech' throughout the period. Such local practice is considered to resist the identity of sexual schoolgirls emitted by 'schoolgirl speech.' As the case of '*teyo dawa* speech' shows, however, the subversive force of this resistance can be easily appropriated by a larger political process.

Second, ideology *provides resources for* practice as well as *restricting* it. The language ideology of 'schoolgirl speech' provided resources to construct the identity of schoolgirl in practice. By using particular sentence-final particles and foreign words, anybody, either women and men, could construct a schoolgirl identity. Middle-aged male writers constructed their schoolgirl characters by using 'schoolgirl speech' in writing novels. At the same time, ideology restricts practice in that socially acceptable identities, which can be constructed in practice without anticipating social sanctions, are constrained. The use of 'schoolgirl speech' was associated with sexuality. The use of a polite style was associated with the identity of a future good-wife-wise-mother. The use of 'schoolboy speech' was severely condemned. No resource was provided to present the identity of an intelligent, modern female student.

Chapter 23

Don Kulick

2003

NO

PERFORMATIVITY AS A THEORY is most closely associated with the American philosopher Judith Butler, who in a number of well-known books has developed what she calls a performative approach to language and culture. The cornerstone of this approach is of course J.L. Austin's concept of the performative, which is concerned with language as action, language that in its enunciation changes the world – it brings about a new social state. The archetypal performatives with which Austin begins his discussion are utterances like 'I bet' or 'I promise'. However, by the conclusion of *How to Do Things with Words*, Austin has collapsed the distinction between performatives and constatives that he established at the beginning, and he declares that even constative utterances are in fact performatives: 'there can hardly be any longer a possibility of not seeing that stating is performing an act', he wrote (Austin 1997: 139).

This collapse of the distinction between performative and constative was the dimension of Austin's theory that Butler developed in her work. Focusing on gender, Butler claimed that utterances like the 'It's a girl' delivered by a doctor to a mother who has just given birth are not merely descriptive. Like the priest's 'I now pronounce you man and wife', an utterance like 'It's a girl' performs an act. It *does something* in Butler's analysis. That act of naming 'initiates the process by which a certain girling is compelled', she wrote (Butler 1993: 232). It requires that the referent so designated act in accordance with particular norms and create, in doing so, the appropriate gender in every culturally legible act that the person so designated performs, from sitting in a chair, to expressing her desire, to deciding what she ought to eat for dinner.

The relevant part of this story for the argument I will develop here is what happened next. After the publication of Butler's 1990 book *Gender Trouble*, performativity suddenly became all the rage. It entered the lexicon of literary studies, history, sociology and anthropology, and it even merits a separate entry in Alessandro Duranti's recent collection *Key Terms in Language and Culture* (Hall

2001). Now for sociolinguists and linguistic anthropologists, this might appear somewhat odd, because while 'performativity' was busy hypercirculating in other disciplines, another, older, term that seemingly referred to precisely the same thing – or at least it sounded pretty similar – already existed. That term was 'performance'.

But performance is not the same as performativity. The difference is this: performance is something a subject does. Performativity, on the other hand, is the process through which the subject emerges (Butler 1993: 2, 7, 95). This is a crucial distinction that was completely missed by many critics of Butler's work. Early rejections of her framework were based on a reading of performativity as perform-ance; on the idea of an entirely self-aware and volitional actor who could choose to put on or take off genders the way people put on or take off clothes (see e.g. Weston 1993). This is wrong. Performance is one dimension of performativity. But performativity theory insists that what is expressed or performed in any social context is importantly linked to that which is not expressed or cannot be performed. Hence, analysis of action and identity must take into account what is not or cannot be enacted. Furthermore, a performative approach to language inter-rogates the circulation of language in society – not so much who is authorized to use language (which was Austin's concern, as it was a major concern of Pierre Bourdieu, e.g. Bourdieu 1991), as how particular uses of language, be they autho-rized or not, produce particular effects and particular kinds of subjects in fields or matrices of power.

Performativity is not a linguistic concept – Austin was not a linguist, he was a philosopher, as is Butler – and this may be one reason why there are really very few linguistic studies that might be said to be performative. There are lots of studies of performance, but few of performativity. The difference between the two perspec-tives is something I hope to illustrate in this paper. I propose to do this through an examination of the linguistic token of rejection or refusal, the word 'no'. My interest is in how the enunciation (or not) of 'no' in particular social situations works to produce those situations as sexual, even as it materializes particular subjects as sexual subjects. I am also interested in how the enunciation of 'no' is structured by certain absences, certain other enunciations that cannot or must not be expressed. I will illustrate my arguments by discussing the occurrence of 'no' in three seem-ingly very different contexts, which I will link. The three situations I will discuss are situations of (1) sexual harassment and rape, (2) instances where the so-called Homosexual Panic Defense, which I will explain shortly, is invoked, and, finally, (3) sadomasochistic sex.

Sexual harassment and rape

The foremost context for the analysis of 'no' in sexual situations is research that examines the language of sexual harassment and rape. This important research focuses on the fact that a woman's 'no' is constrained by cultural expectations and demands of femininity (Ehrlich 1998, 2001; Lees 1996; Kitzinger and Frith 1999; Matoesian 1993; McConnell-Ginet 1989). The strongest articulation of this posi-tion is the assertion that a woman's refusal of sex simply cannot be heard in patriarchal culture (MacKinnon 1993). In a culture that relentlessly objectifies and sexualizes women, the illocutionary force of a woman's 'no' to sex is consistently thwarted and distorted to mean 'keep trying', or even its inversion, 'yes'. Hence, men can claim that they misunderstood women's refusal, and women who are raped can be blamed for not having conveyed their refusal clearly enough. This is particularly the case when there is no physical evidence, such as bruises or broken bones, that the woman refused the man's advances.

Phrased in terms of performativity theory, what linguistic analyses of sexual harassment and rape trials demonstrate is that the subject position 'woman' is produced in part by the normatively exhorted utterance 'no' when encountering male desire for sex. This differs from the subject 'man', who, in contrast, is normatively exhorted to *never* say 'no' when confronted with female desire. Indeed, for a male to say 'no' to female desire for sex would threaten to signify him as a homosexual. In order to block this signification, extenuating circumstances need to be asserted, such as extreme physical unattractiveness in the female. All of this configures a cultural grammar in which saying 'no' is part of what produces a female sexual subject, and not saying 'no' produces a male sexual subject. 'No' in both its present and absent manifestations facilitates the production of heterosexual subjectivities and heterosexual sexuality. Its utterance invokes a domain in which one interactant can performatively produce himself as a man by responding to it by prolonging the encounter and ideally finally transforming it into a 'yes', and the other interactant can performatively produce herself as female by facilitating – willingly or not – that extension and prolongation of the sexual scene.

Any performative approach to language will ask: 'where does a particular signifying system run up against its own limits'? One place 'no' meets its limits is when a woman does not utter it, and says 'yes' without persuasion. Now, while Conversation Analysts have shown us that a 'yes' is an interactionally preferred response, as a woman's response to a sexual advance, it is culturally a *dispreferred* one. Accordingly, the sexual subjects produced through 'yes' are *marked* in the linguistic, Jakobsonian sense; they are not just women; there are many other names for them, most of them pejorative. A 'yes' to sex can also produce female subjects as being outside heteronormativity, when that 'yes' occurs as a response to the advances of a woman (who, of course, is also marked in this discursive system). As an aside, I can also note that women who say 'yes' to sex are also marked in our academic texts, in this case through their virtual absence – we have several excellent studies on how women say 'no' to sex, but little information on how they say 'yes'. One paper we do have, interestingly enough, indicates that many women say 'yes' to (hetero)sex precisely by saying 'no'. This was a questionnaire study done in the late 1980s, which asked 610 female undergraduate students if they had ever said 'no' to sex, even though they 'had every intention of and were willing to engage in sexual intercourse'. It turns out that 68.5% of these women reported saying 'no' when they meant 'maybe', and 39.3% reported saying 'no' when they meant 'yes'. When asked why they said 'no' when they meant 'yes', women answered either that they were afraid of appearing promiscuous, or they felt inhibited about sex, or they wanted to manipulate the male – they were angry with him, they wanted to make him more aroused, or more physically aggressive (Muehlenhard and Hollabaugh 1988).

The field of sexuality produced by 'no' also runs up against its limits when a man says 'no' to a woman. As I have already mentioned, this appearance of 'no' threatens to signify the subject as marked 'gay'. But interestingly, this 'no', rather than quashing sexuality, also invites its prolongation. Movies like *The Opposite of Sex* (a 1998 film in which the main female character plots to seduce her brother's boyfriend, who says 'no' to her advances, telling her he is gay) make explicit and exploit this domain of possibility raised by a man's 'no' to female desire.

The most striking place where this system of sexual positionings runs up against its own limits is in instances when a man is solicited by another man. The marked subjectivity here is not so much the man doing the pursuing – men are subjects who pursue others sexually, and cultural stereotypes insist that men who pursue other men are the most fully sexed subjects of all (hence the most repellent hetero-sexual men in the world feel no embarrassment announcing that homosexuality is 'OK' with them, as long as the homosexuals don't try to seduce them . . .). In this particular erotic choreography, the marked subjectivity is the man who says 'no'. Precisely by saying 'no', this speaker performatively materializes the position reserved in heteronormative praxis for women. By having to utter 'no', the speaker produces a feminine subject; one that importantly does not reject sex so much as facilitate it, by invoking a matrix of persuasion. In other words, the 'no' here ensnares and constrains the male speaker in the same bind that it raises for female speakers who produce it. The fact that 'no' ensnares both women and men in this way is one reason why analysis should not concentrate, I think, on the *performance* of 'no'. What is important to interrogate is the way particular iterations of language performatively produce particular subject positions; positions which may in fact undermine the performance of a coherent gender identity.

The Homosexual Panic Defense

That 'no' is precisely *not* just 'no', and that the performative force of 'no' facili-tates, rather than ends, a sexual scene, is explicitly highlighted in the form of a phenomenon popularly known as the Homosexual Panic Defense. The Homosexual Panic Defense is the name of a legal defense invoked on behalf of men who have murdered other men who they claim made sexual advances towards them. In effect, the Homosexual Panic Defense argues that a sexual advance is in itself an act of aggression, and that the defendant was justified in responding to it with violence.

The Homosexual Panic Defense is based on something called 'acute homo-sexual panic'. This is a psychiatric condition that was first proposed in 1920. In its original formulation, 'homosexual panic' did not refer to a fear due to advances by other men. Instead, it referred to cases where men who had been in intensively same sex environments became aware of homosexual desires that they felt unable to control, and unable to act on. The original formulation of the disorder was based on diagnosis a small number of soldiers and sailors in a US government mental hospital after WWI (Kempf 1920). These men were not violent – they were, on the contrary, passive. The disorder was characterized by periods of introspec-tive brooding, self-punishment, suicidal assaults, withdrawal, and helplessness. So 'homosexual panic' was generally understood not as a temporary, violent episode, but, rather as an ongoing illness that comprised severe bouts of depression. Patients suffering from it were catatonic, not violent. Basically, 'homosexual panic' was the diagnosis given to men who we today would try to get to 'come out' and accept their homosexuality. In fact, some early psychiatrists recognized that the best treatment for the disorder was for the patient to accept his homosexual desires and act on them.

What happened during the course of the 1900s is that the original understanding of this condition shifted, and it came to be applied even to men who reacted violently in situations where homosexual desire was made explicit. In other words, it became used to explain situations where a man allowed himself to be solicited or seduced by another man, but then suddenly turned on that man and beat or even murdered him. In the psychiatric literature, there is no consensus that 'homosexual panic' should or can be used to explain sudden violent outbursts like these. But to the extent that the fury is identified as 'homosexual panic', the violence is explained by latent homosexual cravings and a challenge to or collapse of a heterosexual self-image.[1]

The Homosexual Panic Defense builds loosely on this later understanding of homosexual panic. It argues that there is a scientific and medical reason for, and, hence, a justification of, the behavior of defendants who murder gay men. The literary scholar Eve Sedgwick (1990: 19) has noted that the very existence of such a category rests on an assumption that hatred of homosexuals is a private and atypical phenomenon. But think about it, she says. To what extent would anyone accept 'race panic' as an accountability-reducing illness for a German skinhead who bludgeoned a Turk to death? Or 'gender panic' for a woman who shot a man who made an unwanted advance to her? (Consider how many bodies would be swept out of bars and clubs every morning.) The fact that the Homosexual Panic Defense exists at all indicates that far from being an individual pathology, hatred of homosexuals is actually more public and more typical than hatred of any other disadvantaged group.

The defense is applied in English speaking countries like the US, Australia and Canada in two ways. One is as an insanity defense – that is, a defense that argues that the accused is in a condition or state where they cannot tell right from wrong or not understand the character of their actions. Legal scholars have argued that in pure legal terms, the Homosexual Panic Defense should not qualify as an insanity defense at all, first of all because to the extent that individuals can be said to panic at homosexuality, they do so precisely because they believe that homosexuality is 'wrong'. Second, cases that invoke the Panic Defense do not assert that defendants do not realize the likely consequences of shooting their victims in the heart, hacking them with meat cleavers, jumping on their heads or beating them with clubs – to take some more charming examples of the cases where the defense has been invoked. It is never asserted that defendants who do these things are unaware that they may kill the victim.

The second way the defense is applied is as a response to provocation. This defense relies on and promotes a view that there is no difference between a sexual advance and a sexual attack. In fact, the Homosexual Panic Defense argues that a sexual advance from a homosexual male is definitionally a sexual attack, and that the accused is justified in responding violently to such an act of aggression.

In practice, the Homosexual Panic Defense is used in ways that often bear almost no resemblance to any version of the psychiatric disorder. For example, the psychiatric criterion that homosexual panic is related to latent homosexuality in the accused is often disregarded. The most famous case of the Homosexual Panic Defense in recent years was a man named Jonathan Schmitz. Twenty-six-year-old Schmitz was brought onto an American television program called the *Jenny Jones* show, which is a kind of *Ricki Lake* or *Jerry Springer* show where people surprise their friends, family and lovers by revealing unexpected and often scandalous secrets about themselves on national television. Jonathan Schmitz had been told by the *Jenny Jones's* show's producers that someone he knew was secretly in love with him, and would reveal this crush on the air. It turned out that the person who was secretly in love with Schmitz was a 32-year-old gay man named Scott Amedure. Amedure greeted Schmitz when he appeared on the television stage and professed his attraction. Three days after the taping of the show, Schmitz bought a shotgun, drove to Amedure's home and shot him twice through the heart.

In the subsequent trial, Schmitz blamed the murdered Amedure for his actions – and this is how the Homosexual Panic Defense is increasingly being used. In other words, Schmitz's lawyers did not claim that Schmitz is a latent homosexual who panicked at the collapse of his heterosexual self image. Instead, they claimed that Scott Amedure's public revelation of his desire in itself constituted an 'ambush'.[2] Schmitz's lawyers argued that Amedure's public revelation of an infatuation with Schmitz was, in and of itself, an act of aggression that excused a violent retaliation. The jury agreed with this line of reasoning and found Schmitz guilty not of first-degree premeditated murder, but of the lesser charge of second-degree (i.e. not premeditated) murder.

Now let's look for a moment at the Homosexual Panic Defense in relation to what I have already argued about 'no' in cases of sexual harassment and rape. At first glance, the two kinds of cases seem very different, which may be one reason why I have not seen them discussed together in any detail. In the case of rape, the victim of violence is the woman who rejects the sexual advance of a man. In the case of Homosexual Panic, the victim of violence is the man who (is reported to have) made the sexual advance.

What links the two cases, I am arguing, is 'no'. In both cases, a sexual advance acts as an interpellation, a calling into being of a sexual subject. Like Louis Althusser's famous example of the policeman's call 'Hey, you there!' that produces a subject in the person who turns around (Althusser 1971: 174) – a subject who did not pre-exist the call, but who becomes constituted as a subject upon responding to it – a sexual advance calls into being a sexual subject. And in the case of both rape and Homosexual Panic, from the perspective of performativity theory, a 'no' is not just a refusal of that subjection. It is also an acknowledgement of it; a response to the interpellative call that even in disputing it affirms it. It is a 'no' that says 'I refuse to acknowledge that I am being called into being as a sexual subject'. But a refusal to acknowledge something is already a form of acknowledgment. In structural terms, therefore, a 'no' to a sexual advance is – must be – both a 'no' and a 'yes' at the same time.

This dual indexicality of 'no' is what allows men to claim that they misunderstood a woman's 'no', even as it also facilitates their assertion that sexual solicitation by another man in itself was an act of violence that justified a violent response. Remember that part of what produces the masculine sexual subject is the 'no' of the other. To have to utter that 'no' oneself is to be forced to produce oneself as a non-masculine subject. I think that it is for this reason that in cases in which the Homosexual Panic Defense is invoked, there is often no evidence that any verbal refusal ever even occurred. The word 'no' is not – in a sense, cannot be uttered. Instead, the sexual interpellation is acknowledged non-verbally, with vicious physical violence.

I hope it is becoming clear where this argument is leading. My point is that 'no' is essential not so much for the production of a sexual scenario (after all, a 'yes' can produce that), but for the materialization of *a particular kind of sexual scenario* in which the sexual subjects so produced are differentially empowered and differentially gendered. In other words, 'no' produces a sexualized, gendered field of power. As a final empirical example, I offer a situation that crystallizes all this, namely sadomasochistic sex.

Sadomasochistic sex

Sadomasochistic sex is an extremely straightforward example of a case where 'no' is self-consciously used to constitute a sexualized, gendered field of power. To see this, it is important to understand that any description or analysis of S/M discusses what is called a 'safeword'. This is a word or phrase that is negotiated in advance of the sexual scene and used by either the submissive bottom or the dominant top whenever either of them wants to stop some activity. The most important dimension of this for us is the fact that one of the very few words which cannot function as a safeword is, precisely, 'no'.

'Consider . . . this dialogue', readers are instructed by one S/M manual, in a section on safewords:

> Top: 'Seems to me you deserve a good spanking with this hairbrush, my little slut.' Bottom (in role as obedient slave): 'If it pleases you, sir or madam' – or bottom (in role as reluctant victim): 'No! Please! Not the hairbrush!'[3]

'In either case', the manual explains, 'the top has no guide to the bottom's real feelings' (Easton and Hardy 2001: 39). Why is this? The same authors go on to explain:

> The reason we need [a safeword] is that lots of us like to pretend we don't want to have all these amazing things done to us, and we may pretend by joyously shrieking 'Nononononono', so we need another word to mean that.
>
> (Easton and Hardy 2001: 44)

Another S/M manual (Henkin and Holiday 1996: 89, italics in original) puts it like this:

> Words other than No, Stop, or Slow Down are usually designated [as a safeword] because SM is a *consensual* eroticism in the realm of *erotic theatre*. If a bottom could just say 'Stop' to end a [sexual] scene, the illusion that the Top has total control might be threatened. Besides, many bottoms enjoy the fantasy of nonconsenuality and scream 'No, no, please stop!' – or words to that effect – when the scene is going very well; they would be upset, confused, and even angry if a Top actually did stop in response to their outbursts.

Another S/M manual explains that 'A plea to "Stop beating me" may well mean "I love it. Keep going"' (Lee 1983: 186).

It is clear that 'no' in these situations means its inversion, 'yes'. For that reason, manuals explain that safewords should be anything other than words like 'no', 'stop', or 'don't' – that is to say, any words other than negations or expressions of pain. Most manuals recommend either contextually jarring words like 'PICKLE' or 'RADISH', or words that invoke associations to traffic lights: 'YELLOW', meaning 'lighter or slower', and 'RED' meaning 'stop'.

In any case, my point is that S/M sex self-consciously exploits the performative potential of 'no' to facilitate and extend sexual scenes. It recognizes the dual indexicality of 'no' and deploys it to produce a domain of sexuality; a domain of sexuality that is, moreover, saturated with power. Because whatever else it may be about, all practitioners and observers of S/M are agreed that it is an eroticization and staging of power. S/M manuals all discuss power. The title of one of the first and most famous S/M manuals ever published, by the lesbian-feminist S/M support group, Samois (1981), was the pun: *Coming to Power*. A common definition of S/M is 'consensual exchanges of erotic power' (e.g. Henkin and Holiday 1996: 72). One manual elaborates a distinction between 'power-over', which is power obtained at the expense of others, and 'power-with', which is 'the idea that we can all become more powerful by supporting each other in being more powerful' (Easton and Hardy 2001: 24–5). S/M, this manual explains, is a play with power for the fun of it; hence, a 'power-with' in which erotic pleasure is produced by skillful manipulations of forms of power that are invested with new content. This same manual proposes that all bottoms ought to see themselves as what it calls 'full-power bottoms'.

We can debate the extent to which concepts like 'full-power bottoms' are reasonable ones. But even those who reject them – for example radical feminists who insist that S/M practitioners merely reinscribe the very structures of power they claim to transcend – do not contest that what happens in sadomasochistic sex is an erotic staging of power.

The central role that 'no' plays in this staging is not fortuitous or arbitrary. On the contrary, the structuring role of 'no' in the production of a sadomasochistic sex scene is a distillation and elaboration of 'no's role in wider arenas of social life. And that role, as I have been arguing, is not so much about performance as it is production. 'No' performatively materializes specific kinds of erotic domains, ones in which power is channeled through and constitutive of specific social positions. Those positions are gendered in the sense that they are differently positioned in relation to 'no' – as I mentioned earlier, the subject position 'woman' is produced in part by the normatively exhorted utterance 'no' when encountering a sexual interpellation. This contrasts with the subject 'man', who is normatively exhorted to never say 'no' to sex, and whose position as masculine is produced in part through the 'no' of the other. S/M sex invokes this plane in order to exploit the disruptive potential of the erotic to manipulate and invert these positionings. Hence, it provides a space for the male body to temporarily (and socially inconsequentially) inhabit the 'no' that is otherwise disallowed it; just as it provides a space for the female body to inhabit the position that is materialized through the enunciation of the 'no' of the other. (It is no secret to anyone that the overwhelming majority of submissive bottoms are males – frequently the same males who exercise a great deal of social power outside the dungeon. Nor is it a secret that the tops that these men pay a lot of money to dominate them are female dominatrixes – how's that for a linguistically *marked* category?). The erotic plane that S/M sex constructs for itself also recognizes the violence that inheres in sexual domains invoked by 'no', and it produces that violence. But it produces it not as realism or tragedy, but, rather, as melodrama, a genre that is characterized by the exteriorization of conflict and psychic structures in dramatic excess (see Gledhill 1987: 31).

Conclusion

One of the points of this essay has been to suggest what I see as a difference between performance and performativity, and the relationship of those two perspectives to language. At several junctures, I noted where I think that a performance perspective differs from a performativity perspective. But there is a particular difference, a crucial one in my view, with which I would like to end. That difference is this: whereas studies conceived of in a performance framework have a tendency to see language in relation to *identity*, research framed as performative will concentrate more on *identification*. The difference is between identity, which in sociolinguistic and linguistic anthropological work is conventionally presented as a more or less conscious claim-staking of a particular sociological position, and identification, which is concerned with the operations through which the subject is constituted. A psychoanalytic truism about identifications is that they do not constitute a coherent relational system. Nor are they entirely conscious. On the contrary, identifications are just as much structured by rejections, refusals and disavowals as they are structured by affirmations. Because they are not the same thing, it is important to not collapse identification into identity. A performative approach to linguistic phenomena does not start or end with identity. Instead, a performative approach would examine the processes through which some kinds of identifications are authorized, legitimate and unmarked, and others are unauthorized, illegitimate, and marked. I have tried to do this here with 'no', examining it not by asking: who says it? but, rather: what does saying it – or not saying it – produce? That question leads me to another, more consequential one, namely: instead of a sociolinguistics of identity, what would happen if we began imagining a sociolinguistics of identification?

Notes

6 Gayspeak

1   No previous study of gay language has attempted this method. Previous efforts are mostly lexicons without any rigorous analysis (Farrell 1972; [Penelope] Stanley 1970, 1974; Rodgers 1972). Farrell, Rodgers, and [Penelope] Stanley (1970) provide mostly word lists, although Rodgers is quite exhaustive for gay men's language. [Penelope] Stanley (Chapter 4, this volume) is an excellent presentation of the radical perspective.

2   Although I refer in several places to the language of both gay men and women I am speaking primarily about *gay men*. My experience in the lesbian community is not sufficient to delineate a special dialect among gay women.

3   The term setting is intended to mean something more than Gumperz's concept of community (Gumperz 1962). I am not speaking here so much of a 'community of interaction' as I am of a 'situated context'. A gay liberationist, for instance, might normally belong to a counterculture 'speech community' but might still use secret Gayspeak in certain contexts (e.g., in family 'setting'). Whatever his politics or convictions, his language is usually appropriate to a given context.

4   It is most important to emphasize that there are no easily defined boundaries between the three settings singled out. Gays may use special language in certain contexts but never in others. For instance, men who wish to appear 'serious' or 'masculine' might use radical-activist or neutral language with one set of friends although they might abandon this role in order to *camp it up* with another set of friends.

5   The term is taken from Humphreys 1972: 74–6.

6   These few examples are selected from a much lengthier list in Rodgers 1972: 164–5.

7   The two most famous discussions of camp are Sontag 1964 and Brien 1967. Neither one is addressed especially to the use of camp in the gay community; such a complex analysis still remains to be done.

8   Among members of the gay liberation movement there is an especial emphasis on desexualizing the term gay: 'Being *gay* no longer simply refers to loving one's own sex, but has come to designate a state of political awareness in which one no longer needs the narrowly defined sex-role stereotypes as bases for identity' ([Penelope] Stanley, Chapter 4, this volume, p. 54). Similarly, James Foratt writes of *homosexual*:

'I find the word hard to relate to because it puts me in a category which limits my potential. It also prescribes a whole system of behavior to which I'm supposed to conform which has nothing to do with the reallity of my day to day living' (Foratt 1970: 16). The position paper of the Paris *Front Homosexual d'Action Revolutionnaire* states that 'homosexuality doesn't exist. It is only in the minds of those who see themselves as heterosexuals or those who have been persuaded they are gay by the would-be heteros' (Broadside translated by the group, 1972).

8 Can there be gay discourse without gay language?

1   Sapir wrote, for example: 'The genuine culture is . . . inherently harmonious, balanced, self-satisfactory. It is the expression of a richly varied and yet somehow unified and consistent attitude toward life, . . . a culture in which nothing is spiritually meaningless, in which no important part of the general functioning brings with it a sense of frustration, of misdirected or unsympathetic effort' (1949: 314). These criteria enable Herdt and Boxer (1993: 27–36, *passim*) to question whether there was an authentic gay culture in Chicago prior to the Stonewall rebellion and its aftermath.

13 Supermodels of the world, unite!

1   Critiques of drag as misogynistic based on the assumption that only men perform drag (e.g. Williamson 1986) do not necessarily hold for this research. In the bar where the majority of this research took place, drag king performances (i.e. drag performed by lesbians) occurred with almost the same frequency as drag queen performances.

2   Although *Paris is Burning* deals with both transsexuals and drag queens, it does not distinguish the two, leading many critics to confuse the groups. As the focus of this work is on drag queens, I will refer only to drag queens in the remainder of the paper.

3   'African American English,' refers to a particular (structurally-defined) linguistic variety (sometimes called Black English Vernacular) with cultural associations to African American identity. Although many African Americans do not speak AAE (and not all speakers of AAE are African American) there is a symbolic association between AAE and African American culture, so that use of AAE may serve to index a person's identity as an African American.

4   By gay English, I mean to imply a set of structural linguistic characteristics and lexical choices that might be perceived as markers of gay identity.

5   Gay bars in Texas are often (but not always) segregated either through practice or through explicitly racist carding practices.

6   A 'butt-fucking tea' is anything that is exceptionally good.

14 'Speaking as a heterosexual'

1   In a survey of language use among gay men, Harvey (1997: 68) found that four of the 53 respondents reported referring to their same-sex partner as their 'wife' or 'husband' – a usage he describes as 'parodic appropriation'. I have no recorded naturalistic data in which someone in a same-sex couple can be heard as referring to a same-sex partner using the terminology appropriate to a different sex spouse (i.e. 'wife' from a gay man or 'husband' from a lesbian). Those instances in which a woman refers to her same-sex partner as her 'wife' (see Land and Kitzinger 2005) result in major interactional difficulties.

2   The only talk *about* non-heterosexual people I have found in the data corpora are: talk about actors who play 'fags' in the movies, including what is apparently a quote from some such movie ('Tell them I'm not a fag') (Chicken Dinner); a news-reporting about 'fags' in Detroit ('Isn't that the place they say where if two fags split up one's got to pay the other one alimony?'; 'Too way ahead out there') (Chicken Dinner); and what Drew (1987: 224) describes as 'three teasing attributions to Vic of homosexuality' (Upholstery Shop) – to which Vic's retort is that he'd rather be a 'faggot' than marry the female prostitute with whom he reports having been sexually involved.

16 The discursive reconstruction of sexual consent

1   The pool of tribunal members consists of three faculty members and three students nominated by the Dean of the university's Law School, three faculty members nominated by the Governing Council of the university's residential colleges, three students nominated by the Undergraduate Student Union and three faculty members and three students nominated by the Vice-President, Campus Relations.

2   Criminal charges against the defendant reached some resolution in the spring of 1995, when he was convicted of one of the two charges of sexual assault and sentenced to 6 months in jail.

3   All of the examples in this section come from the alleged instance of acquaintance rape that occurred with another couple in the room.

4   All names used to designate individuals involved in the tribunal are pseudonyms.

5   Transcription conventions (adapted from Jefferson 1978) are as follows:

.	sentence final falling intonation
,	clause-final intonation (more to come)
?	rising intonation followed by a noticeable pause
. . .	pause of 1/2 second or more
=	no interval between adjacent utterances (second is latched to the first)
[a lot	
I see]	overlapping utterances
-	a halting, abrupt cutoff
:	an extension of the sound or syllable it follows
italics	emphatic stress
((sniff))	details of the conversational scene or vocalizations

6   Despite Matt's claims to the contrary, some of his comments suggest that he wasn't sure that Marg welcomed his sexual advances. For instance, on lines 27–8 of example (2), Matt says that 'he wasn't looking for consent', a comment that Matt's representative hurriedly cuts off.

19 Why defining is seldom 'just semantics'

1   Bayles contrasts instrumentalists (who believe that definitions should further certain purposes) with realists (who see definitions as specifying what really exists), conventionalists (specifying extant or earlier conventions), and reductionists (who want to eliminate one kind of term in favor of some other). His endorsement of an instrumentalist stance does not mean he thinks that judges should be free to offer whatever definitions they personally favor: there are constraints embodied in the idea of a 'justifiable legal system.'

2   Some states still have 'marital rape exemption' provisions that absolve a man from rape charges in certain cases when he is married to the woman assaulted.

20 'I went to bed with my own kind once'

1   The inclusion of 'drag queen' in this list is a particular choice on my part, and not one that all transgender-identified people or drag queens might agree with. Indeed, I include it here, somewhat reluctantly, only because many of my informants do so in their explanations of what 'transgender' encompasses. As will become apparent later in this paper, 'drag queen' is a central category in thinking about the relationship between identity and desire.

2   I use the construction 'transgender-identified' to mark the ways in which people both take on the category transgender as something meaningful about themselves; as well as the sense of being identified by others to fall into a category. This is a useful way of dealing with the conceptual mismatches I will be talking about in this paper, but it also speaks to the ways that self identity and identification by others of the self are not separate but complexly related phenomena.

3   Given my argument, one might imagine that Nora would have said 'gender' rather than 'sexuality' here. At the same time, however, her use of 'sexuality' indicates the slippage between these categories in talk and practice, and points to the gaps produced by needing to talk about desire in discrete categories.

4   This argument does not intend to draw away from the organizing and advocacy engaged in by transgender-identified people in claiming this category; nor is it intended to contest the political gains achieved under this category. My goal here is to point to a particular cultural logic that underpins contemporary understandings of both gender variance and homosexuality in order to consider the deeper implications of these politics.

21 Writing desire in Nepali love letters

1   This excerpt and all others taken from love letters or conversations were translated from Nepali by the author. For the entire text of this letter and many others, see the online appendices of Ahearn (2001a) at http://www.press.umich.edu/webhome/ahearn/index.html. In keeping with anthropological convention, all names in this article are pseudonyms.

2   Three dots with spaces in between them indicate omitted words. A series of eight dots indicates an ellipsis that was in the original letters.

3   For a comparable love letter guidebook featured at a Borders Bookstore Valentine's Day display in the 1990s, see Lovric (1995).

22 Creating indexicality

1   The construction of indexicality through the language-use of fictional characters is not confined to women's language. Most Japanese have knowledge, for example, of how Martians talk and what they say. They are supposed to say, *wareware wa uchuu-jinn da* 'We are aliens from outer space' with a flat intonation in a shrill, mechanical voice. Kinsui (2003) points out that Japanese language has many linguistic features, although no Japanese actually uses them in conversation, which are firmly associated with particular social identities in comics and folk stories, and calls this 'virtual Japanese'.

2   According to Koyama (1991: 58), the ideology of good-wife-wise-mother is not the old Confucian notion but 'the key concept in the process of synthesizing women into citizens of the modern state'. Industrial development divided workplace from residence in a modern society, in which men were expected to work and women were

expected to stay home. New abilities were required for women to manage households and reproduce workers and soldiers.

3   The following is a list of abbreviations used in the transcripts.

GEN   genitive particle
GOAL   goal marker
HON   honorific marker
NEG   negative
NOM   nominative particle
OBJ   object marker
PAST   past marker
QUOT   quotative particle
SFP   sentence final particle
SFX   verb suffix
TOP   topic marker

4   Although *shosei kotoba* literally means 'student language', I call it 'schoolboy speech' because in actuality it refers specifically to the usage of schoolboys.

5   These particles were first used to translate the speech of Western girls. The writer Futabatei, translating a work by Turgenev in 1885, 'was having such difficulty . . . At the time, there was no suitable language to describe Western women such as the "schoolgirl speech" we have today' (Tsubouchi and Uchida 1965 [1909]: 489). 'At the time, in translation, we [novel writers] could not use middle-class language, especially women's language which was full of polite words' (Tsubouchi 1977 [1933]: 419). The choice of these particles by novel writers to represent the speech of Western girls shows their associations with Westernization and modernization.

6   Some claim that '*teyo dawa* speech' was entirely the creation of novelists, but people were commenting on the use of *teyo* and *dawa* at least seven to eight years before they began to appear in novels.

7   Neither the author nor the publication year of the story has been determined, since pornography was strictly censored by the state at the time. It is assumed to have been published between 1907 and 1911, and the author has been variously said to be Oguri, his teacher Ozaki, or his student Nakagawa.

23 No

1   See the following sources on homosexual panic and the Homosexual Panic Defense: Bagnall *et al.* (1984), Comstock (1989), Freiberg (1988), Glick (1959), New South Wales Government (1998), Suffrendi (2001), Hart (1958).

2   Michigan Court of Appeals (1998). 586 N.W. 2d 766, 768.

3   For the uninitiated, I should note that the terms 'top' and 'bottom' in S/M culture denote, respectively, the dominant and submissive partner in a sexual scene.

Bibliography

Abe, H. 2000. *Speaking of Power: Japanese Women and their Language*. Munich: Lincom Europa.

Abelson, R. 1968. Definition. In P. Edwards (ed.) *Encyclopedia of Philosophy*. New York: Macmillan, Vol. 1, 314–24.

Abrahams, R. 1976. *Talking Black*. Rowley, MA: Newbury House.

Abrams, K. 1989. Gender Discrimination and the Transformation of Workplace Norms. *Vanderbilt Law Review* 1183: 1203.

Abu-Lughod, L. and C.A. Lutz, 1990. Introduction: Emotion, Discourse, and the Politics of Everyday Life. In C.A. Lutz and L. Abu-Lughod (eds) *Language and the Politics of Emotion*. Cambridge: Cambridge University Press, pp. 1–23.

Ackroyd, P. 1979. *Dressing Up: Transvestism and Drag: The History of an Obsession*. New York: Simon & Schuster.

Aeba, K. 1988 [1888–9]. *Momiji [Maple]*. In *Shoonen en (fukkoku ban) dai 1 kan [Shoonen en (Reprint) Vol. 1]*, 5: 13–4. Tokyo: Fuji Shuppan, No. 5, 13–14.

Agar, M. 1980. Stories, Background Knowledge and Themes: Problems in the Analysis of Life Story Narratives. *American Ethnologist* 7: 223–39.

Ahearn, L.M. 2001a. *Invitations to Love: Literacy, Love Letters, and Social Change in Nepal*. Ann Arbor, MI: University of Michigan Press.

Ahearn, L.M. 2001b. Language and Agency. *Annual Review of Anthropology* 30: 109–37.

Almeida, M. Vale de. 1996. *The Hegemonic Male: Masculinity in a Portuguese Town*. Providence, RI: Berghahn Books.

Althusser, L. 1971. Ideology and Ideological State Apparatuses (Notes Towards an Investigation). In *Lenin and Philosophy and Other Essays*. London: Monthly Review Press, pp. 127–88.

Ashburn, K. 2000. Mainstream Perceptions of SF [Science Fiction]. Panel discussion at Minicon 35, Minneapolis.

Austin, J.L. 1997 [1962]. *How To Do Things With Words, second edition*. Cambridge, MA: Harvard University Press.

Bagnall, R.G., P.C. Gallagher and J.L. Goldstein. 1984. Burdens on Gay Litigants and the Bias in the Court System: Homosexual Panic, Child Custody and Anonymous Parties. *Harvard Civil Rights-Civil Liberties Law Review* 19 (2): 487–559.

Baker, P. 2002. *Polari: The Lost Language of Gay Men*. London: Routledge.

Baker, P.and R. Marcus. 1998. Experts Scoff at Perjury Loophole Proposed for Clinton. *Washington Post*, 15 August: A6.

Barrett, R. 1997. The 'Homo-genius' Speech Community. In A. Livia and K. Hall (eds) *Queerly Phrased: Language, Gender and Sexuality*. Oxford: Oxford University Press, pp. 181–201.

Bawer, B. 1993. *A Place at the Table: The Gay Individual in American Society*. New York: Poseidon Press.

Bayles, M.D. 1991. Definitions in Law. In J.H. Fetzer, D. Shatz and G.N. Schlesinger (eds) *Definitions and Definability: Philosophical Perspectives*. London: Kluwer Academic Publishers, pp. 253–67.

Beck, U. 1992. *The Risk Society: Towards a Different Modernity*. London: Sage.

Begle, E.G. 1954. *Introductory Calculus with Analytic Geometry*. New York: Henry Holt and Company.

Bell, A. 1984. Language Style as Audience Design. *Language in Society* 13: 145–204.

Bell, A. 1997. Language Style as Audience Design. In N. Coupland and A. Jaworski (eds) *Sociolinguistics: A Reader and Coursebook*. New York: St Martin's Press, pp. 240–50.

Benor, S.B. 2001. Sounding Learned: The Gendered Use of /t/ in Orthodox Jewish English. *University of Pennsylvania Working Papers in Linguistics* 7.

Berger, C.R. and J.S. Bradac. 1983. *Language and Social Knowledge: Uncertainty in Interpersonal Relationships*. London: Edward Arnold.

Berger, P.L. and T. Luckman. 1967. *The Social Construction of Reality*. Garden City, NY: Anchor Books.

Besnier, N. 1995. *Literacy, Emotion, and Authority: Reading and Writing on a Polynesian Atoll*. New York: Cambridge University Press.

Billig, M. 1999. *Freudian Repression: Conversation Creating the Unconscious*. Cambridge: Cambridge University Press.

Black's Law Dictionary, sixth edition. 1990. St Paul, MN: West Publishing Co.

Blackwood, E. 1995. Falling in Love with an-Other Lesbian: Reflections on Identity in Fieldwork. In D. Kulick and M. Willson (eds) *Taboo: Sex, Identity, and Erotic Subjectivity in Anthropological Fieldwork*. New York: Routledge, pp. 51–75.

Boellstorff, T. 2006. *The Gay Archipelago: Sexuality and Nation in Indonesia*. Princeton, NJ: Princeton University Press.

Bolig, R., P.J. Stein and P.C. McKenry 1984. The Self-advertisement Approach to Dating: Male–Female Differences. *Family Relations* 33: 587–92.

Bolton, R. 1995. Sex Talk: Bodies and Behavior in Gay Erotica. In W.L. Leap (ed.) *Beyond the Lavender Lexicon: Authenticity, Imagination and Appropriation in Lesbian and Gay Languages*. New York: Gordon and Breach, pp. 173–206.

Bormann, E.G. 1969. *Discussion and Group Methods*. New York: Harper & Row.

Bourdieu, P. 1991. Authorized Language. In *Language and Symbolic Power*. Cambridge, MA: Harvard University Press, pp. 107–16.

Bowden, F. 1994. Operation Love: Finding a Lonely Heart. *Daily Mirror*, 19 February: 18.

Bram, J. 1955. *Language and Society*. New York: Random House.

Brien, A. 1967. Camper's Guide. *New Statesman* 23: 373–4.

Briggs, C.L. 1986. *Learning How to Ask: A Sociolinguistic Appraisal of the Role of the Interview in Social Science Research*. Cambridge: Cambridge University Press.

Bright, N. n.d. *Lively Love Letters*. New Delhi: Goodwill Publishing House.

Brown, P. and S. Levinson. 1987. *Politeness: Some Universals in Language Usage*. Cambridge: Cambridge University Press.

Browning, F. 1993. *The Culture of Desire: Paradox and Perversity in Gay Lives Today*. New York: Crown.

Bucholtz, M. 1996. Geek the Girl: Language, Femininity, and Female Nerds. In J. Ahlers, L. Bilmes, M. Chen, M. Oliver, N. Warner and S. Wertheim (eds) *Gender and Belief Systems*. Berkeley, CA: Berkeley Women and Language Group, pp. 119–32.

Butler, J. 1990. *Gender Trouble: Feminism and the Subversion of Identity*. New York: Routledge.

Butler, J. 1993a. *Bodies that Matter: On the Discursive Limits of 'Sex'*. New York: Routledge.

Butler, J. 1993b. Sexual Inversions. In J. Caputo and M. Yount (eds) *Foucault and the Critique of Institutions*. University Park, PA: Pennsylvania State University Press, pp. 81–98.

Byron, S. 1972. The Closet Syndrome. In K. Jay and A. Young (eds) *Out of the Closets: Voices of Gay Liberation*. New York: Pyramid.

California Style Collective. 1993. Variation and Personal/Group Style. Paper presented at New Ways of Analyzing Variation 21, Ottawa.

Cameron, D. 1992. *Feminism and Linguistic Theory*, 2nd edn. New York: St Martin's Press.

Cameron, D. 1996. The Language-Gender Interface: Challenging Co-optation. In V. Bergvall, J. Bing and A. Freed (eds) *Rethinking Language and Gender Research: Theory and Practice*, London: Longman, pp. 31–53.

Cameron, D. 1998. Performing Gender Identity: Young Men's Talk and the Construction of Heterosexual Masculinity. In J. Coates (ed.) *Language and Gender: A Reader*. Oxford: Blackwell, pp. 270–84.

Cameron, D. 2006. Language, Sexism and Advertising Standards. In *On Language and Sexual Politics*. London: Routledge, pp. 27–42.

Cameron, D. and D. Kulick. 2003. *Language and Sexuality*. Cambridge: Cambridge University Press.

Campbell-Kibler, K., R.J. Podesva, S.J. Roberts and A. Wong (eds). 2002. *Language and Sexuality: Contesting Meaning in Theory and Practice*. Stanford, CA: CSLI Publications.

Cargile, J. 1991. Real and Nominal Definitions. In J.H. Fetzer, D. Shatz and G.N. Schlesinger (eds) *Definitions and Definability: Philosophical Perspectives*. London: Kluwer Academic Publishers, pp. 21–50.

Carnap, R. 1962 [1950]. *Logical Foundations of Probability*. Chicago: University of Chicago Press.

Cartier, D. 1973. A Dyke's Manifesto. *The (Lesbian) Tide*, Vol. 2: 19.

Case, S.E. 1993 [1989]. Toward a Butch-Femme Aesthetic. In H. Ablove, M.A. Barale and D.M. Halperin (eds) *The Lesbian and Gay Studies Reader*. New York: Routledge, pp. 294–306.

Chauncey, G. 1994. *Gay New York: Gender, Urban Culture, and the Makings of the Gay Male World*. New York: Basic Books.

Cheepen, C. 1988. *The Predictability of Informal Conversation*. London: Pinter.

Chesebro, J.W. 1972. Rhetorical Strategies of the Radical-Revolutionary. *Today's Speech* 20: 37–44.

Chesebro, J.W., J.F. Cragan and P. McCullough. 1981. Consciousness-Raising Among Gay Males. In J.W. Chesebro (ed.) *Gayspeak: Gay Male and Lesbian Communication*. New York: Pilgrim Press.

Chierchia, G. and S. McConnell-Ginet. 2000. *Meaning and Grammar: An Introduction to Semantics*, 2nd edn. Cambridge, MA: MIT Press.

Chillman, C.S. 1983. *Adolescent Sexuality in a Changing American Society*. New York: John Wiley & Sons.

Coates, J. 1998a. *Language and Gender: A Reader*. Oxford: Blackwell.

Coates, J. 1998b. Gossip Revisited: Language in All-female Groups. In J. Coates (ed.) *Language and Gender: A Reader*. Oxford: Blackwell, pp. 226–53.

Collier, J.F. 1997. *From Duty to Desire: Remaking Families in a Spanish Village*. Princeton, NJ: Princeton University Press.

Comstock, G.D. 1989. Developments: Sexual Orientation and the Law. *Harvard Law Review* 102: 1508–51.

Connell, R.W. 1987. *Gender and Power: Society, the Person and Sexual Politics*. Stanford, CA: Stanford University Press.

Cormack, A. 1998. *Definitions: Implications for Syntax, Semantics, and the Language of Thought*. New York: Garland.

Cory, D.W. and J.P. LeRoy. 1963. *The Homosexual and His Society*. New York: Citadel.

Coulmas, F. 1981. *Conversational Routine: Explorations in Standardised Communication Situations and Prepatterned Speech*. Amsterdam: Mouton.

Coupland, J., N. Coupland and J. Robinson. 1992. 'How Are You?'. Negotiating Phatic Communion. *Language in Society* 21: 201–30.

Coupland, J., J. Robinson and N. Coupland. 1994. Frame Negotiation in Doctor-Elderly Patient Consultations. *Discourse and Society* 5 (1): 89–124.

Coupland, N. and H. Giles. 1988. Communicative Accommodation: Recent Developments. *Language and Communication* 8: 175–327.

Coupland, N. and J. Nussbaum (eds). 1993. *Discourse and Lifespan Identity*. Newbury Park, CA: Sage.

Coupland, N., J. Coupland and H. Giles. 1991. *Language, Society and the Elderly: Discourse, Identity and Ageing*. Oxford: Blackwell.

Crawford, M. 1995. *Talking Difference: On Gender and Language*. London: Sage.

Crenshaw, K. 1992. Whose Story is it Anyway?: Feminist and Antiracist Appropriations of Anita Hill. In T. Morrison (ed.) *Race-ing Justice, En-gendering Power*. New York: Pantheon Books, pp. 402–40.

Crist, S. 1997. Duration of Onset Consonants in Gay Male Stereotyped Speech. *University of Pennsylvania Working Papers in Linguistics* 4 (3): 53–70.

Dart, J. 1975. Closet Atheists Urged to Tell Beliefs. *Los Angeles Times*, 20 February II: 12.

Davis, A. 1983. *Women, Race and Class*. New York: Random House.

Davis, S. 1990. Men as Success Objects and Women as Sex Objects: A Study of Personal Advertisements. *Sex Roles* 23 (1/2): 43–50.

de Munck, V.C. 1998. *Romantic Love and Sexual Behavior: Perspectives from the Social Sciences*. Westport, CT: Praeger.

Dobash, R.E. and R.P. Dobash. 1992. *Women, Violence and Social Change*. London: Routledge.

Donham, D.L. 1998. Freeing South Africa: The 'Modernization' of Male-Male Sexuality in Soweto. *Cultural Anthropology* 13 (1): 3–21.

Drew, P. 1984. Speakers' Reportings in Invitation Sequences. In J.M. Atkinson and J. Heritage (eds) *Structures of Social Action: Studies in Conversation Analysis*. Cambridge: Cambridge University Press, pp. 129–51.

Drew, P. 1987. Po-faced Receipts of Teases. *Linguistics*, 25: 219–53.

Drew, P. and E. Holt. 1988. Complainable Matters: The Use of Idiomatic Expressions in Making Complaints. *Social Problems* 35: 398–417.

Dunbar, R. 1995. Are You Lonesome Tonight? *New Scientist* 11 February: 26–31.

Dynes, W. 1990. Effeminacy, Historical Semantics of. In W. Dynes (ed.) *Encyclopedia of Homosexuality*. New York: Garland Publishing, pp. 347–9.

Easton, D. and J.W. Hardy. 2001. *The New Bottoming Book*. Emeryville, CA: Greenery Press.

Eckert, P. 2000. *Linguistic Variation as Social Practice*. Malden, MA: Blackwell.

Eckert, P. and S. McConnell-Ginet. 1992. Think Practically and Look Locally: Language and Gender as Community-based Practice. *Annual Review of Anthropology* 21: 461–90; also reprinted in C. Roman, S. Juhasz and C. Miller (eds). 1994. *The Women and Language Debate*. New Brunswick, NJ: Rutgers University Press, pp. 432–60.

Eckert, P. and S. McConnell-Ginet. 2003. *Language and Gender*. Cambridge: Cambridge University Press, p. 201.

Edelsky, C. 1981. Who's Got the Floor? *Language in Society* 10 (3): 383–422.

Ehrlich, S. 1998. The Discursive Reconstruction of Sexual Consent. *Discourse & Society* 9 (2): 149–71.

Ehrlich, S. 2001. *Representing Rape: Language and Sexual Consent*. London and New York: Routledge.

Ephron, N. 1983. *Heartburn*. New York: Alfred Knopf.

Ervin-Tripp, S. 1969. Sociolinguistics. In L. Berkowitz (ed.) *Advances in Experimental Social Psychology*, Vol. 4. New York: Academic Press, pp. 93–107.

Estrich, S. 1987. *Real Rape*. Cambridge, MA: Harvard University Press.

Fairclough, N. 1995. Critical Discourse Analysis and the Marketization of Public Discourse: The Universities. *Discourse & Society* 4 (2): 133–68.

Farrell, R.A. 1972. The Argot of the Homosexual Subculture. *Anthropological Linguistics* 14: 97–109.

Featherstone, M. 1991. *Consumer Culture and Postmodernism*. London: Sage.

Feldman L., P. Holowaty, B. Harvey, K. Rannie, L. Shortt *et al.* 1997. A Comparison of the Demographic, Life-style, and Sexual Behaviour Characteristics of Virgin and Non-virgin Adolescents. *Canandian Journal of Human Sexuality* 6: 197–209.

Fetzer, J.H., D. Shatz and G.N. Schlesinger. 1991. *Definitions and Definability: Philosophical Perspectives*. London: Kluwer Academic Publishers.

Foratt, J. 1970. Word Thoughts: Homosexual. *Come Out!*, *New York Times*, 16.

Foucault, M. 1981. *The History of Sexuality, Vol. I: Introduction*. London: Pelican Books.

Foucault, M. 1985. *The Use of Pleasure*. Harmondsworth: Penguin.

Franzen, J. 2002. Books in Bed. In *How To Be Alone*. New York: Harper Perennial, pp. 270–85.

Freiberg, P. 1988. Blaming the Victim: New Life for the 'Gay Panic' Defense. *The Advocate* 24 May: 10–13.

Frye, M. 1983. *The Politics of Reality: Essays in Feminist Theory*. Trumansburg, NY: The Crossing Press.

Fukaya, M. 1966, 1998. *Ryoosai kenbo shugi no kyooiku* [*Education of the Good-Wife-Wise-Mother*]. Tokyo: Reimei Syobo.

Futabatei, S. 1962 [1906]. *Sono omokage* [*Her Silhouette*]. In *Nihon gendai bungaku zenshuu 4: Tsubouchi Shooyoo and Futabatei Shimei* [*A Complete Collection of Japanese Modern Literature 4: Tsubouchi Shooyoo and Futabatei Shimei*]. Tokyo: Koodan Sha, pp. 298–379.

Gagnon, J.H. and W. Simon. 1967. Pornography: Raging Menace or Paper Tiger? *Transaction* 4: 41–8.

Garber, M. 1992. *Vested Interests: Cross Dressing and Cultural Anxiety*. New York: Routledge.

Garfinkel, H. 1967. *Studies in Ethnomethodology*. Englewood Cliffs, NJ: Prentice-Hall.

Gates Jr, H.L. 1988. *The Signifying Monkey: A Theory of African-American Literary Criticism*. Oxford: Oxford University Press.

Gaudio, R.P. 1994. Sounding Gay: Pitch Properties in the Speech of Gay and Straight Men. *American Speech* 69 (1): 30–57.

Gaudio, R.P. 1997. Not Talking Straight in Hausa. In A. Livia and K. Hall (eds) *Queerly Phrased: Language, Gender and Sexuality*. Oxford: Oxford University Press, pp. 416–29.

Giallombardo, R. 1966. *Society of Women: A Study of a Women's Prison*. New York: John Wiley & Sons.

Giddens, A. 1991. *Modernity and Self-identity: Self and Society in the Late Modern Age*. Cambridge: Polity Press.

Giles, H. and P.F. Powesland. 1975. *Speech Style and Social Evaluation*. London: Academic Press.

Gledhill, C. 1987. The Melodramatic Field: An Investigation. In C. Gledhill (ed.) *Home Is Where the Heart Is: Studies in Melodrama and the Woman's Film*. London: British Film Institute, pp. 5–42.

Glick, B.S. 1959. Homosexual Panic: Clinical and Theoretical Considerations. *The Journal of Nervous and Mental Disease* 129: 20–8.

Goffman, E. 1959. *The Presentation of Self in Everyday Life*. Garden City, NY: Anchor.

Goldberger, R. 1973. Rita Right-On: Radical Rhetoric. *The (Lesbian) Tide,* Vol. 2: 7.

Goldhaber, G. 1977. Gay Talk: Communication Behavior of Male Homosexuals. *Gai Saber*, Vol. 1.

Goodwin, J.P. 1989. *More Man than You'll Ever Be: Gay Folklore and Acculturation in Middle America*. Indianapolis, IN: Indiana University Press.

Gough, K.H. 1959. The Nayars and the Definition of Marriage. *Journal of the Royal Anthropological Institute* 89: 23–34.

Gray, J. 1992. *Men are from Mars, Women are from Venus*. New York: HarperCollins.

Grice, H.P. 1975. Logic and Conversation. In P. Cole and J.L. Morgan (eds) *Syntax and Semantics 3: Speech Acts*. New York: Academic Press, pp. 41–58.

Guild Dictionary of Homosexual Terms. 1965. Washington, DC: Guild Press.

Gumperz J.J. 1962. Types of Linguistic Communities. *Anthropological Linguistics* 4 (1): 28–40.

Gumperz, J.J. 1982. *Discourse Strategies*. Cambridge: Cambridge University Press.

Habermas, J. 1984. *The Theory of Communicative Action, Vol. 1*. London: Heinemann.

Hagaki shuu [Collection of Postcards]. 1902. *Yomiuri Newspaper*, 26 December.

Hagiwara, M. (ed.). 1997. Sexuality. *Anise* 3: 24–7.

Hall, K. 1992. Women's Language for Sale on the Fantasy Lines. In K. Hall, M. Bucholtz and B. Moonwomon (eds) *Locating Power: Proceedings of the Second Berkeley Women and Language Conference, Vol. 1*. Berkeley, CA: Berkeley Women and Language Group, pp. 207–22.

Hall, K. 1995. Lip Service on the Fantasy Lines. In K. Hall and M. Bucholtz (eds) *Gender Articulated: Language and the Socially Constructed Self*. London: Routledge.

Hall, K. 2001. Performativity. In A. Duranti (ed.) *Key Terms in Language and Culture*. Oxford: Blackwell, pp. 180–3.

Hall, K. and M. Bucholtz (eds). 1995. *Gender Articulated: Language and the Socially Constructed Self*. London: Routledge.

Hall, K. and V. O'Donovan. 1996. Shifting Gender Positions among Hindi-speaking Hijras. In V. Bergvall, J. Bing and A. Freed (eds) *Rethinking Language and Gender Research: Theory and Practice*. London: Longman, pp. 228–66.

Halliday, M.A.K. 1976. Anti-language. *American Anthropologist* 78 (3): 570–84.

Halliday, M.A.K. 1978. Language as Social Semiotic. In *Language as Social Semiotic*. Baltimore, MD: Edward Arnold, pp. 108–26.

Hart, H.H. 1958. Fear of Homosexuality Among College Students. In B.M. Wedge (ed.) *Psychosocial Problems of College Men,* New Haven, CT: Yale University Press, pp. 200–13.

Harvey, K. 1997. Gay Men, Straight Men and a Problem of Lexical Choice. In K. Harvey and C. Shalom (eds) *Language and Desire: Encoding Sex, Romance and Intimacy*. London: Routledge, pp. 60–82.

Harvey, K. 2000. Describing Camp Talk: Language/Pragmatics/Politics. *Language and Literature* 9(3): 240–60.

Hempel, C. 2001 [1970]. On the 'Standard Conception' of Scientific Theories. In J.H. Fetzer (ed.) *The Philosophy of Carl G. Hempel: Studies in Science, Explanation, and Rationality*. Oxford: Oxford University Press.

Henkin, W.A. and S. Holiday. 1996. *Consensual Sadomasochism: How to Talk About It and Do It Safely*. Los Angeles, CA: Daedalus.

Henley, N.M. and C. Kramarae. 1994. Gender, Power, and Miscommunication. In C. Roman, S. Juhasz and C. Miller (eds) *The Women & Language Debate*. New Brunswick, NJ: Rutgers University Press, pp. 383–406.

Herdt, G. and A. Boxer. 1992. Introduction: Culture, History and the Life-course of Gay Men. In G. Herdt (ed.) *Gay Culture in America*. Boston, MA: Beacon, pp. 1–28.

Herdt, G. and A. Boxer. 1993. *Children of Horizons*. Boston, MA: Beacon.

Herold, E.S. and L. Way. 1983. Oral-genital Sexual Behavior in a Sample of University Females. *Journal of Sex Research* 19: 327–38.

Hertzler, J.O. 1966. Social Uniformation and Language. *Sociological Inquiry* 36: 298–312.

Heywood, J. 1997. 'The Object of Desire is the Object of Contempt': Representation of Masculinity in *Straight To Hell* Magazine. In S. Johnson and U.H. Meinhof (eds) *Language and Masculinity*. Oxford: Blackwell, pp. 188–207.

Hodge, R. and G. Kress. 1988. *Social Semiotics*. Cambridge: Polity Press.

Hoffman, M. 1968. *The Gay World*. New York: Basic Books.

Holmes, J. 1984. Hedging Your Bets and Sitting on the Fence: Some Evidence for Hedges as Support Structures. *Te Reo* 27: 47–62.

Honda, M. 1990. *Jogakusei no keifu: Saishiki sareru Meiji* [*The Genealogy of Schoolgirls: Painted Meiji*]. Tokyo: Seido Sha.

hooks, bell. 1992. *Black Looks: Race and Representation*. Boston, MA: South End Press.

Horii, R. 1993. Joseigo no seiritsu [The Formation of Women's Language]. *Nihongo Gaku* 12: 100–8.

Horn, L.R. 1988. Pragmatic Theory. In F.J. Newmeyer (ed.) *Linguistics: The Cambridge Survey I, Linguistic Theory: Foundations*. Cambridge: Cambridge University Press, pp. 113–15.

Horvath, B. 1987. Text in Conversation: Variability in Story-telling Texts. In K. Denning, S. Inkelas, F. McNair-Knox and J. Rickford (eds) *Variation in Language: NWAV-XV at Stanford. Proceedings of the Fifteenth Annual Conference on New Ways of Analyzing Variation*. Stanford University Linguistics Department, pp. 212–23.

Humphreys, L. 1972. *Out of the Closets: The Sociology of Homosexual Liberation*. Englewood Cliffs, NJ: Prentice-Hall.

Hyden, M. and I.C. McCarthy. 1994. Women Battering and Father-Daughter Incest Disclosure: Discourses of Denial and Acknowledgement. *Discourse & Society* 5: 543–65.

Ide, R. and T. Terada. 1998. The Historical Origins of Japanese Women's Speech: From the Secluded Worlds of 'Court Ladies' and 'Play Ladies'. *International Journal of the Sociology of Language* 129: 139–56.

Ide, S. 1979. *Onna no kotoba, otoko no kotoba* [*Women's Language, Men's Language*]. Tokyo: Nihon Keizai Tsushinsha.

Ide, S. 2003. Women's Language as a Group Identity Marker in Japanese. In M. Hellinger and H. Bussmann (eds) *Gender Across Languages*. Amsterdam: John Benjamins Publishing Company, pp. 227–38.

Inoue, M. 2002. Gender, Language, and Modernity: Toward an Effective History of Japanese Women's Language. *American Ethnologist* 29 (2): 392–422.

In the Matter of XXX: Reasons and Judgement of the University Discipline Tribunal. 1994. York University.

Irigaray, L. 1985. *This Sex Which is Not One*. Ithaca, NY: Cornell University Press.

Irvine, J.T. 1989. When Talk Isn't Cheap: Language and Political Economy. *American Ethnologist* 16 (2): 248–67.

Irvine, J.T. 2001. Style as Distinctiveness: The Culture and Ideology of Linguistic Differentiation. In J. Rickford and P. Eckert (eds) *Stylistic Variation*. Cambridge: Cambridge University Press.

Iwamoto, Y. 1885. Baika joshi no den [The Story of Miss Apricot Scent], *Jogaku Zasshi* 4: 68–71.

Iwamoto, Y. 1887. Shoobi no kaori [The Scent of Rose], *Jogaku Zasshi* 74: 78–9.

Iwamoto, Y. 1890. Josei no kotoba tsuki [Women's Speech]. *Jogaku Zasshi* 221: 594.

Iwaya, S. 1985 [1889]. *Jibore musume sakka* [*Conceited Woman Writers*]. In M. Iwata (ed.) *Genyuusha kei zasshi shuusei: Garakuta bunko 2 (6)* [*Collection of Magazines of Genyuusha Group: Garakuta Bunko 2 (6)*]. Tokyo: Yumani Shobo, pp. 371–6.

Jackson, P. 2004. *Gay* Adaptation, *Tom-Dee* Resistance, and *Kathoey* Indifference: Thailand's Gender/Sex Minorities and the Episodic Allure of Queer English. In W.L. Leap and T. Boellstorff (eds) *Speaking in Queer Tongues: Globalization and Gay Language*. Urbana, IL: University of Illinois Press, pp. 202–30.

Jacobs, G. 1996. Lesbian and Gay Male Language Use: A Critical Review of the Literature. *American Speech* 71: 49–71.

Jacobs, G., H. Rogers and R. Smyth. 1999. Sounding Gay, Sounding Straight: A Search for Phonetic Correlates. Paper presented at New Ways of Analyzing Variation 28, Toronto.

Jankowiak, W. (ed.). 1995. *Romantic Passion: A Universal Experience?* New York: Columbia University Press.

Jay, K. 1972. Foreword. In K. Jay and A. Young (eds) *Out of the Closets: Voices of Gay Liberation*. New York: Pyramid.

Jefferson, G. 1978. Sequential Aspects of Storytelling in Conversation. In D. Scheinkein (ed.) *Studies in the Organization of Conversational Interaction*. New York: Free Press, pp. 219–48.

Jefferson, G. 1984. On Stepwise Transition from Talk about a Trouble to Inappropriately Next-positioned Matters. In J.M. Atkinson and J. Heritage (eds) *Structures of Social Action: Studies in Conversation Analysis*. Cambridge: Cambridge University Press, pp. 191–222.

Jesperson, O. 1946. *Mankind, Nation and Individual From a Linguistic Point of View*. Bloomington, IN: Indiana University Press.

Jogakusei no heifuu 3 [Bad Custom of Schoolgirls 3]. 1891. *Yomiuri Newspaper*, 8 September.

Jogakusei to gengo [Schoolgirl and Language]. 1905. *Yomiuri Newspaper*, 16 March.

Johnson, M. 1997. *Beauty and Power: Transgendering and Cultural Transformation in the Southern Philippines*. London: Berg.

Jolly, M. and L. Manderson. 1997. Introduction: Sites of Desire/Economies of Pleasure in Asia and the Pacific. In L. Manderson and M. Jolly (eds) *Sites of Desire, Economies of Pleasure: Sexualities in Asia and the Pacific*. Chicago: University of Chicago Press, pp. 1–26.

Kanamaru, F. 1997. Ninshoo daimeeshi/koshoo [Person pronouns and address terms]. In S. Ide (ed.) *Joseigo no sekai* [*The World of Women's Language*]. Tokyo: Meiji Shoin, pp. 15–32.

Karasawa, T. 1958. *Nihon no joshi gakusei* [*Japanese Female Students*]. Tokyo: Dai Nihon Yuuben Kai Koodan Sha.

Katz, J.N. 1995. *The Invention of Heterosexuality*. New York: Dutton.

Kawamura, K. 1993. *Otome no inori: Kindai josei imeeji no tanjoo* [*The Maiden's Prayer: The Birth of the Image of Modern Women*]. Tokyo: Kinokuniya Shoten.

Kempf, E.J. 1920. *Psychopathology*. St Louis, MO: C.V. Mosby Company.

Kikuchi, Y. 1969 [1903]. *Chi kyoodai* [*Bosom Sisters*]. In *Meiji bungaku zenshuu 93: Meiji katei shoosetsu shuu* [*A Complete Collection of Meiji Literature 93: Meiji Family Novels*]. Tokyo: Chikuma Shobo, pp. 89–240.

Kim, W., J. Branega, J. Carney, J.F.O. McAllister and V. Ralnert. 1998. When Sex Is Not Really Having Sex. *Time Canada* 151: 22.

Kinsui, S. 2003. *Baacharu Nihongo: Yakuwari go no nazo* [*Virtual Japanese: The Mystery of Social Role Word*]. Tokyo: Iwanami Shoten.

Kitzinger, C. 2005. Heteronormativity in Action: Reproducing the Heterosexual Nuclear Family in 'After Hours' Medical Calls. *Social Problems* 52(4): 477–98.

Kitzinger C. and H. Frith. 1999. Just Say No? The Use of Conversation Analysis in Developing a Feminist Perspective on Sexual Refusal. *Discourse & Society* 10 (3): 293–316.

Klapp, O. 1962. *Heroes, Villains, and Fools*. Englewood Cliffs, NJ: Spectrum.

Klein, M. and J.R. Petersen. 1996. *Playboy's* College Sex Survey: A Most Stimulating Look at Lust on Campuses Across the Country. *Playboy* 43: 64.

Koestner, R. and L. Wheeler. 1988. Self-presentation in Personal Advertisements: The Influence of Implicit Notions of Attraction and Role Expectations. *Journal of Social and Personal Relationships* 5: 149–60.

Komatsu, S. 1974. Toosei shosei katagi no edogo teki tokushoku [The Edo Language Characteristics in *Toosei shosei katagi*]. *Saitama Daigaku Kiyoo* 9: 17–28.

Komatsu, S. 1988. Tokyo-go ni okeru danjosa no keisei: Shuujoshi o chuushin toshite [The Formation of Sex Differences in the Tokyo-language: Centering on the Sentence-final Particles]. *Kokugo to Kokubungaku* 65: 94–106.

Koyama, S. 1991. *Ryoosai kenbo toiu kihan* [*The Norms of Good-Wife-Wise-Mother*]. Tokyo: Keiso Shobo.

Kramarae, C. and P.A. Treichler (eds). 1985. *A Feminist Dictionary: In Our Own Words*. London: Pandora Press.

Kress, G. and R. Hodge. 1979. *Language As Ideology*. London: Routledge & Kegan Paul.

Krige, E.J. 1974. Woman-Marriage, with Special Reference to the Lovedu: Its Significance for the Definition of Marriage. *Africa* 44: 11–37.

Kulick, D. 1998. *Travesti: Sex, Gender, and Culture among Brazilian Transgendered Prostitutes*. Chicago: University of Chicago Press.

Kulick, D. 1999. Transgender and Language: A Review of the Literature and Suggestions for the Future. *GLQ* 5 (4): 605–22.

Kulick, D. 2000. Gay and Lesbian Language. *Annual Review of Anthropology* 29: 243–85.

Kulick, D. 2002. Queer Linguistics? In K. Campbell-Kibler, R.J. Podesva, S.J. Roberts and A. Wong (eds) *Language and Sexuality: Contesting Meaning in Theory and Practice*. Stanford, CA: CSLI Publications, pp. 65–8.

Kulick, D. 2003. Language and Desire. In J. Holmes and M. Meyerhoff (eds) *The Handbook of Language and Gender*. Oxford: Blackwell.

Kusamura, H. 1969 [1902]. *Hamako* [*Hamako*]. In *Meiji bungaku zenshuu 93: Meiji katei shoosetsu shuu* [*A Complete Collection of Meiji Literature 93: Meiji Family Novels*]. Tokyo: Chikuma Shobo, pp. 3–88.

Labov, W. 1966. *The Social Stratification of English in New York City*. Washington, DC: Center for Applied Linguistics.

Labov, W. 1972. *Sociolinguistic Patterns*. Philadelphia, PA: University of Pennsylvania Press.

Lakoff, R. 1975. *Language and Woman's Place*. New York: Harper & Row.

Land, V. and C. Kitzinger. 2005. Speaking as a Lesbian: Correcting the Heterosexual Presumption. *Research on Language and Social Interaction* 38(4): 371–416.

Lave, J. and E. Wenger. 1991. *Situated Learning. Legitimate Peripheral Participation*. Cambridge: Cambridge University Press.

Layer, J. 1975. Communicative Functions of Phatic Communion. In A. Kendon, R.M. Harris and M.R. Key (eds) *The Organisation of Behaviour in Face-to-face Interaction*. The Hague: Mouton, pp. 215–38.

Layer, J. 1981. Linguistic Routines and Politeness in Greetings and Partings. In F. Coulmas (ed.) *Conversational Routine*. The Hague: Mouton, pp. 289–304.

Lazar, M. 1999. Family Life Advertisements and the Narrative of Heterosexual Sociality. In P. Chew and A. Kramer-Dahl (eds) *Reading Culture: Textual Practices in Singapore*. Singapore: Times Academic Press.

Leach, E.R. 1955. Polyandry, Inheritance and the Definition of Marriage With Particular Reference to Sinhalese Customary Law. *Man* 199: 182–6.

Leap, W.L. 1996. *Word's Out: Gay Men's English*. Minneapolis, MN: University of Minnesota Press.

Leap, W.L. (ed.). 1995. *Beyond the Lavender Lexicon: Authenticity, Imagination and Appropriation in Gay and Lesbian Languages*. New York: Gordon & Breach.

Leap, W.L. and T. Boellstorff (eds). 2004. *Speaking in Queer Tongues: Globalization and Gay Languages*. Urbana, IL: University of Illinois Press.

Lee, D. 1992. *Competing Discourses: Perspective and Ideology in Language*. London: Longman.

Lee, J.A. 1983. The Social Organization of Sexual Risk. In T. Weinberg and G.W.L. Kamel (eds) *S and M: Studies in Sadomasochism*. New York: Prometheus Books, pp. 175–93.

Lee, Y. 1996. *Kokugo toiu shisoo* [*The Ideology of National Language*].Tokyo: Iwanami Shoten.

Lees, S. 1996. *Carnal Knowledge: Rape on Trial*. London: Hamish Hamilton.

LePage, R.B. and A.Tabouret-Keller. 1985. *Acts of Identity: Creole-based Approaches to Language and Ethnicity*. Cambridge and New York: Cambridge University Press.

Lerman, P. 1967. Argot, Symbolic Deviance and Subcultural Delinquency. *American Sociological Review* 32: 209–24.

Levinson, S.C. 1983. *Pragmatics*. Cambridge: Cambridge University Press.

Lewin, E. 1993. *Lesbian Mothers: Accounts of Gender in American Culture*. Ithaca, NY: Cornell University Press.

Liang, A.C. 1997. The Creation of Coherence in Coming-out Stories. In A. Livia and K. Hall (eds) *Queerly Phrased: Language, Gender, and Sexuality*. New York: Oxford University Press, pp. 287–309.

Lindholm, C. 1995. Love as an Experience of Transcendence. In W. Jankowiak (ed.) *Romantic Passion: A Universal Experience?* New York: Columbia University Press, pp. 57–71.

Livia, A. 1995. 'I Ought to Throw a Buick At You': Fictional Representations of Butch/Femme Speech. In K. Hall and M. Bucholtz (eds) *Gender Articulated: Language and the Socially Constructed Self*. London and New York: Routledge, pp. 245–78.

Livia, A. and K. Hall (eds). 1997. *Queerly Phrased: Language, Gender and Sexuality*. New York: Oxford University Press.

Lovric, M. 1995. *How to Write Love Letters*. New York: Shooting Star Press.

Lurie, A. 1981. *The Language of Clothes*. New York: Random House.

Lycan, W.G. 1991. Definition in a Quinean World. In J.H. Fetzer, D. Shatz and G.N. Schlesinger (eds) *Definitions and Definability: Philosophical Perspectives*. London: Kluwer Academic Publishers, pp. 111–31.

Lynn, M. and R. Bolig. 1985. Personal Advertisements: Sources of Data about Relationships. *Journal of Social and Personal Relationships* 2: 377–83.

Lynn, M. and B.A. Shurgot. 1984. Responses to Lonely Hearts Advertisements: Effects of Reported Physical Attractiveness, Physique, and Coloration. *Personality and Social Psychology Bulletin* 10 (3): 349–57.

McCollum, C. 1998. American Narratives of Falling in Love from the Perspective of Relational Psychoanalysis. Paper presented at the Society for Psychological Anthropology Reunion, Emory University, 23 October.

McConnell-Ginet, S. 1988. Language and Gender. In F. Newmeyer (ed.) *Linguistics: The Cambridge Survey, Vol. IV*, Cambridge: Cambridge University Press, pp. 75–99.

McConnell-Ginet, S. 1989. The Sexual (Re)production of Meaning: A Discourse-based Theory. In F. Frank and P.A. Treichler (eds) *Language, Gender, and Professional Writing*, New York: Modern Language Association, pp. 35–50.

McConnell-Ginet, S. 1995. Can Linguists Help Identify Sexual Harassment? Paper presented at Linguistic Society of America Symposium: Linguistic Perspectives on Sexual Harassment. Linguistic Society of America's Annual Meeting January. New Orleans, LA.

McIlvenny, P. (ed.). 2002. *Talking Gender and Sexuality*. Amsterdam: John Benjamins.

MacKinnon, C. 1987. *Feminism Unmodified*. Cambridge, MA: Harvard University Press.

MacKinnon, C. 1993. *Only Words*. Cambridge, MA: Harvard University Press.

MacLean, J. 1995. An Afternoon with My If-There-Were-A-Laws. In K. Jay (ed.) *Dyke Life: A Celebration of the Lesbian Experience*. New York: HarperCollins, pp. 23–6.

McLemore, C.A. 1991. The Pragmatic Interpretation of English Intonation: Sorority Speech. Unpublished Ph.D. dissertation, University of Texas at Austin.

Mahoney, E.R. 1980. Religiosity and Sexual Behavior Among Heterosexual College Students. *Journal of Sex Research* 16: 87–113.

Makino, S. and M. Tsutsui. 1986. *A Dictionary of Basic Japanese Grammar*. Tokyo: Japan Times.

Malinowski, B. 1972. Phatic Communion. In J. Layer and J. Hutcheson (eds) *Communication in Face-to-Face Interaction*. Harmondsworth: Penguin, pp. 146–52.

Maltz, D.N. and R.A. Borker. 1982. A Cultural Approach to Male-Female Communication. In J. Gumperz (ed.) *Language and Social Identity*. Cambridge: Cambridge University Press, pp. 196–216.

Manahan, N. 1982. Homophobia in the Classroom. In M. Cruikshank (ed.) *Lesbian Studies: Present and Future*. New York: The Feminist Press, pp. 66–9.

Manalansan, M.F. 1997. In the Shadows of Stonewall: Examining Gay Transnational Politics and the Diasporic Dilemma. In L. Lowe and D. Lloyd (eds) *The Politics of Culture in the Shadow of Capital*. Durham, NC: Duke University Press, pp. 485–505.

Manohar. n.d. *Love Letters*. New Delhi: New Light Publishers.

Martin, S. 1975. *A Reference Grammar of Japanese*. New Haven, CT: Yale University.

Matoesian, G.M. 1993. *Reproducing Rape: Domination Through Talk in the Courtroom*. Chicago: University of Chicago Press.

Maynard, S.K. 1987. *Japanese Conversation: Self-contextualization Through Structure and Interactional Management*. Norwood, NJ: Ablex.

Meyer, M. 1994. Introduction: Claiming the Discourse of Camp. In M. Meyer (ed.) *The Politics and Poetics of Camp*. London: Routledge, pp. 1–22.

Meyerowitz, J. 2002. *How Sex Changed: A History of Transsexuality in the United States*. Cambridge, MA: Harvard University Press.

Michigan Court of Appeals. 1998. 586 N.W. 2d 766, 768.

Milroy, J. and L. Milroy. 1985. *Authority in Language: Investigating Language Prescription and Standardisation*. London and New York: Routledge.

Mitchell-Kernan, C. 1971. *Language Behavior in a Black Urban Community*. Monograph no. 2, Language-Behavior Research Lab. Berkeley, CA: University of California.

Miyake, K. 1971 [1888]. *Yabu no uguisu* [*Bush Warbler*]. In *Gendai Nihon bungaku taikei 5: Higuchi Ichiyoo, Meiji joryuu bungaku, Izumi Kyooka shuu* [*The Great Collection of Contemporary Japanese Literature 5: Higuchi Ichiyoo, Meiji Female Writers, and Izumi Kyooka*], Tokyo: Chikuma Shobo, pp. 125–45.

Mohr, R.D. 1992. *Gay Ideas: Outing and Other Controversies*. Boston, MA: Beacon.

Moonwomon-Baird, B. 1997. Toward the Study of Lesbian Speech. In A. Livia and K. Hall (eds) *Queerly Phrased: Language, Gender, and Sexuality*, New York: Oxford University Press.

Morford, J. 1987. Social Indexicality in French Pronominal Address. *Journal of Linguistic Anthropology* 7: 3–37.

Morgan, R. and K. Wood. 1995. Lesbians in the Living Room: Collusion, Co-contruction, and Co-narration in Conversation. In W.L. Leap (ed.) *Beyond the Lavender Lexicon: Authenticity, Imagination and Appropriation in Lesbian and Gay Languages*. New York: Gordon and Breach, pp. 235–48.

Movsesian, A.J. 1993. *How to Write Love Letters and Love Poems*. Bombay: Jaico Publishing House.

Muehlenhard, C.L. and L.C. Hollabaugh. 1988. Do Women Sometimes Say No When They Mean Yes? The Prevalence and Correlates of Women's Token Resistance to Sex. *Journal of Personality and Social Psychology* 54 (5): 872–9.

Murray, S.O. 1979. The Art of Gay Insulting. *Anthropological Linguistics* 21: 211–23.

Myers-Scotton, C. 1993. *Social Motivations for Code-switching: Evidence from Africa*. Oxford: Oxford University Press.

Nakamura, M. 2001. *Kotoba to jendaa* [*Language and Gender*]. Tokyo: Keiso Shobo.

Nakamura, M. 2002. The Dynamic Model of Language and Gender Studies. *Nature-People-Society* 32: 1–26.

Nakamura, M. 2003a. Discursive Construction of the Ideology of 'Women's Language': From *Kamakura, Muromachi* to *Edo* periods (1180–1867). *Nature-People-Society* 34: 21–64.

Nakamura, M. 2003b. Discursive Construction of the Ideology of 'Women's Language': Women's Disciplinary Books/Moral Textbooks and the Unification of Written and Spoken Languages in the Meiji/Taisho Periods (1868–1926). *Nature-People-Society* 35: 1–39.

Nakamura, M. 2004. Discursive Construction of the Ideology of 'Women's Language': 'Schoolgirl Language' in the Meiji Period (1868–1912). *Nature-People-Society* 36: 43–80.

Nakamura, M. 2005. Construction of 'Men's National Language' in Japan (1968–1926). *Nature-People-Society* 38: 91–125.

Nanda, S. 1989. *Neither Man Nor Woman: The Hijras of India*. Belmont, CA: Wadsworth.

Natsume, S. 1961 [1905]. *Wagahai wa neko de aru* [*I Am a Cat*]. In *Nihon gendai bungaku zen-shuu 23: Natsume Sooseki shuu 1* [*A Complete Collection of Modern Japanese Literature 23: Natsume Sooseki 1*]. Tokyo: Koodan Sha, pp. 5–201.

Nestle, J. 1981. Butch-Femme Relationships: Sexual Courage. *Heresies* 12: 21–4.

New South Wales Government, 1998. Homosexual Advance Defence: Final Report of the Working Party. Available from www.lawlink.nsw.gov.au/clrd1.nsf/pages/had.

Newton, E. 1979 [1972]. *Mother Camp: Female Impersonators in America*. Chicago: University of Chicago Press.

Ochs, E. 1991. Indexing Gender. In A. Duranti and C. Goodwin (eds) *Rethinking Context*. Cambridge: Cambridge University Press, pp. 335–58.

Oguri, F. 1998 [1907–11]. *Sode to sode* [*Sleeve to Sleeve*]. Tokyo: Kawade Shobo Shinsha.

Okada, Y. 1957. Konogoro no kotoba [Language Use Today]. *Gengo Seikatsu* 64: 45.

Okamoto, S. 2004. Ideology of Linguistic Practices and Analysis: Gender and Politeness in Japanese Revisited. In S. Okamoto and J.S. Shibamoto Smith (eds) *Japanese Language, Gender, and Ideology: Cultural Models and Real People*. New York: Oxford University Press, pp. 38–56.

Okano, H. 1964 [1902]. Hyoojungo ni tsuite [On Standard Language]. In S. Yoshida and Y. Inoguchi (eds) *Meiji ikoo kokugo mondai ronshuu* [*Collection of Papers on National Language Issues After Meiji*]. Tokyo: Kazama Shobo, pp. 509–14.

The Opposite of Sex. 1998. D. Roos (Director), D. Kirkpatrick, M. Besman (Producers), SONY Pictures Classic Release.

Osa, S. 1998. *Kindai Nihon to kokugo nashonarizumu* [*The Modern Japan and the Nationalism of National Language*]. Tokyo: Yoshikawa Kobunkan.

Otsuki, F. 1905. Nihon hoogen no bunpu kuiki [The Distribution of Japanese Dialects]. *Fuuzoku Gahoo* 318: 12–17.

Oxford English Dictionary, 2nd edn. 1989. New York: Oxford University Press.

Ozaki, K. 1965 [1897]. *Konjiki yasha* [*Gilded Demoness*]. In *Meiji bungaku zenshuu 18: Ozaki Kooyoo shuu* [*A Complete Collection of Meiji Literature 18: Ozaki Kooyoo*]. Tokyo: Chikuma Shobo, pp. 127–327.

Ozaki, K. 1994 [1888]. Hayari kotoba [Trendy Words]. In *Kooyoo zenshuu 10* [*A Complete Collection of Koyoo 10*]. Tokyo: Iwanami Shoten, pp. 4–5.

Painter, D.S. 1981. Recognition Among Lesbians in Straight Settings. In J.W. Chesebro (ed.) *Gayspeak: Gay Male and Lesbian Communication*. New York: The Pilgrim Press, pp. 68–79.

Parker, R. 1999. *Beneath the Equator: Cultures of Desire, Male Homosexuality, and Emerging Gay Communities in Brazil*. London: Routledge.

Penelope [Stanley], J. 1970. Homosexual Slang. *American Speech* 45 (1–2): 45–59.

Penelope [Stanley], J. 1977. Paradigmatic Women: The Prostitute. In D.L. Shores and C.P. Hines (eds) *Papers in Language Variation*. Tuscaloosa, AL: University of Alabama Press, pp. 303–21.

Penelope, J. 1990. *Speaking Freely: Unlearning the Lies of the Fathers' Tongues*. New York: Teachers College Press.

Penelope J. and S.J. Wolfe. 1979. Sexist Slang and the Gay Community: Are You One, Too? *Michigan Occasional Paper No. XIV*. Ann Arbor, MI: University of Michigan.

Penman, R. 1990. Facework and Politeness: Multiple Goals in Courtroom Discourse. In K. Tracy and N. Coupland (eds) *Multiple Goals in Discourse*. Clevedon: Multilingual Matters, pp. 15–38.

Philips, S. 1992. A Marx-influenced Approach to Ideology and Language: Comments. *Pragmatics* 2: 377–85.

Plummer, K. 1992. Speaking Its Name: Inventing a Lesbian and Gay Studies. In K. Plummer (ed.) *Modern Homosexualities: Fragments of Gay and Lesbian Experiences*. New York: Routledge.

Potter, J. and M. Wetherell. 1987. *Discourse and Social Psychology*. London: Sage.

Queen, R. 1997. 'I Don't Speak Spritch': Locating Lesbian Language. In A. Livia and K. Hall (eds) *Queerly Phrased: Language, Gender, and Sexuality*. New York: Oxford University Press.

Quine, W. 1951. Two Dogmas of Empiricism. *Philosophical Review* 60: 20–43.

Quinn, N. 1982. 'Commitment' in American Marriage: A Cultural Analysis. *American Anthropologist* 9: 755–98.

Quinn, N. 1996. Culture and Contradiction: The Case of Americans Reasoning about Marriage. *Ethnos* 24: 391–425.

Random House Unabridged Dictionary, 2nd edn. 1993. New York: Random House.

Reijo saikun no kotoba [Language of Daughters and Wives]. 1896. *Waseda Bungaku*, February: 148.

Reinisch, J.M., C.A. Hill, S.A. Sanders and M. Ziemba-Davis. 1995. High-risk Sexual Behavior at a Midwestern University: A Confirmatory Survey. *Family Planning Perspectives* 27: 79–82.

Reinisch J.M., S.A. Sanders, and M. Ziemba-Davis. 1988. The Study of Sexual Behavior in Relation to the Transmission of Human Immunodeficiency Virus: Caveats and Recommendations. *American Psychologist* 43: 921–7.

Reiss Jr, A.J. 1961. The Social Integration of Queers and Peers. *Social Problems* 9: 102–20.

Rich, A. 1980. Compulsory Heterosexuality and Lesbian Existence. *Signs: Journal of Women in Culture and Society* 5 (Summer): 631–60.

Robinson, R. 1954. *Definition*. Oxford: The Clarendon Press.

Rodgers, B. 1972. *The Queens' Vernacular: A Gay Lexicon*. San Francisco, CA: Straight Arrow.

Rogers, H., R. Smyth and G. Jacobs. 2000. Vowel and Sibilant Duration in Gay- and Straight-sounding Male Speech. Paper presented at the International Gender and Language Association Conference 1, Stanford University, Stanford, CA.

Romano, R. 2003. *Race Mixing: Black-White Marriage in Post-war America*. Cambridge, MA: Harvard University Press.

Rosanoff, A. 1927. *Manual of Psychiatry, Sixth Edition*. New York: Wiley.

Rubin, G. 1984. Thinking Sex: Notes for a Radical Theory of the Politics of Sexuality. In C.S. Vance (ed.) *Pleasure and Danger: Exploring Female Sexuality*. London: Pandora, pp. 267–319.

Russo, V. 1976. Camp. *The Advocate*, 19 May. Reprinted in M.P. Levine (ed.) *Gay Men: The Sociology of Male Homosexuality*. New York: Harper & Row, pp. 205–10.

Sacks, H. 1972. An Initial Investigation of the Usability of Conversational Data for Doing Sociology. In D. Sudnow (ed.) *Studies in Social Interaction*. New York: Free Press, pp. 31–74.

Sacks, H. 1974. An Analysis in the Course of a Joke's Telling in Conversation. In R. Bauman and J. Sherzer (eds) *Explorations in the Ethnography of Speaking*. Cambridge: Cambridge University Press, pp. 337–54.

Sacks, H. 1984. On Doing 'Being Ordinary'. In J.M. Atkinson and J. Heritage (eds) *Structures of Social Action: Studies in Conversation Analysis*. Cambridge: Cambridge University Press, pp. 413–29.

Sacks, H. 1995a. *Lectures on Conversation: Volume I*. Oxford: Blackwell.

Sacks, H. 1995b. *Lectures on Conversation: Volume II*. Oxford: Blackwell.

Samois (ed.). 1981. *Coming to Power: Writings and Graphics on Lesbian S/M*. Boston, MA: Alyson Publications.

Sanday, P.R. 1996. *A Woman Scorned: Acquaintance Rape on Trial*. New York: Doubleday.

Sapir, E. 1949 [1924]. Culture, Genuine and Spurious. In D. Mandelbaum (ed.) *Selected Writings of Edward Sapir*. Berkeley, CA: University of California Press, pp. 308–31.

Sato, H. 1999 [1941]. *Kokugo no junka bika* [*The Refinement and Beautification of National Language*]. In *Teihon Sato Haruo zenshuu 22* [*Authentic Texts: A Complete Collection of Sato Haruo 22*]. Tokyo: Rinkawa Shoten, pp. 166–77.

Schegloff, E.A. 1992. Repair After Next Turn: The Last Structurally Provided Defense of Intersubjectivity in Conversation. *American Journal of Sociology* 97: 1295–1345.

Schegloff, E.A. 1996. Some Practices for Referring to Persons in Talk-in-Interaction. In B.A. Fox (ed.) *Studies in Anaphora*. Amsterdam: John Benjamins, pp. 437–85.

Schegloff, E.A. 2000. On Granularity. *Annual Review of Sociology* 26: 715–20.

Scherer, K.R. and H. Giles. 1979. *Social Markers in Speech*. Cambridge: Cambridge University Press.

Schiappa, E. 2003. Defining Reality: Definitions and the Politics of Meaning. In D. Blakesley (ed.) *Rhetorical Philosophy and Theory*. Carbondale and Edwardsville, IL: Southern Illinois University Press.

Schulz, M.R. 1975. The Semantic Derogation of Women. In B. Thorne and N. Henley (eds) *Language and Sex: Difference and Dominance*. Rowley, MA: Newberry House.

Schwartz, G. and D. Merten. 1967. The Language of Adolescence: an Anthropological Approach to the Youth Culture. *American Journal of Sociology* 72: 453–68.

Sedgwick, E.K. 1990. *Epistemology of the Closet*. Berkeley and Los Angeles, CA: University of California Press.

Seidman, S. 1991. *Romantic Longings: Love in America, 1830–1980*. Routledge: New York.

Sexual Assault and Harassment on Campus. n.d. York University Sexual Harassment and Complaint Centre.

Sheeran P., D. Abrams, C. Abraham and R. Spears. 1993. Religiosity and Adolescents' Premarital Sexual Attitudes and Behaviour: An Empirical Study of Conceptual Issues. *European Journal of Social Psychology* 23: 39–52.

Shepperd, J.A. and A.J. Strathman. 1989. Attractiveness and Height: The Role of Stature in Dating Preference, Frequency of Dating, and Perceptions of Attractiveness. *Personality and Social Psychology Bulletin* 15 (4): 617–27.

Sherzer, J. 1987. A Discourse-centered Approach to Language and Culture. *American Anthropologist* 89: 295–309.

Shokeid, M. 1995. *A Gay Synagogue in New York*. New York: Columbia University Press.

Shotter, J. and K. Gergen. 1989. *Texts of Identity*. Newbury Park, CA: Sage.

Silverstein, M. 1972. An Open Letter to Tennessee Williams. In K. Jay and A. Young (eds) *Out of the Closets: Voices of Gay Liberation*. New York: Pyramid, pp. 69–72.

Silverstein, M. 1996. Indexical Order and the Dialectics of Sociolinguistic Life. In R. Ide, R. Parker and Y. Sunaoshi (eds) *SALSA III: Proceedings of the Third Annual Symposium About Language and Society, Austin*. Austin, TX: University of Texas, Department of Linguistics, pp. 266–95.

Simmons, R. 1991. Some Thoughts on the Challenges Facing Black Gay Intellectuals. In E. Hempfil (ed.) *Brother to Brother: New Writings by Black Gay Men*. Boston, MA: Alyson, pp. 211–28.

Simon, W. and J.H. Gagnon. 1967. Homosexuality: The Formulation of a Sociological Perspective. *Journal of Health and Social Behavior* 8: 177–85.

Smitherman, G. 1977. Talkin' and Testify-in': The Language of Black America. Boston, MA: Houghton-Mifflin.

Soga, T. 1875. Kaika hyaku baka no yon [A Hundred Fools of Civilization 4]. *Yomiuri Newspaper*, 3 October.

Sonenschein, D. 1966. Homosexuality as a Subject of Anthropological Inquiry. *Anthropological Quarterly* 39: 73–82.

Sonenschein, D. 1968. The Ethnography of Male Homosexual Relationships. *Journal of Sex Research* 4: 69–83.

Sontag, S. 1964. Notes on Camp, *Partisan Review* 31: 515–30.

The Starr Report: *Referral to the United States House of Representatives Pursuant to Title 28. United States Code §595(c)*. Available from www.icreport.house.gov/icreport. Submitted by the Office of the Independent Counsel, 9 September 1998.

Stevenson, C.L. 1944. *Ethics and Language*. New Haven, CT: Yale University Press.

Strait, G. 1964. *The Lavender Lexicon*. San Francisco, CA: Strait.

Suffrendi, K.S. 2001. Pride and Prejudice: The Homosexual Panic Defense. *Boston College Third World Law Journal* 21 (2): 279–314.

Sullivan, A. 1995. *Virtually Normal: An Argument About Homosexuality*. New York: Alfred A. Knopf.

Taguchi, K. 1969 [1904]. *Meoto nami* [Husband and Wife Wave]. In *Meiji bungaku zenshuu 93: Meiji katei shoosetsu shuu* [A Complete Collection of Meiji Literature 93: Meiji Family Novels]. Tokyo: Chikuma Shobo, pp. 241–364.

Takeuchi, H. 1907. Tokyo fujin no tsuuyoogo [Common Speech of Tokyo Ladies]. *Shumi* 2 (11): 24–6.

Talbot, M. 1998. An Explosion Deep Inside Her. In K. Harvey and C. Shalom (eds) *Language and Desire: Encoding Sex, Romance and Intimacy*. London: Routledge.

Tannen, D. 1990. *You Just Don't Understand: Women and Men in Conversation*. New York: Morrow.

Terasaki, Alene, K. 2004 [1976]. Pre-announcement Sequences in Conversation. Reprinted in Gene H. Lerner (ed.) *Conversation Analysis: Studies from the First Generation*. Amsterdam: John Benjamins.

Teyo dawa monogatari [The Story of *teyo dawa*]. 1906. *Tokyo Pack*, 1 January: 13.

Thorne, B. 1993. *Gender Play*. Buckingham: Open University Press.

Tohsaku, Y.-H. 1999. *Yookoso: Continuing with Contemporary Japanese*. Boston, MA: McGraw-Hill College.

Treichler, P.A. 1989. From Discourse to Dictionary: How Sexist Meanings Are Authorized. In F.W. Frank and P.A. Treichler (eds) *Language, Gender, and Professional Writing:*

Theoretical Approaches and Guidelines for Nonsexist Usage. New York: Modern Language Association, pp. 51–79.

Tsubouchi, S. 1969 [1886]. *Shoosetsu shinzui* [*The Essence of the Novel*]. In *Meiji bungaku zenshuu 16: Tusbouchi Shooyoo syuu* [*A Complete Collection of Meiji Literature 16: Tsubouchi Shooyoo*], 3–58. Tokyo: Shikuma Shobo.

Tsubouchi, S. 1977 [1933]. *Kaki no Heta* [*The Calyx of Persimmon*]. In *Shooyoo Senshuu: Bessatsu 4* [*The Selected Works of Shooyoo: Separate Volume 4*]. Tokyo: Diichi Shobo, pp. 393–670.

Tsubouchi, S. and R. Uchida. 1965 [1909]. Hasegawa Kun no Seikaku [Personality of Mr Hasegawa]. In Y. Masahide (ed.) *Kindai buntai hassei no shiteki kenkyu* [*The Historical Study of the Emergence of Modern Style*]. Tokyo: Iwanami Shoten.

Twaddell, W.F. 1935. On Defining the Phoneme. *Language Monograph 16*. Baltimore, MD: LSA.

Tyler, C.A. 1991. Boys Will Be Girls: The Politics of Gay Drag. In D. Fuss (ed.) *Inside/Out: Lesbian Theories, Gay Theories*. New York: Routledge, pp. 32–70.

Uchida, R. 1986 [1894]. *Bungakusha to naru hoohoo* [*How to Become a Novel Writer*]. In *Uchida Roan Zenshuu 2* [*The Complete Collection of Uchida Roan 2*]. Tokyo: Yumani Shobo, pp. 175–299.

Vaid, U. 1995. *Virtual Equality: The Mainstreaming of Gay and Lesbian Liberation*. Doubleday: New York.

Valentine, D. 2000. 'I Know What I Am': The Category 'Transgender' in the Construction of Contemporary US American Conceptions of Gender and Sexuality. Ph.D. dissertation, Department of Anthropology, New York University.

Valentine, D. 2003. The Calculus of Pain: Violence, Anthropological Ethics, and the Category Transgender. *Ethnos* 68 (1): 27–48.

Valentine, J. 1997. Pots and Pans: Identification of Queer Japanese in Terms of Discrimination. In A. Livia and K. Hall (eds) *Queerly Phrased: Language, Gender, and Sexuality*. New York: Oxford University Press.

Vance, C. (ed.). 1984. *Pleasure and Danger: Exploring Female Sexuality*. New York: HarperCollins, pp. 267–319.

Wakakuwa, M. 2001. *Koogoo no shoozoo: Shooken kootaigoo no hyooshoo to josei no kokuminka* [*The Portrait of Empress: The Representation of Empress Shooken and the Nationalization of Women*]. Tokyo: Chikuma Shobo.

Walters, K. 1981. A Proposal for Studying the Language of Homosexual Males. Austin, TX: University of Texas, unpublished manuscript.

Warner, M. 1999. *The Trouble with Normal: Sex, Politics, and the Ethics of Queer Life*. The Free Press: New York.

Warren, C.A.B. 1974. *Identity and Community in the Gay World*. New York: John Wiley & Sons.

Watanabe, M. 1990. *Uuman Rabingu* [*Women Loving*]. Tokyo: Gendai Shokan.

Webster's Third New International Dictionary of the English Language Unabridged. 1993. Springfield, MA: Merriam-Webster.

Weeks, J. 1981. *Sex, Politics, and Society: The Regulation of Sexuality Since 1800*. London: Longman.

Weinreich, U. 1953. *Language in Contact*. Hague: Mouton.

Wenger, E. 1998. *Communities of Practice. Learning, Meaning and Identity*. Cambridge: Cambridge University Press.

Wernick, A. 1991. *Promotional Culture*. London: Sage.

Weston, K. 1991. *Families We Choose: Lesbians, Gays, Kinship*. New York: Columbia University Press.

Weston, K. 1993. Do Clothes Make the Woman? Gender, Performance Theory, and Lesbian Eroticism. *Genders* 17: 1–21.

White, E. 1980. *States of Desire: Travels in Gay America*. New York: E.P. Dutton.

Wieringa, S. and E. Blackwood. 1999. Introduction. In E. Blackwood and S. Wieringa (eds) *Female Desires: Same-sex Relations and Transgender Practices Across Cultures*. New York: Columbia University Press, pp. 1–38.

Williamson, J. 1986. *Consuming Passions: The Dynamics of Popular Culture*. London and New York: Marion Boyars.

Wittman C. 1972. Refugees from Amerika: A Gay Manifesto. In J.A. McCaffrey (ed.) *The Homosexual Dialectic*. Englewood Cliffs, NJ: Prentice-Hall.

Wood, K. 1997. Narrative Iconicity in Electronic-mail Lesbian Coming Out Stories. In A. Livia and K. Hall (eds) *Queerly Phrased: Language, Gender, and Sexuality*. New York: Oxford University Press.

Wood, R. 1977. *Another Kind of Love*. Chicago: Thomas More Press.

Yasuda, T. 1997. *Teikoku Nihon no gengo hensei* [*The Language Organization of the Japanese Empire*]. Kanagawa: Seori Shobo.

Young, A. 1974. On Human and Gay Identity: A Liberationist Dilemma. *Gay Sunshine* 31–2: 31.

Zimmerman, D.H. 1992. The Interactional Organization of Calls for Emergency Assistance. In P. Drew and J. Heritage (eds) *Talk at Work: Interaction in Institutional Settings*. Cambridge: Cambridge University Press, pp. 418–69.

Zwicky, A. 1997. Two Lavender Issues for Linguistics. In A. Livia and K. Hall (eds) *Queerly Phrased: Language, Gender and Sexuality*. Oxford: Oxford University Press, pp. 21–34.

General index

African American English (AAE) 151–63, 295 n.13.3; and code-switching 156–7; and signifying 155
The American Dictionary of Slang 39
anti-language 15
Antioch College Sexual Offense Policy 218–21
authenticity: in gay experience 92–3; in gay men's English 88–9; in lesbian and gay cultures 81–8

'bitch' 126–7, 191
'bitch boy' 127–8

camp 22, 71, 81
'chicken' 22
classism 52
code-switching: and AAE 156–7; indexing identity 156; and power relations 157
'come out' 22
commodification of the self 102, 103, 114
communication: of desire 241, 247; non-verbal 83–4; styles 203; *see also* language; miscommunication
communities of practice 8, 118, 189
consent 5, 166, 198; as defined by Antioch College 218; and temporality 198, 200; terms of 217; verbal 215; *see also* heteronormativity; 'no'; sexual acts

conversation analysis (CA) 169
cooperative discourse 91
counterculture 72
'cruise' 21, 23
cultural system 47
'culture of desire' 90

dating advertisements: audio recordings 108–10; conventional structure 105–8; personalizing potential 111; *see also* commodification of the self
desire 6, 12; African American men and white women 160; and attributes listed in personal ads 114; and categorization 242; and code-switching 156; 'culture of desire' 90; definitions of 241–2, 245, 254; as desirable 243, 260; as expressed in speech 248; and girls 191; heterosexual 119, 121, 171, 187, 203; homosexual 4, 30, 34, 52, 246, 247, 254–5, 288–90; homosocial 118; and identity categories 242, 245; intelligible and unintelligible 242, 245–57; interracial 160; 'ki-ki' 27; and Kulick 241, 246; and labeling 253, 297 n. 20.3; and language 10, 242, 247–8, 257; lesbian 40; and modernity 269; and 'no' 287, 288; and non-Western sexual practice 245; and politics 248; and power 254; to remain covert 77;

and representation 10; as rupturing identity categories 254; and self-fashioning 243; and sexuality 245; and slang 50; as something needing to be communicated 10, 241; as something private 10; and truth 254; to be white 152, 163; women's 154; and writing 258–69

The Dictionary of Underworld Lingo 39

discourse 86; of heterosexuality 118; of homosexuality 63; about homosexuals in CA data sets 296 n. 14.2; of sexuality and gender 251–2, 255

domination: of men 130; symbolic 126–7, 163; of women 125

drag 40, 51; critique of racist stereotypes 160–1; glam drag 151; high drag 151; and race 153; restructuring gender norms 155

drag queens: African American 151–63; performing femininity 98; and relationship between identity and desire 297 n. 20.1; and white women's language 153–5; *see also* gender

Epistemology of the Closet 63

feminism: and authenticity 93; and distinction between 'gender' and 'sexuality' 248, 255; and marriage 233, 234; and opposition to cross-gender reference 60–2; and 'reasonable person' standard 212–13; and sadomasochism 293; and self-naming 54–5, 72–3; and sexual consent 166, 217; *see also* politics; radical feminism

fraternities 99, 118

'fuck-story' 98, 122–4; as narrative performance 122; in Portuguese 130

gay 26, 36, 40, 246

gay activism 49, 54, 55, 82, 150, 254

Gay English 87, 88–92, 295 n. 13.4; and women-centered imagery 90

Gayspeak 18, 39, 64, 68–77; as camp 81; critique of 64, 78–85, 141–2; dysphemism 76; euphemism 35, 74, 76; and gay men 294 n. 6.2; as ironic 75; kinship terminology 74, 295 n. 14.1; multiple types of 150; and parody 72; rank terminology 74

gay studies 78–9; idiographic approach 83

gender: differentiation 130, 190; drag performances as reactionary 55, 295 n. 13.1; performance 122; as performative 9, 285; and power dynamics 214

Gender Trouble 97, 285

'greek' societies 118; *see also* fraternities

hanky-code 84

heteronormativity 9; and consent 166, 287; definition of 170; expressions of 165; and language-use 165; and organization of gender and sexuality 256; *see also* queer theory

heterosexism 92, 152, 155, 163, 181

heterosexual: adolescent development 193; desire 121; identity as naturalized 165; ideology 129; marketplace 189–91; privilege 187; self-presentation 170; sexual relations 121; style 194

heterosexual relationships: and adolescents 193–5; as naturalized 166; and power 217

heterosexuality: as aspect of socially constructed identity 129; in Conversation Analysis (CA) data sets 169; discourse of 118; as naturalized 170; and 'no' 287; performance of 99, 101–17, 118–31, 165, 187; production through dominance relationships 126; production through talk 170, 177, 287; as social imperative 190, 217; *see also* homosociality

history, subcultural 79

homosexual: as foreign 34; ontology 66, 85

The Homosexual in America 16

homosexual language 17, 45, 65; and class variation 46; development of 33; and geographic variation 38; phonetic features 146; pitch range 146; vocabulary 43

Homosexual Panic Defense 244, 288–91, 298 n. 23.1; and interpellation 290; *see also* 'no'

homosociality 99, 121

Hothead Paisan 18

'husband' 175, 185, 195

identification: gay male with women 58; of persons through language 79; processes of 293

identity: and actions 97; as constructed 100; as constructed through personal ads 102; as constructed through phonetic features 145–50; gender 11; identity-management processes 114; and language use 37, 68; male 129; multiple 124, 251; and performance framework 293; as performed 97; sexual 11, 67, 122; and style 144, 194–5
index categories 144
indexicalization 243, 270, 297 n. 22.1
insult 90, 126–7; gendered dimensions 202
'invert' 35

Jenny Jones show 290

Kinsey Institute for Research in Sex, Gender, and Reproduction Studies 223
kinship terminology 175; see also Gayspeak

language: and categorization 70, 256–7; as communication 56; community 47; and constitution of sexual acts 5; and definition 85; and gay authenticity 88; and gay men 86–7; and hetero-normative social arrangements 165, 168; and heterosexuality 171–86; and homosexuality 7; of homosexual life 33–40; and identity construction 100, 132; ideology 271; of Japanese women 271–2; as medium of representation 5, 34; nationalization as gendered in Japan 273; nonverbal communication 83–4; and self-concept 48; and self-presentation 9, 37; and self-styling 98–9; and sexual identity 67, 79; sexual registers 57; and status production within gender groups 128–30; and stigmatized groups 15, 33, 77; used by gay people 92; of women 72, 151; see also Gay English; homosexual language; slang
lesbian feminism 54, 64, 73, 81; see also Radicalesbians
lesbian/lesbianism: and camp 22; and drag 52; as 'factitious' 20; and gay male slang 49, 53; as gender inverts 59; identity 140, 246; language 15, 17–18, 20, 50, 79; language use (as compared to gay

men's) 12, 18, 20; and Mae West 80; relations with gay men 49, 55, 61, 81, 85; relation to onabe 4, 133–4; terms for 34, 45, 53; in Tokyo bars 9, 99; in women's prison 17; and word 'gay' 38, 54; see also onabe; rezu
love: as beyond agency or control 261; and courtship 260, 266–9; and family 238; heterosexual 116, 193; homosexual 35, 36, 47; as ideology 265; and individualism 243; and Japanese 'schoolgirl' speech 281; lesbian 51, 73, 134; and literacy 258–69; love letter guidebooks 264, 297 n. 21.3; love letters 258–9, 264; and marriage 234–5, 237–8, 259, 262, 269; and modernity 259, 269; 'mother-love' 28; Nepali understandings of 243, 260–3; and Nepali women 243, 259, 265; and pets 101; revealed on Jenny Jones show 290; romantic love in Nepal 243, 258–69; as Western construct 243, 258–69

marriage 167, 172; anthropological conceptions of 231–2; changing definitions of 239; consequences of definition 227–40; Defense of Marriage Act 227, 239; definition of 228; extralegal associations of 236–8; about family and children 237–8; Goodridge decision 235, 238; legal definitions 234–6; as 'sacred' 236–7; social values and practices 234
masculinity 51; gay male intensification 57–8
Mattachine Society 16
Men are from Mars, Women are from Venus 166
miscommunication 167, 204; deficiency model 196, 206–7, 209–10; in sexual assault 196
misogyny: and drag queens 98, 151–4, 160–2, 295 n.13.1; and gay slang 7, 90–1; see also sexism

narrative: of sexual difference 129; see also cultural system
'no' 166; and consent 215; dual indexicality 291–2; effects of its enunciation 244; and hegemonic masculinities 202–3; and Homosexual

Panic Defense 288–91; illocutionary force 287; and mechanics of heteronormative praxis 288; production of heterosexuality 287; and production of sexual situations 286; and rape 244, 290; as response to sexual advance 287; and sadomasochistic sex 291–3

onabe 133–5; bars 134; construction of self 134–5; linguistic behavior and interaction 135–40; social and emotional identity 134, 140; styling through speech 99–100
orders of indexicality 129
orgasm 26, 31, 226; faked 5–6

Paris is Burning 152–3, 162, 295 n. 13.2
parody 72, 91, 153
passing 74
pederasty 16, 36
performativity 285; as distinct from performance 286, 293
personal ads 99; *see also* dating advertisements
politics: feminist 18, 54–5; of gay liberation 64, 72, 294 n. 6.8; radical 17, 73, 98; of separation 55; of visibility 12
power 138
practice 97; and ideology 272, 283–4; linguistic 141, 191–2
priests 61
prostitution 20

The Queens' Vernacular: A Gay Lexicon 49
queer theory 8, 10; *see also* heteronormativity

race: African American drag queens as 'wanting to be white' 152–3; in dating advertisements 107–8, 113, 117; interracial marriage 171; and linguistic domination 128; and performance 157; 'race panic' 290; and survey about sex 223; use of 'white woman's language' by African American drag queens 151–63
racism: in gay vocabulary 50, 55; and marriage in the US 239; and sexuality 249; white fear of black men 161; 'white woman style' as critique 162

radical feminism: criticism of Antioch College Sexual Offense Policy 217; and sadomasochism 292; *see also* feminism
Radicalesbians 74
rape 6, 7, 196, 197, 202, 209, 210–12, 217, 219–20, 286–7, 290; acquaintance rape 197, 296 n. 16.3; changing definitions 230; on college campuses 166; 'date' rape 197; and the enunciation of 'no' 244; legal criteria 212; legal definitions 196; marital rape 230, 296 n. 19.2; and resistance 201, 206, 208–7, 209, 213; simulation 160–2
rezu (*rezubian*) 99
RuPaul 158–9

safewords 291; *see also* 'no'
'schoolgirls' and 'female students' 273–4
'schoolgirl' speech 243; categorization of 272–4; construction of 272, 275; derogation 275; and 'family novels' 280; as gendered differentiation 275–7, 282; imitation of 272, 282; and modernization 273, 298 n. 22.5; relationship to 'schoolboy' speech 275–7; and social class 281; use of foreign words 279; and Westernization 274, 298 n. 22.5
scientific terminology 35
secrecy 69, 79
semiotics 242
'sex': heteronormative definition of 167; and oral sex 222, 225; as penile-vaginal intercourse 225
sexism: and gay slang 17–18, 50–1, 55, 60–2, 72, 74–5, 81; and Japanese 281; and speech community 202; *see also* misogyny
sexual acts 4; attitudes toward 223, 225; and consent 215–26, 198–202; definitions of 222; gay lexicon 76; of gay men 53; heterosexual 122; slang 20–32
sexual aggression 202, 212
sexual harassment 5, 196–8, 212–13, 219–20, 286–7, 290
sexual identity 3; indigenous forms 4
sexuality 2–3
sexualization 243, 280

slang 19–32; for cruising 21; for cunnilinctus 25; for female genitals 23, 25; for heterosexuality 30, 37; homosexual 41, 42, 49; for homosexual desire 27; for homosexuality 34; for male genitals 21, 28; for male homosexual 24; for pederastic desires 29; for promiscuity 28; for prostitution 29; for sexual acts 20–32; *see also* Gayspeak; indexicalization; 'schoolgirl' speech

social meaning: as constructed by dominant groups 169; as produced through practice 141; as shared 142; and style 143

Society of Women 17

stereotypes 160–1; gay-as-effeminate 18; gay world 75; gender 51; sexual 215

'straight' 37

styles 141; in co-construction of identity 144; and code-switching 157; definition of 142–3; flamboyantly gay 149; gay 145, 150; as interpersonal audience accommodation 143; as linguistically constructed 150; white woman's 159

'trade' 30, 31, 38, 52

transgender 11, 247, 249, 255

'transgender-identified' 247, 256, 297 n. 20.1, n. 20.2, n. 20.4

When Harry Met Sally 5

'wife' 175

Word's Out: Gay Men's English 65

You Just Don't Understand 66, 166

Index of names

Abe, Hideko 99
Abu-Lughod, Lila 261
Ahearn, Laura M. 242
Althusser, Louis 98, 290
Austin, J. L. 8, 285

Bayles, Michael 234, 296 n. 19.1
Bell, Allan 143
Blackstone, William 239
Bush, George W. 238, 239
Butler, Judith 8, 97–8, 100, 152,
    285–6
Byron, Stuart 83

Cameron, Deborah 11, 142–3, 166–7
Campbell-Kibler, Kathryn 100
Clinton, Bill 167, 222, 227
Cory, Donald W. 15; see also Edward
    Sagarin
Coupland, Justine 99
Crew, Louie 15, 18

Darsey, James 64

Eckert, Penelope 165, 166, 189
Ehrlich, Susan 166–7
Evans-Pritchard, Edward E. 231

Fairclough, Norman 102–3, 115
Foucault, Michel 3–4, 98, 245

Franzen, Jonathan 1

Gallagher, Maggie 238
Giallombardo, Rose 18
Giddens, Anthony 102, 111
Goffmann, Erving 46
Gough, Kathleen 232
Gray, John 166
Grossman, Joanna 235

Hale, Matthew 230
Hayes, Joseph J. 64, 79–82, 85
Hoffman, Martin 83–4
Hyams, Paul 237

Irvine, Judith 144

Kiesling, Scott F. 99
Kitzinger, Celia 165
Klapp, Orrin 47
Krige, Eileen Jensen 231–2
Kulick, Don 166, 187, 241, 244,
    246

Lakoff, George 76
Lakoff, Robin 154
Lave, Jean 189
Leach, Edmund 231
Leap, William 7, 65–7
Legman, Gershon 15, 17

Livingston, Jennie 152
Lutz, Catherine 261

McConnell-Ginet, Sally 167, 189
MacKinnon, Catherine 202–3, 213, 287
Marshall, Margaret H. 235, 238
Mohr, Richard 90

Nakamura, Momoko 243
Newton, Esther 254

Ochs, Elinor 144, 270
O'Hair, Madalyn Murray 76

Penelope [Stanley], Julia 15, 17, 72
Perkins-Gilman, Charlotte 234
Podesva, Robert J. 100

Quinn, Naomi 234

Roberts, Sarah J. 100

Sagarin, Edward 16
Sapir, Edward 88, 295 n. 8.1
Sedgwick, Eve Kosofsky 63
Silverstein, Michael 129
Sonenschein, David 16–17
Stevenson, Charles L. 233
Sullivan, Andrew 238

Tannen, Deborah 66, 166

Vaid, Urvashi 255
Valentine, David 242

Wenger, Etienne 189
Wood, Richard 61

Young, Allen 72

Forthcoming Title

Language and Gender:
An advanced resource book
Jane Sunderland

'This book marks a timely intervention in the field of language and gender research and provides students and researchers alike with essential primary materials. The book contains articles from a very wide range of disciplines; if you think that this book will contain all of the usual suspects, then prepare to be surprised - there are extracts on masculinity, corpus linguistics, post-structuralist linguistics, fairy tales, ELT textbooks, queer theory, and social networks. This would make an ideal textbook for gender and language courses.' *Sara Mills, Sheffield Hallam University, UK*

Routledge Applied Linguistics is a series of comprehensive resource books, providing students and researchers with the support they need for advanced study in the core areas of English Language and Applied Linguistics.

Language and Gender:

- presents an up-to-date introduction to language and gender;

- includes diverse work from a range of cultural, including non-Western, contexts, and represents a range of methodological approaches;

- gathers together influential readings from key names in the discipline, including: Deborah Cameron, Mary Haas and Deborah Tannen.

Written by an experienced teacher and researcher in the field, *Language and Gender* is an essential resource for students and researchers of Applied Linguistics.

ISBN10: 0–415–31104–7 (pbk)
ISBN10: 0–415–31103–9 (hbk)
ISBN10: 0–203–45649–1 (ebk)

ISBN13: 978–0–415–31104–5 (pbk)
ISBN13: 978–0–415–31103–8 (hbk)
ISBN13: 978–0–203–45649–1 (ebk)